Methods and Strategies for Teaching in Secondary and Middle Schools

Kenneth T. Henson
University of Alabama

Longman
New York & London

Methods and Strategies for Teaching in Secondary and Middle Schools

Longman Inc., 95 Church Street, White Plains, N.Y. 10601

Associated companies:
Longman Group Ltd., London
Longman Cheshire Pty., Melbourne
Longman Paul Pty., Auckland
Copp Clark Pitman, Toronto
Pitman Publishing Inc., New York

Executive editor: Raymond O'Connell
Senior Production editor: Ronni Strell
Text design: Steven August Krastin
Cover design: Paul Agule Design
Text art: J & R Services, Inc.
Production supervisor: Judith Stern

This book was previously published as *Secondary Teaching Methods*.

A special thanks to Dr. Bob Alley, Associate Dean of the College
of Education, Wichita State University, Wichita, Kansas; to the
Wichita School District for providing the case data on matching
learning styles and teaching styles; and to Sharon Henson for all
the photography in this book.

Library of Congress Cataloging-in-Publication Data

Henson, Kenneth T.
  Methods and strategies for teaching in secondary and
middle schools.

  Includes bibliographies.
  1. Teaching.   2. Education, Secondary—United States.
I. Title.
LB1025.2.H4565   1988   373.11'02   87-4006
ISBN 0-8013-0017-7 (instructor's manual)
ISBN 0-582-28676-X (pbk.)

Compositor: TC Systems
Printer: R. R. Donnelley and Sons Company

88 89 90 91 92 9 8 7 6 5 4 3 2

CONTENTS

CASES

PREFACE

Methods and Strategies for Teaching in Secondary and Middle Schools is designed to prepare prospective middle through senior high school teachers and to help in-service teachers to improve their teaching skills. Chapter 1 examines the dynamic profession of teaching and what it means to you. It includes a critique of several educational reform committee reports and a critique of American schools.

Part I is a thorough guide to planning. Chapter 2 introduces the reader to curriculum development, or long-range planning. Chapter 3 shows how daily lesson plans can be designed to achieve the goals of long-range plans, and Chapter 4 guides the reader in using and writing performance objectives in all domains and at all levels of the taxonomy.

Part II explains how you can put your plans into action most effectively. Chapter 5 introduces a variety of teaching methods, ranging from the lecture to inquiry, presents the strengths and limitations of each, and tells how the teacher can incorporate each method into an overall teaching strategy. Chapter 6 explains how the teacher can use both verbal and nonverbal communications to enhance the methods and strategies.

Recognizing that learning occurs in different ways for different people, Part III begins with a chapter on individualizing instruction and explains how this can best be applied to students with special needs and talents (Chapter 8) and to groups of students with diverse cultural backgrounds (Chapter 9).

For teachers to be effective in today's society, they must know how to apply modern technology to improve instruction. Part IV is devoted to this important goal. Chapter 10 explains the role that imagery plays in learning and shows how teachers can apply media technology to improve instruction. The subject of Chapter 11 is the microcomputer, which has established itself in our schools and is accepted as a permanent feature in present and future education. The chapter tells how teachers can, without fear or other discomforts, use computers to enhance their teaching effectivensss and the level of thinking in the classroom.

Without good classroom management, motivation, and discipline skills, teachers cannot effectively implement their lesson plans. Part V examines the research on techniques of motivation and classroom management. Chapter 12 helps teachers integrate findings from studies on motivation with their own personalities and teaching strategies to stimulate student interest. Chapter 13 examines several discipline and management models from within education and from outside disciplines. The emphasis is on helping teachers develop their own management and discipline strategies for the classroom.

Never before have American teachers been so accountable for the achievement of their students. Part VI is written to help teachers develop, administer, and score their own tests (Chapter 14) and to help teachers understand and use evaluation techniques to promote learning, improve instruction, and assess student achievement (Chapter 15).

Each chapter is organized to motivate the reader by direct involvement throughout each chapter. At the very beginning of each chapter, a list of chapter objectives tells the reader exactly what to expect from the chapter. A "Pretest" then thrusts the reader into the major concepts of each chapter, asking the reader to agree or disagree with a few pertinent statements.

From time to time, boxes titled "Let's Ponder," "Let's Talk," or "Do This" interrupt the main text. These deal with important or controversial information, or provide thought-provoking exercises pertinent to the subject under discussion. The Let's Ponder boxes end with questions to elicit reader reactions to the statements. The main body of the chapter is followed by a "Recap of Major Ideas," presented as a list of concise statements.

A "Posttest," which asks the same questions as the Pretest, enables individual students to measure changes in their own perceptions as a consequence of having read the chapter.

Next there is a set of "Cases" that show the major principles in the chapter in action. Each case is a true experience taken from a real-life situation. It tells how principles were applied in classroom settings and the results that each application had. At the end of each case are a few questions related to each experience and a discussion of these questions.

A college course should always be considered a beginning. This course and this book will stimulate you to go far beyond the bounds of each. A set of "Activities" will help you pursue further topics introduced in the chapter. Students should use these activities to individualize their learning programs. Put simply, this section invites students to select activities they find most interesting or most useful to their future teaching.

Each chapter ends with a list of "Suggested Readings." This list is very current. The chapters of this book cite and use information from more than 400 sources, a high proportion of which are research studies. The "Suggested Readings" lists include all these references, plus many additional sources that contain further information about the content in each chapter. This section too will be helpful as students continue to investigate topics related to the profession.

An Instructor's Manual is provided to complement this book. The manual is designed for use with the overhead projector. It contains a discussion of each question on the pretests, a set of multiple-choice test items for each chapter, a set of essay items for each chapter, and suggestions for introducing each chapter. Transparency prints are provided to add clarity and interest to the lessons.

Kenneth T. Henson

C H A P T E R *1*

Teaching and You

Objectives

- Name at least one major recommendation of each education reform report.
- Identify weaknesses and errors in the recommendations offered in reform reports.
- Identify major strengths in the recommendations of reform reports.
- Identify and criticize the major curriculum determiner in the United States.
- Explain the teacher's responsibility for using research.

"If an unfriendly foreign power had attempted to impose on America the medio-cre educational performance that exists today, we might well have viewed it as an act of war." These words are from *A Nation at Risk,* a report by the National Commission on Excellence in Education, one of the many commissions of the 1980s that sought to reform teacher education drastically in the United States. This report describes the condition of the schools as "a rising tide of mediocrity."

Another report of the early 1980s, titled *Action for Excellence,* speaks of "a need for survival." It uses the words *emergency* and *urgency.* The aim of these early "reform reports," which were often named after the commissions that wrote them, was to reform American schools. Most of the reports called for a total revision of undergraduate programs.

By the mid-1980s, other reports came up with even more drastic recommen-dations. Because of a pervasive belief that teacher education students have failed to master their content areas, *Time for Results,* written by the National Governors Conference (1986), and *Teaching in the 21st Century: A Nation Prepared* (1986), by the Carnegie Foundation, advocated that undergraduate teacher education programs be abolished and replaced with fifth-year programs.

These recent criticisms have not come without warning. They are built on a growing general dissatisfaction of the public. For 16 out of the 18 years that Gallup surveyed public attitudes about public schools, the major concern was discipline. In 1986 the leading perceived problem in the schools was drug abuse (Gallup, 1986). The list in Chapter 13 of the major problems in the schools today, con-trasted to the major problems in 1942, will surprise you.

Where does this leave you? Whether you are an undergraduate teacher edu-cation major, a graduate student pursuing one of the new fifth-year programs, or an in-service teacher pursuing a higher degree, many of these reports should be disturbing to you. It is time for teachers to take a proactive stance. Don't wait for others to jump in and correct the conditions.

But there is also good news about today's schools. Other measuring devices show that our schools have been extremely effective. One example of this is that Americans have received a disproportionate share of Nobel Prizes. Since the Nobel program began in 1901, Americans have won one-third of all Nobel Prizes—seven times as many as those won by Soviet citizens and twice as many as citizens of any other nation. American schools have also educated a larger proportion of the nation's youth than has any other educational system in the world, making special efforts to reach the poor, the minorities, and the handicapped. And Ameri-cans are capable of developing a system that is excellent in every respect.

This optimism is shared by other educators. In her introduction to the 1986 yearbook of the Association for Supervision and Curriculum Development, Karen Zumwalt (1986) writes:

> Teacher education programs have been declared inadequate, inefficient, and, in some cases, totally irrelevant and detrimental to the entry of quality people into the profession. A rather dismal picture producing an even more dismal picture. Yet, amid this depressing scene is a bright light; the public has rediscovered something most educators have always known—the importance of the teacher.

There can be no excellence in education without first-rate teachers. One can change the curriculum, beg more materials, refurbish the physical environment, lengthen the school day, but without good teachers, change will not produce the desired effect. (p. VII)

But you and thousands like you are acquainted with the conditions of teaching, and you did not turn away from the challenge. You realize that our schools need to improve significantly in some areas, and although you know that the job is tough, you choose to be part of the solution. Because of your determination to improve our schools, you are a bright light of hope that will enable our schools to become all that they can be.

THE REFORM REPORTS

Educators know that the reports in the 1980s had both positive and negative impacts on education. When education is ignored, support for it is lost. Because the federal government has no national system, such as that in England and many other countries, the responsibility for supporting the schools is distributed among the people in each state. When the schools are operating effectively, there is a tendency to leave well enough alone or, worse, to interpret the success as an indication that schools are receiving adequate support. The reform reports have come at a critical time—when the schools are suffering drastically from inadequate funding, and these reports are stimulating major investments in the form of career ladders and other incentive programs for teachers. This is good.

All the reform reports state that our public schools need substantial improvement. The most common word used in these reports is *excellence*. This demand for higher-quality instruction is a valuable service. Clearly, there is much room for improvement. But the reports also have major flaws. Most of the reports were written by special-interest groups, which gives them a narrow perspective and stimulates them to sell the public the idea that education is an instrument of national policy, or an instrument of survival, or an instrument of economic growth, or that education is only for the gifted or that it is only for teachers who major in the sciences, languages, or mathematics. But as Stinnett and Henson (1982) state,

Fortunately Americans have never believed any of these [narrow goals] for long, only as a spur-of-the-moment impulse or under the influence of super salesmanship. Deep down, they know in their hearts that education exists for the cultivation of talents of the individual. And any society—be it a democracy, an autocracy, or a collectivist one—that insists upon viewing the child as a resource, or a weapon, or a tool, or an instrument will end up by treating him as such, and no more. (p. 292)

A second flaw in many of the reports is their narrow and unfounded recommendations for raising the quality of education. Many of these reports downplay the role of a professional education, suggesting that pedagogy be replaced by an increased number of courses in the teacher's content area. But will this improve the effectiveness of teachers? Not according to a recent national study of middle school teachers (Henson, Chissom, & Buttery, 1986), which found that 86 percent of all middle school teachers in the United States are comfortable with their knowledge in their subject fields. But they do admit that they need help in other areas. For example, almost one-third of the teachers say that they have inadequate knowledge in the areas of the psychology of learning and human growth and development. These teachers also reported areas of even greater needs. As many as 70 percent said that their knowledge of discipline is insufficient (Chapter 13 is devoted to this topic), and 44 percent of the teachers in the study said they need to know more about methodology. The new fifth-year programs should not neglect this important area.

The reports also offer other questionable advice for attaining excellence. For example, both *A Nation at Risk* and *Action for Excellence* recommend extending the length of both the school year and the school day. But as you will see in Chapter 3, merely assigning more instructional time would not raise the level of achievement. Studies show that although the length of time that teachers keep students focused on the lesson does correlate positively with achievement, the amount of *assigned* time for studying a topic does not correlate positively with student achievement. The common belief that the reason Japanese students outperform Americans in mathematics is that they spend more time studying mathematics is also dispelled. Although Japanese students attend school for five-and-a-half days a week, they study mathematics only every other day. Consequently, their total time on mathematics instruction is less than the time American students spend with the subject.

Another error in many of these reports is the recommendation that student electives and studies in the fine arts be reduced or eliminated. One report even calls for the return to lectures and recitation. But electives offer students opportunities to discover themselves—what they like and what disciplines they want to spend their lives pursuing. And through the fine arts they learn how to express themselves—an important skill. Bel Kaufman (1966) explains:

> I've run the gamut of every kind of school from the toughest to the so-called best. But, whatever the class, whatever the student—whether he was a window smasher or an apple polisher—each one it seems to me, in his own private wilderness, was crying: "Listen to me, look at me, pay attention to me, care about me."

The Bicentennial Committee of the National Education Association found that one of the top three things high school students want to learn in school is how to express their feelings (Shane, 1977). By studying the humanities, we learn to become human beings. No civilized nation can afford to eliminate the fine arts or the humanities from its curricula.

The reform reports have still other shortcomings. Most of them fail to recommend methods for organizing or teaching content; they also fail to mention the need for additional planning periods or facilities for teachers.

Although the reports are loaded with poor advice, they do contain a number of insightful and constructive ideas. For example, John Goodlad's *A Place Called School* (1984) is a different type of report and offers many excellent suggestions. One suggestion, missing in the other reports, is that teachers should identify and teach the *major concepts* of each discipline. When they do this, their students achieve more. A series of studies over the past 60 years has validated this approach, yet teachers seldom use it. Chapter 2 will show you how to identify the major concepts in your content areas and build your curriculum around them.

Another major report, by former U.S. commissioner of education and current Carnegie Foundation president Ernest Boyer (1983), portrays *communication skills* as the area of greatest need. Chapter 6 explains the teacher's role in both verbal and nonverbal communications and shows how teachers can trap themselves by unconsciously sending nonverbal messages. When you know about this "hidden curriculum," you can use it to help promote cooperation and learning in your classes. The report titled *Action for Excellence* was the only report that emphasized the need to motivate students (see Chapter 12 of this book).

THE TEACHER'S ROLE

Teachers can make a difference. If you cannot accept this premise, you should not pursue teaching as a career. You may be surprised when you read in Chapter 6 just how much a teacher's attitude can affect the level of student achievement. And it is imperative that you communicate to your students your belief that you can make a positive difference. Even the sequence of your activities on the first day of school is a critical factor in communicating your competence.

Did you ever consider that students have a perspective that is very different from that of their teachers? According to Stake and Easley (1978), students do not think of themselves as mastering knowledge, but rather they work to achieve for the teacher or the test. You must learn how to teach students to achieve for themselves and to demand the best for themselves. As stated by Stake and Easley, "teachers are the key to what happens in the classroom."

MOST TEACHERS DO NOT USE RESEARCH

More than 400 studies were used in writing this book, and each is capable of making you a better teacher. Unfortunately, the research also shows that teachers generally fail to use such knowledge effectively, if at all. Egbert (1984) noted, "Teachers ignore research and overestimate the value of personal experience" (p. 14). The result is that the ordinary classroom limits what students can do.

Never before have teachers had at their disposal so much knowledge about factors that affect achievement. Yet teachers usually do not base their planning on the factors that affect achievement. In Chapter 3 you will learn that effective teachers separate important information and salient information, and then simplify these major concepts for their students. Less-effective teachers tend to deal with more issues. Which will you do?

THE MAJOR CURRICULUM DETERMINER

Did you know that the major determiner of curriculum has been and continues to be the textbook? Teachers consider the textbook as the major and often only source of content. Yet, as you will see in Chapter 2, the most widely used textbooks cover as few as 8 percent of the major concepts required to master their discipline, and more than 90 percent of the content in the textbooks is written at the lowest cognitive level. A study of 61,000 questions asked in workbooks and teacher's manuals found that more than 95 percent of the questions were at the lowest cognitive level.

The topic of asking questions is itself a story that surprises many. Recent research shows that teachers can use questions in ways that increase the level of student achievement, yet they rarely apply this knowledge. For example, one well-known study showed 12 significant benefits from waiting only two seconds longer than normal for students to respond to questions. These 12 benefits are listed in Chapter 5. It is difficult to believe that, after directing questions to students, teachers move on to other content and other students so quickly, giving students almost no time to respond to their questions. Even the time when a question is asked can determine whether students remember the major ideas found in the lesson.

A FINAL CAUTION

Now you are aware of some of the errors in recent recommendations for improving education in the United States, and you know some of the real problems in our schools. Hope for improving poor schools rests more with teachers than with any other group. In fact, if the job is to be done, it will be the teachers who do it.

Teachers must stop relying so much on personal experience and must begin using the research data that is so abundant. But not all solutions come easily, and some problems do not lend themselves to a single, linear application of research. As you apply the results of more studies to your lessons, you will find that the results with any method may vary, just as each group of students is unique. The important thing to recognize is that teachers who have a repertoire of methods and who are aware of new findings will learn how to apply and adjust these resources to improve their lessons. This will also give them a number of alternatives from which to choose when the first selected method fails.

SUMMARY

These are turbulent times for teachers. Most Americans believe in the importance of quality education, but they do not think that today's schools are providing the excellent education that is needed.

The reform reports of the early 1980s were, in general, negative. They called the schools mediocre or worse and recommended major revisions in undergraduate teacher education programs. They provided a service by calling the public's attention to the often-neglected schools and by calling for badly needed improvement in instruction. But most of the reports reflect the narrow interests of the commissions and task forces that wrote them. And many of their recommendations, such as increasing the length of the school day and the school year and abolishing electives and fine arts, are educationally unsound. Some even recommend abolishing undergraduate teacher education programs.

Most of the reports recommend reducing the number of courses in pedagogy and replacing them with additional courses in subject areas. But today's teachers are comfortable with their content field knowledge. They want more knowledge about teaching methods, the psychology of learning, classroom management, and discipline. Most of the reports focus only on the hard sciences, foreign languages, and mathematics, and some recommend the deletion of the fine arts.

Some of the reform reports do make some good recommendations. These include teaching teachers to identify and teach the major concepts in their disciplines (covered in Chapter 2), teaching communications skills (Chapter 6), and learning how to motivate students (Chapter 12).

Recent studies support the claim that instruction in our schools needs improvement. As you review the studies discussed in this book, you should learn how to use their findings to plan and execute lessons, to construct tests, to manage and discipline your classes, and, in general, to become the very best teacher you can.

SUGGESTED READINGS

Alder, M. J. (1982). *The Paideia proposal*. New York: Macmillan.

Alexander, Lamar. (1986, November). Time for results: An overview. *Phi Delta Kappan, 68*, 202–204.

Bellon, C. B., Bellon, J. J., & Blank, M. A. (1986). *What really works: Research based instruction*. Knoxville, Tenn.: Bellon & Assoc.

Boyer, E. L. (1983). *High school*. New York: Harper & Row.

Carnegie Foundation (1986). *Teaching in the 21st century: A nation prepared*. Washington, D.C.: The Forum.

Fantini, M. D. (1986). *Regaining excellence in education*. Columbus, Ohio: Merrill.

Gallup, A. M. (1986). The 18th annual Gallup poll of the public's attitudes toward public schools. *Phi Delta Kappan, 68*, 43–59.

Goodlad, J. I. (1984). *A place called school*. New York: McGraw-Hill.

Henson, Kenneth T. (1986, March). Reforming America's public schools. *U.S.A. Today*, 75–77.

Henson, K., Chissom, B., & Buttery, T. (1986). Improving instruction in middle schools by attending to teachers' needs. *American Middle School Education, 9*(2), 2–7.

Johnson, W. J. (1985). *Education on trial*. San Francisco: ICS.

Joyce, B. R. (1985). *Improving America's schools*. New York: Longman.

Kaufman, B. (1966, December). Education and social change: Symposium. *Teachers College Record*, 230–231.

National Commission on Excellence in Education. (1983). *A nation at risk*. Washington, D.C.: U.S. Department of Education.

Shane, H. (1977). *Curriculum change toward the 21st century*. Washington, D.C.: National Education Association.

Stake, R. E., & Easley, J. A. (1978). Eds. Case studies in science education. Urbana, Ill.: Center for Instructional Research and Curriculum Evaluation, vol. 1, p. 29. See also, Rhodes, G. L. and Young, D. B. (1981). Making curriculum development work again. *Educational Leadership, 38* (8), 627–629.

Stinnett, T. M., & Henson, K. T. (1982). *America's public schools in transition*. New York: Teachers College Press.

Task Force for Economic Growth. (1983). *Action for excellence*. Denver: Education Commission of the States.

U.S. Department of Education. (1986). *What works: Research about teaching and learning*. Washington, D.C.: Department of Education.

Zumwalt, K. (1986). Introduction. In K. Zumwalt (Ed.), *Improving teaching,* (pp. vii–viii). 1986 Association for Supervision and Curriculum Development Yearbook. Alexandria, Va.: Association for Supervision and Curriculum Development.

PART I

PLANNING

The teacher's paramount purpose is to help students learn. Effective planning is a prerequisite to achieving this all-important goal.

Although school systems and state departments of education frequently provide teachers with curriculum guides and courses of study, teaching is a highly autonomous profession. Ultimately it is the teacher who determines what will be taught and what objectives will be pursued. Chapter 2 will help you examine the curriculum over a long period and design units to achieve the year's goals. Chapter 3 shows how you can plan to reach each day's objectives by selecting appropriate content and activities and by sequencing these in a way that will facilitate mastery of the content.

Good planning requires a working knowledge of behavioral objectives. Chapter 4 prepares you to write good objectives at all levels of all three domains of the educational taxonomies.

C H A P T E R **2**

Long-Range Planning

Objectives

- List several sources for selecting curriculum content.
- Give three reasons teachers should plan their own curricula and explain the student's role in curriculum development.
- Describe the role of the teacher's philosophy in curriculum planning.
- Explain the relationship between curriculum objectives and content and between curriculum content and student activities.
- List three unique characteristics of Taba's Inverted Curriculum Model.
- Develop a learning-teaching unit for a subject and grade level that you plan to teach.

PRETEST

	Agree	Disagree	Uncertain
1. All teachers have responsibility for determining the curricula for their classes.	____	____	____
2. The textbook usually determines the curricula in secondary school classes.	____	____	____
3. Teachers should not plan more than a few days (or at most a few weeks) in advance.	____	____	____
4. Each state has curriculum guides for teachers to use.	____	____	____
5. Textbooks should not be used to select content for courses.	____	____	____
6. Principles and concepts are more important than facts in selecting curriculum content.	____	____	____
7. Students do not have the expertise they would need to become involved in curriculum planning.	____	____	____
8. Because units must be kept very practical, philosophy has limited value in unit planning.	____	____	____
9. Going to another teacher for advice on curriculum matters is a professional mistake.	____	____	____
10. Teachers are responsible for covering material the students will need to progress in the subject next year.	____	____	____

Middle-Level Message

Middle-level teachers often have heavier and more diversified teaching assignments than teachers of high school subjects. The increased number of preparations required, coupled with the diversity of assignments, makes it necessary for middle-level teachers to have expertise in a range of subjects. Sometimes this leaves middle-level teachers feeling frustrated and hopeless.

One way to meet the need for expertise in a number of teaching fields is to continue your formal and informal education. A 1986 survey of middle-level teachers showed that they benefit from a variety of educational experiences. Middle-level teachers reported that they received significant advantages by attending college courses taken for credit, workshops taken for college credit, and noncredit workshops. They also reported that they learned much about curriculum development from participating on committees in their schools.

This chapter gives you the opportunity to learn about curriculum development. Relate each principle and each example to the grade levels and subjects you plan to teach. Appendix A will refresh your memory about the nature and goals of the middle school and the characteristics of middle-level learners.

Have you ever wondered who decides the nature of each course—What content will be covered? What will be the general goals? What experiences will be part of the course? Will there be field trips, guest speakers, or other special events? Who determines whether there will be one or two units of composition in an English class? Will the geometry class spend six weeks or six months studying solid geometry as opposed to plane geometry?

Is the decision based on the number of chapters devoted to each topic in the textbook? If so, who chooses the textbook? Surely not the principal or the super-intendent. As you might suspect, the teacher plays a significant role in making all these important decisions. According to Joyce (1979, p. 75), most of the important decisions by teachers are long term in their influence, as opposed to the influence of lesson-by-lesson planning. This means that the quality of education each of your future students (and these may number in the thousands) will receive will depend on how much you are involved in long-term planning.

Some teachers are willing to follow their textbooks, chapter by chapter, and bring little or no supplementary material to class. But allowing textbook authors to be the sole determiners of curricula is unwise. The authors know nothing about your particular students—their aspirations and their strengths and weaknesses, for example. Furthermore, they do not know what resources your community has. Are there facilities for good field trips? Are there people in the area who can give excellent talks? Is there a good zoo, a museum, a park, an industry that would offer valuable learning experiences? And does the textbook content correspond to *your* background, so that you can use your own expertise? Or perhaps your own preparation has gaps that will prevent you from teaching textbook content that you do not understand.

Because of these limitations, most teachers choose to become involved in the long-term planning of each course they teach. Yet most teachers know how important it is to have continuity throughout the year. "More recent research has shown the increased effectiveness in learning when experiences are organized to enable students to progress from unit to unit, in which each subsequent unit builds on the preceding ones" (Tyler, 1984, p. 36). Although most teachers do not have total freedom to make all these decisions alone, they have considerable influence.

Through experience, teachers can learn how to increase their influence in the total planning of their courses.

THE QUESTION OF CONTENT

At the beginning of the year, one of the first and greatest decisions will be what content to cover. Teachers often let their own likes and dislikes serve as the sole basis for content selection. For example, Scheville and colleagues (1981) report that an elementary school teacher who enjoyed teaching science taught 28 times more science than one who said she did not enjoy teaching science (Berliner, 1984, p. 53). Like most teachers, you will probably feel some obligation to cover the content that students will need as background for courses the next year. But an even greater concern for a teacher is that students gain the *understandings* and *skills* that will be needed the following years—and throughout their lives.

By now you may be wondering how teachers determine what students should learn in each class. Take a moment and make a list of 10 ways a teacher can find out what students will need to learn in a particular class. You might title it "Ways to Identify Content." No two teachers will have identical lists.

One logical place to begin this search is the state curriculum guide. Each state produces its own guides. These guides are important because they consider a course's content in relation to the previous year and the following years. In other words, the developers of state curriculum guides consider the total content needed by students throughout the entire K–12 school program. Another important feature of state curriculum guides is their focal points. They begin with broad goals and identify general understandings that students are expected to acquire and develop at each grade level.

A second source of information is the syllabi that local teachers of the next grade up use to teach your subject. By paying special attention to the beginning of each unit of study, you can see what the students are expected to know when they leave *your* class.

One popular source of information about what should be covered each year is textbooks. While you should not let a single textbook dictate your total curriculum, looking at several texts will remind you to incorporate certain important content from each. Start by examining several current texts at your own grade level and make a content-comparison chart. This way you can determine any deficiencies of your own text and compensate for them. Table 2.1 is an example of a chapter comparison of general secondary methods texts.

Although making chapter comparisons is a broad and therefore crude assessment of textbook content, it is a step in the right direction. A close examination of the texts in your field can help you identify the major concepts or principles in each content area. For example, a junior high earth science textbook should cover the following major areas of study: astronomy, geology, meteorology, oceanography, and physical geography. You may be surprised that Figure 2.1, which compares four popular texts, shows only a small percentage of pertinent principles

TABLE 2.1. CONTENT COMPARISON

Chapter Topics	Book A	Book B	Book C	Book D	Book E	Book F	Book G	Book H
Adolescence and learning	X	X	X	X	X			X
Planning	X	X	X	X	X	X	X	X
Classroom management	X	X	X	X	X	X	X	X
Evaluation	X	X	X	X	X	X	X	X
Teaching styles	X	X	X	X	X			X
Motivation	X	X						X
Multicultures or disadvantaged		X		X	X			X
History and aims		X						X
Audiovisuals		X		X				X
Teaching special pupils		X	X					X
Communications			X					X

represented in each book. Such poor coverage is not at all uncommon, however. In fact, the actual coverage of these texts ranges from about 8 percent to about 33 percent (see Figure 2.2).

The failure of textbooks to cover all important principles and concepts makes any textbook (or even a combination of texts) an incomplete source for determining what should be included in a course. Textbooks should be one of *many* curriculum determiners.

Another common weakness of textbooks is the sparsity of content at the higher levels of the cognitive domain. Most textbook content is written at the bottom levels. Studies by Davis and Hunkins showed that more than 85 percent of textbook content is written on the recall level (Orlich et al., 1980). An analysis of more than 61,000 questions in workbooks, texts, and teachers' manuals accompanying nine world history textbooks showed that more than 95 percent of those questions were lower-order (Trachtenberg, 1974, pp. 55–57).

It is important that the students themselves discover and develop some content generalizations. As Doyle (1983) explains, "Students must be given ample opportunities for direct experience with content in order to derive generalizations and invent [learning] algorithms on their own. . . . Gaps are left which students, themselves, must fill." This means that, whatever the sources, content selection must never be done in isolation from students and from the instructional process.

Researchers at Michigan State University found still other factors that influence the selection of content. These include the perceived *effort* required to teach a subject matter area, the perceived *difficulty* of the subject matter area for students, and the teacher's personal *feelings of enjoyment* while teaching a subject matter area (Scheville et al., 1981). Personal preferences of teachers can and often

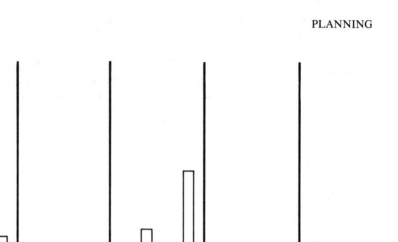

Figure 2.1 Variance in Representation of Principles among Four Basic Science Textbooks

do dominate selection of content. This is one reason you should involve all your students in curriculum planning. Hilda Taba (1962) developed a way to do this in the 1950s. In contrast to the other curriculum-planning models, which are developed outside the school, Taba's model is developed by teachers and their students. It is different in that it starts at the bottom—in the classroom—and moves

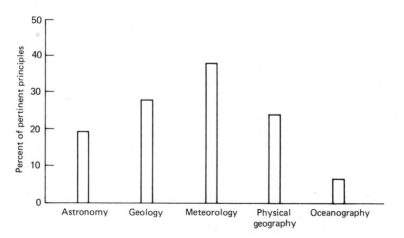

Figure 2.2 Mean Representation of Pertinent Principles for Each Subject

upward, and it has come to be known as Taba's Inverted Model. Taba's model has the advantage of taking into consideration the desires and abilities of your students, and because it is developed by you, the teacher, you will be more likely to use it, and more effectively, than if you were using a unit that had been developed externally.

Another unique feature of Taba's model is that it connects curriculum with instruction. Taba achieved this by making the learning unit the center of her model. In other words, you and your students will choose major *topics* of study, such as astronomy or geology. Then you, by yourself, will develop for each topic a unit lasting from a few days to several weeks. For convenience, most units are designed to be the same length as a grading period. Since most secondary and middle school systems report grades every six weeks, most units are six weeks long, but there is nothing wrong with having two three-week units in a grading period.

THE UNIT PLAN

For each major objective you hope to accomplish during the year, you should have a specific plan. This is the unit plan. For example, a teacher of junior high earth science would probably want each student to acquire some understanding of astronomy, ecology, geology, meteorology, oceanography, paleontology, mineralogy, and physical geography. For each of these areas, the teacher should plan a unit of study that will last from a few days to a few weeks and contain the topics that the teacher believes are essential to a general understanding of earth science.

Planning the Unit

Once you have selected your unit topics, you can plan each unit. The planning can be a joint effort by you and your students, but this does not mean that you and your students should have an equal role in the planning. Before you approach the class with the project of planning a unit of study, you will want to determine exactly what your role will be and what theirs will be.

Your extensive study of the subject gives you insights into what students need to know about the subject of the unit—insights that your students do not have. Therefore, a major part of your role in planning a unit is to identify some of the important ideas or concepts that will be developed in the unit and to explain the importance of this material to the students. Students may want to have some ideas or sections of the unit deleted solely on the basis of a dislike for certain material, but if you believe these concepts are essential, you will not allow the material to be omitted.

A second function of your role in planning a unit is to give students an opportunity to include areas within the unit that *they* think should be studied. Even though you might think certain topics are less important than some others that are not being included, consider that the mere fact that students find a topic interesting makes it relevant and meaningful to them. Involving students in planning has another important advantage: It helps avoid the sequential approach that often limits learning. According to Hart (1983, p. 77), "Because the ordinary classroom does not provide this richness in learning and, in most instances, limits what the brain can do, students become addicted or habituated to this limited, sequential approach." Involving students can also increase their emotional commitment to the material, which is important because it enhances their learning of that material. According to Levy (1983), "If students are engaged [in learning activities, as opposed to remaining passive], both sides of the brain will participate in the educational process regardless of subject matter."

A third part of your role in planning a unit is to help the class select activities necessary for developing an understanding of the unit. The activities are the vehicles through which students will learn the content. Doyle (1979) expressed the importance of activities when he said, "The immediate test of teaching in classrooms is that of gaining and maintaining the cooperation of students in activities that fill the available time." This does not mean that the teacher selects some of the activities and the students independently select others. When you present the problem of selecting class activities, have on hand a list of activities from which the class can choose. This provides a start in the desired direction. But if the students want to add other activities that are feasible, why not let them? You might ask yourself about each proposed activity: Is it contrary to school policy? Is it dangerous or harmful to me, to the students, or to others? Is it something I should first check with the principal? Is it worthwhile? And finally: Is it something we could try? If so, it may prove worthwhile because the students are interested in that particular activity.

Parts of the Unit Plan

The learning unit, or unit plan, is much more than an outline of the subject material to be explored within a certain topic. Although there are many variations, most unit plans contain most of the following parts: a title; a statement of philosophy, goals, objectives, and content to be covered; teacher and student activities to enhance the attainment of the objectives; and a method for evaluating the degree of understanding developed while studying the unit. The unit plan may also include a list of resource people (consultants) and resource materials (bibliography).

The learning unit or unit plan is an outline of the subject material to be explored within a certain topic; and it is much more. Although there are many variations, most units contain the following parts: a statement of philosophy, a list of general objectives or purposes, a list or outline of content, a description of activities for students to engage in, and an evaluation system (see Figure 2.4). The significance of involving students in planning is stated well by Doll (1978, p. 393): "Despite the imperfections and general functioning one can find in instances of teacher-pupil planning, the dividends that such cooperative planning pays in pupil

Philosophy → Purposes → Content → Activities → Evaluation

Figure 2.3 Anatomy of a Learning Unit

interest and achievement have resulted in its acceptance as a valid instructional process.''

The statement of philosophy is merely a declaration of the teacher's beliefs about such issues as the purposes of the school, the nature of adolescence, how adolescents learn, and the purposes of life in general. Because teachers spend too little time reflecting on their beliefs about these all-important issues, it is the most neglected part of learning units. Yet the first question teachers hear at the beginning of a new unit is often ''Why do we have to study this stuff?'' Only by thinking through these broad issues can you prepare to answer this question intelligently.

The statement of purposes is a list of general expectations that you want the unit to achieve. For example, a tenth-grade unit in government may include such general expectations as an understanding of how a bill is introduced, more tolerance of the opinions of others, or an appreciation of democracy as a type of government. Unlike the performance objectives used in daily planning, which are stated in specific, observable, and measurable terms, the statement of purposes for a unit should be much more general.

Your selection of content for any unit should be based on three broad considerations: (1) the *significance* of the content in attaining the purposes of the particular unit (in other words, it must be content that is necessary to master in order to reach the general objectives), (2) the importance of the content to society, and (3) the needs and interests of the learners.

Choose the activities on the same basis; select experiences that will enable students to learn the content. Do not feel obligated to select one activity for each objective, for some of the best activities serve multiple purposes and lead to the attainment of several objectives. For example, one activity for a senior English class might be to write a composition contrasting Shelley's poetry with that of Lord Byron. Such an activity would undoubtedly provide opportunities for both gaining writing skills and sharpening concepts of an author's style by contrasting it with another author's. Some teachers believe they do not have time for achieving multiple objectives in their classes, but they should realize that several objectives can be met simultaneously. Planning activities that have multiple objectives does not necessarily promote inefficiency (Zais, 1976, p. 357). Each learning unit should contain two types of student performance and include different types of measurement, such as written tests, oral tests, debates, term projects, homework assignments, classwork, and perhaps performance in class or group discussions. This type of evaluation, which examines the quality of a product, is called *product evaluation*.

Another type of evaluation that should be applied to each learning unit is called *process evaluation*. This is merely a description of the effectiveness of the teaching or the unit. Process evaluation analyzes the various parts of the unit in isolation to determine whether the unit needs improvement. It also involves looking at all parts together to see how they relate to one another. Ask yourself such questions as, Is my philosophy sound? Does it convince these students that the unit is important? Are the purposes important? Am I being realistic in expecting these students to achieve them in this length of time? Is the content in this unit what is needed to achieve the unit's stated purposes? Are these activities helpful in attaining these objectives? Is the evaluation fair to everyone? Does it discriminate between those who have met the objectives and those who have not?

Learning units should include certain practical information too. Besides the title, subject, and grade level, they should contain a list of resources—consultants, equipment, facilities, and supplies—needed to teach the unit, especially audiovisual aids. They should also include a list of references that support the unit and can be used to pursue the topic further. Finally, each unit should contain performance objectives that (1) are stated in terms of student behavior, (2) describe the conditions, and (3) specify the minimum acceptable level of performance.

Let's Ponder

Read the following statements and respond to the questions below.

Don't Fix It If It Ain't Broke

TEACHER A

Too much attention is given to instructional planning, evaluating lessons, and replanning. Some of the most effective lessons occur as spur-of-the-moment insights that teachers have on the way to class. But this can occur only when teachers are mentally free from overly structured lesson plans. In fact, the cookbook approach to teaching often results in boring the students. Anyway, aren't lessons supposed to serve the students' needs rather than the teacher's needs?

TEACHER B

You had better not listen to that gibberish. Those words probably come from a teacher who is too lazy to plan lessons adequately. Granted, spur-of-the-moment insights may occur, but how often does that really happen? No sensible teacher will sit around and wait for an inspiration. It's far better to overplan than underplan—if indeed one can overplan at all.

1. List some benefits of instructional planning.
2. Think about a former teacher who evidenced little or no planning. Was this teacher able to relate to students better? Describe the amount of learning that occurred in this teacher's class.
3. Can instructional planning serve the needs of students? How?
4. In Chapter 3 we will see that effective teachers have the ability to be flexible and yet return to the focus of the lesson. How does planning affect teacher flexibility?

Sample Unit Plans

Examine the following unit plans. Notice that the title describes the unit; the statement of purpose or objectives describes a desired change in the students; and the evaluation is stated in terms of the objectives stated at the beginning of the unit.

METEOROLOGY UNIT PLAN: WHAT METEOROLOGY MEANS TO YOU

I. Purpose
   A. Knowledge: To understand—
      1. The different types of weather
      2. The principles of weather formation
      3. The role of the weatherperson
      4. The names and principles of commonly used weather instruments
      5. Weather vocabulary
   B. Attitudes: To appreciate—
      1. The damage weather can do
      2. The advantage of good weather
      3. How weather affects our daily behavior
      4. The rate of accuracy of weather predictions
      5. The precision use of weather instruments
      6. The fallacies of superstitions about the weather
   C. Skills: To develop the ability to—
      1. Read and interpret weather instruments
      2. Read and interpret weather maps
      3. Predict future weather

II. Daily Lessons
   A. Definition of weather
   B. Precipitation
      1. The different types of precipitation
      2. How each type of precipitation is formed
   C. Reading the weather map
   D. Reading weather instruments
   E. Predicting weather
   F. Effects of geographic location on weather
   G. Effects of the earth's rotation on weather
   H. Effects of the earth's tilting on weather
   I. How to change weather that can hurt you

III. Materials
   A. Weather reports from newspapers
   B. Weather maps
   C. Equipment for making fog: air pump, water, jar
   D. Barometer, thermometer, anemometer, wind vane
   E. Graph paper for each student

IV. Evaluation
   Tests for each section of the unit: approximately one test per week's study of the topic.

The above unit plan was chosen for its brevity and simplicity. This does not make it a superior plan, but such brief units are often used. Do you think the unit is too skimpy? What do you think about this format? Is the outline adequate? Figure 2.5 shows the parts commonly found in a unit. Which of the parts in the figure are missing from the sample unit above?

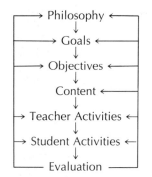

Figure 2.5 Diagram of a Learning/Teaching Unit

Did you notice that the meteorology unit has neither a statement of philosophy nor a statement of rationale to show the significance of the unit? Many educators feel that a statement of philosophy will help you clarify your own basic beliefs about life, school, and adolescents and how they learn. Goals and objectives should coincide and should reflect your basic beliefs. Other educators prefer to have a statement of rationale instead of a statement of philosophy. When you write a statement of rationale, you justify the unit to yourself; then you can use the rationale to convince students that the unit is worth *their* time and energy.

The meteorology unit has no sections titled "Teacher Activities" or "Student Activities." This is unfortunate, because at this time the teacher should be making decisions about activities, such as taking the class to a weather station and showing films on meteorology. The weather station may need advance notice, and for field trips students will have to identify in advance what information they will attempt to obtain during the visit. Films must be scheduled and ordered in advance so that they will be available when you need them, and you will need time to preview them. You can probably identify other weaknesses in this unit plan.

Below is a sample chemistry unit designed for use in an eleventh-grade class. This more comprehensive plan has fewer weaknesses (but you will be the judge of that). It has most of the parts that educators consider essential to any unit, but as you study it, note both its strengths and its weaknesses. Pay particular attention to the unit's overall structure and organization. Can you improve it?

CHEMISTRY UNIT PLAN: THE ORGANIZATION OF CHEMISTRY

I. Statement of Purpose. The chapters covered in this unit are designed to introduce the beginning chemistry student to the basic background and structural knowledge needed for further studies in chemistry. Topics include Atomic Structure and the Periodic Table.

Let's Talk

A statement of general purpose, aims, goals, or rationale is helpful for orienting the teacher to the unit, and can be used to introduce the unit to the students. The overall purpose can also include general changes in student behavior. But because the reason for teaching is to change students' behavior, a much more specific list of performance objectives is used to explain precisely what the teacher expects the students to be able to do after studying the unit. Because this particular unit is built around two chapters, the following list of objectives will be for both chapters.

II. Performance Objectives
    A. Chapter 1: Atomic Theory. The eleventh-grade general chemistry student will be able to—

Lesson 1
1. Define an atom correctly in a closed book test.
2. Give the size of an atom in the unit posttest.
3. Identify the parts of an atom by name and describe them, given an unlabeled diagram of the atom. Four of five parts must be correctly labeled and described.
4. Match the mass of the parts of the atom to the correct path, given a list of masses.

Lesson 2
1. Define the atomic number of an atom.
2. Define the mass number of an atom in a closed book test.
3. Utilize the concept of isotopes by correctly grouping given atoms into isotopic groups.
4. Apply the concept of energy level shells by designating the number of electrons in each shell, given an atomic number.

Lesson 3
1. Correctly define atomic mass in a closed book test.
2. Define Avogadro's number in a closed book test.
3. Apply the concept of a mole by the amount of a substance in a mole of a given substance.
4. Define the atomic weight of an atom in a closed book test.
5. Apply the concepts of atomic number, Avogadro's number, mole, and gram atomic weight in solving simple stoichiometric problems. Given the problem and required information, the student must solve for the asked-for information, correctly answering 80 percent of the problems to receive credit. (Partial credit given for correct setups.)

Let's Talk

Each performance objective should contain four parts. Check the above objectives against these criteria. It is as simple as A, B, C, D.
Audience: The student should be the subject of each objective.
Behavior: The student's behavior should be the verb of each objective.

Conditions: The objective should describe the conditions under which the student is expected to perform.

Degree: The degree or level of performance required of the students should be specified.

B. Chapter 2: Periodic Table. The eleventh-grade general chemistry student will be able to—

Lesson 1:
1. List at least three of the four basic elements.
2. Identify the common elements by symbol. This will be shown by correctly giving the elements or symbol asked for in 15 of 18 questions in two in-class quizzes.

Lesson 2
1. Obtain atomic numbers of elements from the periodic table with an accuracy level of 80 percent.
2. Obtain the mass number of elements from the periodic table with an accuracy level of 80 percent.
3. Obtain a given element's electron configuration from the periodic table.

Lesson 3
1. Define periodic law.
2. Define "group of elements."
3. Define "period of elements."
4. Distinguish the characteristics of families of elements by matching the correct family with the given characteristic with a minimum accuracy level of 80 percent.
5. With 80 percent or above accuracy, match the correct family with the given element.

III. Attitudinal Objective. The eleventh-grade general chemistry student will be able to participate in class discussions. This objective will be met when 80 percent of the class answers general questions, directed to the class as a whole, during the course of the discussion.

Let's Talk

Below are lists of concepts and content generalizations under topics to be studied. A check to see whether students know these terms can help the teacher begin at the appropriate level. The second list—generalizations—is even more important. These are the major understandings that should come from the unit. Notice that they are essential for achieving the preceding objectives.

IV. Concepts and Generalizations
    A. Topic 1: Atomic Structure

Concepts	*Generalizations*
Atomic theory	Atomic theory has been developed to support
Atom*	observations.
Proton*	Each subparticle composing the atom (electron,
Neutron*	neutron, proton) has certain characteristics and
Electron*	is unique in energy levels or shells.
Nucleus*	Each atom has its electrons arranged.
Element	
Mole	
Avogadro's number	
Angstrom, Å	

B. Topic 2: Arrangement of Electrons in Atoms

Concepts	*Generalizations*
Orbitals	Quantum numbers describe the
Orbital notation	orientation of an electron in an
Electron configuration notation	atom in terms of (a) distance from
Electron dot notation	the nucleus; (b) shape; (c) position
	in space with respect to the three
	axes (x, y, z); and (d) direction of
	spin.

C. Topic 3: Periodic Table

Concepts	*Generalizations*
Periodic table	The periodic table organizes the elements;
Series (period)	properties can be predicted from the elements'
Group (family)	positions.
Noble gas family	Elements with similar arrangements of outer shell
Sodium family	electrons have similar properties.
Calcium family	
Nitrogen family	
Oxygen family	

Let's Talk

Now that we have identified a purpose for the unit, set down the objectives for the lesson, and selected the major concepts and content generalizations that are needed to achieve those objectives, it is time to plan the daily activities. These should include the teacher's activities and the activities in which the students will be involved. Chapter 3, on planning daily lessons, will cover the planning of meaningful ways to involve students.

---

* Students should already be familiar with these concepts.

RECAP OF MAJOR IDEAS

1. In selecting content, teachers should seek out the generalizations that are essential to understanding the subject.
2. Teachers can use their own expertise but also involve students in selecting content and activities.
3. Hilda Taba's Inverted Curriculum model is considered superior because it is built in the classroom by teachers around teaching units.
4. Learning activities are the vehicle through which students develop the generalizations needed to understand a subject.
5. Teachers can add consistency to their lesson planning by beginning their units with a written statement of their own philosophy toward life, school, and learning.
6. Each part of a learning unit should relate to the other parts. This is called coherence.
7. When beginning a unit, teachers have at their disposal many sources—for example, teachers at the next grade level, textbooks, curriculum guides, and students.
8. Used by themselves, textbooks are an inadequate source of information for curriculum planning.
9. Long-term planning is essential for maximum learning opportunities.

POSTTEST

Now that you have read the chapter, take a moment to respond to the following statements again.

	Agree	Disagree	Uncertain
1. All teachers have responsibility for determining the curricula for their classes.	____	____	____
2. The textbook usually determines the curricula in secondary school classes.	____	____	____
3. Teachers should not plan more than a few days (or at most a few weeks) in advance.	____	____	____
4. Each state has curriculum guides for teachers to use.	____	____	____
5. Textbooks should not be used to select content for courses.	____	____	____
6. Principles and concepts are more important than facts in selecting curriculum content.	____	____	____
7. Students do not have the expertise they would need to become involved in curriculum planning.	____	____	____
8. Because units must be kept very practical, philosophy has limited value in unit planning.	____	____	____
9. Going to another teacher for advice on curriculum matters is a professional mistake.	____	____	____
10. Teachers are responsible for covering material the students will need to progress in the subject next year.	____	____	____

CASES

The focus of this chapter is the teacher's role in long-term planning. The chapter offers guidelines and suggestions for planning learning units for periods that may range from a few days to a few weeks. But blanket statements that dictate step-by-step planning have been avoided. These guidelines and your own experience will enable you to develop a system that you will be comfortable with and that will let you provide learning experiences your students will need.

This is not to suggest that you will have no problems or struggles. The following cases are examples of the dilemmas teachers can encounter as they plan teaching units.

Case 1: Should Lesson Planning Be Sequential?

Bongo Nagatah was realizing his dream of attending an American university where he could learn to become a master teacher and return to his native land for a lifetime of service. Bongo applied himself totally. He had indeed mastered his chosen teaching field, mathematics, which he enjoyed for its preciseness and structure, and he had done equally well in his professional education courses. In spite of all this, however, he ran into problems. Ironically, much of his frustration resulted from his love of structure.

When his methods course began developing learning units, Bongo looked for guidelines or rules that would help him come up with a learning unit. He wrote a brief statement of philosophy for the unit but was not sure about the next step. The professor had instructed the class to follow the statement with a list of general goals for the unit, but Bongo felt that he was leaving out some important content and that perhaps he should make a content outline before identifying the goals. Later, when he began identifying content and activities, the same dilemma emerged: If he selected the activities first, how could he be sure that content was being adequately covered, but if he selected the content first, how could be take advantage of opportunities that he wanted to offer his students—field trips, speakers, and civic activities? He especially wanted to encourage his students to enter projects in the regional science and mathematics fair.

Discussion

1. Is there a definite sequence for developing a unit?
   In a general sense there is. Your statement of philosophy should be written first. The goals should precede the behavioral objectives, and the objectives should precede the selection of content and activities. Most teachers find this sequence helpful, but many believe that following it in all situations is restrictive and could even damage their units.
2. How can you ensure complete content coverage and also take advantage of opportunities to involve students in valuable learning experiences?
   Because a general sequence of design can be helpful, you may prefer to follow the accepted sequence until you have a specific reason for changing it. Many teachers find that skipping a step and going back to it later can be useful in some situations.

Case 2: A Principal Requires Six Months' Advance Planning

When I moved from teaching in a rural school to my first urban school, I learned the true meaning of planning. In the smaller, rural school lesson-planning had never been mentioned, but during my first faculty meeting at the urban school the principal handed each teacher a 300-page spiral book for entering lesson plans for the following six months. Because I had never planned for more than a week or two in advance, I was overwhelmed, but my fellow faculty members accepted the principal's request without question.

After the meeting, I asked whether the principal ever actually checked the plans to see if they were completed so far in advance and was told that there would probably be a surprise check once or twice a year. In addition, my lesson plan book would have to be left in the office in case I was absent, so a substitute teacher could use it.

The other teachers assured me that there was no required length for each lesson and suggested that I list only the name or title of each lesson without attempting to describe it. Because even this would consume several hours and appeared to be a waste of time, I decided to take a chance and enter only two weeks of plans in advance. I followed this procedure throughout the year. My hunch was correct. The lesson plan book was never checked, and fortunately I was not absent. The following year no mention was made of the six-month policy.

Discussion

1. How far in advance should teachers plan?
   Teachers should plan far enough in advance that when emergencies arise they can meet them without disrupting the continuity of the classes. This will help prevent regular and substitute teachers from having to meet their classes poorly prepared. By planning a few weeks in advance, the teacher can arrange logical continuity in class experiences.
2. What are some reasons teachers should not be required to plan months in advance?
   If teachers are forced to plan months in advance, they are being encouraged to plan merely for the purpose of satisfying their administrators. This can result in plans that look impressive on paper but are not functional in the classroom. Moreover, because each class is unique and because student interests change, the teacher should be flexible enough to challenge new interests as they emerge. A set of lesson plans extending throughout the year would probably not provide such flexibility. Can you think of other disadvantages of requiring teachers to plan lessons months in advance?
3. Why did my principal "misuse" lesson plans?
   I believe that he saw lesson planning from an administrator's rather than the learner's point of view. He saw the lesson plan as an instrument to force teachers to upgrade their teaching. Some administrators tend to view everything in terms of ease of provision, expense, and other administrative terms, but it is the teacher's responsibility to see everything in terms of the effect it has on students. Teachers should try to find a way to satisfy both the administrator and the needs of the students.
4. Was my decision to disregard the rules justified?
   Probably not. Although I was determined to refrain from doing what I thought would be detrimental to my teaching, I should have found a way to satisfy the demands of my administrator too. How would you respond to such a requirement?

ACTIVITIES

The "Objectives" at the beginning of the chapter promised that you would learn how to develop a complete learning unit. If you are ready for this challenge, select a topic in one of your teaching fields and apply your skills as follows:

1. Write a brief statement of your philosophy of education. Include your beliefs about the general purposes of secondary schools, the nature of adolescence, and the nature of learning.
2. Write at least three broad goals for a unit of three to six weeks.
3. For each goal, write a few behavioral objectives.
4. Outline the major content generalizations for the unit.
5. Select some teacher activities and student activities to facilitate attainment of these objectives.
6. Design a grading system and a system for evaluating the effectiveness of this unit. Consider whether it has all the essential parts; also check the sequence of these parts.

SUGGESTED READINGS

Beauchamp, G. A. (1975). *Curriculum theory* (3rd ed.). Wilmette, Ill.: Kagg.

Berliner, D. C. (1984). The half-full glass: A review of research on teaching. In P. A. Hosford (Ed.), *Using what we know about teaching*. Alexandria, Va.: Association for Supervision and Curriculum Development.

Casciano-Savignano, C. (1978). *Systems approach to curriculum and instructional improvement*. Columbus, Ohio: Merrill.

Curtis, T. E., & Bidwell, W. W. (1977). *Curriculum and instruction for emerging adolescents*. Reading, Mass.: Addison-Wesley.

Doll, R. C. (1978). *Curriculum improvement: Decision making and process* (4th ed.). Boston: Allyn & Bacon.

Doyle, W. (1979). Making managerial decisions in classrooms. In D. L. Duke (Ed.), *Classroom management,* 78th Yearbook of the National Association for the Study of Education, part II. Chicago: University of Chicago Press.

Doyle, W. (1983). Academic work. *Review of Educational Research* (Washington, D.C.: American Educational Research Assoc.), *53*(2), 176–177.

Firth, G. R., & Kimpston, R. D. (1973). *The curriculum continuum in perspective*. Itasca, Ill.: Peacock.

Foshay, A. (Ed.). (1984). *Considered action for curriculum improvement*. Alexandria, Va.: Association for Supervision and Curriculum Development.

Hart, L. A. (1983). *How the brain works*. New York: Basic Books.

Hass, G. (1980). *Curriculum planning: A new approach* (3rd ed.). Boston: Allyn & Bacon.

Joyce, B. (1979). Toward a theory of information processing in teaching. *Educational Research Quarterly, 3*. 66–77.

Levy, J. (1983). Research synthesis on right and left hemispheres: We think with both sides of the brain. *Educational Leadership, 40,* 66–71.

Miller, J. P., & Seller, W. (1985). *Curriculum: Perspectives and practices*. New York: Longman.

Oliva, P. (1981). *Developing the curriculum*. Boston: Little, Brown.

Oliver, A. I. (1974). *Curriculum improvement: A guide to problems, principles, and procedures*. New York: Dodd, Mead.

Orlich, D. C., et al. (1980). *Teaching strategies: A guide to better instruction*. Lexington, Mass.: D. C. Heath.

Orlosky, D. E., & Smith, B. O. (1978). *Curriculum development: Issues and insights.* Chicago: Rand McNally.

Rubin, L. (1979). *Curriculum handbook.* Boston: Allyn & Bacon.

Scheville, J., et al. (1981). Teachers as policy brokers in the content of elementary school mathematics. National Institute of Education Contract No. P-80-0127. East Lansing: Institute for Research on Teaching, Michigan State University.

Schubert, W. H. (1985). *Curriculum: Perspective, paradigm, and possibility.* New York: Macmillan.

Steeves, F. L., & English, F. W. (1978). *Secondary curriculum for a changing world.* Columbus, Ohio: Merrill.

Taba, H. (1962). *Curriculum development: Theory and practice.* Orlando Fla.: Harcourt Brace Jovanovich.

Trachtenberg, D. (1974). Student tasks in text material: What cognitive skills do they tap? *Peabody Journal of Education, 52,* 54–57.

Trump, J. L., & Miller, D. F. (1979). *Secondary school curriculum improvement: Meeting challenges of the times (3rd ed.). Boston: Allyn & Bacon.*

Tyler, R. W. (1984). Curriculum development and research. In P. A. Hosford (Ed.), *Using what we know about teaching.* Alexandria, Va.: Association for Supervision and Curriculum Development.

Wulf, K. M., & Schave, B. (1984). *Curriculum design.* Glenview, Ill.: Scott, Foresman.

Zais, R. S. (1976). *Curriculum: Principles and foundations.* New York: Crowell.

C H A P T E R *3*

Planning Daily Lessons

Objectives

- Define and differentiate between *daily lesson plan* and *unit plan*.
- Describe four major steps in developing a unit plan.
- Write a unit plan in your area of specialty.
- List four essential qualities of a behavioral objective and write five behavioral objectives.
- List in order six pertinent parts of a daily lesson plan.
- Write a plan for each of two daily lessons.

PRETEST

	Agree	Disagree	Uncertain
1. All lesson plans should begin with a list of the subject content to be learned.	___	___	___
2. A lesson plan that works well with one group may not work well with another group.	___	___	___
3. The best lesson plans are those drawn up by outside experts (as opposed to teacher-made plans).	___	___	___
4. To be effective, a lesson must cause students to change their behavior.	___	___	___
5. A lesson is a failure unless it gives students new skills.	___	___	___
6. Student activities are essential to all lesson plans.	___	___	___
7. Most teachers begin planning by identifying the goals and objectives to be attained.	___	___	___
8. Most changes in teaching that come as teachers interact with students are based on lesson objectives.			

Middle-Level Message

This chapter shows that the amount of time allocated to a subject does not necessarily affect achievement, but that the amount of time students are engaged with the subject does. This can become a handicap for middle-level classes, because the energy level for this age-group is so high that keeping them on task often becomes difficult. But their high energy level can be used as a positive learning force since the time students spend developing concepts (instead of just studying the concepts) does correlate positively with achievement.

It is especially important that middle-level teachers not try to suppress the high activity level of these students, but rather channel their energy toward developing concepts. Middle-level teachers should challenge students to learn the concepts that comprise their chosen disciplines.

In Chapter 2 you saw how important planning is to teaching. You learned to begin each year by identifying the goals you hope to achieve along the way and to select content accordingly. You also learned how to design learning units through which you and your students could achieve these goals. As essential as they are, however, goals by themselves remain no more than illusive glittering generalities. To make them attainable, you must design daily lesson plans that include these general expectations (goals) but that can also be translated into more specific terms. Each daily lesson plan should be developed to achieve a particular part of the unit; in fact, most units contain a series of daily lesson plans.

THE DAILY LESSON PLAN

Because the teaching unit is usually content oriented and may not specify the experiences needed for learning each day's lesson, you will need to develop daily strategies for helping students move nearer to the unit goals. For most teachers, this is the daily lesson plan. A teacher who attempts to teach without a lesson plan is like a pilot taking off for an unknown destination without a map. Like the map, the lesson plan provides direction toward the lesson objectives. If the lesson begins to stray, the lesson plan brings it back on course. This may be difficult without a lesson plan. According to Walter (1984, p. 55), however, despite the emphasis teacher education places on the "ends-means" approach, there is now much evidence that experienced teachers do not begin the planning process by determining objectives. Studies show that teachers begin by determining the content to be covered, and then design or select learning activities for students (Zahorik, 1975; Walter, 1979; Shavelson & Stern, 1981). One study, which examined planning in middle-level laboratories, found that teachers spend most of their planning time with content, a moderate amount of time selecting strategies, and the smallest amount of time on objectives (Peterson, Marx, & Clark, 1978). Furthermore, even when teachers modify their teaching approaches, they seldom consider the lesson objectives (Clark & Peterson, 1986, p. 269).

Factors Affecting Achievement

Other recent data provide a framework for developing daily lesson plans. Romberg and Carpenter (1986) reviewed studies of mathematics classes and discovered three significant variables associated with student achievement. First, instead of teaching the concepts needed to understand their subject, teachers of the same subject and grade level may cover very different materials. This unfortunately reduces the time spent studying the important concepts, and "classes in which less time is allocated to mathematics instruction (or instruction in any subject) are likely to have relatively poorer achievement in the subject" (Romberg, 1983, p. 60). Yet as we saw in Chapter 2, the most frequent determiner of content–the textbook–usually does a poor job covering concepts that are essential to understanding a discipline. In a similar study of content coverage by textbooks, Schville and colleagues (1983) examined the three most commonly used fifth-grade math textbooks; more than half of the 290 topics common to one or more books were unique to a single book (p. 376).

A second factor in daily lesson planning is the amount of *engaged* time teachers spend on a topic or concept compared to the time that is allocated for the subject. For example, during the same allocated 50-minute period, one class may spend 20 minutes on the day's lesson (engaged time), while another class may spend 40 minutes on the lesson. The later class is likely to achieve more. Thus it is obvious that each lesson should be planned so that it engages students with the important concepts and skills for that subject.

A third factor that affects achievement is the time students spend *developing* particular concepts, as opposed to the time they spend just *studying* the concepts. In the developmental portion of a lesson, students spend time discussing such issues as why the concept is true, how skills or concepts are interrelated, and how to use these broader relationships to estimate answers to problems. In other words, developmental time puts the important concepts and skills in a broader context in an attempt to extend the students' understandings of those ideas.

Unfortunately, teachers usually do not base their planning on the factors that affect achievement (Carnahan, 1980, p. 140). Furthermore, clear concepts in each discipline, and effective models and strategies for teaching them, have not been available because they were not identified. As Armento (1986) stated recently, "Methodological advances have outpaced conceptual advances in the last 10 years" (pp. 948–949). Although Armento was referring to the field of social studies, the same is true of all disciplines. But there is hope, because more studies that identify important concepts in disciplines are being conducted today, and there is an increase in metacognitive studies, which will help determine more effective ways to teach students to analyze their individual conceptual development processes. For the present, prospective teachers should seek out concepts and skills needed to achieve the objectives of each lesson, and plan to use them as focal points for studying. These concepts and principles should become the content portion of each lesson plan.

What Makes a Good Lesson Plan?

Lesson plans come in many sizes and varieties. The length or style of the plan does not make one plan better than another. A good lesson plan can be a comprehensive outline that is worded formally, neatly typed on bond paper, and enclosed in a plastic binder, or it can be a brief outline written in pencil on three-by-five-inch cards. The styles of good lesson plans vary as much as their length. A good lesson plan contains material that will challenge students throughout the hour and activities that involve every student. The format will be easy for you to follow with only a glance and you will never have to stop the lesson to read it.

Arguing about which type of lesson plan is best would be a waste of time. The lesson plan should be thought of as a tool, and like any tool it will be only as effective as the person using it; yet, the worker who has good machinery has an advantage over the worker who has faulty equipment. The important point is that you develop and correctly use a lesson plan that works for you.

Setting Objectives

As in planning an entire unit, planning a daily lesson always begins by thinking as follows: In what ways do I want this lesson to change my students? Or, what will they be able to do as a consequence of the lesson? When stated at the outset, these proposed behavioral changes can give direction to daily activities. Because writing performance objectives was discussed in Chapter 2, it will not be repeated here.

Organizing Materials

Having decided what material to include in the lesson, you must next decide on the sequence in which you will present the material. Sometimes the nature of the subject dictates the order of presentation, so you should check the major ideas you want to cover to determine whether there is a natural sequence.

For example, a physical education teacher who wants to provide experiences that are essential for learning to drive a golf ball will think, "What few ideas are important to understanding this process?" The answer is: "Addressing the ball, the backswing, the downswing, and the follow-through." The answer to the question of what sequence to follow is obvious because a natural process is involved. Another example would be the home economics teacher planning a lesson on how to bake a chiffon cake. Again, the process dictates the sequence of the content. A history teacher, too, would prepare many lessons involving historical events in which the sequence of the content would follow in chronological order.

If the four or five objectives of the day's lesson have no natural order, you can try to determine whether a particular sequence would make the lesson more easily understood. For instance, a chemistry teacher would probably not teach the formula of a compound until the students had learned to recognize the symbols of the elements contained in the compound.

THE CURRICULUM

The word *curriculum* comes from a Latin word meaning "race course" (Zais, 1976, p. 6), but the concept of curriculum has changed considerably since the emergence of the American school system. At first, *curriculum* meant "program of studies." The curriculum, then, was the same as a list of the courses being offered. Later the meaning of the word changed to denote the content of these courses. But today many educators define the word in terms of learning experiences. One such contemporary definition is: "the formal and informal content and process by which learners gain knowledge and understanding, develop skills and alter attitudes, appreciations, and values under the auspices of the school" (Doll, 1978, p. 6).

In other words, most contemporary educators view the curriculum as the content and experiences planned by the schools for the students. It can mean either the plan (the document) itself or the actual functioning curriculum (Beauchamp, 1975, p. 7). For the purposes of this text, we should think of *curriculum* in this more recent context. *The curriculum is the purposefully planned content and experiences selected to help students achieve the goals and objectives set by the school.*

Selecting Experiences

Our definition of curriculum (in Chapter 4) includes planned experiences that the school provides the student. Generally, more emphasis is placed on experiences than on content, because today's educators recognize that the experiences students have are major avenues for learning. For this reason, a lesson plan must describe what experiences the teacher expects to use to teach the content. Students often complain that their lessons have no relevance, so educators tell us that we must provide *meaningful* experiences. How can you make experiences meaningful so that, in turn, your classes will be relevant? And because students should not engage in an activity without knowing what they are trying to accomplish, how will you plan their involvement?

Review the partially completed lesson plan. You have stated how you wanted the lesson to change the students—that is, the objectives of the lesson. Little (1985) found that objectives can be used as advance organizers to improve student achievement. You have also selected and organized some major ideas you want to develop. Now you are ready to plan involvement by assigning a task that will require the students to *use* each of the major ideas in the lesson.

The English teacher who is planning a lesson on "How to Capture the Reader's Attention" would assign tasks that make the students use what they have just learned. Presented with several compositions, the students could be asked to identify the principles of capturing the reader's attention each time they occur. Later in the hour, each student will write the lead paragraph of a composition, employing the five techniques of capturing the reader's attention introduced earlier in the hour.

The physical education teacher who wants to teach the correct procedure for driving a golf ball may demonstrate each step and ask students to identify mistakes that the teacher deliberately makes in each phase. Eventually, the students go through the process themselves, while other students critique. A vocational shop teacher would follow a similar process, as would math, science, history, English, music, and art teachers.

Notice that each of these experiences is an assigned task. Each requires students to do things they could not do correctly unless they understand the content taught in the earlier part of the lesson.

IMPLEMENTING THE LESSON PLAN

The results of any lesson are likely to be no better than the daily lesson plan. Yet the lesson plan does not guarantee learning success. Even the best plans may need modification as the students interact with the materials and activities (Green & Smith, 1982). In summarizing several studies on planning, Shavelson (1984) suggests that prolific planning may be counterproductive if the teacher becomes single-minded and does not adapt the lesson to the students' needs. As you develop planning skills, consider ways to alter your plans in case they are not effective with a particular group at a particular time.

Effective teachers separate important information and salient information (Corno, 1981) and simplify these major concepts for their own students; less-effective teachers attempt to deal more with issues (Morine & Vallance, 1975). Because beginning teachers often lack the ability to simplify and make sense of classroom events (Calderhead, 1981), the time you spend identifying the major principles and concepts in your discipline will be a wise investment.

SUMMARIZING THE DAILY LESSON

End your lesson plan with a review of the *main ideas* covered in the lesson. The summary should not be an attempt to review every detail covered in the lesson, nor should it merely list the main parts of the lesson. The review should show the relationships among the major ideas, tying together the parts of the lesson.

For example, the physical education teacher planning a lesson on how to drive a golf ball would include in the review each of the major ideas—the address, the backswing, the downswing, and the follow-through—and review the major issues related to each. The review would begin with the first idea, how to address the golf ball, and include the major points involved in the proper address as they were mentioned in the lesson. Likewise, the English lesson on "How to Capture the Reader's Attention" would include each point and its development.

Let's Ponder

Hunter's Design for Effective Teaching

Madeline Hunter (1984) offers the following seven-step approach to designing lessons. After reading the steps, respond to the questions below.

1. *Anticipatory set*. The teacher causes students to focus on the lesson *before* the lesson begins. Example: "Look at the paragraph on the board. What part do you think is most important to remember?"
2. *Objective and Purpose*. The teacher states explicitly what will be learned and how it will be useful. Example: "Sometimes you find it difficult to know what to study and hard to remember the important parts. Today, we're going to learn ways to identify what's important, and then we'll practice ways we can use to remember important things."
3. *Input*. Students must acquire new information about the knowledge, process, or skill they are to achieve. The teacher must have task-analyzed the final objective to identify needed knowledge and skills.
4. *Modeling*. To enhance creativity, several examples should be a routine part of most lessons. These might include live or filmed demonstrations of process and products.

5. *Checking for Understanding.* The teacher should check to see that students understand the tasks before they become involved in lesson activities. This checking may occur before or during activity or during student activity.
6. *Guided Practice.* Students practice their new knowledge or skill under teacher supervision. New learning is like wet cement: it is easily damaged. An error at the beginning can easily "set" so that is is harder to eradicate than had it been apprehended immediately.
7. *Independent Practice.* Independent practice is assigned only after the teacher is reasonably sure the students will not make serious errors.

1. How can the teacher know which parts of the lesson are most important? List two or three criteria for judging the importance of content and skills.
2. Describe two different ways to establish anticipatory set.
3. Name one important concept in your discipline, list all the tasks that are needed to teach this concept, and name some understandings and skills the students will need to develop before mastering the concept.

SAMPLE DAILY LESSON PLANS

Following are some sample daily lesson plans. They differ in style, but each contains a few major ideas and is arranged in a sequence that facilitates learning. Note that each major idea is followed by an assigned task that requires students to use the idea. Note also that each sample lesson ends with a review that ties together the major ideas in the lesson.

The parts of each plan (statement of purpose, introduction, student activities, and summary) vary from plan to plan. Make a list of all the parts you find in these plans. Put an asterisk next to the parts you believe will be helpful to you when you teach. Use the results as an outline to make a lesson plan in your subject area.

Lesson Plan 1

PHYSICAL EDUCATION: GRADE 9

   I. Purpose: To develop the ability to score a complete bowling game.
  II. Materials: Scoresheet and lead pencil with eraser for each student.
 III. Equipment: Overhead projector.
 IV. Main ideas
      A. How to score and add an open frame.
      B. How to score and add a spare.
      C. How to score and add a strike.
      D. How to score and add the last frame.
  V. Procedure
      A. Five-minute explanation of each concept.
      B. Demonstration of scoring a game.
 VI. Assignment: Each student is to score and add the following game at his desk.

4-2	4-/	8 /	9 /	X	X	4 /	X	X	2-3	4 /	2

VII. Summary: The teacher will show a transparency of the game on the over-head screen and use questions to lead the class in filling out each step in the game.

Discussion of Lesson Plan 1. Do you like the lesson plan? Is it clear? Among its strongest assets are its initial statement of purpose telling immediately what the lesson should do for the student, its clear statement of the ideas being taught, and its summary. The task is also stated clearly. Notice that the teacher selected as an example a game that starts with the simplest ideas and moves to progressively more complex ideas until everything one needs to know to score a bowling game is covered. Note also that because the game contains all the essential ideas of scoring, it provides a satisfactory review of the whole lesson.

How could this plan be improved? Notice the procedures. Would the plan be easier to follow if the time limits were stated alongside the activities? Can you think of other ways to improve it?

Lesson Plan 2

Mr. Hulsey   ***Class: Tenth-grade Business***
Date: December 2

I. Descriptive Title: "How to Prepare a Balance Sheet"
II. Concepts in Logical Sequence
    A. The balance sheet tells what is owned, what is owed, and what the owner is worth on a specific date.
    B. Assets and liabilities determine owner's equity.
    C. Assets are entered in the left column, and liabilities and owner's equity are entered in the right column.
    D. The total of both columns must be equal. If they do not balance, an error has been made.
III. Presentation: Discussion is the method to be used in presenting the concepts while working through a sample balance sheet on the board.
IV. Assign Task: Each student will prepare a balance sheet to determine what the student owns, owes, and is worth.
V. Summary: Go back over the four concepts, having students check to be sure they have followed these concepts in preparing their balance sheet.

Discussion of Lesson Plan 2. Compare the format of this plan with Lesson Plan 1. Which is easier to follow? Notice that this plan has no time indicated for any part of the lesson. Is that good, or would you need time limits to determine how long you should spend on each part?

Lesson Plan 3

Mr. Alfred Harding   *Class: Speech, Grade 12*

1. Title: "How to Use *Time* When Reading with Expression."
   Establish set by reading a poem ("Richard Cory") aloud as monotonously and ineffectively as possible, no pauses, no variation in speed.
2. The essential concepts of time: pause, rate, duration. Introduce these concepts (pause, rate, and duration) in that order because we go from time where no words are involved to time that involves several words, down to time that involves just one word.
3. (a) Pause—the pregnant space of time when no sound is uttered, the dramatic pause after a heavy statement—give an example; the anticipating pause—slight hesitation before key word, often used both in dramatic and comedy punch line—give an example.
   (b) Duration—the amount of time spent on just one word. Used for emphasis and imagery. Show how one can stretch out a single word and how it highlights the meaning of a passage.
4. Assignment: Go around the room and have each one say "Give me liberty, or give me death" using the three concepts of time for more expression.
5. Summary: Read same poem ("Richard Cory") as in beginning, only read it well and with expression. Then ask class if they've heard it before. Tell and then show how important the proper use of those three concepts is for effective communication. In the second reading, demonstrate how those three concepts worked.

Discussion of Lesson Plan 3. What is your major criticism of this plan? Do you find the format complicated and involved? This lesson plan has some definite assets. Can you recognize them? The introduction would be effective in almost any class. The lesson content is divided into three clear categories, so the class would not be overwhelmed with too much content. The summary is very good because it allows students to compare and actually see the value in the main ideas developed–pause, rate, and duration. Can you think of ways to improve this lesson plan?

Lesson Plan 4

CLASS: MR. ROBERT PABST, SOCIOLOGY, GRADES 11 AND 12

 I. Topic: The Social Problem of Population
II. Objectives: To give the students a new awareness and knowledge of the population problem from various viewpoints, relating causal factors and discussing possible solutions. This lesson and the unit as a whole should provide students with practical knowledge to help them do their part to help control or solve the population problem.

III. Content and Activities

Content	Activities
A. The population problem	Introductory remarks by teacher.
1. Decline in death rate	Question/answer discussion about benefits of concepts to be gained by this unit. Check of student opinion and responses to this subject. Distribute handout study guide for this lesson.
a. Man's expanded knowledge of himself and his environment has enabled him to exert some control over the death rate of our population.	
(1) Industrialism	Brief lecture by teacher on the major concepts of population.
(2) Scientific advances	
2. Problems in the United States	
a. Rapid growth—World War II birth boom	Discussion by class on feasibility of solutions.
b. Food production—factors of economics and technology	Distribute booklet "This Crowded World."
c. Attitudes and socioeconomic factors	Show filmstrip "A Matter of Life and Death."
3. Possible solutions	Summarize and review major points.
a. Family size	
b. Birth control	Give a 10-point quiz on population lesson for task and evaluation.
(1) Role of religion	
(2) Role of government	
IV. Assignment:	Read booklet distributed in class and make a brief outline of major points (written in longhand, about one page) to be turned in. Read at least the first 10 pages of chapter titled "Population" in the text. Make notes on major points and topics you found interesting. These notes should be written neatly in the semester notebook and turned in later.

Discussion of Lesson Plan 4. You probably noticed that this lesson plan includes a statement of the lesson's objectives. Are these objectives too general? (How could you test the class to see whether these objectives were attained?) They could be improved by stating them in more specific terms—for example, the expression "various viewpoints" could be spelled out.

This lesson plan is longer than the previous ones. Is it too long? Do you like having the activities listed in a vertical column corresponding to the content? Note that this enables the teacher to see at a glance what activity will be used to teach each unit of content. Is there anything missing in this plan?

Lesson Plan 5

Mr. Robert Bullen   *Equipment: None*
Class: Business   *Facilities: None*
Grade: 12   *No. in class: 30*
Date: June 30

    I. Title of Lesson: How to Read and Analyze a Newspaper's Financial Page Effectively.
  II. Reason for Lesson: To show how a stock exchange allows people to put their capital to work whenever and however they choose.
III. Points to be reviewed
    A. Just what common stock is
    B. What common stock means to an issuing corporation
    C. What common stock ownership means to the investor
    D. Advantages and disadvantages of common stock
IV. Content and Activities

Content	*Activity*
A breakdown of the different headings contained in the stock quotes.	Each student will be asked in advance of my explanation as to their meanings.
The prices will be analyzed as to what they actually mean.	Different prices will be put on the board with students giving the answer in dollars and cents.
Actual examples from a newspaper will be analyzed as to their meanings in relation to other stock quotes.	Each student will recite the quotes from a newspaper handout and will tell what they mean.

Summarizing the above concepts:
  V. Evaluation: A simple quiz on the material just covered and the review work will be given. A simulated paper quote will be provided so that I can test whether they understand all the aspects of the heading and the prices contained in the quote.
VI. Assignment: They will be given a project of keeping the daily price quotes of a particular stock, which will be turned in at the end of the week and evaluated. Each student will be assigned a different stock.

Discussion of Lesson Plan 5. Did you notice anything in this plan that was not part of the other plans? Note the section titled "Reason for Lesson." What advantage is there in having this a part of the actual lesson? Do you think students want to know why they are studying certain content? They do, and unless you can give them a meaningful reason, they may be very casual or even bored throughout the lesson.

This plan provides a means for evaluating the lesson. It could be improved by stating the objectives in terms of expected student behavior and gearing the evaluation to measure the degree to which students have met the originally stated objectives.

Lesson Plan 6

Mrs. Grace Bishop
Class: English, Grade 9
  I. Objective: The student should understand the importance of using proper grammar.
 II. Objective: Teach students to identify nouns and know their classes.

(5 min.)	A. Introduce subject: Grammar.

  (5 min.)   A. Introduce subject: Grammar.
                         1. Give a brief outline of the plan of study.
                         2. Announce the noun as the first part of speech you will study.

 (10 min.)   B. Present the idea that proper use of grammar is important.
                         1. Give one example.
                         2. Ask students for other examples.

 (15 min.)   C. Give the definition of nouns and explain classes.
                         1. Common.
                         2. Proper.
                         3. Abstract.
                         4. Concrete.
                      Give an example of each on the board.
                      Ask students to give other examples and add to list.

 (15 min.)   D. Have each student make a list of 15 nouns naming objects seen in the classroom (3 min.).
                         1. List the four classes on the board.
                         2. Call on students for nouns and have them designate the proper list of each case.

  (5 min.)   E. Summary
                         1. Conduct a brief questioning period reviewing the definition and classes of nouns.
                         2. Evaluate the effectiveness of the lesson by the response of the students. Did they understand the various classes? Could they easily choose the appropriate list for each noun?

Discussion of Lesson Plan 6. What is your reaction to the time indicators in this plan? Would they help you teach this lesson, or would they make you uncomfortable? Perhaps they are too restrictive. The teacher's activities and the students' activities are listed in steps. Do you like this? Notice the objective stated in the beginning. How could it be improved? There is no written evaluation at the end. Would this make it difficult to evaluate the accomplishment of the stated objective, "To understand the importance of using proper grammar?" Can you rewrite the objective, stating it in performance terms?

Lesson Plan 7

Mr. Redlhammer
United States History—U.S. Civil War 1863–65
Grade 11

  I. Aim: Discuss some major battles and the effect each had on the outcome of the war.

 II. Battles covered: Battle of Gettysburg
                         Battle of Vicksburg
                         Appomattox

    A. Confederates were the farthest north they had ever been.
    B. Union and Confederate forces happen to meet and clash at a little town called Gettysburg.
    C. Battle itself wasn't one big battle, but a series of small skirmishes.
    D. Union took a position on Cemetery Ridge and Confederates on Seminary Ridge.
    E. First day of battle ended with no headway.
    F. July 2 started with intense fighting, and by evening the South was winning.
    G. July 3: North shifted position and occupied both Seminary and Cemetery ridges.
    H. Confederates led the famous Pickett's Charge and were massacred.
    I. Ask why this battle was important and list reasons on board.
    J. July 4: Vicksburg fell, another Union victory.
    K. Vicksburg was a key and strategic position that the South held on the Mississippi River.
    L. Vicksburg located on high cliffs. Why did the city's location make it a key point?
    M. Grant tried attacking from the river, but was defeated.
    N. Grant planned to go 20 miles down river and come back to attack by land.
    O. Grant encircled the city, cutting off all food supplies, and starved the city to surrender. Do you think that Grant was fair in using this tactic?
    P. What do you think was the significance of this battle?
    Q. Last brave struggle of the South was at Appomattox.
    R. South forced to surrender because of dwindling forces. What do you think caused this reduction in their army? Could this reduction have been prevented?
    S. Grant and Lee met at Appomattox to discuss peace terms.

T. Terms of surrender were lenient.
U. South may have lost the fighting, but not their pride. Discuss this last statement.
V. Summarize important points.
III. Activities: Get in discussion groups and discuss this statement: "If the South had won the war . . ."
IV. Assignment: From the ideas discussed, write a short report on what the South would be like if it had remained split from the U.S.

Discussion of Lesson Plan 7. What is your reaction to the length of this lesson plan? It was used by a prospective teacher to teach a lesson in a secondary education methods class. The lesson was interesting and well organized, but it was too long for one period. The discussion should have continued for the next several lessons.

The group discussions were the climax of the lesson. Following the group discussions, a representative from each group gave a capsule report of the conclusions of the group. This report is not included under "Activities." Should it be?

RECAP OF MAJOR IDEAS

1. Daily lesson plans are essential for attaining the expectations set forth in units.
2. Teachers should not become enslaved to lesson plans to the point of reading them step-by-step to students. On the other hand, teachers cannot afford to ignore the value that planning offers in giving necessary direction as each lesson progresses.
3. Like any other tool, the value of a lesson plan depends on how it is used.
4. Lesson plan design should begin by identifying desirable changes in student behavior.
5. All lesson plans should contain activities to involve students.
6. Content should be organized according to natural sequences, simple to complex, or sequences that facilitate understanding of the material.
7. Each lesson plan should end with a review of the major concepts found in the lesson.
8. Teachers seldom use objectives when beginning lesson planning and when changing their approaches.

POSTTEST

Now that you have read the chapter, take a moment to respond to the following statements again.

	Agree	*Disagree*	*Uncertain*
1. All lesson plans should begin with a list of the subject content to be learned.	_____	_____	_____
2. A lesson plan that works well with one group may not work well with another group.	_____	_____	_____
3. The best lesson plans are those drawn up by outside experts (as opposed to teacher-made plans).	_____	_____	_____
4. To be effective, a lesson must cause students to change their behavior.	_____	_____	_____
5. A lesson is a failure unless it gives students new skills.	_____	_____	_____
6. Student activities are essential to all lesson plans.	_____	_____	_____
7. Most teachers begin planning by identifying the goals and objectives to be attained.	_____	_____	_____
8. Most changes in teaching that come as teachers interact with students are based on lesson objectives.	_____	_____	_____

CASES

The importance of planning cannot be overemphasized. No teacher can be successful without adequate planning, but *good* planning is important too. Poor planning, overstructuring, and planning lessons that are too short or too long can lead to serious problems. The following cases are examples of problems from inadequate planning.

Case 1: A Teacher Attempts to Be Democratic in Planning

It was a year to remember: 1976, the nation's bicentennial. Mr. Henry, a first-year teacher, was dedicated to establishing a completely democratic classroom atmosphere. Although he was young and inexperienced, he was determined to develop a feeling of freedom within each student so that everyone could better understand the true meaning of democracy.

Mr. Henry's approach to creating this atmosphere was sensible. From the first day, he incorporated democratic machinery into his tenth-grade democracy classes. Every controversial idea was put to a vote. The opinion of the majority always determined the class's direction and behavior. To say that the students enjoyed his classes is an understatement, at least throughout the first term.

The students decided to determine subject content on a completely individual basis. Some of the more studious quickly identified their area of interest and immediately began their projects. Some of the slower students did not reach definite decisions for several days, but they did not worry about it. Mr. Henry was patient and helped when asked to do so.

All was well, and everyone was happy as the term got under way. Many students were thrilled with this new approach and the complete freedom it provided—something they had not experienced in other classes. The first students to become concerned—and later doubtful—about whether the approach was "right for them" were the high-performing students. Since most members of this group were planning to attend college and would take courses in American democracy, they began to wonder if they were getting the foundation that they would need for college. Mr. Henry assured them they need not worry because they would probably be even more adequately prepared than their fellow students in future democracy classes. He brought to his classes some studies showing that several nondirective and open-ended mathematics and science classes had prepared students so well that they outscored their counterparts in traditional classes on standardized college entrance examinations. This pacified some of the students, but it failed to erase their doubts.

As the end of the first grading period approached, the students who had been concerned began worrying again. When they asked how their grades would be determined, Mr. Henry replied, "How do you want your grade to be determined?" They soon realized that the competitive exams to which they were accustomed were not adequate to test the content in this class. When Mr. Henry proposed that each student provide evidence of his academic progress and let fellow class members determine the appropriate grade, the students rejected the proposal.

The class appeared to be in trouble, and so did the teacher. This approach had not produced the uniformity of content found in traditional classes. Mr. Henry wondered how he could have democratic classes and yet avoid these problems.

Discussion

1. How much freedom should a secondary school class have in selecting content?
   The idea of providing complete freedom for any group of people (youth or adults) is a misguided one. People who have guidelines are the freest of all—far more so than people who have no rules to follow. Individuals who have no regulations find themselves wandering aimlessly without purpose or direction. The teacher who attempts to

give a class absolute freedom of choice and behavior usually finds that the students do not appreciate such a completely nonstructured approach.

From professional education courses and practical experience, teachers can learn to identify certain information that the students need in order to prepare for the future. By sharing essential experiences, which is the teacher's right and responsibility, the teacher can then help students select other content and experiences.

2. Should Mr. Henry discontinue using democratic procedures in the classroom and teach the principles of democracy as content rather than as practice?

Definitely not. Democracy should be practiced in all classes. Teaching the rules of democracy is essential, but the best way to do this is to have the students practice them. Aristotle once said, "We learn virtue by being virtuous." Democracy is a way of treating others as you would have them treat you. This cannot be achieved through learning rules, principles, and definitions.

3. How could Mr. Henry retain structure in the class and yet involve the students in the planning?

The teacher's role is to guide the students in selecting content appropriate to the class. One method would be first to discuss with the students the objectives that the teacher expects the class to achieve, showing why each objective is needed. Then the teacher could let the students decide how they want to achieve these objectives.

The matter of the content to be covered is less important than developing understanding. If Mr. Henry is more concerned with the ultimate goals of the class—and he should be—he will not worry so much about content, but will concentrate on objectives and planned experiences that will keep the students working toward those goals. You can probably think of other ways to let students share the planning responsibility.

4. What can you say about the time the evaluation system was determined?

Mr. Henry waited too late to decide how the grades would be determined. Students should know this from the beginning in order to direct their activities and help them prepare for evaluations.

Case 2: A Teacher Uses Note Cards for Planning

Every student in the school liked Mr. Little, the teacher who supervised my student teaching experience. Mr. Little's classes were both entertaining and successful. Learning seemed to occur automatically in his classes. During the three months I spent in this teacher's classes, I never once saw a detailed lesson plan.

During class, Mr. Little—who coincidentally was small in stature—always sat in front of the room perched on a high stool. As he talked, joked, and laughed with his students, he continually shuffled a few three-by-five cards, glancing at them while carrying on a dialogue with the students. After his introductory lesson on rocks and minerals, I examined Mr. Little's note cards. (see Figure 3.1).

Although the cards were not detailed or impressive, they did provide structure to the lesson. Each item was mentioned briefly. Key words and phrases, rather than complete sentences, were used. This system enabled Mr. Little to glance at his notes without taking his attention away from the students, and I believe it contributed significantly to his unusually effective teaching.

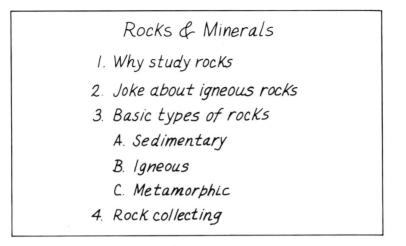

Figure 3.1 Three-by-Five-Inch Card Used for Planning

Discussion

1. What are some advantages of brevity in lesson plans?
   When lesson plans are briefly worded, the teacher will be less likely to "read" the lesson to the class. Brief plans also make room for flexibility; the teacher has time to let the students pursue both the planned topics and any related topics and materials that interest them. Another advantage is that a brief plan leaves time for students to become involved.

2. What are some dangers in lesson plans that are too brief?
   If a lesson plan is too brief, the teacher may run short of material and find there is time left with nothing planned. In addition, a brief lesson may be "shallow"; it may not challenge students to think.

3. Can a lesson be too highly structured?
   Yes—if this means too detailed. When the lesson is too detailed, the teacher is likely to dominate the class, leaving the students no opportunity to ask questions and to comment on the lesson. If you interpret this question literally and answer no, I would have to agree with you. The more structure a lesson has, the more likely students will be to reach the set goals. Although we often stress the value of pupil-centered, discovery approaches, we should realize that this method cannot succeed unless there is much planning and hidden structure. Although pupil-centered classes may appear to have little structure, the successful ones are usually more highly structured in terms of objectives and activities than are traditional classes.

Case 3: A Teacher Fails to Use Objectives

Our college biology teacher had a style of her own. Each hour Mrs. Woods promptly opened her notebook and began the lesson. She wrote everything she said on the board in perfect outline form. Her speaking speed was equaled only by her writing speed; not a moment during the hour was wasted. Students were amazed by how neat, organized, and professional her approach to every lesson was.

Mrs. Woods always kept to the objectives for the day. Once when she was absent, her husband, who was also a biology teacher, took over for the day. Having specified no objectives, he kept students wondering when he was going to get into the lesson. They complained that his remarks had nothing to do with the topic being studied. Mr. Woods understood biology, but his lecture seemed to confuse students.

Some of the best students in school got their lowest marks in Mrs. Woods' classes. Furthermore, they said they learned very little about biology. Students were surprised that they had benefited so little in the class of a teacher who was not only brilliant in her subject but also extremely well prepared for every lesson.

Discussion

1. Did Mrs. Woods' lessons lack structure?
   By no means. Every minute of her classes was thoroughly planned in advance. Her classes lacked variety, student involvement, and student interaction, but they did not lack structure.
2. Why did the students feel so lost in Mr. Woods' class?
   Mr. Woods made the mistake of trying to teach without first identifying lesson objectives. Even when teachers do not share the list of objectives with their students, the objectives often become apparent because they cause the teacher to structure the lesson systematically.

Case 4: A Teacher Gets Lost in His Own Lessons

Each day, when students came to my class after their music class, they complained to me about their music homework assignments. I heard complaints like "This assignment has nothing to do with what we studied in class today," "I don't see the value in this," and "Why does Mr. Marshall make us do this?" I reminded them that they should not direct their criticisms to me, because it would be unprofessional and unethical for me to discuss the issue with them. I refused to comment, but I continued to hear complaints: "Mr. Marshall rambles," "He skips around with the material so much that it doesn't make sense."

Finally, the complaints reached administrators, who spoke with Mr. Marshall about the issue. I do not know what was said during the meeting, but it apparently produced a change in Mr. Marshall's teaching because the complaints were fewer and fewer. I always wondered how Mr. Marshall managed to change so quickly and to improve his teaching so effectively.

Discussion

1. Teachers of special subjects, such as music, art, and physical education, are usually assigned to teach several sections of the same class. This often contributes to a teacher's forgetting just what was covered with each group, which was apparently what happened to Mr. Marshall. What would you do if you ever found yourself forgetting where you ended the previous class and exactly what you had covered in it?

This problem is common, and you should not be surprised if some day you experience it. Because it can be very frustrating to you and to your students, give it some thought before it happens. One precaution is to be practical. Do not try to impress students with your ability to remember everything about the previous lesson. One simple solution is to draw an arrow with the class hour on the lesson plan, indicating where yesterday's lesson stopped. You might also develop the habit of beginning each lesson with a review of the main ideas covered in the preceding lesson. Encourage students to let you know if and when you cover material in the review that was not in a previous lesson.

2. When teaching multiple sections of the same class, should you make separate lesson plans for each section?
   This depends on the difference in the ability of the classes. If the difference is great, it will probably be impossible to use the same plans for multiple sections.

3. Are there times when a teacher should stray from the planned lesson?
   Yes. Often a class will become very interested and enthusiastic about a particular part of the lesson. When this happens, you should be willing to deviate from your plan and let the class explore their interests. On the other hand, when the planned lesson seems boring to a particular class, change your approach drastically.

   The lesson plan should never be considered an end in itself. Rather, it is a means to an end—the objectives of the lesson. If you see that another way of reaching these objectives could be more effective than your first strategy, do not hesitate to put the planned activities aside and pursue the desired objectives another way.

4. Does a teacher's ability to plan improve with experience?
   Not necessarily. With experience you can assess how fast a class will grasp material, and so your ability to judge the appropriate length of a lesson improves. However, experience alone will not make your lessons clearer and more interesting. These qualities come only when you study your approach and deliberately adjust your lessons to improve them.

ACTIVITIES

1. Develop a daily plan in your own major teaching field. Specify the subject and grade level and include performance objectives, content generalizations, activities to help students attain the objectives, and a summary of the most significant ideas in the lesson.

2. Write a unit plan in your area of specialty. Begin by writing a brief statement of your philosophy of education. For each curriculum component, write one sentence to explain how your particular philosophy should affect each component.

3. Identify a topic you might select for a lesson. Now write several student activities to use during the hour. Finally, order these in the best possible sequence. Explain why you put each activity in its selected sequence.

4. Examine all the sample lesson plans in this chapter. For each plan, select one or more features you would change if you were to use the plan in your classes. Explain your reason for making each change.

SUGGESTED READINGS

Armento, B. J. (1986). Research on teaching social studies. In M. C. Wittrock (Ed.), *Handbook of research on teaching* (3rd ed.). New York: Macmillan.

Bloom, B. S. (1956). *Taxonomy of educational objectives: The classification of educational goals, Handbook I: Cognitive domain.* New York: McKay.

Bloom, B. S., Hastings, J. T., & Madaus, G. F. (1971). *Handbook on formative and summative evaluation of student learning.* New York: McGraw-Hill.

Calderhead, J. (1981). *Research into teachers' and student teachers' cognitions: Exploring the nature of classroom practice.* Paper presented at the annual meeting of the American Educational Research Association, Montreal, Canada.

Carnahan, R. S. (1980). *The effects of teacher planning on classroom processes.* Unpublished doctoral dissertation, University of Wisconsin at Madison.

Clark, C. M., & Peterson, P. L. (1986). Teachers' thought process. In M. C. Whittrock (Ed.), *Handbook of research on teaching* (3rd ed.). New York: Macmillan.

Clark, L. H., & Starr, I. S. (1976). *Secondary school teaching* (3rd ed.), Chapter 5. New York: Macmillan.

Corno, L. (1981). Cognitive organizing classrooms. *Curriculum Inquiry, 11,* 359–377.

Green, J., & Smith, D. (1982). *Teaching and learning: A linguistic perspective.* A paper presented to the Conference on Research and Teaching, Airlie House, Va.

Hager, H. K. (1973). *First steps in secondary education.* Columbus, Ohio: Merrill.

Hoover, K. H. (1976). *The professional teacher's handbook* (2nd ed.), Chapter 3. Boston: Allyn & Bacon.

Hunter, M. (1984). Knowing, teaching, and supervising. In P. L. Hosford (Ed.), *Using what we know about teaching,* 175–176. Alexandria, Va.: Association for Supervision and Curriculum Development. Abstracted with the author's permission.

Kim, E. C., & Kellough, R. D. (1974). *A resource guide for secondary school teaching.* New York: Macmillan.

Krathwohl, D. R., Bloom, B. S., & Masia, B. B. (1964). *Taxonomy of educational objectives, Handbook II: Affective domain.* New York: McKay.

Little, D. (1985). *An investigation of cooperative small-group instruction and the use of advance organizers on the self-concept and social studies achievement of third-grade students.* Doctoral dissertation, University of Alabama.

Mager, R. F. (1962). *Preparing instructional objectives.* Palo Alto, Calif.: Fearon.

Morine, G., & Vallance, E. (1975). *Special study B: A study of teacher and pupil perceptions of classroom instruction.* Technical Report No. 75-11-6. San Francisco: Far West Laboratory.

Mosston, M. (1972). *Teaching: From command to discovery.* Belmont, Calif.: Wadsworth.

Oliva, P. F. (1972). *The secondary school today* (2nd ed.). San Francisco: Intext.

Oliva, P. F. (1984). *Supervision for today's schools.* New York: Longman.

Peterson, P. L., Marx, R. W., & Clark, C. M. (1978). Teacher planning, teacher behavior, and student achievement. *American Educational Research Journal, 15,* 555–565.

Renner, J. W., Bibens, R. F., & Shepard, G. D. (1972). *Guiding learning in the secondary school.* New York: Harper & Row.

Romberg, T. A. (1983). *Allocated time and content covered in mathematics.* Paper presented at the annual meeting of the American Educational Research Association, Montreal, Canada.

Romberg, T. A., & Carpenter, T. P. (1986). Research on teaching mathematics: Two disciplines of scientific inquiry. In M. C. Wittrock (Ed.), *Handbook of research on teaching* (3rd ed.). American Educational Research Assoc. New York: Macmillan.

Scheville, J., Porter, A., Billi, G., Floden, R., Freeman, D., Knappan, L., Kuhs, T., & Schmidt, W. (1983). Teachers as policy brokers in the content of elementary school mathematics. In L. S. Schulman & E. G. Sykes (Eds.), *Handbook of teaching and policy*. New York: Longman.

Shavelson, R. J. (1984). *Review of research on teachers' pedagogical judgments, plans, and decisions.* Los Angeles: Rand Corporation and University of California. Reported in R. L. Egbert & M. M. Kluender (Eds.), *Using research to improve teacher education,* pp. 132–133. Lincoln, Neb.: American Association of Colleges for Teacher Education.

Shavelson, R. J., & Stern, P. (1981). Research on teachers' pedagogical thoughts, judgments, decisions, and behavior. *Review of Educational Research, 51,* 455–498.

Tyson, J. C., & Carroll, M. A. (1970). *Conceptual tools for teaching in secondary schools.* Boston: Houghton Mifflin.

Walter, L. J. (1979). How teachers plan for curriculum and instruction. *Catalyst, 2,* 3.

Walter, L. J. (1984). A synthesis of research findings on teaching, planning, and decision making. In R. L. Egbert & M. M. Kluender (Eds.), *Using research to improve teacher education.* Lincoln, Neb.: Clearinghouse on Teacher Education.

Zahorik, J. A. (1975). Teacher planning models. *Educational Leadership, 33,* 134–139.

Zais, R. S. (1976). *Curriculum: Principles and foundations.* New York: Crowell.

Using Performance Objectives

Objectives _____

- Explain three advantages of using objectives in daily planning.
- Differentiate between educational aims, goals, and objectives.
- Discuss the three domains of educational objectives.
- Write an objective for each level of all three domains.
- List three criteria essential to all performance objectives.
- Explain how performance objectives and daily lessons fit into the total curriculum.
- Give an example of a well-known educational aim, and explain why aims are needed.
- Write one goal appropriate for the subject and grade level you plan to teach.
- List three ways to involve students in curriculum planning.
- Give three guidelines for using homework.

PRETEST

	Agree	Disagree	Uncertain
1. Generally, teachers have both the freedom and the responsibility to plan their own lessons.	____	____	____
2. Aims, goals, and objectives are terms that are used in education to mean the same thing.	____	____	____
3. The more concisely and precisely an objective is written, the better it will be.	____	____	____
4. Every lesson should have some written objectives that have to do with student attitudes.	____	____	____
5. Every lesson should have objectives that are written at all levels of the taxonomy.	____	____	____
6. A major purpose of an objective is to help the teacher communicate to the student exactly what is expected of the students.	____	____	____
7. At the end of any lesson, students should be able to do some things they could not do at the beginning of the period.	____	____	____
8. Objectives can be used to raise the level of thinking in a classroom.	____	____	____
9. Classroom discussions usually remain at the lowest level of thinking.	____	____	____
10. Every lesson plan should include some questions from all three educational domains.	____	____	____

Middle-Level Message

Middle-level students enjoy discussions, because discussion provides opportunities for them to be active and these students need opportunities to work off their energy. But there is another reason that middle-level students like discussions. Discussions give them room to express their opinions. However, middle-level students should use discussions to absorb more information, rather than merely to disseminate their opinions. When conducting middle-level discussions, press students to give examples to support what they are saying.

Because some middle-level students tend to dominate a discussion and others choose to remain passive and uninvolved, you should try to involve every student in discussions.

One of the first decisions you will have to make as a teacher has to do with the content you will cover in each class. Some school systems regulate content so closely that they virtually dictate what each teacher will teach. By providing externally designed curriculum plans, guides, and syllabi, they may even specify the exact content to be covered each day. Curriculum directors, supervisors, assistant superintendents, and assistant principals in charge of curricula may periodically visit classes to make sure that each class is indeed studying the prescribed lessons. But even within such dictatorial systems, there is much flexibility in how you teach the lessons.

At the opposite extreme are the many school systems that do no more than provide general guidelines that are merely suggestive. In fact, some teachers are not given anything more than a textbook from which to design their curricula. Fortunately, most school systems operate somewhere between these two extremes. They realize that teachers need suggestions and guidelines, but they also realize that teachers need to be free to select content and plan their curricula according to the needs and interests of their students and the desires and resources of the community.

The question "How do teachers plan?" is quite different from the question "How should teachers plan?" In their education programs and in the professional literature, most teachers are told to use a curriculum planning model introduced by Ralph Tyler (1949). Tyler's model is often called the "ends-means" model because it stresses that desired learning outcomes (objectives) be identified *before* instructional methods or activities are selected.

Unfortunately, "most teachers [ignore this model and] begin the planning process by determining the content to be covered and then design or select learning activities for students" (Walter, 1984, p. 55). Walter adds, "Once teachers begin lessons for groups of students, they are very reluctant to change those lessons, even when things are going poorly" (p. 60). More attention should be given to assist beginning teachers in developing high-quality tasks for their initial lessons as they begin to teach. According to Walter, we need to help teachers develop a wide repertoire of instructional tasks, so that teachers have a range of alternatives to consider when the activities are not successful with a group of students and so that teachers can seek to optimize instruction (Walter, 1984, pp. 61–62).

EDUCATIONAL EXPECTATIONS: AIMS, GOALS, OBJECTIVES

To some degree you will be responsible for developing the curriculum for your classes. Since the resulting curriculum should be consistent with what you, the school, and the community want to achieve, you should examine these expectations at various levels. Educational expectations—aims, goals, and objectives—have different degrees of immediacy and specificity. The following discussion begins with the broadest and most general expectations—aims—and progresses toward the most immediate and most specific—objectives.

Aims

Educational aims are the most general expectations of all. In fact, they are so distant and so general that they can never be fully achieved. A good example of educational aims is the list of the "Seven Cardinal Principles of Secondary Education":

1. Health
2. Development of Moral Character
3. Worthy Home Membership
4. Citizenship
5. Worthy Use of Leisure Time
6. Vocational Efficiency
7. Development of the Fundamental Processes

Each of these expectations can never be completely fulfilled or attained (for example, people have to work all their lives to preserve their health, to develop their morality, or to be good citizens), and this is true of all educational aims. They are essential for providing long-term direction, but they can never be completely fulfilled or attained.

Goals

Educational goals are expectations that take weeks, months, or even years to attain. A particular high school may have as one of its goals that all students will be literate by the time they graduate. This goal may or may not be realized for every student, yet probably most will achieve this goal.

But a goal need not take 6 or 12 years to reach. For example, a biology teacher may set a goal that all students will appreciate all forms of life by the end of the school year (a year-long goal). Or the teacher whose students spend six weeks studying endocrines may set as a student goal the understanding of the different processes of reproduction, transportation, and respiration. Clearly, then, an educational goal can be reached (although many students may not reach it), and requires several days to several years to attain. The time frame for reaching a goal is usually set to correspond with a certain program, such as a semester or a six-week grading period.

Objectives

So that educational objectives will not be confused with other types of educational expectations, this book will use the term *objectives* to refer precisely to what is expected of students daily. We might think of these as *performance objectives,* for each refers to the ability of students to perform selected tasks in one or more specific ways. As Wulf has said, when objectives are used "there are no unexpected or surprise results since both parties have agreed upon the end product'' (Wulf & Schane, 1984, p. 117). Because performance objectives are the most specific of all expressions of educational expectations, they must be written very specifically. The following sections introduce the techniques of writing performance objectives.

CRITERIA FOR WRITING PERFORMANCE OBJECTIVES

Depending on the use of the objectives and the content involved, each college instructor of education courses teaches students how to write objectives in his or her (the instructor's) own unique way. Yet most authorities appear to agree that all statements of performance objectives must meet at least three criteria:

1. Objectives must be stated in terms of expected student behavior (not teacher behavior).
2. Objectives must specify the conditions under which the students are expected to perform.
3. Objectives must specify the minimum acceptable level of performance.

Look again at the list of three criteria for writing objectives. Stating objectives in terms of expected student behavior is important because all teaching is directed toward the students. The success of the lesson will depend on what happens to the students. To be more precise, the school exists to change the behavior of students—mentally, physically, socially, emotionally, and even morally. When you state all objectives in terms of desired student performance and use specifics that are observable and measurable, you and your students will better understand what is expected and the degree to which these expectations are being met. The lists of terms in Figure 4.2 shows types of verbs that describe specific, observable, and measurable actions (see the Yes column) and those that are too general and vague to be accurately observed and measured (see the No column).

Because students can grasp only a limited number of major ideas in a period of 45 or 50 minutes, the daily lesson plan should contain only four or five major ideas. Suppose you are an English teacher who wants to teach composition writing. You could select four or five of the most important ideas about capturing and holding the readers' attention. These will become the content for the first day's lesson in a unit titled ''Composition Writing.'' You may determine that five ideas are essential to capturing the readers' attention and that four ideas are essential to holding it, once captured. If so, you could plan one lesson on how to capture the readers' attention and a subsequent lesson on how to hold the readers' attention.

Your objectives should be written in terms of desired student behavior. The emphasis should be not ''Today I'll teach'' but ''As a result of the lesson, each

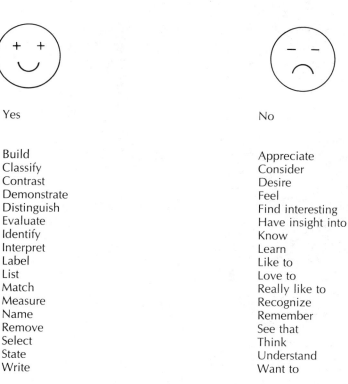

Yes	No
Build	Appreciate
Classify	Consider
Contrast	Desire
Demonstrate	Feel
Distinguish	Find interesting
Evaluate	Have insight into
Identify	Know
Interpret	Learn
Label	Like to
List	Love to
Match	Really like to
Measure	Recognize
Name	Remember
Remove	See that
Select	Think
State	Understand
Write	Want to

Figure 4.2 Performance Terms: Specific and Measurable (Yes); Vague not Measurable (No)

student will be able to. . . ." Second, you should state the conditions under which the students are expected to perform ("When given a list containing vertebrates and invertebrates . . ."). Third, state the expected level of performance ("with 80 percent accuracy" or "without error"). Finally, avoid using verbs that cannot be observed or measured, such as *learn, know,* and *understand.* Instead, your plan should contain such specific, action-oriented verbs as *identify, list, explain, name, describe,* and *compare.*

PERFORMANCE OBJECTIVES
IN THE THREE DOMAINS

Some of the aims and goals of education deal with thinking (for example, command of the fundamental processes), others involve attitudes (for example, development of moral character), and still others focus on physical skills (for example, physical education). You should establish performance objectives in each of these domains (cognitive, affective, and psychomotor) for each class. Let us look now at writing objectives at varying levels of difficulty in each domain.

WRITING OBJECTIVES IN THE COGNITIVE DOMAIN

The first real systematic approach to helping teachers write objectives at specified levels came in 1956 when Benjamin S. Bloom and a group of students at the University of Chicago came up with a taxomony of educational objectives in the cognitive domain that included six levels (Bloom, 1956):

Level 1: Knowledge
Level 2: Comprehension
Level 3: Application
Level 4: Analysis
Level 5: Synthesis
Level 6: Evaluation

In order to involve students in tasks that require them to operate at these different levels, you must be able to write objectives for each level.

Level 1: Knowledge

The simplest and least demanding objectives are those that require only memorization of facts. Before students can move on to more advanced levels of tasks, they must first know certain basic facts. For example, many secondary mathematics problems require students to multiply. Learning the multiplication tables can probably be done best by simple rote memorization. Unfortunately, many secondary classes fail to go beyond this most elementary level. There is nothing dishonorable about introducing assignments or tasks at the knowledge level, as long as such assignments have a purpose and do not dominate the curriculum.

An example of an objective written at the knowledge level would be: "When given a list of 10 elements and a list of atomic weights, the student will be able to correctly match 8 of the 10 elements with their correct atomic weights." Another example is: "When given a list containing 10 vertebrates and 10 invertebrates, the student will correctly identify 8 of the 10 invertebrates."

Notice that both objectives begin with a statement of the conditions under which students are expected to perform the task ("When given . . .") and are written in terms of desired student performance ("the student will . . ."). In addition, both objectives contain action-oriented verbs that can be observed and measured ("match," "identify") and end with a statement of the minimum acceptable level of performance ("8 of the 10").

Level 2: Comprehension

Objectives at the comprehension level require that the students do more than mere memorization. They require students to translate, interpret, or predict a continuation of trends (Bloom, 1956, p. 149).

For example, an English teacher who wants students to know the differences between phrases and clauses may set the following objective: "When given a paragraph containing two clauses and three phrases, the student will correctly underscore the phrases using a single line and underscore the clauses using double lines.'' Can you tell what the minimum acceptable level of performance is for this objective? Actually, because there is no mention of an acceptable level, it must be assumed that the students are expected to perform with 100 percent accuracy.

See if you can write one objective in your teaching field at the comprehension level that requires the students to *translate,* one objective that requires them to *interpret,* and one that requires them to *predict.* (Hint: you may want to use charts, maps, graphs, or tables.)

Level 3: Application

Objectives written at the application level require students to use principles or generalizations to solve a concrete problem.

For example, a mathematics teacher might write the following objective for geometry students: ''Given the lengths of both legs of a right triangle, the student will use the Pythagorean theorum to solve the length of the hypotenuse.'' Or an English teacher might write the following objective: ''Given the beats and measures in iambic pentameter, the student will write a five-verse poem in iambic pentameter without missing more than one beat per verse.''

The advantage of writing objectives at this level is that once students learn to apply a principle to one situation they can then apply it to multiple situations to solve many other problems.

Level 4: Analysis

Like the application level objectives, analysis level objectives require students to work with principles, concepts, and broad generalizations—but the students must do this themselves. Students are required to break down the concepts and principles in order to understand them better, and to do this they must understand not only the content but also its structural form.

For example, a government teacher might write the following objective for a class that is studying how a bill becomes a law: ''Given a particular law, students will trace its development from the time it was first introduced as a bill, listing each major step without missing any.''

A teacher of auto mechanics might write the following objective for a group of students who have been studying the electrical system in an automobile: ''Starting with the positive battery terminal, the student will trace the current throughout the automobile until it returns to the negative battery terminal, stating what happens in the coil, alternator, distributor, and condenser without getting more than one of these steps out of sequence.'' A biology teacher might ask students to trace the circulatory system in a similar manner.

Suppose you are teaching the circulatory system to a biology class. See if you can write an objective that will enable students to understand the sequence in which the blood travels throughout the body. (Hint: You may want to designate one of the heart's chambers as a beginning point.)

Check your objective to see whether it includes the three designated criteria:

Is it written in terms of expected student performance? If so, underscore the part of the objective that identifies both the performer and the performance. Does the verb you used express action? Can it be observed or measured? Is your statement of conditions clear? Circle it. Does it accurately describe the conditions under which you expect the student to perform? Did you begin the objective with a statement like "Given . . ." or "When given . . ."? (This is an easy way to be sure you have included a statement of conditions in each objective.) Is your statement very general, such as "When given a test" or "following a lesson"? Can you make it more specific? Can you think of a way to alter the task, making it easier to perform, simply by changing the conditions?

Finally, examine your objective to see whether it includes a statement of minimum acceptable level of performance. Draw a box around this statement. Does it tell the student exactly how accurately the task must be performed before it will be acceptable? Does it contain a percentage or fraction, such as "with 80 percent accuracy" or "four out of five times"? Can you think of other ways to express your concept of minimum acceptable level of performance without using percentages or fractions?

By now you probably would like to start over and rewrite your original objective, improving each part.

Level 5: Synthesis
In a way, the synthesis level objective is the opposite of the analysis level objective because it requires the student to take several parts and put them together. But the synthesis level objective is more demanding because it requires students to form a *new* whole. Unlike the analysis level objectives, synthesis level objectives require students to use divergent thinking and creativity.

The student's attitude is especially important at the synthesis level. Synthesis requires experimentation—investigating the new. Furthermore, the student must understand that the teacher does not have in mind a definite solution or preconceived notion for the student to reach.

For example, a history teacher who wants students to understand the problems faced by the settlers of this country might preface the unit with an assignment involving the following objective: "Suppose you are a member of a team of explorers that is going to another inhabited planet to start a new colony. List at least 10 rules you would propose to guide the new nationals, making sure that at least five of the rules would serve to protect the interests of all the native inhabitants."

Because of their divergent and creative nature, synthesis level questions are difficult to write. You may need practice before you feel comfortable and competent writing objectives at this level.

Suppose you are an art teacher. In your class, you have studied such concepts as cubism (using cubes to form objects) and pointism (using pencil points to form objects). Can you write an objective at the synthesis level? (Hint: You might begin by identifying a particular effect you would like your students to achieve through the use of cubism and pointism; this might be a specific feeling or mood.)

One example of such an objective might be as follows: "While looking at some examples of cubism in Picasso's paintings and at some of Renoir's paintings that reflect the use of pointism, the student will combine these two techniques and a new technique to create at least three of the following feelings: happiness, surprise, sadness, anger, love.

At the synthesis level, be sure to provide enough structure to make the assignment meaningful and yet allow students enough freedom to put themselves into the work.

Level 6: Evaluation

The highest level in Bloom's cognitive domain is the evaluation level. Here the student is required to make judgments, but judgments based on definite criteria, not just on opinions. Evaluation level objectives contain various combinations of elements in the first five levels.

A speech teacher might use the following objective with students who are studying diplomatic and persuasive techniques: While viewing a video recording of a president's two most recent public addresses, each student will rate the speeches in terms tact and persuasion, pinpointing in each address at least three areas of strength and three areas of weakness.

Or a physical education instructor who is teaching bowling may want to write an objective that involves the starting position, delivery, and follow-through. Can you help this teacher by writing an objective at the evaluation level? If you do not bowl, you may substitute another activity that involves the same three steps, such as golf or diving.

Now examine your evaluation level objective. Does it require that the judgment be based on supportive data or on internal or external standards?

The ability to write objectives at each cognitive level is crucial since this is the only way you can be sure your students will learn to develop intellectual skills at each level. Because this is the most important work a teacher does to effect learning, you must be able to state objectives clearly. You may want to ask a classmate to read a few of your objectives to see whether they do indeed communicate clearly.

WRITING OBJECTIVES IN THE AFFECTIVE DOMAIN

Educators have recently become more concerned with the effect of schooling on the attitudes of students. This concern has been stimulated in part by the students' own acknowledgment of the differences between their attitudes and values and those of "the system." Such differences began to show up in the 1950s with the "beatniks," who were rebelling against the material wealth syndrome that was sweeping the nation. Everyone seemed determined to get ahead of the Joneses by building a larger house and owning a larger car or boat. The youth of the 1960s expressed their dissatisfaction about U.S. involvement in Vietnam by burning draft cards and holding moratoriums and demonstrations. Further dissent was expressed in civil rights marches.

In recent years the community at large has blamed the schools for such social ills as pollution of the environment, exhaustion of natural resources, and economic recession. But the greatest accusation currently aimed at the schools is their failure to teach students basic skills (cognitive domain), and of even greater concern is the schools' failure to discipline today's youth (affective domain).

Our schools will never rid society of all social ills, but if our society, and the world itself, is to survive, the schools will play a major role in affecting how students feel about such important issues as the equality of all people, world peace, honesty, integrity, and the value of life itself.

But, you may ask, exactly what is the role of the school or the teacher in governing the values of students? You may even ask whether the teacher has any right to purposely try to influence the values of students. First, it must be noted that you cannot avoid affecting your students' values. And all teachers should attempt to perpetuate such values as honesty, fairness, and good citizenship. On the other hand, you should not try to persuade students to accept your own religious, political, and cultural or ethnic values.

Another important role of the school and the teacher in the realm of values is to help students become aware of their own values, to question these values, and to discover the basis for those values, be they factual and logical, or prejudiced and illogical.

David R. Krathwohl led in the development of a system to categorize values. The outcome was a hierarchy of objectives in the affective domain (Krathwohl et al., 1964):

Level 1: Receiving
Level 2: Responding
Level 3: Valuing
Level 4: Organization
Level 5: Characterization

Level 1: Receiving

Receiving refers to the students' being aware or alert to new information or experiences. Students receive information in varying degrees. In a single class, some may not receive the information at all, while others attend or receive at a low level of awareness. Still others may be very selective, attending only to the things that are most meaningful to them. Of course, students can be encouraged and taught to develop attention skills.

All teachers want their students to listen carefully to their lessons and to be aware of the feelings of their peers. Can you write an objective that would enable you to measure the degree to which students were paying attention to a lesson? Now examine your objective. Does it include a statement of the conditions under which you want the students to perform? Does it specify a minimum acceptable level of performance? Is it observable and measurable? An example might be: "When participating in a group discussion, the student will ask every other student at least one question."

Can you write an objective at the receiving level for a ninth-grade art class that is taking a field trip to a local art museum?

Level 2: Responding

At the responding level, the student reacts to whatever has attracted his or her attention. This requires physical, active behavior. Some responses may be overt or purposeful behaviors, as contrasted to the simple, automatic responses. A student who becomes involved at the responding level might at the teacher's instruction, or even voluntarily, go to the library and research the issue further. Or the student may obey the rules set forth in the class. Can you write an objective at the responding level? Try a responding objective for a homework assignment. You choose the subject and grade level.

Examine your objective to determine whether it involves active student participation. Does it reflect the student's attitude(s)? It should. Specifically, performance of this objective should show a commitment to the homework assignment that a student who does not complete the objective might not have.

Level 3: Valuing

A value is demonstrated when someone prizes a behavior enough to be willing to perform it even in the face of alternatives. A value is not necessarily reflected when a person reacts without having had time to think. In other words, if people really value a behavior they are likely to perform it even though they know the results it may bring, and they will do so repeatedly (Simon et al., 1972).

For example, a mathematics teacher whose students are learning to use simulation games might write the following valuing objective: "When given free time at the end of each period next week to read, play simulation math games, talk to friends, or sleep, each student will voluntarily choose to play simulation games at least two out of the five days." Note that the objective requires students to choose individually of their own free will and to repeat that choice. Also notice that there are other alternatives from which to choose.

Level 4: Organization

The organization level of behavior requires individuals to bring together different values to build a value system. Whenever there is conflict between two or more of their values, they must resolve the conflict. For example, secondary and middle school students constantly encounter conflicting expectations of friends and parents. As students mature, it is hoped that they will not always react according to the expectations of the people they are with at the moment, but will learn to combine the two different sets of values with their own existing beliefs and knowledge about themselves. They will respond to the orderly composite of the combined values, developing their own value system. At this level students may change their behavior or defend it.

For example, a teacher might assign students to defend opposing positions on a controversial issue. By defending both sides, each student will in effect compare the two points of view and may even learn to compromise between the two extremes.

A teacher of a class in U.S. government might introduce a hypothetical bill and have students form two teams, one composed of those who favor the bill, and one of those who oppose it. The objective might read: "After having had the opportunity to support the bill, and the opportunity to try to defeat it, the students will combine all the information and write a statement that expresses their feelings for and against the bill. Given the opportunity, the students will choose to modify the bill to make it fit better with their own value systems."

Level 5: Characterization by a Value or a Value Complex

At the characterization level, students have already developed their own value systems. They are so consistent in the way they behave that they are predictable. At this level, students also demonstrate a degree of individuality and self-reliance.

An example of an objective written at the characterization level: "Each student will bring one newspaper article or news report to class and explain at least two ways in which the article caused the student to change his or her mind from a previously held position on a controversial issue." Does this objective prove that the student has really changed values? What if the student just says that the change has occurred? At the moment the student may believe this, but what about a week from now or a year from now? Can you rewrite this objective so that this doubt will be removed or reduced?

WRITING OBJECTIVES
IN THE PSYCHOMOTOR DOMAIN

The psychomotor domain involves development of physical skills that require coordination of mind and body. It is especially relevant to such courses as physical education, art, drama, music, and vocational courses, but all subjects provide many opportunities for development of psychomotor skills.

Although this domain was the last to have a taxonomy developed for it, at least two scales have now been developed. The following taxonomy is based on a scale developed by E. J. Simpson (1972):

Level 1: Perception
Level 2: Set
Level 3: Guided response
Level 4: Mechanism
Level 5: Complex overt response
Level 6: Adaptation
Level 7: Origination

Level 1: Perception

Purposeful motor activity begins in the brain, where phenomena received act as guides to motor activity. The performer must first become aware of a stimulus, pick up on cues for action, and then act upon these cues. For example, a writer discovers that she is separating her subjects and verbs, thus diluting the impact of her themes. Or a baseball batter notices himself flinching and taking short steps away from the plate when striking, causing him to miss the ball. Or a piano student learns that he is failing to reduce the interval between double notes.

A sample objective at the perception level would be: "Following a demonstration, a geometry student who has been confusing x and y axes in plotting graphs will notice that the x axis always runs horizontally and the y axis always runs vertically."

Level 2: Set

In the psychomotor domain, *set* refers to an individual's readiness to act. It includes both mental readiness and physical and emotional readiness. For example, a high-diver is always seen pausing before a dive to get a psychological, emotional, and physical set. Emotionally she must feel confident about her ability to make a safe and accurate dive. Psychologically, although she may have performed the same dive hundreds of times, she still takes the time to think through the sequence of steps before each dive. Physically, she must ready her muscles in order to respond quickly and accurately. On a less dramatic scale, a student preparing to take notes or do a writing assignment may be seen flexing his fingers or rubbing his eyes—in short, getting set to perform at his best.

An example of a psychomotor objective at this level for piano students is: "Upon the signal 'ready,' each student will assume proper posture and place all fingers in correct keyboard position." Is there a minimum level of performance specified in this objective? Can you rewrite this objective to assign a more meaningful type of behavior? Taking a moment to think about this objective, list two ways you could establish minimum levels of performance.

Does either of your objectives explain what is meant by "correct posture" or "correct keyboard position"? Do both of your suggested changes help make the act measurable?

Level 3: Guided Response

Once the students see the need to act and ready themselves to act, they may find that whenever the act involves complex skills they will need guidance through their first few responses. For example, students in the photography club may need oral guidance as they process their first negatives.

An example of an objective to enhance the development of these skills would be: "When given step-by-step directions in the darkroom, each student will open the film cylinder, remove the film, and, without touching the surface of the film, wind it on a spool so that the surface of each round does not touch previous rounds."

Level 4: Mechanism

This level involves performing an act somewhat automatically without having to pause to think through each separate step. For example, the above photography teacher might want students eventually to be able to perform the entire sequence of development operations while simultaneously counting the number of seconds required to wait between each step. Or a chemistry teacher might write the following objective at the mechanism level: "Given a series of compounds to analyze, the student will operate the electron microscope without having to pause even once to think about the sequence involved in mounting the slide, focusing the projector, and changing the lens size."

Level 5: Complex Overt Response

The level of complex overt response is an extension of the previous level, but it involves more complicated tasks. For example, a driver education teacher may write an objective at this level such as: "When given an unexpected and abrupt command to stop, the student will immediately respond by applying the correct amount of pressure to the brakes, giving the correct signal, and gradually pulling off the road."

Level 6: Adaptation

At this level the student is required to adjust performance as different situations dictate. For example, to allow for an icy surface the driver would adjust her brake pressure and swerve. Or the cook would adjust the timing when going from an electric stove to a gas stove. A boxer would alter his style to adjust for a left-handed opponent.

An example of a psychomotor objective at the adaptation level is: "When planning a budget vacation, the student (without being reminded of the gas supply shortage and cost increase) will eliminate the unnecessary automobile travel and substitute gas-saving strategies."

Level 7: Origination

At the origination level, the highest level of the psychomotor domain, the student creates new movement patterns to fit the particular situation. For example, the cook adds his own touch of genius, and the pianist alters her style or the music itself.

An art teacher might write the following objective: "Given a mixture of powders and compounds of varying textures, the student will use these to accentuate the feeling he is trying to communicate in an oil painting."

OTHER WAYS TO INVOLVE STUDENTS

In addition to varying your lesson plans, you will also need to use a variety of learning avenues, such as textbooks, discussions, field trips, oral reports, term projects, and homework. We now turn to the use of these and the teacher's role in each.

Textbooks

Throughout the history of education in the United States, one type of textbook or another has dominated the curriculum. At first, it was the textbook that determined the content to be studied. There were virtually no experiences other than rote memorization and recitation, which often resulted in a boring, irrelevant curriculum. To a large extent, this is still true: "Teachers consider the textbook as the major (and usually only) source of content" (Walter, 1984, p. 58). Although the twentieth century is changing the textbook's role as sole determiner of content, the textbook still can play an effective role in today's planning.

One common use of a textbook is to build the curriculum around it. The textbook may be the center of the curriculum, but it is supported by other textbooks, journals, magazines, and newspapers. This approach is probably a good choice in communities or school systems that press for traditional education, and in schools that have very limited resources. But it is much more likely to succeed if the teacher includes some contemporary problems and helps students apply the acquired knowledge toward solving them.

Another approach is to use the textbook along with other materials. Instead of letting the textbook lead the teacher, and students, in the selection of content and experiences, the teacher may take the lead in designing the curriculum. For example, the teacher would determine the sequence of topics, instead of following the textbook organization from chapter 1 to chapter 2. The teacher may decide that some chapters are not worth including in the curriculum. Teachers are becoming increasingly competent in curriculum development, and more and more teachers insist on having the freedom to shape the curricula in their classes as they see fit.

But not all school systems provide teachers with such freedom to develop their own curricula. Concern that students may not "cover" all the content needed for the following year or for college is always present. Such concern is legitimate. School administrators know that they are responsible for seeing that the total school curricula do not have major content gaps. Many larger secondary schools hire a curriculum director, a curriculum supervisor, or an assistant principal who is directly responsible for that. Teachers should work with the curriculum leader and/or fellow teachers to avoid curriculum redundancy and gaps.

Other teachers make even less use of the textbook, almost totally avoiding it. They substitute current problems, learning activity packages, or learning units they developed themselves. Of course, these teachers are in school systems that permit an unusually high degree of teacher freedom. Such systems are not typical.

Whatever freedom your system permits you in using the textbook, be sure you do not spend most of the class period reading the text or requiring the students to read it. It is much better to assign a chapter as homework the evening before a lesson and to use class time to discuss what was read.

Discussions

Today's students want to be involved. They feel that their own opinions and judgments are worthwhile, and they want to share them. For this reason the discussion has increased in popularity. A good discussion involves all participants. Everyone has an opportunity to relate the topic to his or her own experiences. This sharing of various perspectives can enrich the knowledge and understanding of individual participants. But discussions that are merely rambling gossip sessions and that do no more than share ignorance should be avoided.

Plan discussions carefully. First, to encourage total participation, group students according to their interest in the topic. This can be achieved by letting students choose discussion topics. Second, avoid assigning both very passive students and aggressive students to the same groups. By putting the reserved students together, you will force one or more to assume leadership, and by placing aggressive students in the same group, some will be forced to learn to yield the floor to others. By assigning roles, such as "discussion moderator" and "recorder," and then varying these roles, you will prompt all group members to participate even further.

Select topics that have answers, although there may be multiple answers, depending upon individual perspective. By letting students know that a definite outcome is expected, you will give them a sense of purpose and responsibility.

If the moderator fails to keep group discussion progressing and on target, you may want to intervene, but too much interference will cause a group to become dependent on your leadership. Take care, also, to assure that the group moderator does not dominate the discussion. In addition, the discussion must reflect the belief that all serious comments are worth a hearing, regardless of how inaccurate or insignificant others may consider them.

A free-flowing discussion provides a valuable opportunity to develop social skills, which is in itself an important goal for secondary and middle-level students. It also helps students identify with their peers. All adolescents need to belong, and all need positive recognition and approval from peers. Group discussions should help fill these needs.

The participants need to know that each person has a definite role in every discussion. First, each participant is obligated to read the assignment so the discussion will begin from a common base. Second, each person is responsible for contributing additional information to the discussion. Opinions and contributions of knowledge are prized only when the participants can present evidence or knowledge to support them. Third, each participant is responsible for listening to others and, when possible, for referring to specific comments of others. This assures all participants that their comments are being considered.

You, the teacher, are responsible for seeing that the environment remains informal, pleasant, and nonthreatening. You are also a facilitator, helping students to locate adequate resources and to plan their discussion. When the discussion is over, you can help them evaluate discussion techniques and redesign their strategies for future discussions.

Field Trips

Like many fine inventions of the past, the field trip has become almost prematurely moribund, even though it still has many unique advantages. The reasons for its loss of popularity are many. First, there has been a growing trend of more lawsuits against schools, and the courts have begun to find more schools liable as charged. Because administrators and teachers can also be found liable, many of them are reluctant to encourage field trips, which are perceived as unnecessary risks.

This is unfortunate, because field trips still have unique potentials. There is no better way for a social studies class to study the habits of an ethnic group than to visit a local community. And a group of students interested in aerodynamics could find nothing more meaningful than a visit to a wind tunnel. An agriculture class may benefit tremendously from a visit to an agriculture education agency, an experimental station, or a local farm.

Before you arrange a field trip, first check school policy, because many schools now forbid field trips of any type. But even if you find yourself teaching at such a school, you might try to bring the "field" to the school. For example, a junior high or middle school earth science teacher might arrange for a few truck-loads of several types of soil and rocks to be dumped on the school grounds so that students can take an on-campus geology field trip.

If your school does permit field trips, you might let your students suggest the need for one—assuming that they are mature enough and self-disciplined enough to be trusted. Some groups of students simply present too great a risk, and a teacher would be foolish to pursue a trip with such students. If the idea comes from the students, they may be willing to work harder and organize better.

Next, you must be sure that the trip is indeed necessary and purposeful. Each student should be assigned, or should assume, definite responsibilities for gathering specific data. Students may also share the responsibility for organizing the trip, clearing it with the principal's office, arranging the visits, filling out the necessary insurance forms, and securing the necessary permissions and finances.

After the field trip, a follow-up lesson in which students report their data and discuss implications will accentuate what the trip accomplished. As with all other instructional approaches, evaluation of each trip will improve the quality of future trips. Evaluations are more effective when done immediately after the trip while the teacher and students still remember specifics.

Oral Reports

For several decades, oral reports have been popular in secondary and middle-level schools, but how successful this technique is depends on its use. When you are considering using oral reports, first decide what their purpose is. Teachers too often give assignments without really thinking through the purpose of the report. Oral reports can have several purposes that may be considered important goals.

For example, you might assign a report to an advanced student who is delving into one aspect of a topic. The report would provide that student with an opportunity to share what he or she has learned while at the same time enabling the rest of the class to benefit from the study. Or you might assign a report to a group of students to give them an opportunity to learn to work together co-operatively. Another teacher might assign reports to give students experience in public speaking.

Each of these purposes is legitimate and worthwhile so long as the teacher communicates the main purpose(s) of the reports to the students. However, assigning a report to punish misbehavior or to substitute for teacher planning is not wise. Students will quickly connect the report with those purposes and probably fail to expect any significant learning to result. This is the case when reports are used at the end of a grading period to give students an opportunity to improve their grades.

Whatever your reason for assigning oral reports, you must communicate to the reporter(s) the primary purposes of the assignment. Other members of the class should be told what is expected of them during the report. Should they take notes? ask questions? take issue with the speaker? Should they ask for clarification when they do not understand? Should they interrupt the speaker with comments, or wait until the end of the presentation? Will they be held accountable on the next test for the information presented orally by their peers? By answering these questions before the report is delivered, you can draw each student into the oral presentations of their peers and thereby maximize interest and involvement.

As a precaution against students' taking reports too lightly, you might have a policy of always assigning credit for oral reports—and perhaps to the rest of the students for their responses. You can do this without presenting a threat to the students. Consider a positive reward system that would let students earn credit for participation in the discussion without penalizing those whose contributions are minimal.

The timing of oral reports can be critical. Avoid scheduling too many reports in succession. The student who is giving the twelfth consecutive report in class is at a definite disadvantage. To avoid the repetition and the boredom that students experience when too many reports are given, spread the reporting out so that no more than two are given in any week.

Students need ample time to prepare reports. Depending on the level of sophistication of the subject, a minimum of one week to several weeks lead time will be needed. Because many secondary school students and some middle school students hold part-time jobs, and extracurricular activities consume much of their out-of-class time, you might allot some class time for preparing oral presentations. This is needed especially when students are planning group presentations.

Teachers should never make assignments without giving students an opportunity to present the results. This would be especially destructive when oral presentations are involved. Of course, a teacher would never intentionally be so callous, but sometimes teachers forget to save enough time in the term for the reports. This can be avoided by scheduling the reporting dates at the time the assignments are made. Then students will not be disappointed, and they will see oral presentations as worthwhile.

Projects

Whatever subject you teach, you will find that assigning projects is valuable. You can choose among many types of projects: long-term projects, which may last for a grading period or even a semester; short-term projects; and individual projects. You have probably considered several types of projects as assignments for oral presentations, but not all projects must end with an oral presentation. Some may conclude with written reports or with presentation of concrete products that have resulted from the assignment. Regardless of product produced, students should be given an opportunity to show their creations. For example, a science teacher may want to arrange a local science fair to display students' insect collections, or a music teacher may want to set up a student recital.

Teachers who offer projects as options (or not required of all students) may use a liberal grading system. One great advantage of projects is that they permit students who for one reason or another do not benefit from didactic forms of instruction to become totally involved. Many teachers take advantage of the opportunity to grade these activities in a way that rewards student effort. Many students who appear to be failures on tests can produce excellent projects. Perhaps it is because they want to do the projects, or perhaps they feel more competent doing something with their hands, or it may be a combination of the two. Therefore, many teachers view projects as an opportunity to provide successful experiences for everyone. You might want to experiment by assigning all As and Bs to the projects for one term. Of course, you are free to let it count as much or as little of the total term grade as you prefer.

Homework

During the 1960s and 1970s, homework for the public school student lost much of its prestige, but by the end of the 1970s it had regained a more positive reputation. In fact, half the secondary school students themselves said that the homework was not challenging (Elam, 1978, p. 700). This is evidence that homework, when properly assigned and utilized, can be meaningful.

But all homework does not necessarily result in improved learning. In a review of 24 studies on the effects of homework given in elementary and secondary schools, Friesen (1979) found that of the 24 studies conducted, 12 reported positive effects on achievement and 11 found no difference or negative effects; the remaining study showed that the homework group did better on investigator-designed tests but worse on standardized tests.

One reason students who have homework often score less well is that teachers often do not have a definite purpose for homework assignments. This can lead to busywork. Here are some of the major uses teachers can make of homework assignments (Lee & Pruitt, 1978, p. 31).

1. Practice—designed to reinforce skills and information covered in class
2. Preparation—given to prepare students to profit from subsequent lessons
3. Extension—provided to determine whether a particular student can extend the concept or skill learned in class to a new situation
4. Creative—designed to require students to integrate many skills and concepts in producing some project

This list shows that homework can be used for different purposes and that it can also be used to develop higher-order skills. The purpose of the homework should determine the teacher's instructional behavior. Teachers should always base a decision to use homework (or not to) on a purpose for which it is suited and should introduce it accordingly. Far too often homework is used only for practice. Because many states now require all teachers to give homework (many actually specifying the number of hours a night), it is imperative that you become familiar with the variety of uses for which homework is suited. The four uses listed above are a good place to begin. The following suggestions will help you design and implement a system for assigning homework that will work well for you.

Clarify the Assignment. Homework assignments must be clear. If they involve problem solving, you may want to give students an opportunity to work at least one problem of each type in class before you ask them to do problems at home. And simply using verbal instructions and explanations may not be enough. Perhaps you can remember a time when as a student you thought you understood how the teacher wanted you to complete an assignment, but when you got home you found that you could not start the problem because you didn't know how to begin. If you had been given an opportunity to work just one problem in class, you could have raised questions at that time.

Individualize Homework Assignments. Students who cannot understand how to do their classwork even with the help of the teacher will benefit little from a homework assignment of more of the same type of problems. The teacher assigning homework must consider the abilities and needs of each student. Certain homework assignments for slower students will help them catch up with the rest of the class, while the more advanced students can explore areas of special interest to them in depth. Such an individualistic approach to homework assignments can help relieve the ever-present dilemma of teachers—how to challenge the brightest students without surpassing the slower students.

Make Homework Creative. Teachers today realize that the old practice of assigning students to "read the next chapter and work the problems at the end of the chapter" is not challenging or stimulating. Homework assignments are more interesting when they contain variety. Students could be asked to respond to something that is on the evening news, in the newspaper, or on an educational television program. Multisensory activities can replace written assignments. Creativity cannot be forced, but you can establish a climate that stimulates and nourishes creativity. Let your students use all their senses and manipulate objects; have them investigate problems that have no fixed answer.

Be Reasonable. Avoid making too many demands on students' time at home. Many students come from homes that have no books or any place that is well lighted or quiet enough for studying. Disruptions from brothers and sisters make homework difficult for many students. Then, too, many secondary school students and some middle school students, use after-school hours for part-time jobs on which their families depend for some essentials. For such students, homework assignments that require a few hours each evening are impossible to complete.

Secondary school teachers must also remember that students have several other courses and may be receiving homework assignments in all of them.

When you evaluate homework, take into account the conditions under which students must perform. As with classroom or term projects, grading of homework should be lenient enough so that students who are faced with the most adverse environments will not become discouraged.

Follow-up. Nothing can be more disheartening than spending time and energy on an assignment only to have the teacher forget about it or push it aside for more critical matters. If you schedule a follow-up time at the time of the assignment, you can prevent these annoying situations.

Overview of Steps for Assigning Homework. The following steps for assigning homework can be used as a summary of this discussion and as a guideline for making homework assignments (Berry, 1977, p. 52).

1. As an alternative, plan for assignments to be completed at some time during the school day in a supervised area.
2. Be sure the purpose of every homework assignment is clear in your mind and that you have made it clear to the students.
3. Try to match assignments with students, making sure each student is treated fairly and equally.
4. Be sure every student knows exactly what is required.
5. Check the assignment when it is due.
6. Don't expect homework to teach a student who is not learning properly in the classroom.
7. Remember that assignments that use a multisensory approach are most effective in teaching.

These seven steps were actually designed for elementary school teachers. Do you think any (or all) of them are adequate guidelines for secondary and middle school teachers?

We have now discussed the uses of textbooks, discussions, field trips, oral reports, term projects, and homework. When making any of these assignments, perhaps the most important question a teacher can ask is: What will this homework assignment permit students to do that they cannot do in class? And how can I (we) design the assignment to benefit the student and perhaps the rest of the class?

RECAP OF MAJOR IDEAS

1. Well-written objectives will help clarify the teacher's expectations.
2. Objectives should be written precisely and concisely.
3. Verbs used in objectives should express action that can be observed and measured.
4. Objectives can be used to raise the level of thinking in the classroom.

5. Textbooks should be only one of several sources of information used in planning.
6. In planning, teachers should first determine the desired ends (aims, goals, and objectives) and then choose the means (content and activities) accordingly.
7. Each objective should (a) be stated in terms of student behavior, not teacher behavior, (b) describe the conditions under which students are expected to perform, and (c) specify the minimum acceptable level of performance.
8. For each lesson plan, teachers should identify objectives at varying levels of all three domains. However, it is highly unlikely that a lesson could or should have objectives written at all levels of all domains.
9. Lessons should use a multitude of planning strategies, including discussion, field trips, oral reports, projects, and homework assignments.
10. Homework assignments should be made creative and reasonable and should reflect student interests.
11. Teachers should always follow up on assignments.

POSTTEST

Now that you have read the chapter, take a moment to respond to the following statements again.

	Agree	Disagree	Uncertain
1. Generally, teachers have both the freedom and the responsibility to plan their own lessons.	＿＿	＿＿	＿＿
2. Aims, goals, and objectives are terms that are used in education to mean the same thing.	＿＿	＿＿	＿＿
3. The more concisely and precisely an objective is written, the better it will be.	＿＿	＿＿	＿＿
4. Every lesson should have some written objectives that have to do with student attitudes.	＿＿	＿＿	＿＿
5. Every lesson should have objectives that are written at all levels of the taxonomy.	＿＿	＿＿	＿＿
6. A major purpose of an objective is to help the teacher communicate to the student exactly what is expected of the students.	＿＿	＿＿	＿＿
7. At the end of any lesson, students should be able to do some things they could not do at the beginning of the period.	＿＿	＿＿	＿＿
8. Objectives can be used to raise the level of thinking in a classroom.	＿＿	＿＿	＿＿
9. Classroom discussions usually remain at the lowest level of thinking.	＿＿	＿＿	＿＿
10. Every lesson plan should include some questions from all three educational domains.	＿＿	＿＿	＿＿

CASE

This chapter covers techniques for writing behavioral objectives. Although most teachers today realize the significance of objectives for teaching, you will undoubtedly hear complaints about objectives among your future colleagues. The following case shows some of the reasons that there are negative feelings about behavioral objectives. As you read it, consider how much you will use objectives in your future lesson planning.

Case 1: A Principal Misuses Objectives

Lincoln High School had the reputation of being one of the most innovative, experimental, and advanced schools in the district. The large number of oil wells in the area made financing one of the least of the principal's worries. When Sondra Bell became principal last year, she promised the board that, with their support, she would lead the school to even greater heights.

As the principal planned her annual report, she realized that the board had delivered their part of the bargain, but she wondered whether they felt as positive about her. The report contained two parts, "In Retrospect" and "In Prospect." Because she thought that the first part looked a little weak, Sondra decided to compensate by planning an impressive "In Prospect" section.

She began spelling out her objectives for the coming year. Could she impress the board by planning everything for the coming year around those performance objectives that she would set for the students? It seemed logical, so she pulled out a taxonomy of educational objectives from the notes in her methods course. For each daily lesson, she wrote an objective at each level of the cognitive domain. But when she began writing objectives for all levels of the affective domain, her task became more difficult. Although she had initially planned to write objectives that represented all levels of all three domains, Sondra gave up in despair long before the task was completed.

Rather than admit failure, Sondra appointed a committee consisting of the department heads and one or two members of each department. She assigned them exactly the same task—to write sample objectives at all levels in all domains for each subject in the entire school curriculum. The faculty was not at all happy with this request. Most teachers were already using objectives in planning their lessons, but they thought this was going too far.

Discussion

1. Was this principal wrong to require her faculty to use objectives in their planning?
   The mistake she made was more in the degree of the requirement than in the decision to require the use of objectives. Certainly all teachers should use objectives to help clarify their expectations of students and to organize their lessons better, but taken to this extreme the objectives could become a nightmare to teachers and to students.
2. Why did Sondra have trouble writing objectives at all levels in all domains?
   It is almost impossible to write so many objectives in all levels for all subjects. The goal itself is admirable, because sample objectives can be very helpful to teachers who do not have extensive experience writing objectives.
3. If you were a teacher at Lincoln High, how would you respond to this requirement?

ACTIVITIES

Most teachers today recognize that carefully written, specific behavioral objectives will help them reach their broader goals.

1. Each teacher has different aspirations for students. Consider your subject and write one broad goal that you believe is absolutely essential for students to understand. Write several specific behavioral objectives to help your students reach this goal.
2. Think about the problems that characterize modern society. Write a general attitudinal goal to eliminate or minimize one of these problems. Now write a few specific behavioral objectives to help students attain this goal.
3. Have you any opinion(s) about the use of objectives that you are willing to share with your classmates? If so, write these down and get a fellow student to listen to your opinion(s). Of course, you will then listen to the same for your fellow student.
4. Choose a topic for class discussion. Write five objectives for the discussion and select a reading for all members. Now identify at least one or two related sources that give information not contained in the student assignment.
5. Plan a field trip for a learning unit in your major field. Start by listing five objectives. Now construct a short questionnaire to evaluate the degree of success of the trip.

SUGGESTED READINGS

Beauchamp, G. A. (1975). *Curriculum theory* (3rd ed.). Wilmette, Ill.: Kagg.

Berry, K. (1977). Homework: Is it for elementary kids? *Instructor, 86,* 52.

Bloom, B. S. (1956). *Taxonomy of educational objectives: The classification of educational goals, Handbook I: Cognitive domain.* New York: McKay.

Bloom, B. S., Hastings, J. T., & Madeus, G. F. (1971). *Handbook on formative and summative evaluation of student learning.* New York: McGraw-Hill.

Doll, R. C. (1978). *Curriculum improvement: Decision making process* (4th ed.). Boston: Allyn & Bacon.

Elam, S. M. (1979, June). Gallup finds teen-agers generally like their schools. Report on a Gallup Poll of teenagers taken in November 1978, *Phi Delta Kappan, 60,* 700.

Firth, G. R., & Kimpston, R. D. (1973). *The curriculum continuum in perspective.* Itasca, Ill.: Peacock.

Friesen, C. D. (1979, January). The results of homework versus no-homework research studies. ERIC ED 167 508.

Girod, G. R. (1973). *Writing and assessing attitudinal objectives.* Columbus, Ohio: Merrill.

Gronland, N. E. (1978). *Stating objectives for classroom instruction* (2nd ed.). New York: Macmillan.

Krathwohl, D. R., Bloom, B. S., & Masia, B. B. (1964). *Taxonomy of educational objectives: The classification of educational goals, Handbook II: Affective domain.* New York: McKay.

Lee, J., & Pruitt, K. W. (1978). Homework assignments: Classroom games or teaching tools? *Clearing House, 53,* 31.

Mager, R. F. (1962). *Preparing educational objectives.* Belmont, Calif.: Fearon.

Oliva, Peter F. (1981). *Developing the curriculum.* Boston: Little, Brown.

Sanders, N. M. (1966). *Classroom questions: What kinds?* New York: Harper & Row.

Simon, S. B., Howe, L. W., & Kirschenbaum, H. (1972). *Values clarification.* New York: Hart.

Simpson, E. J. (1972). The classification of educational objectives in the psychomotor domain. *The psychomotor domain,* Vol. 3. Washington, D.C.: Gryphon House.

Stephens, G. M., & Herman, J. J. (1984, May). Outcome-based educational planning. *Educational Leadership, 41,* 45–49.

Trump, J. L., & Miller, D. F. (1979). *Secondary school curriculum improvement: Meeting challenges of the times* (3rd ed.). Boston: Allyn & Bacon.

Tyler, R. W. (1949). *Basic Principles of Curriculum and Instruction.* Chicago: Chicago University Press.

Walter, L. J. (1984, March). A synthesis of research findings on teacher planning and decision making. In R. L. Egbert & M. M. Lluender (Eds.), *Using research to improve teacher education.* Lincoln, Neb.: Clearinghouse on Teacher Education.

Wulf, K. M., & Schane, B. (1984). *Curriculum design.* Glenview, Ill.: Scott, Foresman.

Yinger, R. (1979, June). Routine in teaching planning. *Theory into Practice, 18,* 163–169.

Zais, R. S. (1976). *Curriculum: Principles and foundations.* New York: Crowell.

PART II

TEACHING STRATEGIES AND COMMUNICATIONS

Effective teachers take a definite approach to teaching each lesson. They select specific methods and develop them into more general and complex strategies. To do this well, a teacher must have a repertoire of methods from which to choose. Chapter 5 presents a variety of teaching methods. To help the teacher select the most appropriate method for each lesson, there is a discussion of the strengths and limitations of each method. To be effective, strategies and methods must come to life in the classroom. The teacher makes this happen through communication. Chapter 6 presents several verbal and nonverbal technical skills to prepare teachers to communicate effectively.

C H A P T E R **5**

Teaching Strategies

Objectives

- Differentiate between *questioning* and *Socratic method*.
- List three unique strengths of simulation gaming.
- List two teaching strategies that are good motivators.
- List two guidelines for teachers who use questions in classroom instruction.
- Give three suggestions to help teachers improve their lectures.
- Define inquiry learning.
- Name one major advantage and one major limitation of inquiry learning.
- List three advantages of the lecture.

PRETEST

	Agree	Disagree	Uncertain
1. Teaching methods are of little importance because good students learn in any setting and poor students do poorly regardless of the teaching method.	_____	_____	_____
2. Some methods are best for some students; others are best for other students.	_____	_____	_____
3. The way a teacher implements a teaching method is more important than which method is selected.	_____	_____	_____
4. The lecture has no place in secondary schools because other methods are superior in every way.	_____	_____	_____
5. Rhetorical questions should be used only when informing students that they are not expected to answer.	_____	_____	_____
6. Games developed by the teacher and students are usually superior to commercial learning games.	_____	_____	_____
7. Inquiry learning is the same as discovery learning.	_____	_____	_____
8. The effectiveness of questioning is enhanced when teachers give students more time to respond, help students reach acceptable answers, and encourage students to ask questions.	_____	_____	_____
9. Simulation-type games are good motivators and lead to increased retention.	_____	_____	_____

Middle-Level Message

The success of any lesson hinges on the teacher's ability to get the students' attention. At the middle level this can be a real challenge. This chapter introduces advance organizers that can help get students' attention at the beginning of the period and hold it throughout the period as new concepts are introduced.

    This chapter also introduces a variety of teaching methods. All teachers need a repertoire of methods from which to choose. Because of the transescent's need for socialization opportunities, middle-level teachers should pay especially close attention to discussions, simulations, and games as teaching methods. Learn when to use each of these methods and how to use them to achieve the full potentials of each method.

Not long ago, teachers could be described according to their particular teaching styles. Prospective teachers spent many hours wondering what their own teaching style would be. Would they use mainly expository teaching—something like the many lectures they had listened to in college? Or would they use an entirely different approach, which would lead students to discover for themselves the important truths of a discipline?

Today's education majors are asking different questions because they recognize that there are many teaching methods—expository, inquiry, questioning, discovery, simulation gaming. The old question "Which *one* should I use?" has given way to a new one: "Which *ones* should I use? and for what purposes?" Education students, who are now exposed to a number of teaching methods, know that certain methods work best with certain objectives.

This chapter looks at several teaching methods and helps you develop the skills needed to select and use each to achieve *particular* goals. "Particular" is emphasized because if the stated goals are too broad there is no advantage in choosing any one particular method. For example, suppose your goal is to select and use the method that will produce maximum learning or understanding. "Of eighty-eight comparisons between traditional lecture and traditional discussion methods, as reported in thirty-six experimental studies, 51 percent favored the lecture method and 49 percent favored the discussion method" (Berliner & Gage, 1975, p.15). In other words, 51 percent of the studies found that the lecture method was superior to the discussion method for effective learning; 49 percent found the discussion method superior to the lecture.

This does not mean that teaching methods are unimportant; it does mean that they are contextual. The success of each method depends on the teacher's ability to relate it to the overall instructional program in a particular classroom with a particular group of students. In fact, hundreds of studies show that, correctly used, each style is superior in its ability to produce certain specific results.

As you study each method, keep these questions in mind: What are the unique potentials of this method? How can this method best be implemented? If I decide to experiment using this method, what precautions should I take? Can I learn to implement this method effectively, along with other approaches, to develop overall instructional strategies that will lead to achievement of my course objectives?

THE LECTURE

The lecture has been the teaching method used most frequently in U.S. classrooms and in most other countries. Although it has received much criticism from contemporary educators, the lecture's survival is evidence that it has some unique strengths as a teaching method.

When to Use the Lecture

When deciding whether to use the lecture, keep in mind the type of students you are teaching. Are your classes college preparatory, elective, or remedial? If they are composed of students whose potential is limited, the lecture would be a poor choice because it requires students to take notes and most students are not good note takers. In fact, under ideal conditions, even college students are able to capture only 52 percent of a lecture's important ideas (Maddox & Hoole, 1975).

The success of the lecture also depends on whether the students are self-motivated, because the lecture itself is a poor motivator. So before you decide for or against using the lecture, consider the interest level of your group of students. Many students prefer the lecture because it demands little direct participation and involvement. Less-capable students tend to favor the lecture over other modes of instruction that place more responsibility on them (Couch, 1973). Teachers should not lecture frequently to groups of low performers.

Weaknesses of the Lecture

Only well-planned and well-executed lectures are either successful or well liked by the students. Students often say that lectures are boring, do not involve the learner, are poorly organized, focus on the lowest level of cognition, and do not recognize individual differences. Lectures also produce excessive anxiety among students, more than is produced by other teaching methods (Ellis & Jones, 1974). Many teachers use the lecture to show off their own knowledge. Feeding their egos, these teachers tend to be too formal, too authoritative, and too structured. They often stress technical points instead of interpreting or relating information, and they may not be receptive to student comments that question what they are saying. Such domination of students is an example of gross misuse of the lecture.

It has already been suggested that, when properly planned and executed, the lecture works best for students who are capable and motivated. But best for teaching what? Any subject? Best for communicating in general? No. In fact, a review of 91 surveys covering four decades of research on comparative teaching methods found no difference in the effectiveness of the lecture and other methods of teaching (Voth, 1975). The lecture is superior only for certain objectives; it is inferior for others. For example, the lecture is generally not an effective method for stimulating interest, promoting creativity, or helping students develop responsibility or imagination, and it is not a good approach for helping students learn to synthesize, internalize, or express themselves. Compared to educational games, the lecture is only equally as effective for immediate cognitive gain, and it is significantly less effective for retention over a period of three weeks or longer (Lucas et al., 1975).

Strengths of the Lecture

But the lecture has several unique potentials. It is an extremely effective way to introduce a unit or to build a frame of reference (Kyle, 1972). It is also a superior technique for demonstrating models and clarifying matters that may be confusing to students (Thompson, 1974). A short lecture can effectively introduce and summarize the major concepts presented in a lesson. It gives the teacher an opportunity to collect related information and to assemble it into a meaningful and intellectually manageable framework.

Implementing the Lecture

Why are some lectures good, some bad? Why are some teachers stimulating when they dispense information, when others are so boring? Not all lectures are the same. How do they differ, and how can the teacher make them more interesting and informative?

Most successful lectures are relatively short. Few people can concentrate for extended periods of time, so even the best lecturers should limit their lectures to short time periods, occasionally changing to activities that involve students. The next section presents some effective ways for improving the lecture through correct planning and delivery and by combining the lecture with other instructional approaches.

Improving the Lecture

Instructional Objectives. Much attention has recently been given to instructional objectives. But do they really affect learning, and if so, how? Should they be introduced before or after the lesson?

When used either before or after a lecture, instructional objectives do affect students' reactions to the lecture. Instructional objectives introduced at the beginning of the lecture tend to increase intentional learning (that is, learning that the teaching seeks to stimulate); instructional objectives used after the lesson affect the incidental learning by those students. To ensure that students will learn the most important concepts in a lesson, the teacher should always introduce the objectives before the lecture. In this way the objectives become *advance organizers,* giving learners a basis for new concepts.

Tempo. One important variable in any lecture is the tempo, or pace. When the pace of a lecture is too slow, students become bored; when it is too fast, their inability to keep up with and understand the lesson discourages them. The "pall level"—a state of physical, program-related fatigue—is reached when students lose interest because the concept is too simple or too difficult, or when the steps in its presentation are too short or too long. In both cases, students tend to respond by generating their own discussions. Lectures that move at a moderate pace produce less noise than those that move at a slow or fast pace (Grobe et al., 1973). Studies show that most studio-recorded presentations are too slow, that they would produce more learning if the lecturer increased the speed up to three times the normal speed. If the speed is too great, however, the students feel rushed and begin to reject the speaker (Rippey, 1975).

Stimulus Variation. Certain actions during a lecture help prevent student boredom, especially among secondary school students. Stimulus variation—such as the teacher moving through the class or gesturing and pausing—correlates positively with student recall of lectures (Wyckoff, 1973). At the elementary level, however, stimulus variation actually lowers student performance on lecture tests; excessive teacher movement distracts younger students from the lecture content.

Structure. Most lectures can be vastly improved and simplified by (1) organizing the content into only a few (three to five) major concepts, (2) ordering the concepts in a logical or natural sequence, (3) limiting the lecture to 10 or 15 minutes, (4) providing tasks that require all students to use the concepts, and (5) summarizing the major concepts. English teachers often outline the major concepts in a story and put them in a definite sequence; history teachers may use events and dates. Identification and ordering of concepts is equally important in math, science, social studies, and other classes.

Titus (1974) presents the following list of steps for preparing a good lecture:

1. Organization is vital.
2. Stick to a limited number of concepts.
3. Limit time.
4. Use humor.
5. Avoid tangents.
6. Watch your language.
7. Listen to yourself.

Vocabulary. Titus' concern for language in the list above is especially warranted. Too many lectures are loaded with jargon, technical vocabulary, or other unfamiliar language that confuses the learners.

Audiovisual Aids. Titus' recommendation that lecturers practice self-evaluation is reflected by many other educators, such as Whooley (1974) and Frazier and Holcomb (1972). Frazier and Holcomb suggest that videotape recordings be used for this purpose. Commonwealth and Gootnick (1974) express the attitude of many educators that visual aids should accompany all lectures. The overhead projector seems to have replaced the chalkboard as the most popular visual aid in today's classroom. The most effective use of either tool occurs when the lesson is not predeveloped but built up in front of the students, who help develop the concepts by working the problems or by responding to the teacher's questions as the lesson develops. In other words, the most effective delivery depends upon student participation in developing the ideas set out by the lesson plan.

Histrionics. The high anxiety level that is common among students during lectures can be reduced if the teacher tells jokes (Ellis & Jones, 1974). It is interesting to note that students for whom the use of a lecture is appropriate (high-ability, low-anxiety students) also benefit most from humor, whereas their counterparts—the slow, anxious students—retain less from humorous lectures (Weinberg, 1975). In some instances, humor does not affect the immediate cognitive gains, but several weeks later students find that they have retained significantly more concepts from lectures containing humor (Kaplan & Pascoe, 1977).

Altering the Lecture Method. In addition to improving the lecture itself and its delivery, research shows that lectures can be vastly improved by combining them with tutorials and student discussions. When tutorials were added to lectures in an eleventh-grade class, the combination increased immediate cognitive gains and retention measured over an 11-week interval (Rowsey & Mason, 1975). The individualizing effect seems to be of special benefit to the lower-ability and lower-achievement students, whereas increasing emphasis on recitation and problem solving benefits the higher-ability and higher-achieving students (Ott & Macklin, 1975). Adding modeling demonstrations to the lecture tends to increase both the immediate and long-term learning and also improves student attitudes toward the lesson. These studies suggest that the pure lecture method can be improved by adding either tutorials or modeling to the lecture.

But for lecture blending to be effective with students, they must be exposed to nonlecture teaching styles at early ages. By seventh grade, many students are already conditioned to the lecture method, and alternatives should be used earlier (Starr & Schuerman, 1974). For students who are accustomed to the straight lecture, the combining of lectures with student discussion produces little difference in cognitive gain among seventh-graders and may actually damage their attitude toward the lesson. For this reason, teachers should balance their selection of learning methods to improve achievement and attitude.

TUTORING

The act of tutoring dates back many centuries. In England it has been a major, if not *the* major, teaching strategy for many years. It derives its strength from being a one-on-one process, giving the student personal, individual attention. The student receiving the help (the tutee) receives immediate feedback and has continuous opportunity to ask questions.

But tutoring has its limitations. It requires much time from the one who gives the help, the tutor, and because most teachers cannot give so much time to individuals, students are often used to tutor. Students selected to tutor other students are usually the brightest and highest achievers in their classes. Some say that high-achieving students give up their own time that could be better spent pursuing their own learning. Others say that having peer help lowers the self-esteem of the students who need help and raises the "snob level" of the brighter students.

After many years of experience directing the tutoring program at the University of Wisconsin in Madison, Klausmeier (1980) concluded that tutoring probably does little psychological damage to the tutors because their reasons for getting involved are unselfish. They want to help others and tutoring makes them feel needed. Klausmeier suggests that, in order to be fair to the students, only volunteers should be tutors, and they should have the option of stopping whenever they wish.

Combining Tutoring with Grouping

The effect of tutoring on learner achievement has been the focus of research throughout the years. Studies have reported varying results. It is clear that, by itself, tutoring does not always increase learning, so some educators have begun combining tutoring with other teaching strategies. Of notable repute is the work of Benjamin Bloom at the University of Chicago. According to Bloom (1984, p. 6), the most striking finding was that under tutoring, the best possible learning condition, "the average student is two sigmas above the average control student taught under conventional group methods of instruction." This is powerful testimony for tutoring. First, it says that one-on-one tutoring is the very best learning condition we can devise. Second, it says that, on the average, students who are taught using this method outscore their counterparts by two sigmas, or two standard deviations. Another way to express this is to say that the average tutored student outperformed 98 percent of the students in the control class. Bloom (1984, p. 17) offers the following suggestions for all schools and teachers:

1. Improve the student processing of instruction by using the mastery learning feedback–corrective process and/or the enhancement of the initial cognitive prerequisites for sequential courses.
2. Improve the tools of instruction by selecting a curriculum, textbook, or other instructional material that has proven to be very effective.
3. Improve the home environmental support of student learning by beginning a dialogue between the school and the home.
4. Improve instruction in the school by providing favorable conditions of learning for all the students in each classroom as well as by increasing the emphasis on higher mental process learning for all the students.

As you continue your study of instructional strategies and ways of individualizing instruction, identify techniques that can be combined with tutoring to make it more effective in your classroom.

Let's Ponder

Read the following statement and respond to the questions below.

Another Bandwagon

Tutoring is not new. In fact, it's the most primitive type of education, even predating civilization. Today's educators seem to get excited over every bandwagon that comes along. Some of the bandwagons simply don't produce music worth the price of the players, and tutoring is an excellent example. The students who tutor don't need the ego trip they get from being the leader. The tutees already know that they are below-average students— they don't need the additional humiliation. Bright students should not waste their time helping slower students. Instead, the program should be challenging the bright students to achieve even higher goals, but in tutoring they give valuable learning time to do the teacher's job. And if this isn't enough, the studies do not all agree that the tutee is actually helped to achieve more.

1. Do you think that the act of receiving help from peers lowers the self-esteem of students who are tutored? What evidence can you give to support your answer?
2. Do you think that receiving tutorial help exposes a student's performance level, or do students already know the general achievement level of their peers? When you were in secondary or middle school, did you know the performance levels of your peers? Do you think this has changed in recent years?
3. Because student tutors have to be trained by teachers, what effects do you think a tutoring program has on teachers? Why?
4. Do you think tutoring tends to focus on a remedial level and therefore lowers the general levels of expectancy in the classrooms involved? Why or why not?

INQUIRY LEARNING

Inquiry learning is a familiar and popular concept in education today. At all levels and in all subjects, inquiry learning is recognized as a viable teaching strategy. In spite of its popularity and prestige, however, there is confusion over exactly what inquiry learning is. When we consider that inquiry is itself a most complicated style of learning, this comes as no surprise. Furthermore, inquiry is closely related to other similar learning approaches that are often confused with inquiry.

Basic to the complexity of inquiry learning is its paradoxical nature. Inquiry learning is concerned with solving problems, but it does not require solutions. It involves a flexible yet systematic approach toward solutions—systematic in that a set of activities is used, yet highly flexible in that the sequence of the activities, and other activities, can be changed or substituted at any time. The success derived from inquiry learning does not necessarily depend on solving the problems at hand. There is a further paradox that adds to the complexity. Even when inquiry is approached by a group, it continues to be a highly personal experience for each individual involved.

Inquiry learning is a dual learning process. While learning about the topic being investigated, the student simultaneously learns about the process of inquiry. Students of inquiry learning must apply themselves totally. They must use their talents, ideas, and judgments to solve a problem. Even the learner's attitude is of utmost importance, because the student must be self-motivated enough to continue searching for numerous solutions without the comfort and assurance that come with "correct" answers found in more traditional learning settings.

Advantages of Inquiry Learning
An obvious advantage of inquiry learning is the high degree of *involvement* of all who participate in the process. This is by no means unique to inquiry learning, because many other teaching-learning styles (such as simulation gaming, individualized instruction, discovery learning, and problem solving) offer participants an equal amount of involvement. But inquiry offers even more involvement that is more meaningful. It is characterized by early and continuous involvement. In true inquiry learning, the student must be involved from the very beginning, even in setting up the problems (Tathart & Bingham, 1973).

Another major advantage of inquiry learning is its *flexibility*. In attempting to understand their environment, people have fallen into a trap of trying to systematize everything within human awareness. For example, for years our schools required students to learn a certain set of behaviors and were led to believe that this is the "method" used by scientists to discover, invent, and find solutions to all problems. Yet studies failed to show that any specific pattern of thought exists to any reliable degree in problem solving. Inquiry is somewhat systematic, without being as rigid as the "scientific method." Instead of just answering questions, students are also involved in asking questions. Instead of just verifying the truth, students are actually seeking the truth.

The absence of a single, predetermined correct answer in inquiry learning is another advantage, because it frees the investigator to explore diverse, multiple possibilities and because it frees the psyche from fear of failing to achieve that which another expects of him or her. On the contrary, the inquiry learner is motivated positively and by the strongest type of motivation—internal motivation. He learns to work for the joy of learning. Involvement in inquiry learning improves students' attitudes toward the subject and, more important, toward school in general (Jaus, 1977). Students in inquiry learning often become so aroused that they return to class on other days eager to continue pursuing the concepts (Bills, 1971).

The nature of inquiry enhances the development of creative potentials. True inquiry learning provides freedom and encouragement in using the imagination, and the learner is responsible for determining what information to gather and then determining how important it is. These are essential conditions for creative thinking to occur.

The teacher-student relationship in inquiry classes must remain positive. While the teacher must give the students freedom to develop their own hypotheses or hunches, the teacher's role is nevertheless important. In fact, no learner is capable of developing critical thoughts by himself (Brown & Brown, 1971), but pupils can be taught in a way that develops critical and inquiry-oriented thinking. An interesting thing happens to the total perspective and behavior pattern of teachers who use the inquiry approach in their classes: They become student-oriented rather than subject-oriented (Lazarowitz & Lee, 1976). Students also become more cooperative, whereas students in textbook-oriented classes tend to be more competitive (Johnson, 1976).

For those who are concerned primarily with cognitive gains, it is important to note that the relative retention rate of inquiry learning (as opposed to lecture, for example) is extremely high. The highly personal experience involved in inquiry adds meaning to the learning. As Abraham Maslow (1973) explains, true learning is very personal; the most valuable learning always involves our emotions.

Disadvantages of Inquiry Learning

Like all other teaching strategies, inquiry learning has its share of disadvantages. First, it is a slow process for exposing students to material. Teachers who feel obligated to cover certain amounts of content (for example, to get through a textbook) may find the process very inefficient for their goal. A more critical disadvantage of inquiry learning is that it requires that its teachers have a unique type of expertise that most do not have without special training. Today's teachers need more training in inquiry activity.

The Teacher's Role in Inquiry Learning

Because inquiry learning is by nature a flexible process, the teacher may want to set the stage in different ways. Taxey (1975) suggests that heterogeneous sub-groups within a classroom be used to capitalize on unique personalities, interests, and skills so that each individual's potential can be used to contribute to the task at hand. In inquiry learning lessons, the major role of the teacher is that of a catalyst. Teachers must give students the freedom to investigate in their own way. Students must be allowed to develop their own ideas and to discover ways to explain what they observe. Even the questions and problems that are formed are the students', not the teacher's. The teacher passively provides direction by selecting objects, activities, events, problems, or questions. The teacher can provide much closer direction by giving cues and supportive feedback (Wendel, 1973). Teachers are often tempted to give information before it is necessary, but they must resist this temptation and avoid making negative nonverbal communications, such as grimacing (Balzer, 1970).

The student of inquiry should not have to worry about pleasing the teacher. In fact, learners must not be dominated by others. The most impressive precondition for inquiry is undoubtedly the autonomy of the learner. It is important that students be encouraged to form hypotheses and test them on their own initiative (Traugh, 1974). The teacher should encourage students to move toward the recognition that a problem can have many aspects and solutions (Tjosvold & Marino, 1977). Students who participate in inquiry must not be afraid to make mistakes. The teacher must encourage each student to make bold conjectures and then to test them. Any hypothesis that seems at all probable to the student should be pursued.

Participants in inquiry learning are self-motivated. They must learn to work for the joy of learning, even in the absence of feedback—which students in traditional classes get from test scores and grades. Inquiry is a cooperative process, not a competitive one. Even the teacher who becomes involved with inquiry soon becomes student-oriented rather than subject-oriented. The independence and separate responsibility of the student, coupled with the opportunity to pursue learning for the joy of it, produces a high level of motivation. For this reason, the retention rate of inquiry learning is superior to most other teaching strategies and offsets the disadvantages of being slow in content coverage.

Effective inquiry learning does, however, require certain special skills that some teachers simply do not have. Teachers need to be able to match personalities, interests, and skills in order to get the most out of each student. Perhaps most of all, teachers need to learn to give students enough freedom to investigate in their own ways. Teachers must learn to act as catalysts and to provide direction in a passive manner. Above all, they must learn to resist the temptation to give information before it is necessary. The student of inquiry must treasure diversity, and the teacher must be able to encourage and reinforce students who take risks and make bold conjectures and then explore a variety of aspects and solutions.

QUESTIONING

Chapter 12 examines in depth the role that questioning plays in motivation. Here we will look at questioning in a much broader context, that is, at the many ways teachers can use questions in various phases of their teaching methods.

When we think of using questions to teach, Socrates usually comes to mind. One of the greatest teachers of all time, Socrates used a variety of instructional techniques. A master of the art of questioning, he used questions to lead his students down a treacherous path of contradictions. Tricky? Of course. But his students respected and admired him. Socrates knew the importance of self-analysis and of discovering one's own errors.

The Socratic method—that is, teaching by asking questions and thus leading the audience into a logical contradiction—is one style of questioning. Many other questioning strategies are in use today. As a teaching style, questioning is second in popularity and in common use only to lecturing, but the technique of questioning is grossly misused. It is helpful to identify several valid uses of questioning and several ways that teachers can improve their questioning skills.

How Teachers Should Use Questions

Although the textbook is the major curriculum determiner in most classes, most textbooks do not stimulate advanced levels of thinking. The Wisconsin School Improvement Program found that 90 percent of all textbooks are written at the knowledge (recall and memory) level. Therefore, if student thinking is to climb to higher cognitive levels, the teacher must find other means of stimulating it. Studies that use interaction analysis show that most teachers never achieve this goal, that most thinking in the classroom remains at the recall level (Chaudhari, 1975). Of course, some knowledge-level questions can be desirable, so long as they are complemented with higher-level questions. Teachers who ask more higher-order questions have students who achieve considerably more (Redfield & Rousseau, 1981). Chaudhari (1975) suggests the following three-step model:

> **Phase 1:** Encourage students to ask questions.
> **Phase 2:** Emphasize questions requiring convergent thinking (application and analysis).
> **Phase 3:** Emphasize questions requiring divergent thinking (synthesis and evaluation).

Miller and Vinocur (1973) provide the following suggestions for moving up to higher levels of thinking. Miller suggests that the teacher should move from such recall level words as *state, name, identify, list, describe, relate, tell, call, give,* and *locate* to include such evaluation-producing words as *judge, compare, ana-*

lyze, contrast, measure, appraise, estimate, and *differentiate,* and then move on to such creative and stimulating words as *make, design, create, construct, speculate, invent, devise, predict,* and *hypothesize.*

Teachers can use student names to increase student response: they should pause after each question to give the students time to think about it. Studies by Sabol (1975), Rothkopf and Billington (1974), Sund (1971), Santieslebau (1976), and Mary Budd Rowe (1974) reinforce the need for these practices. These studies show that there are a number of advantages to waiting at least three seconds after each question is asked. Sund (1971) lists twelve:

1. The length of children's responses increases.
2. The number of unsolicited but appropriate responses increases.
3. Failure to respond decreases.
4. Confidence of children increases.
5. The incidence of speculative creative thinking increases.
6. Teacher-centered teaching decreases.
7. Pupils give more evidence before and after inference statements.
8. The number of questions asked by pupils increases.
9. Number of activities proposed by the children increases.
10. Slow pupils contribute more.
11. The variety of types of responses increases.
12. There is more reacting to each other.

Santieslebau (1976) found that as wait time increased to at least three seconds the confidence of the slow students increased, speculative thinking increased, the number of experiments by the students increased, and observation and classification skills improved. The price for these advantages appears to be cheap. Just by pausing, and doing nothing, the teacher can stimulate these results. However, a study by Rowe (1974) found that the average wait time in the public school classroom is only one second.

Another common mistake of teachers is overuse of questions. Many lessons begin with a series of cognitive questions, but research shows that it is far more effective to wait until a knowledge base has been established before initiating questioning. For example, a short lecture is a far more efficient means for building this necessary framework. Furthermore, when too many questions are asked students' attitudes are damaged as their attention turns from one subject to other areas (Santieslebau, 1976).

Classroom questions that seek cognitive feedback often lack specificity. For example, the question "What was the cause of the Civil War?" is impossible to answer. In posing such a question just to create an entry into the lesson, the teacher rejects some correct responses—and there are many for that question—in hopes that a student will finally guess the particular desired response. The session proceeds as follows:

Q. What was the cause of the Civil War?
A. Slavery.
Q. Okay, but that's not what I'm looking for.

A. Economics? (This time the student is less certain.)
Q. What about economics? (Another broad question.)
A. The North's economics.
Q. What about it?
A. It was different from the South's.
Q. But what about the North's economy? etc., etc.

Besides increasing the efficiency of the lesson and preventing embarrassment, the teacher's specificity will enhance the recall of other material related to the topic (Rothkopf & Billington, 1974). Shiman and Mash (1974) suggest that, instead of limiting the questions to a series of fact-seeking questions, the teacher should move back and forth among the factual, conceptual, and contextual modes. Factual questions elicit only recall level information, conceptual questions probe, analyze, compare, and generalize, and contextual questions promote judgment. To help increase the number and quality of responses to each question in these categories, teachers should tape or write their questions, testing themselves for the answers. This will remove much ambiguity and generate questions that are more specific and precise.

Some experts believe that students are becoming less curious and less inquisitive—less eager to ask questions. Describing this as a decay of students' minds, Sutton (1977) suggests that teachers work together to produce a reversal of this trend. Far too often a student attempts to answer a question only to hear the response "Yes, but" or a murmured "uh-huh" as the teacher looks quickly to another student for the "correct" answer. To improve students' attitudes toward answering questions, the teacher should help the faltering student with an "Oh, that's interesting. I hadn't thought of it that way" or "Oh, yes, I see what you mean" or "Are you saying . . . ?" Further reinforcement can be provided by returning later to quote the student. For example, "John, what you're saying now seems to agree (or disagree) with Debbie's earlier comment that. . . ." This tells John, Debbie, and everyone else in the class that you do listen to other people's comments.

This does not suggest that all teacher questions should seek to provoke student responses. Rhetorical questions increase motivation and enhance the learning and recall of factual material among audiences with low motivation (Fillman & Cantor, 1973). Yet teachers must resist the temptation to answer all their questions and should let students know, by calling on individuals by name, when they expect an answer.

Questions can also be used effectively before and after a lesson. Bull and Dizney (1973) found that asking questions prior to a reading assignment can stimulate students to remember relevant information. In a similar study, Sanders (1973) found that questions posed after reading a paragraph resulted in increased retention of both relevant and irrelevant material, while questions raised before reading increased retention of only the relevant material. Teachers can apply this knowledge about questioning to reading assignments, field trips, laboratory exercises, and such audiovisual materials as the tape recorder, filmstrips, and films.

Students, too, need to learn to ask productive questions. Alfke (1974) explains that such questions develop skills in learning how to learn, to inquire, and to conceptualize. Teachers can achieve this by providing fewer but better questions of their own and by requiring students to pose more productive questions. The research suggests that all teachers should—

1. Avoid using questions to introduce lessons.
2. Delay questions about content until a knowledge base has been established.
3. Use a combination of levels of questions, extending from recall to evaluation.
4. Pause for at least three seconds following each question.
5. Not expect students to be able to guess what the teacher means.
6. Address questions to individual students, using student names.
7. Keep content-oriented questions specific.
8. Help students by modifying their inaccurate answers until they become acceptable.
9. Encourage students to ask questions.
10. Help students develop skills in asking questions.
11. Listen carefully to student questions and respond, using their content.
12. Prior to making a reading assignment, showing a film, or taking a field trip, pose questions relative to the major concepts or objectives of that experience.

DISCOVERY LEARNING

What is discovery learning? Chances are you have some understanding of, and faith in, the discovery process. Most contemporary students have experienced this approach. The following paragraphs define discovery learning, list its advantages and disadvantages, and provide suggestions for teachers who want to try discovery learning for the first time or improve their skills with planning and implementing discovery learning.

Definition
Most of the literature on discovery learning does not define it at all; this leaves the reader feeling embarrassed about not knowing exactly what it is, and probably ashamed to ask. But discovery learning is not easy to define. There is no single clear-cut definition, just as there is no single process of discovery learning; in fact, there are many. Each experience is unique, ranging from guided discovery to open discovery. Furthermore, each type of discovery has its own advantages, and the management of each is unique. Weimer (1975) lists six types of discovery learning: (1) discovery, (2) discovery teaching, (3) inductive discovery, (4) semi-inductive discovery, (5) unguided or pure discovery, and (6) guided discovery. Notice that these six types are actually degrees in which discovery is controlled.

The term *discovery learning* is frequently but erroneously used interchangeably with two other terms: inquiry and problem-solving. Actually, each of these other terms is or can refer to a specific type of discovery learning. The educational process called inquiry is more accurately defined as guided discovery—that is, during an inquiry lesson the teacher is carefully guiding the student(s) toward a specific discovery or generalization. Discovery learning and problem solving are synonymous when a solution to the problem is discovered. In other words, by definition, problem solving must involve the solving of problems. A good working definition of discovery learning is intentional learning through problem solving and under teacher supervision. In other words, individuals can sometimes solve problems without any leadership, guidance, or supervision; they can also make discoveries quite accidentally. Neither of these activities is discovery learning, for it must be intentional and supervised. At one extreme, it may be carefully guided (inquiry learning); at the other extreme, it is very casually supervised (free discovery). In fact, as Jones (1970) explains, the teacher's main function may be to supply a stimulus, or it may be to organize or arrange tasks (or problems) to make the result obvious (Sickling, 1975). In inquiry learning, the students themselves are involved in setting up the problem as well as in seeking its solution (Baikov et al., 1976).

Advantages of Discovery Learning

Many of the advantages of discovery learning are not unique to discovery learning but are shared by other instructional approaches. For example, the high degree of student involvement is a strong motivator for most students, especially students who find it difficult to remain quiet and passive. There is little evidence to refute the assumption that discovery learning is appropriate for almost all students. Only about one-third of today's college students are able to reason in an abstract, logical way (Mitzman, 1978). An even smaller percentage of secondary and middle school students are able to profit from abstracting. Do most students, then, have the ability needed to benefit from discovery learning? Yes. The Contemporary Cambridge Conference states that anyone can take part in and create experiences in generalizing, testing conjectures, discarding or modifying false hypotheses, and forming rules or theorems (Jones, 1970). A study involving junior high math students (Vance, 1974) found the discovery approach to be a superior motivator in traditional math classes, and inferior only to an experimental laboratory setting.

With an increase in motivation, it is assumed that students' learning and retention will also increase, but the greatest advantage of discovery learning surpasses learning and remembering. Actually, the correlation between a student's knowledge and later success in life is constantly diminishing. Far more important are one's understanding of broad concepts and principles and one's ability to get along with other people. In fact, the Manpower Development Act of 1960 found that as early as 1960 less than 15 percent of all jobs lost in the United States were lost from inability to perform adequately, and that more than 85 percent were lost from inability to get along with superordinates and co-workers (Henson, 1974). When discovery learning involves group work, the socialization is itself clearly a worthy goal.

The discovery process is superior to lecture-type lessons because it offers students an opportunity to focus on major concepts and principles and to develop positive social skills. Discovery learning is a cooperative process. Vance (1974) found no significant difference in the ability of junior high math students in discovery, laboratory, and traditional lessons to score on an exam administered just after the learning. However, the students in the discovery classes scored highest on a special exam designed to measure high-level thinking and problem solving. Another test designed to measure divergent thinking showed that the students in the discovery classes were superior in their ability to relate the new set of materials to the study of mathematics. Students also preferred a learning style that permitted them to work at their own rates and without a teacher always telling them what to do.

Disadvantages of Discovery Learning

It may be difficult to believe that a learning system with so many advantages also has inherent disadvantages, but it does. First, unlike the lecture (which requires little more of students than their attention and an ability to take notes), the discovery method makes more demands of students and teachers. Probably its greatest demand is that both teacher and students understand and adjust to the nature of discovery. At the beginning, teachers and students are uncomfortable because the discovery approach has no constant feedback to show them how well they are progressing. The lack of competition in discovery learning also upsets students. Discovery learning is ideally a cooperative process, not a competitive one. The competition is between the student and the task.

At its best, discovery learning is an inefficient system because it is not a good way to cover large amounts of material (Moulton, 1973). Students and teachers are usually highly concerned about completing the amount of material they are expected to cover in a particular course. College preparatory classes are especially concerned with this limitation of the discovery learning approach.

Methodology

As with any instructional approach, the degree to which discovery learning is successful is determined by the ability of the teacher to plan and execute effectively, that is, manage and supervise the lesson. Sickling (1975) has already suggested that the teacher's task is to organize or arrange tasks (or problems). Rebrova and Svetlova (1976) explain the problem situation as a dilemma, deliberately created by the teacher, which forces students to think, analyze, draw conclusions, and make generalizations. In other words, the teacher's role is to provide a situation that allows students to see a contradiction between what they already know and newly discovered knowledge. Sobel (1975) suggests the following guidelines:

1. Make use of contemporary materials (daily newspaper, comic strips, and the like).
2. Use topics from the history (of the subject).
3. Introduce applications (of the subject).
4. Provide opportunity for guessing.

5. Provide for laboratory experiences.
6. Introduce new topics with innovative teaching strategy.
7. Make frequent use of visual aids.
8. Set the stage for student discovery.
9. Use motivation.
10. Teach with enthusiasm.

Bittinger (1968) makes two suggestions for the teacher in discovery learning. First, the teacher and the textbooks must use unambiguous terms. Second, the student must be allowed to discover generalizations. This suggests that teachers should learn to put more trust in their students and to refrain from interfering with students' work. The many interdisciplinary programs of the 1960s and 1970s stimulated by the Woods Hole Conference were based on generalizations, and the more recent study reported by Goodlad (1984) in *A Place Called School* reiterated the important role that principles and generalizations play in learning.

An Overview of Discovery Learning
Like all teaching-learning approaches, the discovery method has advantages and disadvantages. While discovery learning seems equal to traditional lessons for attaining knowledge, it is superior in motivating students toward learning broad concepts and principles and in developing social skills. Its main disadvantages are that it is not a good way to cover large amounts of material and that it fails to provide constant feedback. Discovery learning is most effective when students are involved in planning the lesson and coming up with their own discoveries, conclusions, and generalizations, and when teachers combine it with the use of visual aids and contemporary, easy-to-read materials.

SIMULATION GAMES

Games have always played a significant role in children's learning; children are quick to mimic adults and to invent games that allow them to assume adult-like roles. As recorded in *The Saber-Tooth Curriculum* (Benjamin, 1939), the first serious use of games for learning occurred during the Great Ice Age, but for those who prefer fact to fiction, the records credit a nineteenth-century schoolteacher, Maria Montessori, with being the first person to realize the potential of games for purposeful use in the school curriculum. By watching children play, Montessori learned to devise games based on the natural behavior of children. Such natural curricula reflected the philosophy of John Locke, Jean Jacques Rousseau, and John Dewey, who believed that children should be actively involved in the curriculum.

Today games are used extensively in industry and in schools to train and educate. The use of games in schools is actually worldwide. For example, more than one-third of all schools in England and Wales now include games in their syllabi (Walford, 1973). The most popular type of game used in educational settings is the simulation game, which offers players the opportunity to experience a variety of roles that are common in life. By definition, a simulation game must imitate some reality and give players the opportunity to compete in a real-life role, yet it is important that the emphasis on competition be kept in perspective. Winning is not the major object of a simulation game. According to Rogers and Goodloe (1973), games offer great socializing potential and should be used to help students learn to empathize with other individuals. Nesvold and his colleagues (1973) agree with this goal and say it is important that every player has a chance to win. Above all, the game should be fun. Hostrop (1972) warns teachers that games using machines tend to become dehumanizing and require special effort by the teacher to counterbalance this with a high level of personal contact with students.

But this does not imply that games are effective only for developing social skills. On the contrary, a good simulation-type game can provide a sound and interesting learning experience (Gillespie, 1973). Maxson (1974) offers the following list of their advantages. Simulation games—

1. Involve the student actively.
2. Create a high degree of interest and enthusiasm.
3. Make abstract concepts meaningful for students.
4. Provide immediate feedback to students.
5. Allow students to experiment with concepts and new skills without feeling the need to be correct at all times.
6. Give students the opportunity to evaluate their mistakes.
7. Allow students to practice communication skills.

Basic to the learning potential for any strategy is motivation. When using a simulation game based on the stock market, Watman (1973) found that by having students work together in small groups and allowing them to discover strategies for playing the game, motivation was increased for low achievers and for students with discipline problems. Shy students became involved, and all students felt the activity was relevant. As for academic achievement, the students quickly mastered the new math concepts, and their work improved in accuracy and neatness.

Simulation games offer special opportunities to learners. Hostrop (1972) found that American history students who used a simulation on the impeachment proceedings of Andrew Johnson learned far more effectively than had they listened to a lecture. Simulation games enable students to interact at their own levels (Lewis, 1972) and to learn how to compete and cooperate with others (Sisk, 1975). But exactly how effective are games compared with more traditional modes of instruction? Wylie (1974) reports on a study in which a simulation game is compared with a programmed text in social studies. After the material was introduced by these two methods, a test showed no significant difference between the learning of the two groups. Two weeks later, however, a retake of the test by the same two groups showed that the students who played the game outscored the control group. It seems, then, that simulation gaming is equal to traditional methods in its ability to produce learning, and is superior in its ability to produce retention. Lucas and colleagues (1975) found that, compared with the lecture, simulation games used to teach mathematics had similar learning and retention results for up to 5 weeks, but after 10 weeks students using the simulation had a significantly higher retention rate. Other studies show that games are especially effective for use with slow learners (Maxson, 1974; Kelly, 1970). Learning itself can be increased during simulations when students work in small groups (Kelly, 1970), when they are permitted to evaluate their own mistakes, and when the vocabulary level is kept simple (Maxson, 1974).

But the question "Is simulation gaming more effective than a textbook?" may not be an appropriate question, because simulation games can be used to supplement the text. Maxson (1974) found that simulations can make the abstract material in a textbook more real and vivid. Taylor (1976) lists the advantages of developing your own simulation:

1. You're able to pick the precise subject matter.
2. You know best the ability level of your students.
3. Time constraints are not a problem.
4. You are there to change or alter it if necessary as the game proceeds.

Of course, the success of any simulation depends upon its design and implementation. To help teachers design their own simulation games, Taylor (1976) gives the following suggestions:

1. Identify your objectives.
2. Decide on a problem or simulation.
3. Define the scope of the simulation.
4. Construct the rules.
5. Identify the participants' goals.
6. Write rules and teacher instructions.
7. Design any additional parts.
8. Develop a debriefing.

The designer of simulation games should consider the management requirements of the teaching situation and the ability of the students. Simulation games are valid only if they teach the desired ideas, values, and facts. Shelly (1973) and Kerr (1974) report that the best game development involves students. When students help develop the game, their level of involvement in playing the game and their attitude toward the game are improved.

Success with the simulation also depends upon how the game is used. In fact, many teachers shun simulations because they are afraid they might not work (Horn & Zuckerman, 1972). Heyman (1976) gives four rules for directing a simulation game:

1. Say no more than the few words necessary.
2. Run the simulation, not the students.
3. Run the game, don't teach.
4. Do not tell the students how to behave.

Suhor (1977) adds one final suggestion to the list: Remember that good classroom management and rapport with students are necessary for good gaming. Finally, Nesvold and colleagues (1973) suggest that anyone who is adapting a game for classroom use should keep the rules simple, keep the game shorter than one class period, and attain a balance between risk, chance, skill, and knowledge in determining victory.

When correctly designed and implemented, simulation games are an effective mode of instruction. Besides being a sound method for learning, simulation gaming is a good motivator and therefore can increase retention. Games also have the ability to promote the development of social skills. Some of the best simulation games were designed by teachers who themselves can select, relate, and adjust the game to their own students. When using a simulation game, the teacher should be sure that it is enjoyable for all class members and should resist the temptation to interfere with the students.

RECAP OF MAJOR IDEAS

1. The lecture should be used with highly motivated students who can take good notes. Most students do not have this ability.
2. The lecture is an effective means of introducing a unit, building a frame of reference, clarifying confusing issues, and summarizing major concepts in a lesson. It is not usually a good motivator, and it does not stimulate imagination and creativity.
3. Most lectures should begin with a clear statement of objectives, be kept short and simple, and proceed at a brisk pace. A lecture should contain only a few major concepts and should provide activities that require students to apply the concepts.
4. Lectures should be supplemented with audiovisual aids, gesturing, joking, and modeling.
5. Tutoring usually helps both the tutor and the tutee. It is more effective when used with other approaches, such as mastery learning.
6. Inquiry lessons offer students opportunities to cultivate their creative talents when they have freedom and flexibility. The absence of continuous feedback and frequent grades in inquiry learning makes it necessary to have students who are self-motivated.
7. The effectiveness of questioning is enhanced when teachers give students more time to respond, help students come up with acceptable answers, and encourage students to ask questions.
8. Simulation games are good motivators and lead to increased retention. Used appropriately, they emphasize cooperation, not competition.

POSTTEST

Now that you have read the chapter, take a moment to respond to the following statements again.

	Agree	Disagree	Uncertain
1. Teaching methods are of little importance because good students learn in any setting and poor students do poorly regardless of the teaching method.	_____	_____	_____
2. Some methods are best for some students; others are best for other students.	_____	_____	_____
3. The way a teacher implements a teaching method is more important than which method is selected.	_____	_____	_____
4. The lecture has no place in secondary schools because other methods are superior in every way.	_____	_____	_____
5. Rhetorical questions should be used only when informing students that they are not expected to answer.	_____	_____	_____
6. Games developed by the teacher and students are usually superior to commercial learning games.	_____	_____	_____
7. Inquiry learning is the same as discovery learning.	_____	_____	_____
8. Questioning effectiveness is enhanced when teachers give students more time to respond, help students reach acceptable answers, and encourage students to ask questions.	_____	_____	_____
9. Simulation-type games are good motivators and lead to increased retention.	_____	_____	_____

CASES

You may have already begun to make some decisions about what your own teaching strategies will be. The following cases will give you some opportunities to refine your ideas.

Case 1: A Methods Course Emphasizes Strategies

Carole Harman had enjoyed her introductory course in education. She had also taken an exploratory course in education that provided interesting field experiences. These courses made her feel more certain than ever that she wanted to be a teacher.

The next year Carole took two courses in her major (chemistry), two in math, and a general secondary methods course. But after only two weeks she was feeling lost in the education course. Her professor had begun talking about educational research and teaching strategies and the relationships between the two. Carole was uncomfortable because she had never taken a course in research methodology and did not have any background in teaching strategies.

Almost from the start the professor began making such comments as "When selecting your strategies . . ." or "You can apply your favorite strategy." Carole had never before thought about teaching strategies, which sounded like unnecessary educational jargon. She wondered whether other class members felt the same way, until one of them nearby mumbled, "How can you have a favorite strategy if you don't know what one is?"

Discussion

1. Why might an education professor assume that students in a general methods course have knowledge of teaching strategies?
Teachers often get so close to their subjects that they expect their students to have more knowledge of and enthusiasm about the subject than they actually do. College professors are just as likely to make this mistake. After all, educational strategies are this teacher's major subject.
2. Why is it important that teachers be familiar with many teaching strategies?
Many teachers believe that a good repertoire of methods is essential for their own survival in the classroom. What works with one group of students may fail to stimulate another group. Familiarity with a variety of methods enables the teacher to shift quickly from one to another when the level of interest drops. (This is only one advantage of having a repertoire of methods. Perhaps you can think of others.)
3. What should the teacher know about each teaching strategy?
To get the most benefit from each strategy, teachers must know the purposes that each method serves best, and the age levels for which it is most appropriate. Besides knowing how to use a strategy, teachers should recognize its strengths and limitations. What else will you want to know about methods that you might use? (You could consider their practicality, cost, and effects on fellow teachers.)

Case 2: Should Teaching in Secondary and Middle Schools Be Fun?

Louis Martinez was the most interesting math teacher ever to come to Jackson High. Before he arrived, three years ago, there weren't enough students interested in math to offer more than the very basic general mathematics, geometry, and first-year algebra. But when school opened this fall, Mr. Martinez had so many students requesting Algebra II that two sections were necessary. In addition, 27 students had signed up for trigonometry, and 15 others wanted a class in first-year calculus. For a school as small as Jackson High, this degree of interest in any single subject was incredible. Happy to see that so many of his students were sharing his enjoyment of mathematics, Mr. Martinez became even more enthusiastic, and his lessons became even more exciting.

The students enjoyed his classes for many different reasons. For one, they never knew what to expect from one day to the next, they just knew it would be different. Most of the lessons involved every student, and usually in a number of ways. Moreover, Mr. Martinez had a great collection of props, audiovisual materials, and games.

Then some of the other teachers began complaining about him. His classes were noisier than most, and though he had more equipment than most of his colleagues, his students were running all over the school borrowing other paraphernalia to use in math class. Basically, though, the other teachers' complaints stemmed from jealousy. Although they would never admit it, they would have tolerated the noise and other minor irritants if they could have their students become that enthusiastic about their classes.

Unfortunately, the complaints reached Mr. Martinez only after they had been spread all over the school and the community. The principal called him in to discuss the complaints and remind him how important it was not to alienate his fellow teachers. Mr. Martinez was perplexed to learn that his successful teaching strategies had begun to cause trouble for him.

Discussion

1. Is having a repertoire of teaching methods likely to get a teacher into trouble?
Although this is possible, most teachers would probably prefer having jealous colleagues to having unmanageable students and unsuccessful lessons.
2. How might Mr. Martinez react to such an accusation?
He would probably profit from admitting that his classes are noisy, but he should then ask the principal whether the complaints are worth sacrificing the success that his students are experiencing. Can you think of an amicable way of convincing the principal?
3. How should Mr. Martinez deal with complaints from fellow teachers?
Regardless of how much the students are achieving in his room, he must realize that the class should not disturb neighboring classes. He should explain this to the students and let them know that they have a responsibility to hold down the level of noise.

ACTIVITIES

In your academic career you have probably experienced both many excellent teachers and others who fall short. Because our viewpoints on any issue represent a combination of our experiences, the following activities will help you classify your own perceptions about good and bad teachers.

1. Think of the best teachers you have ever had—that is, those from whom you think you learned the most. Select one of these favorites and describe his or her (a) methods of establishing cognitive set, (b) methods of involving students, and (c) methods of relating the material to your own experiences.

2. Choosing a concept from your subject area, explain how you can combine some of the methods discussed in this chapter to teach this concept. Consider using one method for the introduction, one or more for involving students, and yet another for summarizing the lesson.

3. Develop a game to use in class to teach the above concept.

SUGGESTED READINGS

Expository Teaching

Birkel, L. F. (1973). The lecture method: Villain or victim? *Peabody Journal of Education, 50,* 298–301.

Bloom, B. S. (1984). The search for methods of group instruction as effective as one-to-one tutoring. *Educational Leadership, 41,* 4–17.

Commonwealth, V., & Gootnick, D. M. (1974). Electrifying the classroom with the overhead projector. *Business Education Forum, 28,* 3–4.

Couch, R. (1973, October). Is lecturing really necessary? *American Biology Teacher,* pp. 391–395.

Ellis, H. P., & Jones, A. D. (1974, Spring). Anxiety about lecturing. *Universities Quarterly,* pp. 91–95.

Frazier, D. T., & Holcomb, J. D. (1972, Autumn). Improving lectures by videotape self-confrontation. *Improving College and University Teaching, 20,* 340–341.

Grobe, R. P., et al. (1973, October). Effects of lecture pace on noise level in a university classroom. *Journal of Educational Research,* pp. 73–75.

Haley, J. H., Lalonde, E., & Rovin, S. (1972). An assessment of the lecture. *Improving College and University Teaching, 22,* 326–327.

Kaplan, R. M., & Pascoe, G. C. (1977). Humorous lectures and humorous examples: Some effects on comprehension and retention. *Journal of Educational Psychology, 69,* 61–65.

Klausmeier, H. J. (1980). Tutoring to increase achievement and motivation. *Theory into Practice, 19*(1), 51–57.

Kyle, B. (1972). In defense of the lecture. *Improving College and University Teaching, 20,* 325.

Lazarowitz, R., and Lee, A. E. (1976, September). Measuring inquiry attitudes of secondary science teachers. *Journal of Research in Science Teaching, 13,* 445–460.

Lucas, L. A., Postma, C. H., & Thompson, S. C. (1975, July). Comparative study of retention used in simulation gaming as opposed to lecture: Discussion techniques. *Peabody Journal of Education,* p. 261.

Maddox, H., & Hoole, E. (1975). Performance decrement in the lecture. *Educational Review, 28,* 17–30.

Ott, M. D., & Macklin, D. B. (1975). A trait treatment interaction in a college physics course. *Journal of Research in Science Teaching, 12,* 111–119.

Rippey, R. F. (1975). Speech compressors for lecture review. *Educational Technology, 15,* 58–59.

Rowsey, R., & Mason, W. H. (1975). Immediate achievement and retention in audio tutorial vs. conventional lecture-laboratory instruction. *Journal of Research in Science Teaching, 12,* 393–397.

Starr, R. J., & Schuerman, C. D. (1974). An experiment in small group learning. *American Biology Teacher, 36,* 173–175.

Thompson, R. (1974). Legitimate lecturing. *Improving College and University Teaching, 22,* 163–164.

Titus, C. (1974, February). The uses of the lecture. *Clearing House,* pp. 383–384.

Tjosvold, D., & Marino, P. M. (1977). The effects of student competition and cooperation on student reactions to inquiry and didactic science teaching. *Journal of Research in Science Teaching, 14,* 281–288.

Traugh, C. E. (1974). Evaluating inquiry procedures, *65,* 201–220.

Voth, R. (1975). On lecturing. *Social Studies, 66,* 247–248.

Weinberg, M. (1975). Humor works in funny ways. *Nation's Schools and Colleges, 2,* 21.

Whooley, J. (1974, Summer). Improving the lecture. *Improving College and University Teaching, 22,* 183.

Wyckoff, W. L. (1973). The effects of stimulus variation on learning from lecture. *Journal of Experimental Education, 41,* 85–90.

Inquiry Learning

Balzer, L. (1970). Teachers' behaviors and student inquiry in biology. *American Biology Teacher, 32,* 26–28.

Bibens, R. F. (1980, Spring). Using inquiry effectively. *Theory into Practice, 19,* 87–92.

Bills, F. L. (1971). Developing creativity through inquiry. *Science Education, 55,* 417–421.

Brown, S. B., & Brown, L. B. (1971). Suggested critical thinking and inquiry techniques in science for middle school teachers. *School Science and Mathematics, 71,* 731–736.

Jaus, H. H. (1977). Activity-oriented science: Is it really that good? *Science and Children, 14,* 26–27.

Johnson, R. T. (1976). The relationship between cooperation and inquiry in science classrooms. *Journal of Research in Science Teaching, 13,* 55–63.

Lazarowitz, R. (1971). Does use of curriculum change teachers' attitudes toward inquiry? *Journal of Research in Science Teaching, 13,* 547–552.

Maslow, A. (1973). What is a taoistic teacher? In L. Rubin (Ed.), *Facts and feelings in the classroom.* New York: Viking.

Tathart, J. R., & Bingham, R. M. (1973). LEIB-IRA: Preliminary report. *American Biology Teacher, 35,* 346.

Taxey, P. J. (1975). Heterogeneous subgroups within a classroom. *American Biology Teacher, 37,* 165–167.

Tjosvold, D., & Marino, P. M. (1977). The effects of cooperation and competition on student reactions to inquiry and didactic science teaching. *Journal of Research in Science Teaching, 14,* 281–288.

Traugh, C. E. (1974). Evaluating inquiry procedures. *Social Studies, 65,* 201–220.

Webb, P. K. (1980, Spring). Piaget: Implications for teaching. *Theory into Practice, 19,* 93–97.

Wendel, R. (1973). Inquiry teaching: Dispelling the myths. *Clearing House, 48,* 24–28.

Questioning

Alfke, D. (1974). Asking operational questions. *Science and Children, 11*, 18–19.

Bull, S. G., & Dizney, H. F. (1973). Epistemic—curiosity—arousing pre-question: Their effect on long-term retention. *Journal of Educational Psychology, 65*, 45–49.

Carmichael, D. (1975). I'm sick of Socrates. *Improving College and University Teaching, 23*, 252.

Chaudhari, U. S. (1975, January). Questioning and creative thinking: A research perspective. *Journal of Creative Behavior*, pp. 30–34.

Henson, K. T. (1974). *Secondary teaching: A personal approach*. Itasca, Ill.: Peacock.

Miller, H. G., & Vinocur, S. M. (1973). How to ask classroom questions. *School and Community, 59*, 10.

Redfield, D. L., & Rousseau, E. W. (1981). A meta-analysis of experimental research on teacher questioning behavior. *Review of Educational Research, 51*, 237–245.

Rothkopf, E. F., & Billington, M. J. (1974). Indirect review and previewing through questions. *Journal of Educational Psychology, 66*, 669–679.

Rowe, M. B. (1974). Wait-time and rewards as instructional variable: Their influence on language, logic, and fate control, part one. *Journal of Research in Science Teaching, 11*, 81–94.

Sabol, J. E. (1975). Do pupils answer, I dunno. *Agricultural Education Magazine, 48*, 114.

Sanders, J. R. (1973). Retention effects of adjunct questions in written and oral discourse. *Journal of Educational Psychology, 65*, 181–186.

Santieslebau, A. J. (1976). Teacher questioning performance and student affective outcomes. *Journal of Research and Science Teaching, 13*, 553–557.

Shiman, D. A., & Mash, R. J. (1974). Questioning: Another view. *Peabody Journal of Education, 51*, 246–253.

Sund, R. B. (1971). Growing through sensitive listening and questioning. *Childhood Education, 51*, 68–71.

Sutton, R. M. (1977). On asking and answering questions. *Physics Teacher, 15*, 94–95.

Zillmann, D., & Cantor, J. R. (1973). Induction of curiosity via rhetorical questions and its effects on the learning of factual materials. *British Journal of Educational Psychology, 43*, 172–180.

Discovery Learning

Baikov, F. I., Kortisky, V. T., & Valsov, M. M. (1976). Correlating the problem-solving approach and other approaches to the teaching of biology. *Soviet Education, 18*, 18–26.

Bittinger, M. L. (1968). A review of discovery. *Mathematics Teacher, 61*, 140–145.

Boyd, H. (1971). Developing an algebra by discovery. *Mathematics Teacher, 64*, 225–228.

Goodlad, J. I. (1984). *A place called school*. New York: McGraw-Hill.

Jones, P. (1970). Discovery teaching from Socrates to modernity. *Mathematics Teacher, 63*, 501–510.

Mitzman, B. (1978, January). Toward a more reasonable physics: The inquiry approach. *Change*, pp. 52–55.

Moulton, P. (1973). The mathematics teacher as a source of experience. *Mathematics Teacher, 73*, 238–243.

Rebrova, L. V., & Svetlova, P. R. (1976). The problem-solving approach: A way to insure solid and thorough learning. *Soviet Education, 18*, 75–84.

Sickling, F. P. (1975). Patterns in integers. *Mathematics Teacher, 68,* 290–292.

Sobel, M. A. (1975, October). Junior high school mathematics: Motivation vs. monotony. *Mathematics Teacher, 68,* 479–485.

Vance, J. H. (1974, February). Mathematics laboratories—More than fun? *School Science and Mathematics, 72,* 617–623.

Weimer, R. C. (1975). An analysis of discovery. *Educational Technology, 15,* 45–48.

Simulation and Other Games

Benjamin, H. (1939). *The saber-tooth curriculum.* New York: McGraw-Hill.

Brown, J. (1974). Recreation: Tic-tac-toe in polar coordinates. *Mathematics Teacher, 67,* 128–129.

Gillespie, J. A. (1973, January). Analyzing and evaluating classroom games. *Social Education,* p. 33.

Hampton, H. F. (1974, March). The concentration game. *Arithmetic Teacher, 19,* 56–67.

Heller, M. M. (1974, March). What are simulation games? *The Instructor,* pp. 9–11.

Heyman, M. (1976). How to direct a simulation. *Phi Delta Kappan, 16,* 17–19.

Holtkamp, L. (1972). The match game. *Arithmetic Teacher, 19,* 221–222.

Homan, D. (1973). Television games adapted to use in junior high mathematics classes. *Arithmetic Teacher, 20,* 219–222.

Horn, R. E., & Zucherman, D. W. (1972, November). Getting into simulation games. *Media and Methods,* p. 65.

Hostrop, R. W. (1972, Autumn). Simulation as stimulus to learning and retention. *Improving College and University Teaching, 20,* 283.

Johnson, L. (1975). Simulations and curriculum. *High School Journal, 37,* 107–111.

Kelly, W. H. (1970, November). Are educational games effective in teaching? *Agricultural Education Magazine, 43,* 117.

Kentucky Group (1973, February). Gaining a perspective on simulation. *National Association of Secondary School Principals Bulletin,* p. 43.

Kerr, D. R., Jr. (1974, March). Mathematics games in the classroom. *Arithmetic Teacher, 21,* 172–175.

Lewis, P. (1972). Games, simulations allow pupils "slice of life." *Nation's Schools, 89,* 80.

Livingston, S. A. (1971, December). Will a simulation game improve student learning of related factual material? *Educational Technology,* pp. 19–20.

Lucas, L. A., Postma, C. H., & Thompson, J. C. (1975, July). Comparative study of cognitive retention used in simulation gaming as opposed to lecture: Discussion techniques. *Peabody Journal of Education, 52,* 261.

Mannix, W. E. (1975). Let's play football. *School Science and Mathematics, 75,* 532–534.

Martin, B., & Reazin, R. (1975). Hinky, pinky, parlez-vous? *School Science and Mathematics, 75,* 637–638.

Maxson, R. C. (1974). Simulation: A method that can make a difference. *High School Journal, 52,* 107–111.

Nesvold, G. T., Gibbons, J., & Campbell, J. R. (1973, May). The teacher made game. *Science Teacher, 40,* 65.

Rogers, V. M., & Goodloe, A. H. (1973, May). Simulation games as method. *Educational Leadership, 30,* 729.

Shelly, A. C. (1973, November). Total class development of simulation games. *Social Education, 37,* 687–689.

Shirts, G. R. (1976, September–October). Ten mistakes commonly made by persons designing educational simulations and games. *Simulation/Gaming,* p. 19.

Sisk, D. (1975, Summer). Simulation: Learning by doing revisited. *Gifted Child Quarterly, 19,* 175–180.

Sommer, J. W. (1973, January). Munificent hexagon: A gaming examination. *Journal of Geography, 72,* 40–48.

Suhor, C. (1977). Hypothesis games can be fun. *English Journal, 18,* 381–382.

Taylor, A. J. R. (1976). Developing your own simulation for teaching. *Clearing House, 50,* 104–107.

Taylor, G. R., & Watkins, S. T. (1974, December). Active games: An approach to teaching mathematical skills to the educable mentally retarded. *Arithmetic Teacher, 21,* 674–678.

Thiagarjan, S. (1974, March). Gamegame II. *Phi Delta Kappan, 55,* 474–477.

Tucker, B. F. (1971, November). Parallelograms: A simple answer to drill motivation and individualized instruction. *Arithmetic Teacher, 18,* 489–493.

Walford, R. (1973, May). Games and simulations. *Times Educational Supplement, 30,* 38.

Watman, M. X. (1973). A simulation game for general mathematics. *Mathematics Teacher, 66,* 23–25.

Wylie, R. E. (1974). Simulation games for general mathematics. *Childhood Education, 54,* 307.

General

Berliner, D. C., & Gage, N. L. (1975). The psychology of teaching methods. In N. L. Gage (Ed.), *The psychology of teaching methods.* Chicago: National Society for the Study of Education.

Caldwell, R. M. (1980, Spring). Improving learning strategies with computer-based education. *Theory into Practice, 19,* 141–143.

Carin, A., & Sund, R. B. (1971). *Developing questioning techniques.* Columbus, Ohio: Merrill.

Dillon, J. T. (1984). Research on questioning and discussion. *Educational Leadership, 42,* 50–56.

Edwards, J., & Marland, P. (1984). What are students really thinking? *Educational Leadership, 42,* 63–67.

Fulkof, L., & Moss, J. (1984). When teachers tackle thinking skills. *Educational Leadership, 42,* 4–10.

Gagne, R. M. (1980, Winter). Preparing the learner for new learning. *Theory into Practice, 19,* 5–9.

Gall, M. (1984). Synthesis of research on teaching questioning. *Educational Leadership, 42,* 40–49.

Gilstrap, R. L., & Martin, W. R. (1975). *Current strategies for teachers.* Santa Monica, Calif.: Goodyear.

Goodlad, J. I. (1984). *A place called school.* New York: McGraw-Hill.

Graham, P. T., & Cline, P. C. (1980, Spring). The case method: A basic approach to teaching. *Theory into Practice, 19,* 112–121.

Grennan, J. (1984). Making sense of student thinking. *Educational Leadership, 42,* 11–17.

Henson, K. T. (1980, Winter). Teaching methods: History and status. *Theory into Practice, 19,* 2–5.

Heyman, M. (1976, November). How to direct a simulation. *Phi Delta Kappan, 58,* 17–19.

Hyman, R. T. (1970). *Ways of teaching* (rev. ed.). Philadelphia: Lippincott.

Joyce, B. R. (1980, Winter). Learning how to learn. *Theory into Practice, 19,* 15–27.

Little, D. (1985). *An investigation of cooperative small-group instruction and the use of advance organizers on the self-concept and social studies achievement of third-grade students.* Doctoral dissertation, University of Alabama.

Livingston, S. A., & Stoll, C. S. (1973). *Simulation games: An introduction for the social studies teacher.* New York: Free Press.

Martin, D. S. (1984). Infusing cognitive strategies into teacher preparation programs. *Educational Leadership, 42,* 68–72.

Rowe, M. B. (1974). Wait-time and rewards as instructional variables: Their influence on language, logic, and fate control, part one. *Journal of Research in Science Teaching, 11,* 81–94.

Shirts, G. R. (1976, September–October). Ten mistakes commonly made by persons designing educational simulations and games. *Simulation Gaming,* 19.

Taylor, J. L., & Walford, R. (1972). *Simulation in the classroom.* Baltimore: Penguin.

Titus, C. (1974, February). The uses of the lecture. *Clearing House, 48,* 383–384.

Torrence, E. P. (1970). *Encouraging creativity in the classroom.* Dubuque, Iowa: Brown.

Wang, M. C. (1980, Spring). Adaptive instruction: Building on diversity. *Theory into Practice, 19,* 122–133.

Weimer, R. C. (1975, September). An analogy of discovery. *Educational Technology, 15,* 45–48.

Weinberger, R. A. (1971). *Perspectives in individualized learning.* Itasca, Ill.: Peacock.

Whimbey, A. (1984). The key to higher-order thinking is precise processing. *Educational Leadership, 42,* 66–70.

Williams, R. O. (1980, Spring). What teaching methods when? *Theory into Practice, 19,* 82–86.

Communications

Objectives

- List three voice qualities that are important to teaching, and explain how each can be improved.
- Give one suggestion for helping a teacher improve the quality of classroom questions.
- Define *set induction* and describe two techniques for establishing it in the classroom.
- Explain how teacher efficacy affects student achievement.
- Describe the difference in communication behavior of effective teachers and less-effective teachers.
- Respond appropriately to an incorrect student response, to a correct confident response, and to a correct doubtful response.
- Describe how review should be used at the beginning of a lesson and at the end.
- Give an example of how the hidden curriculum can communicate positively (usefully) and an example of how it can communicate negatively.

PRETEST

	Agree	Disagree	Uncertain
1. Most beginning teachers talk too quickly.			
2. Teachers should avoid using personal examples in their lessons.	——	——	——
3. Students tend to emulate the behavior of their teachers.	——	——	——
4. Teachers tend to pause too long after asking a question, which bores many students.	——	——	——
5. A teacher's nonverbal communications are more important than what that teacher says.	——	——	——
6. The meaning that results from communication is context-specific (depends on the context in which it is used).	——	——	——
7. Teachers seldom explain what a lesson expects from the students.	——	——	——
8. Effective teachers (those whose students exceed in achievement) spend less time introducing new topics, giving examples, and giving students opportunities for guided practice than do less-effective teachers.	——	——	——
9. When students respond correctly but doubtfully to teacher questions, the teacher should explain the process used to derive the answer.	——	——	——
10. More than 95 percent of the questions in textbooks and similar materials are lower order.	——	——	——
11. Most student responses to higher-order questions are higher order.	——	——	——
12. Teachers should not direct questions to individual students because many students find this embarrassing.	——	——	——

Middle-Level Message

Transescence is a time of life when young people are often confused and mixed up. Just when they get it together it comes apart. They may feel that nobody else understands the problems they face. Too often, they are not capable of effectively communicating their feelings. This leads to further frustration, exacerbating the problems. When asked to do a chore at home and being later called to task for not completing the job satisfactorily, the common request is "Oh, I thought you meant. . . ."

Teachers of this age-group are responsible for clearly communicating what is expected of students in each class. Youths of this age have no criteria to help them decide which concepts are academically important. But when teachers explain how each activity fits into the goals or structures of the lesson, students are no longer at a loss.

Students often have teachers who fail to follow their own advice. Students are advised to behave one way, and then the teachers themselves behave in contrary ways. This adds to the already high state of confusion in this age-group. This chapter shows how verbal and nonverbal communication strategies can be helpful in the classroom.

Teaching is a complex set of activities. Teachers are expected to perform an increasing number of varied roles, but their primary responsibility is to ensure that learning takes place. This role—regardless of the teaching techniques or stategies used—requires communicating. The many other roles of today's teachers also require communicating. Indeed, conversation affects students' thought processes and therefore what they learn (Cazden, 1986, p. 451).

Your ability to produce changes in student behavior—learning or otherwise—depends on your ability to communicate. The difference between teachers who are stimulating and exciting, who cause their students to think, learn, and feel, and dull teachers, who bore students with the subject, is the difference in their ability to communicate.

Students are slow to arrive at Ms. Simms's history class. As the tardy bell rings, there are usually a few still coming in and walking casually to their desks. Equally predictable is the way Ms. Simms will present the lesson. She always begins by mumbling a few words about yesterday's lesson, even while the latecomers are ambling in. Early in the year these students got the impression that Ms. Simms did not really care whether they learned the subject or not. They still do not know if it is because her knowledge of history is inadequate or she is merely unable to communicate.

The scene in Miss Armstrong's class is different. There students arrive quickly, find their seats, and open their books and notepads. The students recognize Miss Armstrong's expertise in her subject—history (her Texas students remarked, "She comes to class with her pistols loaded"). She begins each lesson promptly and assertively. She presents many concepts, but she does this clearly and it is obvious that she wants her students to understand. Furthermore, she seems to know when even one student is confused. Right away she gives an example that clarifies the matter. By the end of the period, she has given a clear picture of the subject under study; the personalities involved have come to life.

Why are some teachers confusing and boring while others, like Miss Armstrong, are clear and interesting? The difference may be not how well the teachers know their subjects but how well they communicate what they know. The teacher who communicates well can make the subject interesting and easy to learn, while the poor communicator is apt to make the lessons boring and confusing.

This chapter will help you focus on your own communication skills. Before you read further, take a few minutes to list your own strengths in communicating, along with any limitations that may need attention. Consider such things as your voice, vocabulary, repertoire of examples and jokes, ability to ask questions, ability to listen to students, ability to use expressions and movements to show others how you feel. Your lists should contain both verbal and nonverbal skills, because both are necessary for effective communication.

Although we may think of classroom communications as a line extending between the teacher and student, that is an oversimplification of what actually happens. The process more closely resembles the pattern shown in Figure 6-1.

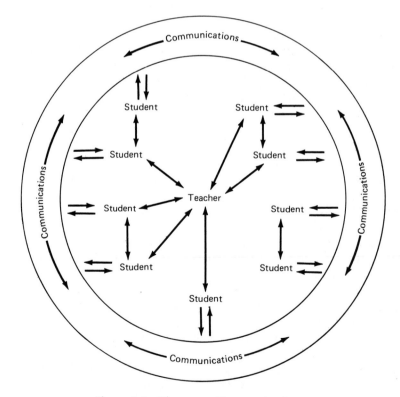

Figure 6.1. Classroom Communications

While the figure may make the teacher's role seem complex, it is accurate. Effective teachers seem to develop a sixth sense that picks up and responds to the many student comments.

Research shows that teachers may engage in more than 1,000 interpersonal exchanges with students in a single day (Jackson, 1968). It requires an acute alertness to students to manage such complex processes. Teachers also learn to respond in ways that serve a number of expressed (and even unexpressed) concerns simultaneously. In addition to verbal transmission and responses, teachers learn to communicate in many nonverbal ways. As you read this chapter, see how many new verbal and nonverbal communications skills you can add to the lists you made earlier.

MESSAGES TO COMMUNICATE

An unprecedented number of recent studies reveal several categories of messages that must be communicated for maximum learning to take place. Keep these in mind as you read the rest of this chapter. Think about ways to communicate these messages effectively.

A Sense of Efficacy

An important factor affecting learner achievement is teachers' self-confidence in their ability to cause students to learn. Fuller (1982) was referring to this when he said, "Efficacy—the individual's perceived expectancy of obtaining valued outcomes through personal effort—appears to yield a variety of important effects in school organizations." Secondary and middle-level students need to know that their teachers have the ability and the determination to lead them to attain class goals.

But how does the teacher achieve this confident image? The teacher can do this by setting clear goals for the class, by asserting the leadership needed to get students on task quickly each period, and by managing all phases of the classroom environment toward these ends. Good and Brophy (1984, p. 322) offer the following explanation of efficacy and its importance in teaching:

> Teachers who produce greater learning gains accept the responsibility for teaching their students, believe that students are capable of learning, and believe that they [the teachers] are capable of teaching them successfully. If students do not learn something the first time, they teach it again, and if the supplied curriculum materials do not do the job, they find or make other ones.

Efficacy begins with an attitude—a positive belief in the ability of the students and a belief in the teacher's ability to cause students to succeed. It also involves a determination that says if you don't succeed the first time, don't give up—we've just started. Teachers who display efficacy do not give excuses. If the necessary materials are not available, the teacher with efficacy finds or makes other materials. Such teachers are invaluable to schools and to students. While getting the job done, they silently communicate to students that anything is possible so long as they believe in themselves.

Establishing a definite sequence for one's own activities can contribute to a positive teacher image. Brooks (1985) examined videotapes of seventh-grade math classes on the first day of school and concluded that the sequence of activities on that day was a critical factor in communicating teacher competence. He recommends that teachers follow this sequence: call class to order, take roll, explain rules and procedures, introduce course content, solicit student information, talk about themselves; and, finally, preview tomorrow's lesson.

Classroom environment affects the types of communications that are appropriate and, consequently, the messages that are communicated. Green (1983) drew the following conclusions about communications:

1. Face-to-face interaction, between teacher and students and among students, is governed by context-specific rules.
2. Rules for participating in classroom activities are implicit and are learned through the action itself.
3. The meaning that results from communications is context specific.
4. Over time, frames of reference are developed.
5. The diversity of classrooms makes communications complex and demanding for teachers and students.

A Sense of Meaning

Too often students go through the motions of learning without really understanding what they are doing and why they are doing it. According to Good (1984), "It is essential that direct instruction include explicit attention to meaning, not simply focus on engagement as an end in itself." All students need help in deciding what information is important. Santmire and Frieson (1984) state, "Children have no criteria to decide which are academically important concepts and which are unimportant. But when teachers do explain how each activity fits into the goals or structures of the lesson, students are no longer at a loss." According to Fisher et al. (1980), students "pay attention more when the teacher spends time discussing the goals or structures of the lesson and/or giving directions about what students are to do." But teachers seldom clearly explain what is expected of the students (Bruner, 1981).

Expectations

Several researchers have conducted studies to determine the effects of teacher expectations on learning. The expectation literature is consistently (though not unanimously) interpreted to show that there are powerful effects on performance when teachers communicate their goals for performance to those they are teaching. Unfortunately, there is evidence that often neither students nor teachers appreciate the value of goals. Content goals often appear to have little salience for either students or teachers. Students do not think of themselves as mastering knowledge but rather as achieving those things required by the teacher or test. As capsuled by Stake and Easley (1978), "teachers are the key to what happens in the classroom."

The Role of Research

Practitioners often fail to appreciate and use research findings in their work, and teachers are no exception. In fact, they may be more guilty of neglect than most. This is especially unfortunate because research on classroom teaching during the past few years has produced much data that can be used to improve classroom learning. Smith (1980) explains: "Although the research on general concepts, principles and skills of teaching and classroom management has grown and become more dependable, there is reason to believe that a large portion of the education faculty in most institutions teaches with little knowledge or utilization of that research."

Teachers tend to perceive research as detached from "the real world." Instead of appreciating and using research findings, they are apt to overuse their own experience as a basis for future decisions. According to Egbert (1984, p. 14), "We have valued the personal and cumulative experiential knowledge of our profession all out of proportion to that which could be contributed by research, either research that confirms and illustrates good practice or research that opens the way to improvement in practice beyond the best that we know today." As you continue preparing to teach, you will want to collect research findings that you can apply throughout your teaching career.

VERBAL COMMUNICATION SKILLS

Teachers can develop and refine several technical skills to improve their ability to communicate with students.

Voice Control

Volume. Some teachers have such weak voices that they cannot be heard by most class members, so their valuable planning is largely wasted. How can you be sure you will be heard by everyone? The obvious answer is to speak louder, but this may not be so easy. One way to increase your volume is to look at and talk to the students in the back of the room during the lesson. Even when you are answering a question posed by someone in the front row, you should let members in the back row know that they are not being ignored. Just because a student in the front row asks the question, don't assume the rest of the class already knows the answer. The chances are good that others also need to hear your response.

Another way to help yourself be heard is to reduce sound interference—for example, close the windows and doors to keep distracting sounds out. But if your school does not have air conditioning, you will sometimes need to keep windows and doors open for ventilation. Traffic noises and other unavoidable interference will always require increased voice volume on your part.

Tone. Once you have adequate volume, examine your voice to see whether it is monotonous. Listen to yourself. When you do, you will feel obligated to speak louder, more clearly, and in a more interesting manner. If possible, have one of your lessons videotaped, or make an audiotape of your classes. The advantage of videotape is that you can also begin improving your eye contact (a nonverbal skill) by seeing yourself on tape.

Clarity. An equally common voice problem is lack of clarity, frequently caused by speaking too fast. The teacher should remember to speak slowly enough to give students time to absorb the message. Because of nervous tension, almost all beginning teachers talk too fast, leaving behind confused and discouraged students.

Pauses. At times you should pause for a moment, to give students time to think. When an important idea is introduced, stop for a moment, then continue. Also, when you have asked a question, give students time to collect and organize their answers. Research shows that the most productive time lapse following a question is three seconds, but teachers usually are uncomfortable with silence and rush on after pausing for only one second (Rowe, 1978). Finally, if a student directs a question to you, your answer will be much better if you pause for an instant to think before answering. A poor answer blurted out immediately is still a poor answer; a good answer is worth a moment's wait.

Even now, in your education courses, you may want to tape a short lesson given to a class of your peers. Try to have a minimum of 10 or 12 students spaced throughout the room. Don't be ashamed to let others help you critique your lesson. You might ask one group to observe your voice and another to observe your eye contact.

Teachers must be aware of how they come across to students. Teachers who cannot speak in an interesting way cannot expect much learning to occur. Taking the time and making the effort to improve voice inflection is a responsibility we cannot escape.

Set Induction

A major difference between the beginning teacher's classes and the experienced teacher's classes is often the amount of attention that students give the teacher at the start of the period. The experienced teacher may refuse to begin a lesson until all students give their undivided attention. Getting students to be quiet is necessary because the teacher generally begins a lesson with an explanation of some kind. This could include a description of what is planned, or it may deal with directions for something the students are to do. In either case, the teacher would prefer to give the introduction or directions one time only.

Teachers' strategies for getting students' attention on the lesson are collectively known as *set induction.* How do you get the attention of the whole class? One approach is to face the class silently, looking at those whose attention you must capture. If you begin talking before the others are quiet, the noisy students usually get louder. Once things are quiet, you might say, "It took us a little while to get started. Is there a topic that needs to be discussed before we begin?" Frequently, there is, and a few minutes discussing it will be a good investment.

Another method for getting total class attention is to begin the lesson with a subject that is of vital interest to the group. It may or may not be related to the day's lesson or even to the subject. By listening to the class conversation, you can determine what the students' current interest is and begin the lesson with a discussion of that topic. You need not feel obligated to lead the discussion. Just remark, "Tom, you seem awfully interested in something. How about letting the rest of us in on it?"

Teachers have tricks for getting students' attention. Some teachers begin the period by talking very low, then raise their voice to normal when students get quiet. Students recognize the signal, and with some groups it is effective all year long.

There is merit in relating the attention-getters to the cognitive aspects of the day's lesson. Studies have shown that by involving students cognitively, teachers can elevate student achievement. In secondary school science classes, Riban (1976, p. 10) found that having students define their own problems for investigation, discuss their problem with the teacher, and organize the collection of information, dividing responsibilities among themselves, resulted in increased student achievement that "exceeded any reasonable expectations."

A few days of experience will alert you to times when catching class attention will be difficult. For example, a drastic change in the weather from hot to cold or rainy to fair, or vice versa, is an indicator of forthcoming boisterousness among middle-level students. An important high school event will often have this effect too. By keeping up with the local news, school news, and the weather, you can plan an appropriate entry into the day's lesson, for example, "Who went to the basketball game last night?" or "Did you hear this on the local news. . . ?" Once you let students express their opinions about the topic that holds their interest, they will become free to concentrate on other topics, and then you can introduce the day's planned lesson. Such set induction exercises should be kept brief.

Another effective method for achieving set induction is suspense. Begin the class by letting students guess what a diagram on the board represents, or begin by introducing a hypothetical case that will lead into the lesson. Perhaps you have a model that you can place so all can see it, or you may do a demonstration for the class. Such practices capture attention. You can increase effectiveness by using a few students, or perhaps the entire class, in the demonstration.

Using Examples

Examples can help clarify the lesson and make it a personal experience for each student, if the students can see how they relate to the lesson. It seems obvious that the amount of student learning that will occur depends on how clearly the lesson is presented, but the influence of this single variable may be far greater than expected. One study of the effect of teacher clarity on learning found that this one variable accounted for 52 percent of the variance in mean class achievement (Hines et al., 1982).

Research shows that the use of examples makes an important contribution to achieving clarity in the classroom. For example, effective teachers of mathematics spend more time on presenting new material and guided practice than do less-effective teachers (Evertson et al., 1980; Good & Grouws, 1979). According to Rosenshine (1986), ''The effective teachers used this additional presentation time to give additional explanations and many examples.'' To be sure that the example is understood, you could begin with simple examples, moving to more complex ones until the desired degree of sophistication is achieved.

Middle-level students tend to enjoy lessons that involve the teacher's previous experiences, especially when the examples involve activities that are most interesting to the specific age-group. Students, too, should give examples from time to time. By asking them for examples of the principle just introduced, you can determine how well they understand the lesson. Too often teachers follow information with the question ''Does everyone understand?'' But to say they do not understand would be to admit a weakness that might be embarrassing. By asking an average achiever to give an example, you can gauge how clearly you have presented the lesson.

Using Repetition

Students admire and respect the teacher who takes the time and has enough patience to help those who have difficulty grasping a concept. This frequently requires repetition. When and what should you repeat? Never refuse a serious request to repeat, but do not make the repetition verbatim. Explain the concept in different words. Saying the same thing, word for word, may only elicit the student statement ''I still don't get it.''

Repetition is not only for the student who does not seem to understand. Full comprehension seldom comes when a concept is first introduced. All students benefit from repetition that varies from the introduction. Some classes have students who can restate what you have said well enough that others will learn even better than if you repeated yourself.

Because some students are reluctant to speak up when they are unsure, teachers may overlook the need for repetition. But to repeat everything would be boring, so in the absence of a direct request only important points should be repeated.

Providing Variety

Variety is a key element in good teaching. Every class session should contain several different experiences for each student. Activities such as lecturing (teacher talk) or reading to students should not last for more than 10 or 15 minutes, and immediately afterward students should be invited to contribute.

Variety is also needed from day to day. If most of today's lesson involves lecturing (heaven forbid), tomorrow's lesson should be built around group work, a field trip, a film, assignments at the chalkboard, or another totally different activity. Usually a film or a group discussion should not be used for two consecutive days. The activities should be varied daily, or better yet, within the period.

Using Questions

Students often become bored with lessons that are more teacher talk than student activities. Goodlad (1984) found that, on the average, only 75 percent of class time is devoted to instruction, and most of that time the teacher is giving students information. Goodlad encourages teachers to teach the major principles and generalizations in their subject(s). Much of the information pertinent to any lesson is of a general nature and already known to the students. To prevent monotony, intersperse questions with talking.

The questions asked of students should not always be simple and basic, for questions can be used to make students think. Good questions do not ask students to state a rule or to quote a definition. Instead, they ask to have the rule applied to something. A good classroom question prompts students to use ideas rather than just remember them. Using this type of question is a simple operation. You need only remember to ask the student for more information. "Why?" "How do you know that?" "How do you feel about that?" You will find it helpful to direct questions to an individual; otherwise the questions may go unanswered or the same few students may answer all of them.

Is it fair to embarrass students with direct questions? Suppose you direct a question to a student who cannot provide the correct answer. Once you direct a question to an individual, you are obligated to help that student find an acceptable answer. This will not be difficult if you remember to (1) pause to give time for organization of thoughts, (2) modify the answer until it is acceptable, and (3) provide hints for getting started. When used in this manner, questioning becomes a form of guided discovery. One former teacher recognizes that at times student answers will be incorrect or at best tangential, and that in either case the teacher is obligated to protect the integrity of the students (Mosston, 1972, p. 124). He gives an example of how the teacher can respond effectively to an incorrect or tangential answer: "My question was not clear. Let me try this one. . . ."

Mosston, an expert on guided discovery, used diagrams (see Figure 6.2) to

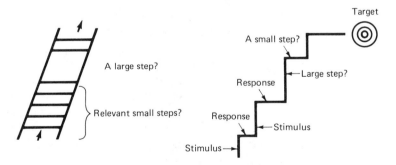

Figure 6.2. Using Questions to Guide Learning
This figure reminds the teacher that it is essential to remain alert to the size of the cognitive steps that are being dealt with. The size of the step determines the pace of the progress. Large steps may require large reinforcements with long intervals, whereas smaller steps may require reinforcements of less magnitude.
Source: Muska Mosston, *Teaching: From Command to Discovery* (Belmont, Calif.: Wadsworth, 1972), p. 124.

show how a series of carefully selected questions can guide students to discover relationships. Note that in Figure 6.2 the size of the steps of progress are not always equal, and neither are the sizes or frequencies of the reinforcements. To some extent these variables are affected by the nature of the subject being discussed, by the ability of the learner to follow a line of pursuit, and especially by the skill of the teacher to guide and reinforce them until they reach the goal being sought. Mosston reminds us that in guided discovery the teacher, never the student, is the cause of failure.

When students respond correctly and confidently, the teacher can simply ask another question or give a short statement of praise while maintaining the momentum of the lesson (Rosenshine, 1986, p. 67). However, if the student response is correct but the student appears doubtful, the teacher should give process feedback that explains the process used to derive the correct answer. For example, ''Yes, Paul, you're correct because. . . .''

CLASSIFYING QUESTIONS

Teachers use questions to achieve very different types of objectives, so we do not rank order them in higher and lower levels or from good to poor. Teachers who ask many higher-order questions (that is, questions that seek to stimulate responses at the upper levels of the cognitive domain) have students whose level of attainment is higher than average (Redfield & Rousseau, 1981). But generally, teachers do not excel in the ability to use higher-order questions.

Considering the level of questions in the most widely used resource, the textbook, this is not surprising. By analyzing over 61,000 questions in textbooks, manuals, workbooks, and tests, Trachtenberg (1974) found that more than 95 percent of the questions were lower order. Even when teachers do ask higher-order questions, their students seldom recognize that the questions are higher order. In fact, Mills and others (1980) found that analysis, synthesis, and application questions elicit responses at these levels only 50 percent of the time. After reviewing the research of Mills and his colleagues, Berliner (1984, p. 64) concluded that ''teachers need experience in learning to classify questions.'' In his book *Strategic Questioning* (1979), Ronald Hyman classifies questions according to cognitive process and other considerations.

The purpose of categorizing questions is to make them understandable. Because no one can design a system to improve the use of questions in the classroom by studying every imaginable question, it is necessary to reduce the number of elements under study by establishing categories of questions. But the number of possible categories is also staggering, so we need to limit the number of categories. The questions could be categorized according to the number of words in the question or the number of words required to answer the question, but such a system would be pointless. A more effective approach would be to group the questions according to the mental processes involved—that is, according to cognitive processes.

Cognitive Process Questions

Three main types of cognitive process questions are used regularly in classrooms: definitional questions, empirical questions, and evaluative questions. No one type is necessarily of a higher order than the others—that is, no hierarchy is implied.

Definitional Questions. Definitional questions require students (or teachers) to define a word, term, or phrase. The following are examples of definitional questions:

1. What is a tornado?
2. Give an example of a verse in iambic pentameter.
3. What does it mean to play "piano"?

Notice that definitional questions search for exact answers or "true" feelings. In other words, you either know the correct answer or you don't.

Empirical Questions. Unlike definitional questions, which ask for a definite, specific answer, empirical questions give respondents an opportunity to express their perception of the world. These questions may ask for facts, generalizations, comparisons, explanations, conclusions, or inferences. For example:

1. Who wrote the play *Hamlet?* (Fact)
2. What generalizations can you make about the lifestyle in Great Britain? (Generalization)
3. How are American football and European football similar? Different? (Comparison)
4. What did Tennyson mean by the lines "Oh, what tangled webs we weave when first we practice to deceive?" (Explanation)
5. What conclusions can you draw when you know that the number of lives lost in traffic accidents decreased by 50 percent following enactment of the 55 mph national speed law? (Conclusion)
6. On any day of the year, the number of drownings in the state of New York correlates significantly with the total sales of ice cream in the state. What do you infer from this data? (Inference)

Each of these empirical questions prompts us to observe the world around us to find answers and proof that our answers are correct.

Evaluative Questions. Evaluative questions ask students to express their opinions or values. They ask the respondent either to express an opinion or to justify one. For example:

1. Who is the greatest living fiction writer? (Opinion)
2. Why do you say that the Rolls Royce is the best car ever made? (Justification of opinion)

Now we will expand the three major types of cognitive process questions into a set of five categories:

1. Definitional
   a. Definitions
2. Empirical
   b. Facts
   c. Relations between facts (generalizations, comparisons, explanations, conclusions, or inference)
3. Evaluative
   d. Opinions
   e. Justification of opinions

Using these five categories, write your categorizing number to the left of each question.

_____ **1.** Which is worse—a tornado or a hurricane?
_____ **2.** What is a sonnet?
_____ **3.** You said that the Edsel was actually a very good car. How do you know this?
_____ **4.** In what year did the revolutionary war end?
_____ **5.** What do you think is the major difference between the Democratic party and the Republican party?
_____ **6.** Who is the greatest U.S. President of the century?
_____ **7.** How fast does light travel?
_____ **8.** What did Patrick Henry mean by "Give me Liberty or give me Death!"
_____ **9.** What is a decibel?
_____**10.** When did the stock market first crash?

Other Types of Questions

We have seen that questions used in the classroom can be effective when they are selected, analyzed, and grouped according to the cognitive processes that the questions provoke. But there are other considerations. For example, what demands does the question place on the respondents? Does it require them to reproduce information given in class, or does it demand that they assemble information to produce their own answers? Another consideration might be the kind of mental activity or process the question requires. With the exception of rhetorical questions—which are intended to draw a response—all questions must tell the respondent what type of behavior is expected of the respondent. A third possible consideration is the type of cue, if any, that the question gives to help clarify the expected type of answer. We now look at each of these considerations.

Productive vs. Reproductive Questions. A productive question is a question that either asks students to produce their own information (a productive question) or asks them to reproduce an answer given earlier by another source, such as the textbook or teacher (a reproductive question). The context of the question will determine whether it is productive or reproductive. For instance, if the question "Why did the issue of Russian military forces in Cuba resurface in 1979?" had been discussed in class, or if reference is made to a certain cause given by specific media, the question would be reproductive. But if the issue has not been previously discussed, students are being asked to create their own explanation, making the question productive.

Information-Process Activity Questions. A second comparison is the information-process activity that you want the respondent to perform. There are three general ways you may expect students to perform: yes/no, selection, and construction. An example of a yes/no question would be: "In the 1984 presidential election, did Walter Mondale carry the state of New York?" Selection questions require the respondent to select from two or more given alternatives—for example, "Is *lonely* an adjective or an adverb?" Construction questions require students to construct their own response: "Explain your position on abortion."

Response-Clue Questions. There are five types of response-clue questions, which give clues to the type of response desired: Wh-words, parallel terms, cited terms, excluded terms, and questions that lead the respondent.

> Questions with *Wh-words,* such as *when, why, what, who,* and *how,* may clue the student to answer in terms of time, reasons, things, people, and number.
>
> Questions with *parallel terms* ask the student to provide more information about the same topic: "Can you give another reason?" "And then what happened?" "Who else was involved?"
>
> Questions with *cited terms* offer a framework for the response—for example, "Who is the best college football team this year, *in terms of cooperative teamwork?*" "What were the major causes of the American Revolution, including social, economic, and political?"
>
> Questions with *excluded terms* tell the respondent what *not* to include in answering—for example, "Other than its cost, why is electricity an undesirable source for heating homes?" "Besides earning good grades, why do you believe it is necessary to learn all you can?"
>
> Questions that *lead the respondent* guide the respondent to a yes or no response—for example, "Don't you agree?" "It's rather humid, isn't it?" "Most American cars aren't subcompacts, are they?"

The Questioning Grid

The questioning grid shown in Figure 6.3 can be used as an observation instrument in the classroom to record and classify questions as they are asked. For this purpose you may wish to record a *T* in the appropriate cells for all questions asked by the teacher and an *S* in the appropriate cells for each question asked by students. Next to each question, list its type. Consider the following sample questions and their classification.

Cognitive Process		Production Type		Information-Process Activity			Wh-Interrogative Words	Response Clue			
		Productive	Reproductive	Yes/No	Selection	Construction		Parallel Terms	Cited Terms	Excluded Terms	Leading the Respondent
Short Set	Expanded Set										
Definitional	Definitions										
Empirical	Facts										
Empirical	Relations between facts										
Evaluative	Opinions										
Evaluative	Justifications										

Figure 6.3. The Questioning Grid
Source: Ronald Hyman, *Strategic Questioning* (Englewood Cliffs, N.J.: Prentice-Hall, 1979), p. 29.

Practice Questions	*Question Type*
1. To convert from centimeters to millimeters, do you divide?	Yes/no; reproductive
2. What is the symbol for silver—Ag or Si?	Selection; Wh-productive
3. What is the best gas to burn in a lawnmower?	Selection; Wh-reproductive
4. Is Athens the capital of Greece?	Construction-reproductive
5. If we exhaust our petroleum, will we turn to using coal?	Yes/no; productive
6. What are the basic differences between the Democratic and Republican parties?	Construction; Wh-productive

REINFORCEMENT

The teacher can frequently elicit desired pupil behavior by using reinforcement. All students want to feel capable of answering questions and performing assigned classroom tasks; they also want to believe that the teacher looks on them favorably. Some students do not believe they can benefit from school because they feel incapable of "fitting in." Such special cases will be dealt with in a later chapter. Here we will look at how a teacher can affect a student's attitude about himself or herself through reinforcement.

Too often the teacher responds to a student with "You're right, but that's not the answer I wanted," leaving the student confused and discouraged. Why not reverse this response, make the correction, and leave the student feeling correct? For example, "Your answer is not what I was looking for, but you are absolutely correct" or "That's interesting. I was expecting you to say . . . but you didn't. You gave an answer I had not even thought about."

To be effective, reinforcement must be sincere and each statement should address specific achievements. Too often teachers get into a rut and use the same reinforcement for every student. For example, they tend to overuse such general expressions as "good" and "okay," making the reward routine and ineffective. Other teachers overemphasize or overdramatize reward, and sensing insincerity the students become skeptical of the teacher.

How can you judge how much emphasis to place on rewarding? The best guide is to consider the age-group and give rewards only when the students have earned them. Overpraising can easily embarrass students from junior-high age upward and produce negative results. The key is to allow each student to feel successful at least one time every day. For some students this will require teacher concentration, but with experience you will learn to create opportunities for students to experience success.

REVIEW

Review is needed at least twice within each lesson—at the beginning and at the end. During the time between one day and the next, many things can intervene and distort the student's memory of the previous lesson. By beginning each lesson with a brief review of the previous day's high points, you can tune students back in to the topic under study.

According to Rosenshine (1986, p. 64), "Effective teachers begin a lesson with a five to eight minute review of previous material, correction of homework, and review of relevant prior knowledge. To make sure that the students possess the prerequisite skills for the day's lesson, the teacher can review concepts and necessary skills to do the next day's homework; have students correct each other's papers; ask about items where the students had difficulty or made errors; and review or provide additional practice on facts and skills that need re-teaching." Review at the end of the period can reemphasize the major points covered during the lesson, clarify the lesson, remove any misconceptions, and give students a feeling of accomplishment. In the review at the end of the period, the teacher should make a special effort to include material that will resurface at a later date. "Daily review is particularly important for teaching material that will be used in subsequent learning, for example, math facts, reading sight words, and grammar and skills such as math computation, math factoring, or solving chemical equations" (Rosenshine, 1986, pp. 64–65).

When reviewing, carefully select and clarify the major concepts developed during the hour. Encourage students to ask questions about concepts they do not understand. This enables them to correct misconceptions and to process further the information they have gained. MacKenzie and White (1982) found that eighth- and ninth-grade students retained information gathered on a geography field trip when the trip was followed by such review activities as small-group discussions, sketching, and tasting leaves they had collected.

Review also contributes to student achievement because it raises the level of students' interaction or involvement with the lesson. Correctly used, reviewing involves explicit instruction. During "explicit" instruction in well-structured areas, the teacher initially takes full responsibility for performing a task but, in order to increase students' alertness, gradually involves them in this part of the lesson.

NONVERBAL COMMUNICATION SKILLS

According to Galloway (1984), "In education we have tended to underestimate the relationship of setting and context to individual behavior. . . . Classroom activity and teacher-student relationships are influenced by levels of nonverbal influence." Students are turned on more by *how* we say things than by *what* we say. They constantly watch for excitement or enthusiasm in the teacher's expression. Even when you are not instructing verbally, students are getting information about how you feel. Your attitudes, likes, dislikes, approval, and disapproval are all communicated through facial expressions and other body language.

Whether they realize or not, some teachers use their desks as walls for protection from their students; others use them as a symbol of authority. Thus, the desk can become a nonverbal psychological barrier to good teacher-student communications. Until the teacher moves from behind it, true communication is not likely to occur.

The next time you are a classroom observer, take notes on the teacher's nonverbal communications. See how many different ways this teacher communicates nonverbally. If before you graduate you have an opportunity to peer-teach a lesson or to teach a lesson to public school students, near the end of the lesson you might ask your students what different ways they believed you were communicating nonverbally with them. Ask how they felt about what you did and about how you did it. Today's students tend to be honest and say what they feel, so you can learn much from them.

Feedback

While the students are receiving nonverbal communications from the teacher, the teacher can simultaneously receive feedback. Alert teachers watch the movements and emotions of students and use what they see to adjust their teaching methods. For example, suppose several students begin yawning while you are teaching. You might open a window or lower the room thermostat. If the drowsiness continues, you might change your teaching style to include more inflection in your voice. Unless you are dealing with students who come from very poor homes—and therefore have poor nutrition and inadequate sleeping facilities—or with students who have night jobs, the yawning can probably be attributed to something you are or are not doing. Again, be aware of any clues the students give you regarding a communication breakdown.

Another way to obtain feedback is to change the bulletin board to let students give their impressions of the teacher. For example, at the end of each lesson or each day, middle-level students might be given a positive "thumbs-up tab" or a negative "purple-shaft tab" to attach to the board to show how the teacher left them feeling on that particular day. High school teachers may prefer to use a closed suggestion box. It is important that the teacher *use* this information to make improvements in teaching style. For best results, the student should be able to put the symbols on the board anonymously, lest some respond the way they *think* you want them to.

Eye Contact

An important nonverbal teaching skill is eye contact. Teaching should be a multichanneled dialogue. Beginning teachers, usually because of insecurity, avoid direct eye contact with students and instead look at their notes. To prevent this, try using fewer notes. A list of the major ideas—or at most a broad outline of the lesson—may work better than a detailed lesson plan. Focus on a few individuals in each conversation. Public school teaching is not lecturing. It is a multicom-municative process between teacher and students and among students.

We all know people who when they talk to us look over our shoulders, above us, or anywhere but directly at us. A little disconcerting, isn't it? We may become so distracted by this annoying behavior that we miss what they are saying. It's no different in the classroom. Without eye contact, teachers experience a communication breakdown and the learning environment becomes far from optimal.

Other Nonverbal Teacher Behaviors

Much of what a teacher does can be characterized as a combination of verbal and nonverbal behaviors. When you ask a student to settle down, you are communicating verbally. At the same time, however, you may be gesturing with your hands or giving a look that is actually more effective in getting your point across. Here are a few examples of such combinations of verbal and nonverbal communication (addressing mainly the nonverbal):

1. You have asked a question to which the student has responded incorrectly. Smiling, you indicate in a nice way that you were seeking a different answer. Your smile alone says, "That's all right. Nobody's perfect."
2. While you are talking, you see a student poking his pencil at a classmate. You pause, tilt your head downward, and look over the top of your glasses. The foolishness stops immediately.

These are examples of occasions when your nonverbal behavior can play an extremely important role in teacher-student relationships. With verbal reprimands only, these relationships would tend to weaken.

Body Movement

The time when teachers hide behind a desk is, we hope, long gone. You need to circulate among your students so you can communicate with each one. Because talking to individual students often disturbs the others, much of the communication must be done nonverbally. Walking throughout the room, pausing momentarily, or giving a smile and a nod of the head can capture the confidence that students should have in their teacher. Older students prefer nods, winks, and hand signals to excessive touching. Even more important, this type of individual recognition can help build self-confidence. Knowing that a teacher is pleased with them helps students feel good about themselves.

Using Silence

Most teachers talk too much. After studying teachers for eight years, Goodlad (1984) reported that, on the average, teachers talk 75 percent of each class period, leaving little opportunity for pupil participation. Learning to remain quiet requires self-discipline.

When advised by her supervisor that she talked too much, a first-year teacher made tapes of her classes and kept a daily log of her experiences. Over a period of time, she was able to analyze, record, and evaluate her progress. However, she did more. On her desk, she put a sign that said in Swedish "Shut up." The teacher explained that she had a tendency to answer her own questions before the students could. She then noted, "The uncomfortable quiet can actually be a time for thinking . . . and if the teacher outwaits the students, one of the latter will begin speaking."

How much silence can you tolerate? How much can *you* refrain from talking? Instead of feeling obligated to respond to student comments, encourage other students to respond. Try to lead rather than dominate the discussions.

You will be asked many questions for which you will not have an answer. To bluff is pure folly, because it can misguide students and destroy your credibility. You should not feel obligated to know all the answers. Admitting your limitations will not show weakness if you show a willingness to seek the answers.

The Hidden Curriculum

The total process of communicating nonverbally, intentionally or not, has a considerable impact on students. Sometimes the effects are positive, sometimes they are negative. Nonverbal communication is part of the *hidden curriculum*. Michal Radz (1978, p. 6) states the significance of the hidden curriculum: "One should not underestimate the knowledge, skills, and attitudes that are acquired through the informal culture of the school. Indeed, the hidden curriculum can reinforce classroom learning or make it a gross hypocrisy. It can promote the development of individual self-esteem or it can crush a fragile self-concept. It can make learning a meaningless experience in gamesmanship."

Teachers can use the hidden curriculum to communicate positive, constructive messages. For example, an orderly, task-oriented classroom routine can socialize students to the world of work (Doyle, 1986, p. 413).

Detecting Boredom

Another group of nonverbal signals that teachers must learn to recognize are those that show boredom. Nierenberg's *How to Read a Person Like a Book* (1971, pp. 122–124) includes in this group resting head in hands, giving a blank stare, and doodling. Other clear indicators of boredom are squirming (because it involves movement of the entire body as one shifts weight from hip to hip while simultaneously repositioning arms, legs, feet, and hands) and yawning, which adds the dimension of sound. Squirming might carry other messages, such as a need to use the restroom, and yawning may indicate a physical need for sleep, but what they probably mean is that communications are breaking down.

Students are also frequently seen resting head in their hands. They may or may not be aware that this gesture also symbolizes boredom. By the time they reach high school, most know that such actions are not polite and have begun substituting more subtle expressions, such as giving a blank stare or silently doodling. A few highly creative individuals do express their creativity through doodling, and a few great thinkers are glassy-eyed when they engage in deep thought, but these are a small minority and their wisdom can be detected by examining their drawings or pursuing their thoughts with questions. Sometimes students may offer fake, hollow stares to trick the teacher, but most students today are quite open, both verbally and nonverbally.

RECAP OF MAJOR IDEAS

1. Teacher efficacy is essential for maximum learning and is established by setting clear goals and objectives, quickly getting all students on task, and keeping them on task until the goals and objectives are attained.
2. Teachers must communicate to students how the activities of each class relate to the class goals. Otherwise, students will not know the purpose of the activities while they are engaged in them.
3. By communicating high but realistic levels of expectations to students, teachers can increase the amount of learning in each class.
4. Teacher educators have failed to impress on prospective teachers the importance of research for classroom teaching. As new information is discovered, teachers can use it to improve their teaching in ways that are currently unknown.
5. Teachers usually give students only one second to respond to questions. By giving them three seconds, the teacher can significantly improve the learning process.
6. By listening to students, teachers can identify topics that prove to be excellent channels of communication.
7. Teachers should not begin or continue a lesson without having the attention of all students.
8. Examples that relate to adolescent experiences should be chosen over those that relate to the teacher's experiences.
9. When directing a question to a student, the teacher is obligated to help the student respond favorably.
10. Nonverbal teacher behaviors communicate important messages to students. Teachers can improve their nonverbal communication skills by observing and critiquing themselves.

POSTTEST

Now that you have read the chapter, take a moment to respond to the following statements again.

	Agree	Disagree	Uncertain
1. Most beginning teachers talk too fast.	_____	_____	_____
2. Teachers should avoid using personal examples in their lessons.	_____	_____	_____
3. Students tend to emulate the behavior of their teachers.	_____	_____	_____
4. Teachers tend to pause too long after asking a question, which bores many students.	_____	_____	_____
5. A teacher's nonverbal communications are more important than what that teacher says.	_____	_____	_____
6. The meaning that results from communication is context-specific (depends on the context in which it is used).	_____	_____	_____
7. Teachers seldom explain what a lesson expects from the students.	_____	_____	_____
8. Effective teachers (those whose students exceed in achievement) spend less time introducing new topics, giving examples, and giving students opportunities for guided practice than do less-effective teachers.	_____	_____	_____
9. When students respond correctly but doubtfully to teacher questions, the teacher should explain the process used to derive the answer.	_____	_____	_____
10. More than 95 percent of the questions in textbooks and similar materials are lower order.	_____	_____	_____
11. Most student responses to higher-order questions are higher order.	_____	_____	_____
12. Teachers should not direct questions to individual students because many students find this embarrassing.	_____	_____	_____

CASES

An earlier chapter portrayed the teacher as a manager of students, equipment, space, and activities. The chapter purposely omitted communications because an entire chapter was needed to explore the teacher's role in managing the complex communications in the classroom. The following experiences will give you an opportunity to see how important good communications are in instruction.

Case 1: Teaching Students, Not Subjects

When Sue began teaching in high school, her students were amazed at how smart she was. She seemed to have the facts, names, and dates all memorized, and she could give from memory every detail of any war. But Sue never tried to show off. She was in fact a borderline introvert. When the beginning bell rang for each period, she seemed to lack the courage necessary to start the lesson. After calling the roll, she would mumble about the homework assignment for several minutes without looking up from her book. A typical lesson started like this:

> (Looking down at her text): All right, class, what did we learn yesterday? What did we say was the cause of World War II? What did we learn about Germany's economic status at the time? Why did the United States stay out of the war for so long?

Discussion

1. Why do you think Sue talked to her book instead of to her students?
   Like all beginning teachers, Sue was nervous. Lacking the courage necessary to face her students, she resorted to looking at the book when she was talking.
2. How could Sue improve her questioning?
   She could begin by directing each comment to a particular student, substituting specific questions about each point emphasized in the lesson for broad, general questions like "What about Germany's economic status?" and "Why did the United States stay out of the war for so long?"

Case 2: A Need for Tact in Questioning

Jack Cobb was a good biology teacher who planned thoroughly. Each day's lesson was highly content oriented but there was room for student participation. Jack claimed to be student centered, but he was not very patient when he asked questions.

In one particular class period he did damage to the self-concepts of three students who were considered slow learners. In each case he had asked a question to which the student responded incorrectly. His response was "That's wrong. Who knows the answer?"

Discussion

1. How can students be made to feel successful when responding incorrectly to a question?
   In this chapter we made it clear that the teacher has both the opportunity and the responsibility for making a student feel successful. No matter how incorrect a response,

a resourceful teacher can guide the student out of despair or embarrassment. Some techniques for doing this have been discussed, but here is another possibility:

Jack Cobb did not realize, or did not care, that his remarks left students feeling inadequate. He could have said, "I don't believe you're totally correct. Would you like some help?" The student would surely have responded affirmatively. Then he could ask for volunteers. When the correct answer was given, Jack could go back to the original student and say, "Do you think that's right?"

This type of response will let a student know that he or she was incorrect but will not exclude that student from the discussion. The student makes the decision to seek assistance and has the final comment, as the teacher returns to him or her for verification of the correct response. A teacher who treats students in a humane manner will earn the respect of the entire class.

2. Should slow learners be asked questions in class?

All students should have an opportunity to respond to questions, or to originate questions of their own, but the teacher should be selective in matching questions to students. Unfortunately, too many questions require short answers of merely yes or no, but this may be the best type of question to ask a student with low achievement. Although shallow questions and responses result in little additional knowledge, they do give the student a chance to be successful.

But slow students should not receive only low-level questions. When a student volunteers to respond to a question that appears too difficult, the student deserves a chance to try. If correct, the student will be pleased, and so will you. The experience might provide the encouragement needed for accepting other challenges.

ACTIVITIES

Good teaching requires good communication, but this does not always happen automatically. Some teachers depend mostly on verbal communications; others, who are less verbose, use more nonverbal strategies to communicate. Every teacher should combine verbal and nonverbal strategies to improve two-way communications in the classroom. The following activities may challenge you to relate these strategies to your own behavior style.

1. How much do you talk? When you are in a one-on-one conversation with a colleague, who dominates the discussion? Think about it. Do you tend to talk too much? Too little? Devise a plan for helping yourself reach a more even balance.
2. Now that you are aware of a number of effective nonverbal strategies for communicating, it is time to relate this knowledge to teaching. Consider your own unique attributes and explain how you can use nonverbal communication techniques in your classroom.
3. From your own previous experiences as a student, can you list any techniques not included in this book that could be effective for classroom application?
4. Check the library for additional recent books and articles on business and speech communications. Try to relate each to teaching, altering it to serve teachers better.

SUGGESTED READINGS

Berliner, D. C. (1984). The half-full glass: A review of research on teaching. In P. A. Hosford (Ed.), *Using what we know about teaching,* p. 66. Alexandria, Va: Association for Supervision and Curriculum Development.

Brooks, D. M. (1985). Beginning the year in junior high: The first day of school. *Educational Leadership, 42,* 76–78.

Bruner, J. (1981, August). *On instructability*. Paper presented at the meeting of the American Psychological Association, Los Angeles.

Cazden, C. (1986). Classroom discourse. In M. C. Wittrock (Ed.), *Handbook of research on teaching methods* (3rd ed.). New York: Macmillan.

Doyle, W. (1986). Classroom organization and management. In M. C. Wittrock (Ed.), *Handbook of research on teaching* (3rd ed.). New York: Macmillan.

Egbert, R. L. (1984). The role of research in teacher education. In R. L. Egbert & M. M. Kluender (Eds.), *Using research to improve teacher education.* Lincoln, Neb.: American Association of Colleges for Teacher Education.

Evertson, C. C., Anderson, G., Anderson L., & Brophy, J. (1980). Relationships between classroom behaviors and student outcomes in junior high mathematics and English classes. *American Educational Research Journal, 17,* 43–60.

Fisher, C. W. (1980). Teaching behavior, academic learning time, and student achievement: An overview. In C. Denham & A. Lieberman (Eds.), *Time to learn,* p. 26. Washington, D.C.: U.S. Department of Education, National Institute of Education.

Fuller, B. (1982). The organizational context of individual efficacy. *Review of Educational Research* (Washington, D.C.: American Educational Research Association), *52*(1), 7–30.

Galloway, C. M. (Ed.). (1984). Nonverbal and teacher-student relationships: An intercultural perspective. *Theory into Practice, 16*(3), 129–133.

Good, T. L. (1984, August). First Annual Conference for Relating Research and Practice. East Lansing, Mich.: Michigan State University.

Good, T. L., & Brophy, J. E. (1984). *Looking in classrooms* (3rd ed.). New York: Harper & Row.

Good, T. L., & Grouws, D. A. (1979). The Missouri mathematics effectiveness project. *Journal of Educational Psychology, 71,* 143–155.

Goodlad, J. I. (1984). *A place called school.* New York: McGraw-Hill.

Green, J. L. (1983). A study of schooling: Some findings and hypotheses. *Phi Delta Kappa, 64,* 465–470.

Hannam, C., Smyth, P., & Stephenson, N. (1971). *Young teachers and reluctant learners.* Baltimore: Penguin.

Hines, C. V., Cruickshank, D. R., & Kennedy, J. J. (1982, March). *Measures of teacher clarity and their relationships to student achievement and satisfaction.* Paper presented at the annual meeting of the American Educational Research Association, New York.

Hyman, R. T. (1979). *Strategic questioning.* Englewood Cliffs, N.J.: Prentice-Hall.

Jackson, P. (1968). *Life in classrooms.* New York: Holt, Rinehart & Winston.

Johnston, W. (1970). *Monday morning father.* New York: Grosset & Dunlap.

Lohman, D. F. (1985). *Teaching higher order thinking skills.* Elmhurst, Ill.: North Central Laboratory for Educational Research and Development.

MacKenzie, A. A., & White, R. T. (1982). Fieldwork in geography and long-term memory structures. *American Educational Research Journal, 19,* 623–632.

Mills, S. R., Rice, C. T., Berliner, D. C., & Rousseau, E. W. (1980). The correspondence between teacher questions and student answers in classroom discourse. *Journal of Experiential Education, 48,* 194–209.

Moldstad, J. A. (Ed.). (1975). Role of technology in improvement of instruction: Symposium. *Viewpoints, 51,* 1–77.

Mosston, M. (1972). *Teaching: From command to discovery.* Belmont, Calif.: Wadsworth.

National Institute of Education (1984). Ten ways to improve writing skills. *Research in Education.* Washington, D.C.: U.S. Department of Education.

Nierenberg, G. I. (1971). *How to read a person like a book.* New York: Pocket Books.

Norris, K. D. (1971). Getting the teacher to shut up. In M. G. McClosky (Ed.), *Teaching strategies and classroom realities.* Englewood Cliffs, N.J.: Prentice-Hall.

Peacock, F., & Patrick, J. (1977, May). Making media fit. *Industrial Education, 66,* 19–20.

Pearson, D. P., & Gallagher, M. C. (1983). The instruction of reading comprehension. *Contemporary Educational Psychology, 8,* 317–344.

Radz, M. A. (1978). Responsibility, education, and the early adolescent. In C. H. Sweat (Ed.), *Responsibility of education in the junior high middle school,* p. 6. Danville, Ill.: Interstate.

Redfield, D. L., & Rousseau, E. W. (1981). A meta-analysis of experimental research on teacher questioning behavior. *Review of Educational Research, 51,* 237–245.

Riban, D. M. (1976). Examination of a model for field studies in science. *Science Education, 60,* 1–11.

Rosenshine, B. V. (1986). Synthesis of research on explicit teaching. *Educational Leadership, 43,* 60–69.

Rowe, M. B. (1978, March). Wait, wait, wait. *School Science and Mathematics, 78,* 207–216.

Rubin, L. J. (Ed.) (1973). Facts and feelings in the classroom. New York: Viking.

Santmire, T. E., & Friesen, P. A. (1984). A developmental analysis of research on effective teacher-student interactions: Implications for teacher preparation. In R. L. Egbert & M. M. Klueder (Eds.), *Using research to improve teacher education.* American Association of Colleges for Teacher Education.

Smith, B. O. (1980). A design for a school pedagogy. Washington, D.C.: U.S. Government Printing Office.

Stake, R. E., & Easley, J. A. (Eds.) (1978). Case studies in science education. Urbana, Ill.: Center for Instructional Research and Curriculum Evaluation, vol. 1, p. 29.

Trachtenberg, D. (1974). Student tasks in text material: What cognitive skills do they tap? *Peabody Journal of Education, 52,* 54–57.

Weil, M., & Joyce, B. (1978). *Social models of teaching.* Englewood Cliffs, N.J.: Prentice-Hall.

Williams, S. S. (1978). Observational system for analysis of classroom communication. *Clearing House, 41,* 346–348.

PART III

PROVIDING FOR INDIVIDUAL DIFFERENCES

Early in their programs, most prospective teachers learn that in order to be successful and attain a high level of achievement in their classes, teachers must meet the needs and interests of all students. They quickly ask how this can be done in a class of 30 or so students whose needs and interests are so different. This is a dilemma that all teachers face. Chapter 7 provides general information to help teachers develop an individualized approach to instruction. Chapter 8 will help you meet the needs of students with exceptional limitations and of those who are exceptionally gifted. Chapter 9 acquaints the reader with the responsibilities and roles of those who teach students who come from different ethnic and cultural backgrounds.

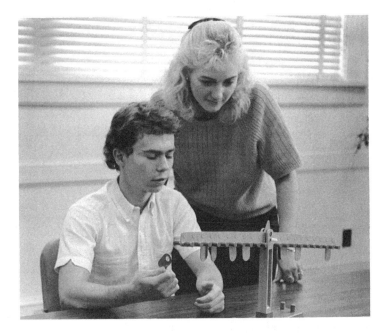

C H A P T E R **7**

Individualizing Instruction

Objectives

- List at least four approaches commonly used to meet individual learning differences.
- Differentiate between two major categories of ability grouping.
- Describe ways to avoid common problems that result from ability grouping.
- Describe ways instruction for low-ability groups should differ from instruction for average groups.
- Name the elements on which success in mastery learning hinges.
- Design a contingency contract.
- Differentiate between teacher-paced and group-paced instruction, and between group-based and individual-based instruction.
- List categories of learner preferences used to determine learning styles.
- Discuss strengths and weaknesses of matching learner and teacher styles.

PRETEST

	Agree	Disagree	Uncertain
1. Individualizing instruction is contextual, which means that the success of a particular approach may vary as the situation changes.	___	___	___
2. The simple act of grouping students according to ability usually increases learning.	___	___	___
3. When using ability grouping, teachers should spend more time with the less-capable students.	___	___	___
4. Ability grouping can be psychologically destructive to high achievers as well as to low achievers.	___	___	___
5. Intraclass grouping produces more competition than interclass grouping.	___	___	___
6. Recent studies show that, given adequate time, motivation, and presentation of material, at least 90 to 95 percent of all high school students can master all the curriculum's objectives.	___	___	___
7. Teaching style has little effect on learner attainment.	___	___	___
8. Teachers should use only the teaching styles their students prefer.	___	___	___
9. In many ways learning is an individual experience.	___	___	___
10. Each teacher should select a teaching style, perfect it, and use it all the time, instead of attempting to master several different styles.	___	___	___

Middle-Level Message

One question prospective teachers usually have is how to plan and teach so that each lesson meets the needs of 20 or 30 students whose abilities range from educationally handicapped to gifted? By the time such a diverse class reaches the senior grades, many of the poor performers drop out of school, and some mediocre performers find themselves and become serious students. But at the middle level this narrowing process has not occurred. At this level the teacher must face the very difficult challenge of meeting a wide range of needs.

Although there is no guaranteed solution to this problem, one approach to meeting individual needs is ability grouping. But sometimes this approach produces disastrous results because teachers mismanage the groups. This chapter explains how grouping can and should be used and identifies common mistakes that teachers make when using groups. Because the general lack of self-confidence among transescents makes them especially vulnerable to psychological damage produced by ability grouping, you will want to learn how to avoid these common effects of the approach.

As prospective teachers begin their involvement in public school classrooms, they quickly are introduced to classes that contain students with a wide range of abilities. They can be overwhelmed by the challenge of designing instruction for students who have not only a broad range of abilities but also levels of motivation that vary over an equally wide range.

Chapter 8 suggests ways to plan instruction that meets the needs of students who vary so much from the average that special, individualized lesson plans are required. Chapter 9 discusses special techniques for teaching students of varying ethnic groups and cultures. This chapter will look at ways to meet the instructional needs of *all* students in secondary and middle school classrooms, but many of the strategies presented in this chapter can be applied to special and multicultural classes.

Individualized instruction can be defined as instruction that meets the needs of all students. Its existence is based on the premise that students are different— indeed, that each student is different and therefore has unique learning needs that each teacher must make special efforts to meet. When teachers fail to plan to take into consideration the variety of student needs, at least two things happen: Some students become bored because they are inadequately challenged; others become discouraged by expectations that are beyond their abilities.

While educators recognize the need to individualize instruction, few agree on how to meet the great range of learning needs. This chapter looks at some common approaches that schools and teachers use to individualize instruction. The approaches discussed are far from all-inclusive, though. Every day new approaches are being applied. Some of the more successful innovations may never get beyond the immediate classroom walls; others are studied and tested and the results are disseminated through the professional literature. This is the case with the approaches described in this chapter.

As you read about each innovation, consider its potentials for your future classes. Make a list of ways to improve each method, and think of ways to modify these approaches to make them more useful for you with your own future students. Remember that most of these approaches had their beginnings in the minds of a few teachers who believed that a method was needed to reach particular students. Explore your own mind, the minds of other educators with whom you come into contact, and the ideas of those who have done research and shared their findings in journals and books.

IN-CLASS ABILITY GROUPING

A common approach to reducing the task of teaching 30 or so students of varying abilities and needs is to form subgroups of students who share abilities and interests. Simple arithmetic would suggest that dividing a class of 30 students into 5 groups of 6 students per group would reduce the range to which the instruction must be adapted to one-fifth the original range. But to conclude that this maneuver would improve the level of performance by a similar margin would be wrong. The results of ability grouping are not usually so monumental. Yet ability grouping does tend to improve student learning. An analysis of more than 40 studies of ability grouping found that grouping makes a small contribution to the improvement of learning and a larger contribution toward improvement of student motivation (Julik, 1981).

Individualizing Instruction

How effectively ability grouping improves learning depends on how the teacher adjusts the instruction to each group. We do know that, in general, less-capable students need more concrete material and examples of ways to apply the newly learned concepts to real-world experiences and that the more-capable students need greater challenges. But the challenges must be of different types. For example, a teacher of ability-grouped math students should not merely assign the upper group a much larger number of the same type of problems given to less-capable groups. Instead, the upper group might receive more creative challenges that require divergent thinking. Advanced groups might even be assigned to develop problems instead of solutions, or to find a variety of solutions to a problem.

The teacher using ability grouping should expect to spend more time with the less-capable students, especially after the more-capable groups get on task. Slower students may require more careful monitoring and guidance. Furthermore, "low-ability students perform less well in school when placed with other low-ability students" (Calfee & Brown, 1979). This is probably partly because teachers usually spend less time with the lower groups. A review of the literature found that the amount of time teachers devote to direct instruction is directly related to student achievement (Centra & Potter, 1980).

Unintentional Differential Treatment

Ability grouping requires different treatment for different groups at different levels, but unintentional differential treatment must be avoided. For example, while it is realistic to expect high-ability students to cover more material faster than lower groups, teachers often make unrealistic differences in the demands of two groups. Shavelson (1983) found that high-ability groups were paced as much as 15 times faster than low groups, increasing dramatically the difference in amounts of material covered by the two groups.

Teachers tend to treat students for whom they hold low expectations in several different ways. For example, Brophy (1983, p. 274) reports that teachers treat these students in the following unique ways. The teacher will—

1. Wait less time for lows to answer questions.
2. Give lows the answer or call on someone else.
3. Provide inappropriate reinforcement.
4. Criticize lows more than highs for failure.
5. Praise lows less than highs for success.
6. Fail to give lows feedback on their public responses.
7. Interact with lows less and pay less attention to them overall.
8. Call on lows less often in class.
9. Ask for lower performance levels from lows.
10. Smile less, have less eye contact, have fewer attentive postures toward lows.

Differences in Evaluation

The teacher may find it desirable to devise nontraditional ways of evaluating advanced students. For example, objective tests may not be able to measure the kinds of growth anticipated for this group. Such methodology as oral discussions or one-on-one questioning may be needed to discover the depth of insights developed by these students. Term projects may be preferable to exams. For example, the teacher of a student who accepts responsibility for writing a computer program to breed plants may find that the resulting product—that is, the computer program—is itself the best measure of success for this assignment.

Precautions

Whenever students are grouped by ability, the teacher must take certain precautions. There is a certain prestige in being affiliated with the upper group(s), while a certain disgrace befalls students who are assigned to the lower group(s). Attempts to disguise the ranking or ordering of groups usually fail. Indeed, students often know the level to which they are assigned even before their teachers know it.

Teachers should not make comments that allow comparisons among ability groups, and they should not allow students to make judgmental or derogatory comments about any group. Sometimes teachers contribute to the caste problem without even realizing their error. Mrs. Bentley's Typing I class had about 30 girls and 10 boys, none of whom had previously taken typing. She had a unique system for reporting individual grades. Along one wall she posted a white sheet of paper with a landscape scene. It had a fence in the foreground and a blue sky above the fence. Higher up, there were beautiful, fluffy cumulus clouds. On the fence sat about 40 bluebirds. Each had the name of a student.

The namesake of the bird called "James" lived in one of the city's worst ghettos. As each student developed the ability to type 25 words a minute, the namesake bird would leave the fence and begin to ascend. Right away, several birds made their departures. These represented students who owned a typewriter and had been familiar with typing at the beginning of the class. This frustrated James because he was still learning the keys when others were typing more than 25 words per minute.

Each day he found himself trying a little harder and making more mistakes (each mistake carried a five-word penalty). By the end of the year, some of the bluebirds were flying into the clouds. James's bluebird was still sitting on the fence.

The high premium set on peer approval in middle and high schools can make emotional damage that can result from ability grouping at these levels greater. Also, upper-level groups tend to become snobbish and condescending toward members of lower groups.

Make a list of at least five ways teachers can limit the amount of psychological damage that ability grouping might cause.

INTERCLASS ABILITY GROUPING

In some schools, ability grouping is done independently of teachers—standardized intelligence tests determine the placement of students in groups. Under these circumstances, teachers are still responsible for protecting the lower groups from ridicule.

Interclass grouping and intraclass (within the class) grouping produce different types of competition. When students are grouped within the same class, they are forced to compete with classmates, but when the grouping is done externally the competition is between two or more classes.

For several centuries schools in England have had "houses." A house is a group of students whose abilities are heterogeneous. In other words, each group (or house) contains students that have a wide range of abilities. The houses frequently compete in oral debates. This encourages cooperation, not competition, among members of a group.

Other schools choose homogeneous ability grouping. For example, five groups of students with similar abilities may be formed, producing five "tracks," each track representing a different level of general ability. Here is an example.

Let's Ponder

Read the following description and respond to the questions below.

A School District Uses Systematic Grouping

You walk into a seventh-grade classroom and see several groups of students throughout the room. On closer observation, you notice that Group A is collecting weather data, using a weather vane, thermometer, and hygrometer, Group B is constructing a U.S. map with a weather symbols key at the bottom, and Group C is shading the map to show general rainfalls, altitudes, and temperatures. Groups D and E are competing vigorously, developing new ways of forecasting the weather one year into the future. On the wall are color-coded charts that show at a glance the group level to which any student belongs.

You notice that Bobby Burns belongs to Group A in English, Group B in social studies and science, Group C in mathematics, and Group D in spelling. A small square is added above Bobby's name as he completes a unit in the appropriate subject. It doesn't seem to bother Bobby that he belongs to groups of different academic levels; his rate of performance in each group appears to be more important to him.

If you were teaching in a school system that was contemplating using a similar approach, and if you had an opportunity to vote for or against a tracking program, how would you vote? Why?

The above example is typical of a classroom in one of the nation's largest and most progressive school systems; all 185 schools use the approach found in this classroom. Several similar approaches to cooperative learning have recently been developed. One system, called Teams-Games-Tournaments (TGT), has heterogeneous groups competing for academic awards (Slavin, 1980). It enables low-ability and high-ability students to contribute the same number of points to the team. TGT has been used in more than 2,000 schools. Group games by Sharon (1980) arrange for each group member to have some of the information needed to solve a problem, ensuring that everyone is responsible for group success.

GRADE CONTRACTS

Grade contracting is a method that recognizes that students are more highly motivated by some topics than others. It permits an individual to place more emphasis on certain topics. Here's how it works.

At the beginning of each unit of study, students are issued a contract. According to the student's ability and interest in the topic, the student agrees to perform a certain amount of work in order to earn a certain grade. A sample contract is illustrated on page 154. As mentioned in Chapter 4, grade contracts can be powerful motivators. In addition to contracting for specific grades, contracts can be used to provide students opportunities to earn free time and other rewards.

MASTERY LEARNING

In 1963 a professor at Harvard University wrote an article titled "A Model of School Learning" in which he challenged the accepted belief that students' IQs are a major factor in determining academic success (Carroll, 1963). Carroll hypothesized that if three conditions were met, at least 90 to 95 percent of all high school students could master class objectives. The three conditions were (1) the student must be given all the time needed by the individual student, (2) each student must be properly motivated, and (3) the subject matter must be presented in a manner compatible with the individual student's learning style.

**12th Grade English
Six-Weeks Writing Unit
Contract**

Grade of B*
The grade of B can be earned through attending the class meetings and contributing to class discussions—especially those that involve critiquing the manuscripts of other participants and preparing a folder containing the following:

_____1. One query letter with all required criteria clearly marked as such
_____2. One cover letter with all required criteria clearly marked as such
_____3. A list of at least three journals selected for this manuscript, with a description of the following characteristics of each journal:
    a. audience
    b. average reading level
    c. average minimum-to-maximum manuscript pages, using an average of 300 words per manuscript page
    d. guidelines for submitting manuscripts
    e. name and address of editor.
_____4. A list of ideas for topics
_____5. A list of your personal writing requirements including preferred time of day, length of writing sessions, physical conditions, and materials and equipment
_____6. A description of at least two strategies that will help you deal with rejection

Grade of A*
Complete all assignments for the grade of B plus
_____1. Submit a second article on this topic rewritten to fit another type of journal, using the same cover-page format as on the first article.
_____2. Explain how this manuscript is more suited to this new audience in terms of the readership and the requirements of this journal.
_____3. Submit a system for tracking your manuscripts.
_____4. In one page, explain how this course has helped you to
    a. improve your writing skills (style)
    b. improve your chance of getting manuscripts accepted.

* All assignments are due and must be submitted on or before the last class session. All materials should be submitted typed and bound in a folder. Part I should contain the B-level assignments; Part II, the A level assignments. Inexpensive cardboard folders with metal tabs inside are preferred.

Using Carroll's model, Benjamin S. Bloom and his students at the University of Chicago developed an education system called Learning for Mastery (LFM). This system is teacher-paced and group-based. In other words, the teacher leads the lessons, and the class as a group follows. But most mastery learning programs are student-paced (that is, the students set the pace) and are individually based. Each student pursues learning individually—at that student's own preferred pace (Guskey & Gates, 1986).

All mastery learning programs have several important characteristics in common. First, they provide students with different lengths of time to master each topic. Second, they give students opportunities to remediate or restudy material that proves difficult, and then to retest without penalty. Third, all mastery learning programs use formative evaluation—evaluation designed to promote learning, *not* to be computed in the grading system. Short daily or weekly tests are given to diagnose learning weaknesses and teaching weaknesses, then teachers and learners adjust to improve the resulting learning. Finally, all mastery learning uses criterion-based evaluation. This means that the criteria essential for success is revealed before the study unit begins. (For further discussion of formative evaluation and criterion-based evaluation, see Chapter 15.)

How effective is mastery learning compared with traditional programs? Burns (1979) examined results from 157 mastery learning studies and discovered that 107 studies found that mastery learning students significantly outscored their traditionally taught counterparts, while 47 of the studies showed no significant differences. Only 3 of the 157 studies reported traditionally taught students outscoring mastery learning students. Burns's (1979) study of mastery learning over 15 years in 3,000 schools concluded that mastery learning was "consistently more effective than traditional curriculums" (Hyman & Cohen, 1979). Guskey and Gates (1986) reviewed 25 studies of group-based and teacher-paced mastery learning in elementary and secondary schools. In all 25 studies, the students in the mastery learning groups outlearned their counterpart control groups.

But mastery learning is not without its critics and criticisms. In a 1984 review of studies on mastery learning, Arlin (1984) reports some of the more popular criticisms. According to this report, some critics claim that the ability of mastery learning to equalize students' learning abilities is an overstatement. Some critics describe mastery learning as a "psychological trap"; many claim that is does not have a proper conceptual base. Some even label mastery learning as a Robin Hood phenomenon that takes from the advanced students and gives to the poor students. Arlin (1984) himself argues that studies that find all students equally capable should be interpreted more cautiously.

When you read professional journal articles, remember that any innovation may experience either astounding success or total failure, depending on the conditions of the moment. The old adage "Never believe anything you hear, and believe only half of what you see" is good advice when interpreted as an admonition to proceed with caution as you continue to learn more about your chosen profession.

MATCHING TEACHING STYLES
AND LEARNING STYLES

Rita Dunn and colleagues (1984) began an article by quoting the following words from a National Association of Secondary School Principals' publication (see Keefe, 1979, p. 132). "Learning style diagnosis . . . gives the most powerful leverage yet available to educators to analyze, motivate, and assist students in school. . . . It is the foundation of a truly modern approach to education." Dunn and her co-workers followed this quotation with another taken from *Redbook* magazine: "You can determine a lot about your own child's learning style, share the information with teachers, challenge any facile diagnosis . . . or any remedial work that isn't working. . . . You can be instrumental in making educators realize that children of different needs need to be taught differently" (Ball, 1982). Like the first quotation, the *Redbook* quotation urges readers to become familiar with techniques for measuring learning styles. For more than a decade, educators conducted research to discover more about various learning styles.

Figure 7.1 shows five major categories of characteristics that affect learning. Notice that these characteristics are grouped into five stimuli categories: environmental, emotional, sociological, physical, and psychological. While the effects of the environment on learning may be obvious, the other elements may affect learning without the teacher's being aware of it.

Several research studies have reported successful applications of the match-

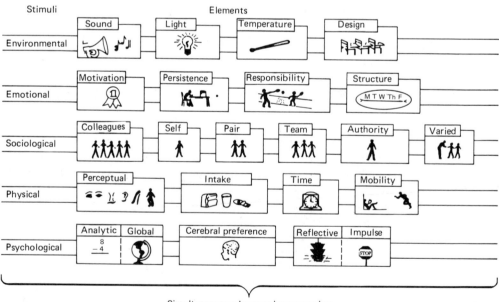

Figure 7.1. Diagnosing Learning Styles (Courtesy, Rita Dunn and Kenneth Dunn.)

ing styles movement. Sixth-graders who were matched with their learning-style preferences had significantly higher reading scores than their counterparts who were not matched with learning-style preferences. Their attitudes were also better (Pizzo, 1981). High school students who were matched with teachers of similar styles had more positive attitudes (Copenhaver, 1979), and in a high school English class, students who were matched with their time-of-day preferences had less truancy (Shea, 1983). Dunn and colleagues (1984) perceive learning-style preferences as strengths teachers can use to design more effective learning experiences. Studies show that such matching consistently increases academic achievement, improves attitudes toward school, and reduces discipline problems. This last finding is consistent with the postulate in Chapter 3; a well-planned lesson is the greatest deterrent to discipline problems (Carruthers & Young, 1980; Dunn, 1981; Hodges, 1982; Hodges, 1983; Lynch, 1981).

How to Match Styles

There are several ways to attain a match between teaching style and learning style. First, teachers can be matched with students who have similar personalities, but there are mixed results with this method. For example, Thelan (1960) found that such personality matches produced more "manageable" classes and increased student satisfaction with classroom activities. Yet Jones (1971) matched introverted teachers with introverted students, and extroverted teachers with extroverted students, and found that these matchings failed to increase dyadic interactions. McDonald (1972) found that mutual attraction between teachers and students did not affect classroom interaction patterns.

A second approach to matching is to have the teacher select teaching methods that correspond to student learning styles. The teacher who discovers that a particular class of students responds favorably to simulations and not to lectures would use more simulations than lectures with that class. Another way to match methods with learning styles is to administer a learning-style inventory to the entire class, which usually results in a variety of preferences. The teacher can then group students according to their style preferences.

Should teachers always try to accommodate students by using instructional methods that the students prefer? Probably not. In fact, to provide students opportunities to develop new styles teachers should purposely expose students to a variety of styles. Of course, this means each teacher must master a variety of teaching styles.

Let's Ponder

Read the following paragraph and respond to the questions below.

The Matching-Learning-and-Teaching-Styles Movement

The movement to match learning styles with teaching styles is a fluke that several educators dreamed up to get attention. Little quality research has been conducted in this area, and some of the limited studies on matching styles found little or no difference in learning.

Some studies suggest that teachers should expose students to several styles, but teachers naturally tend to alter their approaches according to student responses. So matching teaching and learning styles is nothing new—it's the same old wine in a new bottle. To quote Shakespeare, its "much ado about nothing."

1. How consistent must research findings be to be considered conclusive? In other words, must all studies produce the same answer before the answer can be considered factual?
2. Choose one of your favorite teachers. Does this teacher use different teaching styles? List three or four of this teacher's styles.
3. Do you have a single preferred style? To reach an intelligent answer to this question, draw a vertical line down the middle of a sheet of paper. On the left side list variables that enhance learning for you. On the right list variables that impede learning for you.
4. Challenge or defend this statement: All teachers should purposely increase their repertoire of teaching styles.
5. Do you think teachers should spend more or less time developing new styles? Why?

DISCUSSION

This chapter encourages teachers to apply style matching in the classroom. There are indeed a number of advantages to matching teaching and learning styles, but this method is not a solution for all education problems, and teachers should be aware of the limitations and criticisms of this movement. Good and Stipek (1983) identified the four following concerns:

1. There is no single dimension of learners that clearly dictates an instructional prescription. A style which the student may find motivating might not be consistent with the student's ability or prior knowledge. Sometimes, a mismatch might be preferable.
2. Matching styles does not account for the relationship between the student and teacher, the nature of the learning task, and other important variables which affect learning.
3. Such important variables as task clarity, feedback, and opportunities for practice are often ignored; yet, these affect learning.
4. Uniform classroom instructional treatments are often superior to differentiated treatment because they are compatible with the teacher's skills.

These criticisms seem fair, and there are others. The general area of grouping itself may present overwhelming problems. Studies show that many teachers, especially inexperienced teachers, find it too much of a challenge to monitor multiple group arrangements in classrooms (Doyle, 1980; Good & Brophy, 1983). Several studies show that if the major purpose of style grouping is to accommodate students, a degree of discomfort can be an asset in learning, rather than a detriment to be circumvented (Erikson, 1950; Harvey et al., 1963; Piaget, 1952).

Even the term *learning styles* is not clearly defined in the literature. Hyman and Rosoff (1984) say that a clear definition in terms of student performance would be helpful. They further point out that learning style is not static, because learning itself is a highly complex activity. Indeed, learning is such a broad activity that it cannot be contained within the cognitive domain (Stinnett & Henson, 1982).

The study of the effects of matching learning and teaching styles on learning is still in its infancy. The findings hold promise, but students should read these studies and their claims with a critical eye.

Having read pros and cons on the matching of teaching and learning styles, consider your own position. Some critics see the entire movement as a unilateral approach in which the teacher assesses the learning style of the student and prescribes or selects an acceptable teaching style to match with the learner's style. Perhaps the student should be involved in this selection. If you agree, identify some ways to make style matching a bilateral process.

RECAP OF MAJOR IDEAS

1. The instructional needs of students vary greatly from student to student.
2. Ability grouping is one common approach to meeting the needs of individual students.
3. In-class (intraclass) grouping often results in improved learning, but the degree to which it enhances learning is not substantial.
4. Intraclass grouping usually improves motivation more than it improves learning.
5. Attempts to conceal the levels of ability groups almost always fail.
6. Teachers who use ability grouping should take precautions to reduce the psychological damage that can result.
7. Interclass grouping produces group competition, whereas intraclass grouping produces competition between individuals.
8. Given adequate motivation, presentation style, and time, most high school students can master the goals set for high school students.
9. There are instruments available to determine individuals' preferred learning and teaching styles.
10. Teachers should purposely master and use a variety of teaching styles.

POSTTEST

Now that you have read the chapter, take a moment to respond to the following statements again.

	Agree	Disagree	Uncertain
1. Individualizing instruction is contextual, which means that the success of a particular approach may vary as the situation changes.	____	____	____
2. The simple act of grouping students according to ability usually increases learning.	____	____	____
3. When using ability grouping, teachers should spend more time with the less-capable students.	____	____	____
4. Ability grouping can be psychologically destructive to high achievers as well as to low achievers.	____	____	____
5. Intraclass grouping produces more competition than interclass grouping.	____	____	____
6. Recent studies show that, given adequate time, motivation, and presentation of material, at least 90 to 95 percent of all high school students can master all the curriculum's objectives.	____	____	____
7. Teaching style has little effect on learner attainment.	____	____	____
8. Teachers should use only the teaching styles their students prefer.	____	____	____
9. In many ways learning is an individual experience.	____	____	____
10. Each teacher should select a teaching style, perfect it, and use it all the time, instead of attempting to master several different styles.	____	____	____

CASES

The four cases below show how matching learning styles and teaching styles can be used. Each case actually occurred in the Wichita, Kansas, area and describes a real-life application of learning-styles theory. (Friedman & Alley, 1984).

Case 1: An Individual Teacher's Effort

Sometimes teachers have to experiment with new educational theories in the isolation of their classrooms with little support from anyone. But teachers who accept the responsibility not only for what they teach but also for what is learned are eager to use any technique they believe will help them in diagnosis, prescription, and treatment of their students.

One such teacher in Wichita, Kansas, attended a district in-service meeting in 1978, where he learned about learning-styles theory and application. This junior high teacher decided to experiment with the idea and invited a consultant from the teacher center to come to one of his classes and explain the concept to the students. The teacher and consultant spent a considerable amount of time making sure the students understood the implications of learning-styles theory and the teacher's interest in using it.

The teacher administered a learning-styles preference questionnaire, and the students scored the survey, developed their profiles, and shared the results within the class. Students were then encouraged to contribute ideas for classroom organization that would take advantage of the variety of preferred learning modalities within the class. They helped set up auditory areas where students could listen to tapes or form discussion groups. They also arranged visual corners, where other students could read or work on written assignments.

Student enthusiasm was soon reflected at home, and parents became interested. The teacher decided to carry the program further and arranged a parent meeting. He explained the learning-styles concept and how he was implementing it. He then administered the survey to the parents and helped them interpret the results regarding their own preferences. The teacher then began to utilize the parents' learning styles when he conducted parent-teacher conferences.

The results of this experiment were very positive. In this classroom, responsibilities shared by students and teacher in the planning of learning procedures and outcomes increased. Student willingness to accept learning differences in others also increased. In addition, the parent-teacher conferences became more effective and mutually appreciated. The enthusiasm for the process in this particular classroom led this teacher to introduce the procedure in his other classes. Other teachers in the school also began experimenting with the concept in their classrooms.

Discussion

When a teacher wants to initiate a new program or other innovation, is it necessary to sell others on the idea? If so, how can the teacher do this?
Innovations often require additional facilities, materials, space, and program flexibility, so the success of innovators depends on the cooperation received when administrators, teachers, and others understand the importance of the change. A simple approach is first to *inform* others about the process and then to *involve* them with the innovation.

Case 2: A School-wide Individualized Program

In 1974, Cloud Elementary School in Wichita adopted the IGE (Individually Guided Education) program as its basic instructional process. The IGE approach to schooling provides a framework for individualized instruction and continuous progress. Instead of being organized into the usual self-contained classes in which all students of a single age are grouped together, students and teachers are organized into "learning communities." Each learning community is composed of students of several age-groups and teachers of varying talents and backgrounds.

This elementary school program had several goals, one of which was to determine students' learning styles. After experimenting with several assessment techniques, the teachers in the school decided that the locally developed learning-styles inventory gave them usable and practical information that the faculty could easily manage. They arranged for the local district's computer department to put the student data from the instrument onto a computer program. The computer-based analysis was designed to identify students who fell below a previously defined score.

Style data was shared both with the students in the advisement programs and with the parents during conferences. A profile for each student was developed, and the results were used to determine the best way for each student to reach his or her learning objectives. In addition to developing learning objectives to complement each student's learning preference, the teacher identified students whose styles-preference analysis revealed a possible inability to utilize a wide range of learning styles successfully. These students were then given help in expanding their styles. Thus, one major learning goal was to increase "style flex" among students.

Results of the experiment were encouraging. There was increased student achievement and parental satisfaction. Teachers were pleased with the effort because they had acquired an additional tool for individualizing instruction. They also believed that student attitudes toward the classroom were enhanced.

Discussion

If a student has a preferred learning style that works well for that student, why introduce that student to other styles?
Students who have only one preferred learning style are in trouble when they are assigned

to a teacher whose teaching style varies drastically from the student's style. By introducing students to a variety of styles, students have an opportunity to expand their "style flex."

Case 3: *The School within a School*

In response to the career education movement, many high schools throughout the United States established special programs to provide selected students with an opportunity to participate in experience-based learning in the community. This concept provides a less-formal learning environment and more effectively meets the needs of certain students.

The Experience Based Career Education Program at Wichita High School East was one such program. It was organized as a school within a school. Soon after the program began in 1976, its director became aware that the learning-styles concept was being used and applied more and more. After appropriate planning, the program staff decided to include a learning-preference assessment—the Student Learning Styles instrument—as one of the diagnostic procedures utilized as part of each student's admission to the program.

When a student applied for admission to the program, the Student Learning Styles Inventory was administered as one of the standard battery of tests. The results were used to determine the preferred basic learning modalities of the applicants. Faculty served as both teachers and counselors in the program. These teacher-counselors had previously categorized jobs and job skills based on the nine specific characteristics identified in the instrument. The style preferences were strongly considered in the placement procedures and openly shared with prospective employers as an aid to developing learning programs for individual students. (Some employers later requested permission to use and help administer the survey to other employees. They saw it as potentially useful in developing training programs for full-time employees and in hiring procedures.)

The positive outcomes of the program, and the student successes, indicated that the assessment of learning modalities helped the program more completely meet the needs of the students through a closer match of work experience and learning-style preferences. There was also evidence that students' confidence in the success of the program was increased, that the students' self-concepts were enhanced, and that students performed better in other phases of their learning experiences as well.

Discussion

In what ways can teachers in self-contained classrooms increase the experience base of students?

While the most obvious ways to involve students actively are assignments at the board or at their desks, teachers have additional opportunities at their disposal. For example, learning stations can be set up around the classroom, each with specific activities and the directions to guide students through them. Other high-involvement classroom activities are games and simulations. In addition, field trips and assignments in the community provide students opportunities to become fully involved.

Case 4: The Alternative School

Munger Junior High School (now Alcott Alternative Learning Center) was established in 1978 as an alternative for Wichita youth who had experienced considerable frustration in previous learning environments. Some potential students were drug abusers, some were school dropouts, others were family dropouts. All had been discipline problems in school. The staff members for the school were selected because of their special interest in "reluctant learners" and their proven ability to work with them. Each teacher functioned as both teacher and counselor.

The principal and staff decided to administer the locally developed student learning styles survey to determine the learning preferences of the students and to use the information to develop individual learning programs. Many students reported that this was the first time they felt that their own specific needs were being considered. They were very interested in the concept and its outcomes and began to question the teachers regarding their (the teachers') learning styles. As a result, the program was carried one step further to assess the learning styles of the entire staff. Survey results were posted publicly, and students and staff became aware of the various learning styles each represented.

One unexpected additional benefit was the increased communication that occurred as a result of greater awareness of cognitive styles. For example, students who were auditory learners made counseling appointments with staff members who had complementary preferences. When teachers had the opportunity to utilize their own cognitive preferences, they found it easier to work effectively with students. Administration of the learning-styles inventory became a standard procedure for admitting both students and staff members to this alternative junior high school.

Discussion

1. What benefit might there be from a situation where teachers teach students whose learning styles are similar to their own (the teachers') learning styles?
   One possible benefit would be that the teacher might be able to recognize more student problems and limitations. Teachers automatically select methods that they, as learners, find effective.

Case 5: The District-Wide Program

Cognitive-style awareness embraces the concept that both students and instructors are accountable for learning. The Remington district, a small, rural district near Wichita, decided to support the concept by experimenting with learning styles through an expanded application of the process on a district-wide basis. The district took steps to administer the student learning-styles survey to every student in the district.

The initial purpose of the district-wide project represented in this case was to confirm the effectiveness of existing classroom management techniques and teaching strategies. To implement the plan, a Project CITE consultant was scheduled for a series of sessions designed to acquaint the entire professional staff with the concept of learning styles, techniques for administering the specific survey, analysis of the results, and possible teacher-student applications for the classroom.

The survey was then administered to every student in the district. Teachers analyzed the scores of their own students and used them to confirm the various learning groups they had previously established in their classes. To expand the use of survey results further, teachers then met as grade-level committees to develop curriculum goals and instructional processes designed to utilize the styles data available for each student in order to enhance student learning. Where team teaching existed, the results were also used to assign students to team groups that emphasized certain styles.

District-wide use of the learning-styles data was the goal. To date, satisfaction with the process has been high. School officials reported increased student learning, improved self-concepts, and better communication within the district. The district also anticipated that continued improvement in student learning will be evident as students move through a school system in which their learning styles are taken into consideration each year of their education.

Discussion

District-wide implementation of an innovation often increases the success of the innovation by showing that the district supports the change. How might an individual teacher persuade the district office to try a new approach?

First, the teacher needs evidence that the approach is effective. The literature can be used to show the success that other teachers or districts have had with the innovation. Also, the teacher might ask permission to try the innovation at the classroom or department level, collecting test data to show how effective the new approach is compared with the approach currently in use.

ACTIVITIES

1. Because the success of a method that is selected to individualize instruction will depend greatly on the enthusiasm of the teacher who applies it, you are encouraged to select one of the approaches discussed in this chapter—for example, contingency contracts, mastery learning, matching teacher and learner styles, or a type of ability grouping—and further investigate it. Go to the library, research the method, and determine how you would personalize it to fit your own preferences. An alternative would be to use your library's *ERIC System* (or similar reference guide) to discover other approaches to individualizing instruction. Make a list of these

approaches and select one to pursue further, then determine how you
would adjust that approach to fit your own preferences.

2. Make an appointment to visit a school counselor. Ask the counselor to
discuss some students who require special instruction. Do not expect the
counselor to divulge a student's name, but ask for an explanation of how
instruction was altered for that student. Make a list of learning activities
that the counselor found successful.

3. Visit the reading center or a student assistance center on your campus or
at a nearby university or public school. Volunteer your services for as
many hours as you can spare. Keep a record of the techniques you observe in use at that center.

4. Because one of the most common problems teachers face is the need to
teach students with a wide range of abilities simultaneously, you would be
wise to spend a few hours preparing for this task. Visit with several
secondary or middle school teachers and ask them how they teach a heterogeneous class of varying abilities. Make a list of the techniques
they use. Choose one technique and research the literature to learn all you
can about it.

5. Use the Diagnostic Learning Styles model in this chapter to analyze the
prepared learning styles of your classmates. Ask your professor for permission to present the results to the class.

SUGGESTED READINGS

Arlin, M. (1984, Spring). Time, equality, and mastery of learning. *Review of Educational Research, 54,* 71–72.

Ball, A. L. (1982, November). The secrets of learning style: Your child's and your own. *Redbook, 160,* 73–76.

Block, J. R., & Henson, K. T. (1986, Spring). Mastery learning and middle school instruction. *American Middle School Education, 9*(2), 21–29.

Bloom, B. S., Madaus, G. F., & Hastings, J. T. (1981). *Evaluation to improve learning.*
New York: McGraw-Hill.

Bloom, B. S. (1984, May). The search for methods for group instruction as effective as one-
to-one tutoring. *Educational Leadership, 41*(8), 4–18.

Brandt, R. S. (Ed.). (1979, January). Learning styles. *Educational Leadership, 36.*

Brandt, R. S. (Ed.). (1979, November). Mastery learning. *Educational Leadership, 57.*

Brophy, J. (1979). Research on the self-fulfilling prophecy and teacher expectations. *Journal of Educational Psychology, 75,* 631–661.

Brophy, J. (1983). Classroom organization and management. *Elementary School Journal,
83,* 265–285.

Burns, R. B. (1979). Mastery learning: Does it work? *Educational Leadership, 37,* 110–
113.

Calfee, R., & Brown, R. (1979). Grouping students for instruction. National Society for the
Study of Education. Yearbook 78. Pt. 2, 144–148.

Carroll, J. B. (1963). A model of school learning. *Teachers College Record, 64,* 723–733.

Carruthers, S., & Young, A. (1980). Preference of conditions concerning time in learning environments of rural versus city eighth grade students. *Learning Styles Network Newsletter, 1*(2), 1.

Centra, J., & Potter, D. (1980). School and teacher effects: An interrelational model. *Review of Educational Research, 50*, 273–291.

Copenhaver, R. (1979). *The consistency of student learning as students move from English to mathematics.* Doctoral dissertation, Indiana University.

Doyle, W. (1980). *Classroom management.* West Lafayette, Ind.: Kappa Delta Pi.

Dunn, K. (1981). Madison Prep: Alternative to teenage disaster. *Educational Leadership, 39*(5), 386–387.

Dunn, R., Brennan, P., DeBello, T., & Hodges, H. (1984, Winter). Learning style: State of the science. In K. T. Henson (Ed.), *Theory into Practice, 23*, 10–19.

Erikson, E. (1950). *Childhood and society.* New York: Norton.

Friedman, P., & Alley, R. (1984). Learning/teaching styles: Applying principles. *Theory into Practice, 23*(1), 277–281.

Good, T. L., & Brophy, J. (1984). *Looking in classrooms* (3rd ed.). New York: Harper & Row.

Good, T. L., & Stipek, D. J. (1983). Individual differences in the classroom: A psychological perspective. In G. D. Fenstermacher (Ed.), *Individual differences and common curriculum.* Eighty-Second Yearbook of the National Society for the Study of Education, Part I. Chicago: University of Chicago Press.

Guskey, T. R., & Gates, S. L. (1986). Synthesis of research on the effects of mastery learning in elementary and secondary classrooms. *Educational Leadership, 43*(8), 73–80.

Harvey, O. J., Hunt, D. E., & Schroder, H. M. (1963). *Conceptual systems and personality organization.* New York: Wiley.

Henson, K. T. (Ed.). (1984, Winter). Matching learning and teaching styles. *Theory into Practice, 23*.

Hodges, H. (1983). Learning styles: Rx for mathophobia. *Arithmetic Teacher, 30*, 17–20.

Hodges, J. (1982). Madison Prep: Alternatives through learning styles. In *Student Learning Styles and Brain Behavior,* pp. 28–32. Reston, Va.: National Association of Secondary School Principals.

Hyman, J. S., & Cohen, A. (1979). Learning for mastery: Ten conclusions after fifteen years and 3,000 schools. *Educational Leadership, 37*, 104–109.

Hyman, R. T., & Rosoff, B. (1984, Winter). Matching learning and theory styles: The jug and what's in it. In K. T. Henson (Ed.), Matching learning and teaching styles. *Theory into Practice, 23*, 35–43.

Johnson, D., & Johnson, R. (1975). *Learning together and alone.* Englewood Cliffs, N.J.: Prentice-Hall.

Jones, V. (1971). *The influence of teacher-student introversion achievement, and similarity on teacher-student dyadic classroom interactions.* Doctoral dissertation, University of Texas at Austin.

Julik, J. A. (1981, April). *The effect of ability grouping on secondary school students.* Paper presented at the American Educational Research Association, Los Angeles.

Keefe, J. W. (1979). *School applications of the learning style concept: Student learning styles,* pp. 123–132. Reston, Va.: National Association of Secondary School Principals.

Lynch, P. K. (1981). *An analysis of the relationships among academic achievement, attendance, and the individual learning style time preference of eleventh and twelfth grade students identified as initial or chronic truants in a suburban New York school district.* Doctoral dissertation, St. John's University.

McDonald, C. (1972). *The influence of pupil liking the teacher, pupil perception of being liked, and pupil socioeconomic states on classroom behavior.* Doctoral dissertation, University of Texas at Austin.

National Association for Secondary School Principals (1982). *Student learning styles and brain behavior.* Reston, Va.: National Association for Secondary School Principals.

Piaget, J. (1952). *The origins of intelligence in children.* New York: International University Press.

Pizzo, J. (1981). *An investigation of the relationships between selected acoustic environments and sound, an element of learning style, as they affect sixth grade students' reading achievement and attitudes.* Doctoral dissertation, St. John's University.

Sharon, S. (1980). Cooperative learning in small groups: Recent methods and effects on achievement attitudes and ethnic relations. *Review of Educational Research, 50,* 241–271.

Shavelson, R. J. (1983). Review of research on teachers' pedagogical judgments, plans, and decisions. *Elementary School Journal, 83,* 392–414.

Shea, T. C. (1983). *An investigation of the relationship between preferences for the learning style element of design, selected instructional environments, and reading test achievement of ninth grade students to improve administrative determinations concerning effective educational facilities.* Doctoral dissertation, St. John's University.

Slavin, R. (1980). Cooperative learning. *Review of Educational Research, 50,* 503–527.

Stinnett, T., & Henson, K. T. (1982). *America's public schools in transition: Future trends and issues,* Chapter 16, The Human Equation and School Reform. New York: Teachers and College Press.

Thelan, H. (1960). *Education and the Human Quest.* New York: Harper & Row.

C H A P T E R *8*

Teaching Students with Special Needs

Objectives

- Name the main five categories of handicapped students.
- Name the three factors that should always be considered when working with handicapped students.
- List three minimum requirements of all individualized educational programs as set forth by Public Law 94-142.
- Give two definitions of "gifted students."
- Explain why the length of time a specific handicap has existed is important.
- List three characteristics of mildly retarded students.
- Name several rights that Public Law 94-142 gives to handicapped students and their parents.
- Develop an individualized educational program for a hypothetical handicapped student.

PRETEST

	Agree	Disagree	Uncertain
1. Most needs of handicapped students can best be met in an environment where the student is with others who have similar handicaps.	_____	_____	_____
2. Federal law requires that individualized programs be offered to each handicapped student.	_____	_____	_____
3. The length of time a student has had a handicap is irrelevant, because the handicap itself is what must be worked with.	_____	_____	_____
4. People who are not handicapped tend to overestimate the mental abilities of physically handicapped students.	_____	_____	_____
5. Except for certain physical or mental limitations, handicapped students behave no differently from nonhandicapped students.	_____	_____	_____
6. Emotionally disturbed students tend to be either hostile or apathetic.	_____	_____	_____
7. Some traumatic experiences are actually good for emotionally disturbed students.	_____	_____	_____
8. The teacher of students with a sensory handicap should help them learn to ignore their handicaps.	_____	_____	_____
9. Students who have learning disabilities are usually below average in mental ability.	_____	_____	_____
10. Mainstreaming is nothing more than moving handicapped students from special classes back into the regular classroom.	_____	_____	_____
11. The mainstreaming movement will probably remove the need for special-education teachers.	_____	_____	_____

Middle-Level Message

Handicaps among students vary in degree, and the teacher's ability to recognize the severity of a handicap is a critical factor in coping with the handicap. An equally important factor is the ability to recognize and identify developing stages of handicaps. Some handicaps, such as social adjustment problems and emotional problems, develop over a period of years.

Most children are amazingly resilient. They are often able to suppress their pain so well that even their peers do not recognize it. Unfortunately, such damage can be cumulative and continue to build until something snaps. More often than not this occurs near puberty. For that reason, this age-group has the highest rate of suicide and other serious crimes of any age-group.

You should learn all you can from this chapter and from other sources about identifying troubled students. But your responsibility does not stop there. You must learn how to deal with students who have mild adjustment problems, and you must learn how to refer the more severely troubled students to specialists for the help you cannot provide.

Secondary and middle schools should enable all students to develop to their maximum potential. Without a positive attitude toward self, teachers, peers, and school itself, the student cannot reach that potential. But some students have special needs that require additional teacher support to help them realize and develop their potentials.

This chapter covers several categories of "special" students, ranging from several types of handicapped learners to the gifted and talented. As you read, remember that it is good practice to involve all students in planning their programs. Too often educators believe that their role is to do something to the students or for the students rather than to do something *with* them. As Ungerleider (1986) says, "Their parents brought them in for fixin', but they didn't want to be fixed. . . . [But] if we join with them, teach them what they want to know, and give them reasons for learning what they need to know, they will truly learn [what we want them to learn]."

WHAT IS SPECIAL EDUCATION?

Special education is that part of the education process that attempts to meet the needs of youngsters who differ from average children in that, to develop to their maximum potential, they require modification of regularly accepted school practices. The problem is not so much that the student is different but that the educational process needs to be different. "But," you may say, "Isn't this the job of specialists who have been trained to work with these students?" The answer is yes, there are specialists whose training enables them to work with these students, but the classroom teacher is the one who helps them move into the mainstream.

Many contemporary educators believe that the mainstreaming approach to working with handicapped children is the best approach because—

1. Every child has a right to an equal education opportunity, even at the expense of having different education experiences.
2. For most exceptional children, integration, not segregation, is needed.
3. Labeling is an administrative crutch that says nothing about a student's assets and desires to be accepted as a normal person.

For many years American society has recognized that a free or public education is a right of all citizens. While the methods of providing such education are left up to each state, federal legislation does guarantee the right. Because some states have been too casual about providing education for handicapped youngsters, federal legislation now specifies exactly what services must be provided and supplies the funds needed to run these programs. It is essential that you become familiar with some of the more important laws that guarantee quality education for your handicapped students. Professional journals can keep you alerted to new legislation as it occurs.

PUBLIC LAW 94-142

The greatest single legislative action on behalf of handicapped students is Public Law 94-142 (the Education for All Handicapped Children Act, enacted in 1977). This law requires that each state provide special education services for its handicapped students at public expense and under public supervision and direction. These special services must meet state education agency standards; include an appropriate preschool, elementary, and secondary school education; and be provided in conformity with the individualized education program. The law required that by September 1, 1978, all students aged 3 to 19 (later extended to 21) were to be served, including receiving adequate classroom instruction. But the impact of this law on schools continues to grow.

Public Law 94-142 is a complicated law. Nowhere in its many pages does it mention "mainstreaming." Instead it uses the words "least restrictive environment," which does allow for special students to be removed from regular classes if those students are restricted when placed in special classrooms. The thrust of the law seems to be to keep handicapped students in the classroom with nonhandicapped students, as opposed to grouping handicapped students together for instruction. Although the term *mainstreaming* is not used, Public Law 94-142 requires the practice.

The findings that led to enactment of Public Law 94-142 may help us understand the need for this legislation:

1. There are more than 8 million handicapped children in the United States today.
2. The educational needs of handicapped children are not being fully met.

3. More than half the handicapped children do not receive appropriate educational services.

4. One million handicapped children are excluded entirely from the public school system.

5. There are many in regular programs whose handicaps are undetected.

6. Because public school systems lack adequate services, families must find other services at their own expense.

7. With appropriate funding, state and local educational agencies have the knowledge and the methods to provide effective special education and related services.

8. State and local educational agencies have this responsibility, but they have inadequate financial resources.

9. It is in the national interest to help state and local educational agencies provide programs to meet the educational needs of handicapped children *in order to assure equal protection of the law.*

One major provision of this law is that before placement or denial of placement in educational programs, students and their parents must be offered (1) notice of the proposed action, (2) the right to a hearing prior to final action, (3) the right to counsel at that hearing, (4) the right to present evidence, (5) the right to full access to relevant school records, (6) the right to compel attendance of and to confront and cross-examine officials or employees who might have evidence of the basis for the proposed action, (7) the right to an independent evaluation, (8) the right to have the hearing open or closed to the public at the parent's option, and (9) the right to an impartial hearing officer. The hearings are to be held at a place and time convenient to the parents. In other words, students and their parents have a right to question the appropriateness of individual educational plans or programs developed for them.

As a teacher, you will probably be directly involved in complying with the guidelines set forth in Public Law 94-142. This will include developing a program plan each year to show how your school is meeting the requirements. If your school fails to meet these requirements, it will lose its federal funding. One of your responsibilities as a teacher is to help handicapped students get the support to which they are entitled.

MEETING SPECIAL NEEDS
IN THE REGULAR CLASSROOM

Regular classroom teachers have voiced strong concerns about having handicapped students in their classes. One reason for these concerns is the additional responsibilities this law places on classroom teachers. (These responsibilities will be discussed later in the chapter.) But basic to the worries and frustrations that Public Law 94-142 and the resultant mainstreaming have caused is teachers' lack of knowledge about their new role and responsibilities. Put simply, most teachers do not think they are adequately prepared to meet this challenge. Indeed, many insist that their preparatory programs contained little or no information about teaching handicapped students.

Morbeck (1980) investigated this problem and reported that teachers do need in-service education to prepare them for mainstreaming. Studies of the effects of in-service programs designed to inform teachers of their new responsibilities have reported positive results—in-service programs are an effective means of preparing teachers for their responsibilities with handicapped students (Hurtado-Portillo, 1980; Koci, 1980; Althoff, 1981). However, some in-service programs have failed to improve teacher attitudes toward mainstreaming (Doubrave-Harris, 1982). Sometimes additional contact with mainstreamed students improves teachers' attitudes toward handicapped students (Marston & Leslie, 1983), but in other instances additional contact with handicapped students failed to improve teachers' attitudes (McRainey, 1981; Enoch, 1979). Another factor affecting teachers' attitudes toward mainstreaming is the level of support services available to the teachers (Pietroski, 1979).

The most important thing for pre-service teachers to know is that the more information about mainstreaming teachers accumulate before actually becoming involved in the process, the more positive their attitude about mainstreaming will be (Pietroski, 1979). Accordingly, pre-service teachers should seek out opportunities to learn more about handicapped students and about the new roles of regular teachers who have one or more handicapped students in their classrooms. The remainder of this chapter is a good beginning point. The "Activities" section at the end of the chapter will facilitate continuing this pursuit.

CATEGORIZING HANDICAPPED STUDENTS*

We can categorize all handicapped students by type of impairment—physical, mental, emotional, sensory, and neurological—but we could not assign a group of students to these subgroups without noticing much overlap. It is better to view the individual differences as lying on a continuum grouped around a norm. Furthermore, we must keep in mind the *degree of involvement* (mild, moderate, or severe), the *length of time* the student has had the condition, and the *stability of the condition*.

In the following sections, categories of handicaps will be discussed. As you read about each, remember that all the above criteria (degree of involvement, length of time the student has had the condition, and stability of the condition) should be considered when trying to decide how to serve these students best.

---

* Credit is given to Ms. Patricia Haensly and the Department of Educational Psychology at Texas A&M University for the module on preparing teachers to teach the handicapped upon which much of this section is based.

The Physically Impaired

Orthopedically handicapped persons have a crippling impairment that interferes with the normal function of the bones, joints, or muscles, including internal organs and systemic malfunctions. These impairments range from congenital conditions and deformities—such as dwarfism, limb absence, heart defects, hemophilia, cerebral palsy, epilepsy, and spina bifida—to traumatic conditions, such as amputations or burns.

Students with physical impairments may be limited in mobility and in the ability to use certain materials or equipment and may lack motor control. As is true of most categories, the degree of impairment among orthopedically handicapped students varies greatly. If the cause was congenital (a birth defect), as with cerebral palsy, the student may not have had experiences needed for intellectual growth and may now be suffering from secondary handicaps, such as mental retardation. Visual and speech defects are common; poor facial muscle control may cause drooling, giving the false impression of mental retardation. Thus, each handicapped student must be viewed and treated as an individual.

The teacher should be careful to avoid the common tendency of nonhandicapped people to underestimate the abilities of orthopedically handicapped students, because these students are often able to be successful with extremely complicated tasks. Their ability to conceptualize, or ''know how'' to do things, yet not be able to do them because of physical handicaps may lead to frustration on their part. Samuel Kirk (1972) lists behaviors that indicate frustration in orthopedically handicapped students:

1. Verbal aggressiveness
2. Blaming other people
3. Repressing desires
4. Withdrawing into fantasy
5. Degrading the original goals
6. Acting less mature
7. Compensation by shifting to different interests

All students display these behaviors at times, but probably to a lesser degree because their successes minimize their frustrations. The teacher can reduce frustrations in orthopedically handicapped students by providing a climate of success and by accepting and including them in the social activities of the school. Teacher pity, overprotection, and ignoring may perpetuate their condition. These students must become involved if they are to learn to function and become independent. Above all else, the teacher must remember that physical impairment does not automatically mean lowered mental functioning.

The Mentally Retarded

Mentally retarded students have learning rates and potentials that are considerably lower than the average for other students. Depending on the degree of retardation, there are four classifications of mental retardation, based on intelligence test scores. (The score ranges may vary slightly from state to state.)

Mild	55–59
Moderate	40–54
Severe	25–39
Profound	24 and below

Mildly retarded students may appear similar to normal classmates in height and weight, but closer observation reveals that they are lacking in strength, speed, and coordination. They also tend to have more general health problems.

Students who are mentally retarded may experience frustration, especially when they have been expected to function at their chronological age with materials and methods geared above their ability. They often have short attention spans and are unable to concentrate. Antisocial or impersonal behavior can also be attributed to expectations of teachers and others that they perform beyond their abilities.

The Trainable Retarded

Trainable retarded students respond slowly to education and training because their intellectual development is only 25 to 50 percent of normal, yet many can be trained for jobs that require single skills under adequate supervision.

Retarded mental development may include slow maturation of intellectual functions needed for schoolwork. Because the retarded may be significantly low in memory skills, ability to generalize, language skills, conceptual and perceptual abilities, and creative abilities, they should be given tasks that are simple, brief, relevant, sequential, and designed for success.

The Emotionally Disturbed

The emotionally disturbed child is most simply perceived as one who is confused or bewildered. He does not understand his own social stresses, and he feels unaccepted in his efforts to resolve them (Love, 1974). "Aha," you say, "so that is the category used to describe the troublemakers." Often this is true. The emotionally disturbed do tend to be either hostile or apathetic. Seriously emotionally disturbed students require psychological services. Less-seriously or socially maladjusted students do not.

Most students who exhibit apathy and hostility should not be classified as emotionally disturbed. The key element is how frequently they display such behavior. For example, the student who occasionally disrupts or hits a classmate is probably not disturbed, but the one who disrupts a lesson or bothers others several times during the hour may be emotionally disturbed. At the middle and secondary levels, emotionally disturbed students often show oversensitivity to criticism and unusual anxiety because of a weak self-concept. Some may show extreme depression. Again, it is the frequency, duration, and intensity of the behavior that indicate the seriousness of the condition.

In dealing with emotionally disturbed students, the teacher is responsible for arranging opportunities for them to have successful experiences. The teacher must also use a considerable amount of reinforcement and avoid creating a highly threatening climate in the classroom, such as overemphasizing the importance of examinations. Students who appear unusually aggressive or timid should not be forced to speak in front of classmates. The classroom should also be free of threat, ridicule, and other abuses by classmates.

The Sensory Deprived

Students who are handicapped visually and those who have hearing impairments are among the sensory deprived. The visually handicapped category includes the partially sighted and the blind, while the hearing impairment category includes the deaf and the hard of hearing.

Visually handicapped students vary tremendously in the degrees to which they are handicapped; only about 10 percent of the legally blind are actually totally blind. Therefore, the first thing to consider when working with visually handicapped students is important—the degree of the handicap. Another thing to consider—the length of time the student has had the handicap—is also important. Those whose problems have been lifelong will need help developing concepts of space and form, whereas those whose blindness is recent will need help adjusting to their handicap.

Students who have hearing problems range from those who can hear and understand speech with difficulty, using such supports as hearing aids, to the deaf, who at most are able to distinguish only amplified sounds. In considering the extent of the hearing handicap, the teacher should try to determine how much and how clearly the student can hear. Again, how long the student has had the handicap is extremely important, because whether it occurred before or after speech and language comprehension developed makes a difference. The major problem of students who have been deaf since birth is not that they are deaf but that they are unable to develop speech and language comprehension through hearing.

When working with visually and hearing handicapped students, begin by providing psychological support. You can do this by accepting the students in their condition and believing in their ability to adjust to their handicap and to become productive individuals. Indeed students with sensory handicaps can learn to do extremely complicated tasks. The teacher's expression of confidence in the student leads to increased self-confidence.

The teacher is responsible for creating this climate of acceptance among the student's peers. Because both blind students and deaf students are unable to pick up on all the stimuli that provide cues as to how and when people respond, their timing may be off or they may not respond at all. Peers who are sensitive to these limitations may interpret their response (or absence of response) as unfriendly or antisocial. The limited vocabulary of handicapped students may further limit their response. Above all else, do not show pity. On the contrary, the teacher should provide a positive climate that focuses on the abilities and potentials of these students, rather than on their limitations.

The Learning Disabled

Students who are learning disabled have normal intelligence but are unable to process information so that learning can take place. In other words, their problem has to do with a dysfunction and/or emotional disturbance, as opposed to mental retardation or sensory deprivation. Such students may be awkward, hyperkinetic, and impulsive; a few may appear slow. Because most school programs are not designed to accommodate this type of behavior, these students are frequently viewed as having behavior problems. While students with learning disabilities tend to be aggressive, irritable, and highly emotional, some may be even-tempered and cooperative. They may have quick changes of emotional behavior, from high-tempered to remorseful. They may even feel panic in what others see as only mildly stressful situations.

The basis of the problem with learning-disabled students can lie in the psychomotor, visual, or auditory domain. Students who have psychomotor disabilities are likely to be in poor physical condition or may frequently bump into things, for example. Their written assignments can also give clues—handwriting may be unusually large or small and crammed into one corner of the paper.

If the basis of the student's problem is visual, the teacher may notice that the student cannot follow visual directions, may tend to forget things seen, and may be easily distracted by surrounding activities. Furthermore, students may tend to move their eyes excessively or inappropriately. Teachers can recognize auditory disabilities when students fail to follow oral directions, forget directions, are easily distracted by noise, and confuse similar sounds.

THE INDIVIDUALIZED EDUCATIONAL PROGRAM

The current mode of working with handicapped students is to move them from groups consisting of only handicapped students and to put them back into the regular classroom, but this alone does not mean that their special needs will be met. To make certain that the needs of each student are met—and the special needs of each are different from those of others who may share a general problem—Public Law 94-142 requires that a specific individualized program be provided for each handicapped student from the age of 3 to age 21. This approach, called Individualized Educational Programming, calls for a written statement for each handicapped child that identifies the particular needs of that child and describes how those needs are being met.

There must be a special meeting to develop the program for each handicapped student. Attending this meeting will be the representative of the local education authority who will be assigned to supervise the student's program, and the student's teacher(s) and parents. When appropriate, the student will attend the meeting too. In effect, you the teacher will be held responsible for seeing that the services planned are actually rendered. Furthermore, you will be required to see that the program of each handicapped student in your class will be constantly evaluated. The federal law requires that there be at least one progress review each year, and the state may require more. If a parent does not request the review, you, the teacher, should.

The teacher of a handicapped middle school or high school student should try to establish good communications and a good working relationship with the student and parents. Because many handicapped students of this age are capable of participating in the development of their own program, you should try to create a team spirit. By uniting your efforts, you, the student, and the parents can provide a program that is superior to one planned only by you. During conferences with parents, teachers, should avoid using educational jargon. As McNamara (1986, p. 309 explains, "Being clear, precise and up-front with parents will pay high dividends in [your] ability to assist in carrying out the educational plan."

Each individualized educational plan (IEP) must contain, as a minimum, these statements and projections:

1. The child's present level of educational performance.
2. Annual goals and short-term instructional goals.
3. The specific educational services to be provided—by whom, when, and for how long.
4. The extent to which the child will be able to participate in regular educational programs.
5. Appropriate, objective criteria for evaluation, and a schedule for determining (on at least an annual basis) whether instructional objectives are being achieved.
6. The program's beginning and ending dates.
7. A statement of the parents' roles in relation to the plan.
8. Changes that will be needed in the school situation (staffing, in-service education, etc.).

Any member of the planning team, including the student, can make the initial draft of the IEP. The rest of the team can accept the plan, revise it, or develop another plan they feel would be more useful for teachers and other school personnel.

The following is an example of an individualized educational plan. Although each program must include the preceding eight features, no two programs need be or should be exactly alike. Therefore, you should view this not as a model of an ideal program but as what one particular program might look like. The sample forms below were developed by the staff of the Wasioja Area Special Education Cooperative in Minnesota. They include forms for *requesting* an individual educational assessment, for *reporting* assessment findings, and for *recording* an Individual Education Program.

SAMPLE INDIVIDUALIZED EDUCATIONAL PROGRAM*

REQUEST FOR INDIVIDUAL EDUCATIONAL ASSESSMENT/RE-ASSESSMENT FORM

Student's Name: *Sebastian Wynott*   Age: *10-7*   Grade: *5*
School Building: *Sleepy Hollow Elementary*
Date of Conference: *3/15/87*   Teacher/Referrer: *Ms. Portia Streight*

---

* Sample IEP from Maynard C. Reynolds and Jack W. Birch in *Teaching Exceptional Children in All America's Schools* (Reston, Va.: Council for Exceptional Children, 1977), pp. 164–171.

Parent/s Name: *Olga & Ole Wynott*   Address: *114½ Plumb Ave.*

Phone: *CU2-0000*

Rationale For Assessment: *Sebbie has significant difficulty with academics and cannot attend to a task for any length of time. He cannot read any of the classroom material. What can be expected of him and should he be in a special program?*

Pre-assessment/Re-assessment Staffing Team Members (parents, etc.): *Mr. & Mrs. Ole Wynott (parents), Mr. Dilly Dillingham (principal), Ms. Portia Streight (5th grade teacher), Ms. Aggie Knolage (SLBP teacher).*

Objectives To Be Addressed (code to assessment team members):
1. *To determine his capability to learn and the most appropriate styles and modalities to be used in learning processes for him.*
2. *To determine his levels of reading in all components: comprehension, attack skills, etc.*
3. *To determine his levels of academic success in areas other than reading: math, science, spelling, etc.*
4. *To determine his levels of functioning in all areas of perceptual development.*

Assessment Team Members (code responsibility/objectives, when, where to be accomplished: *Ms. Wilma Reedit, Remedial Reading Teacher (2,3)—Dr. Yen, Optometrist (4).*
Mr. Herkimer Humperdinck, Psychologist (1,4)
Ms. Portia Streight, 5th Grade Teacher (1,2,3)
Ms. Aggie Knolage, SLBP Teacher (1,2,3,4)
☐ Additional Data on Attached Sheet.

Assessment: Summarization/Verification Date: *3/30/87*

I (we) consent to the individual educational assessment described above, in order to determine the educational needs of my (our) child.

Signature _____ Mr. and Mrs. Ole Wynott _____ Date *3/15/87*
(Parent/s-student)

I (we) do not consent to the individual educational assessment described above, in order to determine the educational needs of my (our) child.

Signature _____ Date _____
(Parent/s-student)

If the Parent/s-Student Reject the Assessment, State the Reasons and an Acceptable Alternative:

The following RIGHTS and procedures MUST be reviewed prior to the conducting of the individual educational assessment:

Parent's-Student's rights to obtain an independent educational assessment records, information, and results.

Parent's-Student's rights to obtain an independent educational assessment at their own expense.

That Parent's-Student may request assistance in locating the names, addresses, etc., and fee structures of resources that they may go to for an independent educational assessment.

That the student's educational status will not change unless the parent/s have signed the individual educational plan.

That a "conciliation conference" may be requested if the parent/s-student refuse to permit the assessment.

That an "impartial hearing" may be requested if mutual agreement is not reached after the conciliation conference.

Any Objection Should Be Sent To: _____
(Administrator)

Any Objection Must Be Received By: _____
(date)

Address Objection Is To Be Sent To: _____

_____

Date Received: _____
Report Completed By: *Miss Aggie Knolage, Case Facilitator*

Copy of Report To Parent/Student: *3/15/87* Parent/Student: _____O.W._____
(date received) (initialed)

Case Management Log Updated: *3/15/87* Update By: _____Aggie Knolage_____
(name)

INDIVIDUAL EDUCATION ASSESSMENT REPORT

Student's Name: *Sebastian Wynott*
Assessment By: *Miss Aggie Knolage*   *SLBP Teacher*
(name)   (position)
School: *Sleepy Hollow Elementary*   Phone: *CU4-0002*
Date/s Assessment Conducted: *3/16, 18, 20/87*
Specific Objectives Addressed By Specialist:
All (1 thru 4): 1-capability to learn and styles/modalities of learning; 2-reading levels; 3-other academic success; 4-perceptual development.

RESULTS:

a. Indicate Assessment Setting and Materials Used:
   Setting: Sleepy Hollow Elem. School—SLBP room and classroom. Instruments used: Informal observations and tests in classroom and resource room; Detroit Test of Learning Aptitude; Peabody Individual Achievement Test; Key Math Diagnostic Arithmetic Test; Durrell Analysis of Reading Difficulty.

b. Specific Results (indicate by number from "Specific Objectives To Be Addressed")
   1. *Sebbie will need considerable help throughout all learning, emphasis on a tactile kinesthetic approach should be utilized both in the regular classroom and the resource room. Based on informal assessment Sebbie appears to be a very bright child that certainly has the capability to learn.*
   2. *Based on the PIAT, the Durrell, and informal assessment, Sebbie is functioning approximately one year below grade placement. Major areas of difficulty were in listening comprehension, work recognition and analysis, hearing sounds in words, and phonic spelling of words.*
   3. *Based on the PIAT, Key Math, and informal assessment, Sebbie is functioning approximately one year below grade placement in spelling, and approximately five*

months below in math. No attempt was made to measure other areas of academic achievement.

    4. *Based on the Detroit and informal assessment, Sebbie is noted to be having significant difficulty in areas of auditory discrimination and closure.*

c. Additional Comments and/or Recommendations For Additional Assessment(s)/Specialist(s) (specify objectives to be addressed).
Sebbie is very interested in athletics and finds a great deal of success in it, even though he is small. He should be encouraged to participate in any extra-curricular activities of the nature as well as at recess.
Additional assessment may be needed as to physiological and neurological factors.

d. Statement of Constraints On Performance Or On Special Learning Conditions.
Sebbie has difficulty listening and needs to have concrete visual clues presented to him at the same time. He needs concrete, specific directions and repetition of instructions within short time frames. Sebbie works best through direct involvement with tactile/kinesthetic approach.

e. Recommended Application Of Results In Performance Statements.
Sebbie should receive approximately one-third of his educational program from the resource programs. Provisions need to be made between the regular classroom and the resource rooms so that when Sebbie needs a break from the classroom he can go to the resource rooms to do his work. (This should not become a daily ongoing activity.) Sebbie should receive a special reading program provided by the remedial reading teacher dealing with specific skills in phonics and other word attack skills; listening skills, etc. He should be provided services by the SLBP program dealing with math, auditory skills, and attention. Within the classroom expectations should be matched with supplementary services provided by the resource programs. Emphasis should be placed on a tactile/kinesthetic approach to learning. Verbal instructions should be short, to the point and reinforced with visual clues. Parents should be incorporated into the educational plan to help reinforce newly learned skills. This should not be a laborious task.

    ☐ Additional Data On Attached Sheet.

Signature: _____*Aggie Knolage*_____ Date: _____*3/22/87*_____
               (specialist)   (completed)

Copy of Report To Parent/Student: *3/30/87*   Parent/Student _____*O.W.*_____
                                (date received)   (initialed)

Case Management Log Updated: *3/30/87* Update By: _____*Aggie Knolage*_____
                                (date)   (name)

INDIVIDUAL EDUCATIONAL ASSESSMENT/VERIFICATION STAFFING SUMMARY REPORT

Student's Name: *Sebastian Wynott*

Assessment Team Members (name, position, phone, address):
Ms. Wilma Reedit—Remedial Reading Teacher, CU4-0002, Sleepy Hollow Elem.
Ms. Aggie Knolage—SLBP Teacher, CU4-0002, Sleepy Hollow Elem.
Mr. Herkimer Humperdinck—Psychologist, CU2-4000, Sleepy Hollow Admin. Office

Ms. Portia Streight—5th Grade Teacher, CU4-0002, Sleepy Hollow Elem.
Dr. Yen—Optometrist—CU2-4002, Medical Center of Sleepy Hollow
Date Of Meeting: *3/30/87*

Results—Specific Objectives (INDIVIDUAL ASSESSMENT REPORTS MUST
BE ATTACHED)

1. *Sebbie is above average in intellectual functioning and will be functioning academically at grade level within two years as measured by group standardized achievement tests. Learning modalities that are not of a tactile/kinesthetic nature are extremely difficult for him. Visual clues should be used to reinforce any verbal directions.*

2. *Sebbie will make a minimum of at least three months growth by the end of the school year (June 10) in reading. Growth shall be measured based on pre-post assessment conducted by the remedial reading teacher. A special summer program in reading shall be developed and implemented for him, at the end of which he will have made an additional three months gain based on pre-post assessment conducted by the remedial reading teacher. At the conclusion of the summer program he will no longer be in need of special instruction in phonics and other word attack skills, as measured by sampling his oral reading and other appropriate assessment.*

3. *By the end of the year Sebbie will be completing his spelling tests each week, correctly spelling at least 14 of 20 words. Special help will be provided by his 5th grade teacher and reinforced by exercises at home with his parents. Through an individualized math program, Sebbie will be able to demonstrate three months growth in math by the end of the school year, which will be measured by the SLBP teacher with the Key Math Test. The parents will be given supplementary math materials to work with Sebbie during the summer to insure maintenance of the skills that he has gained prior to summer break. (Practice time will not interfere with his summer recreational activities.)*

4. *Sebbie will be able to demonstrate four months growth on the ITPA in auditory skill development by the end of the school year, after receiving individualized instruction from the SLBP teacher.*

5. *By the end of the school year, Sebbie will not be leaving his seat without prior permission. After that time he will be held accountable to a plan that has been agreed to by himself and his teacher/s.*

☐ Additional Summarization Data On Attached Sheet:

Report Completed By: *Aggie Knolage, Case Facilitator*

Copy Of Report To Parent/Student: *3/30/87*   Parent/Student: _____ O.W. _____
                                    (date received)   (initialed)

Case Management Log Updated: *3/30/87*   Update By: *Aggie Knolage*
                              (date received)   (name)

Additional Comments: *The parents are very concerned that no matter what plan is developed that it be carried out and not forgotten about. They have requested that the providers of the program meet with them on at least a monthly basis to review progress and to re-address what they can do to help. Concentration of academics shall be on reading, math, and spelling.*

INDIVIDUAL EDUCATION PLAN

Student's Name: *Sebastian Wynott*   Date Completed: *3/30/87*
Assessment Team Members (Name, position, phone, address):
Ms. Wilma Reedit—Remedial Reading Teacher, CU4-0002, Sleepy Hollow Elem.
Ms. Aggie Knolage—SLBP Teacher, CU4-0002, Sleepy Hollow Elem.
Mr. Herkimer Humperdinck—Psychologist, CU2-4000, Sleepy Hollow Admin. Office
Ms. Portia Streight—5th Grade Teacher, CU4-0002, Sleepy Hollow Elem.
Dr. Yen—Optometrist, CU2-4002, Medical Center of Sleepy Hollow

Description Of Needs: *Sebbie has a prolonged history of poor academic achievement: difficulty with auditory discrimination and closure, reading and spelling levels, year below grade placement, doesn't complete assignments, and can't seem to sit still in classroom.*

Learning Style/Modality: *Sebbie learns best with concrete materials and a tactile/kinesthetic approach. Verbal instructions should be in short time frames and reinforced with visual clues; it may be necessary to repeat several times.*

Measurable Physical Constraints: *Auditory discrimination and closure appears to be the basis of the majority of Sebbie's problems.*

Statement Of Specific Type Of Service Needed: *Sebbie will need special supplementary instruction in reading which shall be supplied by the remedial reading teacher (a summer program shall be supplied). He will receive special help from his regular teacher in the area of spelling and completion of appropriate assignments. The SLBP teacher will supply special help to Sebbie in the areas of math and auditory discrimination and closure. A joint program will be worked out by his classroom teacher, the remedial reading teacher and the SLBP teacher dealing with his staying in his seat, etc.*

Annual Goals: *Sebbie will be able to demonstrate the following gains within 12 months.*
1. No problem with being out of his seat without prior permission.
2. In reading a 12 month gain in functional level.
3. In math to be functioning within 2 months of grade level.
4. In spelling to be within 4 months of grade level.
5. In auditory development to be within 4 months of his age level.

Short Term Objectives With Criteria For Attainment (first 3 months):
1. By June 10, Sebbie will not leave his seat more than twice per day without prior permission of the teacher. The teacher will keep appropriate charts of his behavior.
2. By June 10, after receiving remedial reading instruction, Sebbie will demonstrate at least a 3 month growth in reading level based on pre-post assessment as measured by the remedial reading teacher.
3. By June 10, Sebbie will be able to demonstrate at least a 3 month growth in math skills as measured by pre-post assessment on the Key Math Test. The SLBP teacher will be responsible for carrying out the supplementary services in math.
4. By June 10, Sebbie will consistently complete his spelling tests and spell correctly at least 14 of 20 words on each weekly test. His regular classroom teacher shall be responsible for supplying supplementary instruction in the area of spelling.
5. By June 10, Sebbie will demonstrate a minimum of 4 months growth based on pre-post assessment on the ITPA, after having received special help from the SLBP teacher.

Long-Term Objectives With Criteria For Attainment (beyond 3 months for school year): *Objectives 1, 4, and 5 will be further addressed in the new educational plan that will be developed in Sept.*

2. *By Sept. 1, after receiving special reading instruction throughout the summer, Sebbie will demonstrate a 6 month gain (from this date 3/30/87 in reading as measured by pre-post assessment administered by the remedial reading teacher.*
3. *By Sept. 1, Sebbie will demonstrate that he has maintained the 3 months growth that he had achieved by June 1, through a maintenance program carried out by his parents during the summer. This level of achievement shall be demonstrated by pre-post assessment on the Key Math Test.*

Special Instructional Materials/Supplies/Equipment:
None—

Other Specific Modifications: *Approximately one-third of his individual educational plan shall be carried out in the resource rooms. A special program in reading will be carried out during the summer. The parents will be given special materials to use during the summer to insure that Sebbie maintains his math skills.*

Specify Means Of Coordination With Other Programs (regular classroom, etc.): *SLBP remedial reading and regular classroom teachers will meet at least weekly to review progress on the instructional objectives and to further coordinate activities. Each specialist will spend at least 20 minutes per week in the regular classroom providing assistance in Sebbie's program. Monthly meetings will be held with the parents.*

Personnel Responsible For Providing Service—Include Telephone Numbers, Addresses, etc. (regular classroom teacher, etc.):
Ms. Aggie Knolage—SLBP Teacher, CU4-0002, Sleepy Hollow Elem.
Ms. Wilma Reedit—Remedial Reading Teacher, CU4-0002, Sleepy Hollow Elem.
Ms. Portia Streight—5th Grade Teacher, CU4-0002, Sleepy Hollow Elem.

Location Of Program To Carry Out Plan: *Sleepy Hollow Elem. School—regular classroom and resource rooms.*

Describe Transportation Plan If Needed: *None*

Program Will Begin: *4/1/87* Number Of Days Per Week/Month/Year: *5 days/week; 20 days/month; for the remainder of the year—48 days.*

Daily Duration Of Plan: *2 hrs. 20 minutes per day*

Method And Frequency Of Initial And Periodic Reviews (dates, etc.):
Assessment Team Members—Initial Review—6/9/87
Ongoing monitoring of program with parents and teachers—at least monthly.

Description of Integrated Educational Activities (must be included when the student's primary placement is in special education):
Not pertinent

I (we) do not consent to the individual educational plan described above.

Signature: _____Mr. and Mrs. Ole Wynott_____   Date: *3/30/87*
                          (Parent/s-student)

I (we) do not consent to the Individual educational plan described above.

Signature: _____   Date: _____
                          (Parent/s-student)

If The Parent/s-Student Reject The Individual Educational Plan, State the Reason And An Acceptable Alternative:

Report Completed By: *Aggie Knolage, Case Facilitator*

Copy Of Report To Parent/Student: *3/30/87*   Parent/Student: _____O.W._____
                                  (date received)   (initialed)

Case Management Log Updated: *3/30/87* Updated By: *Aggie Knolage*
                              (date)   (name)

    If the responsibility for meeting the requirements and filling out all the forms seems difficult or strange to you, as a beginning teacher, you will find the following comforting. First, these requirements are equally strange to most experienced teachers, who have seldom if ever been required to keep any type of individualized instruction plan for any students. Second, remember that the purpose of the plan is to assure help for the student; therefore, there is a place for decisions based on common sense.

    Since each IEP is a cooperative effort involving the parents, it will be to your advantage to keep the parents informed at every stage and solicit the parents' ideas, suggestions, and reactions. Assure the parents that if part of the plan proves inoperative or ineffective you will recommend changes that will serve their child better. Ask the parents to let you know how the plan is working at home. A "we" approach will help you minimize any parental resistance and maximize parental cooperation. Parental cooperation is especially important because this is a team project in which you will need suggestions from the parents.

    To enhance your relationship with the parents further, remind them that they have complete access to their child's records. Give them copies of each report, and explain exactly how the assessments are being made. Whenever possible, make the parents team members in the diagnosis, treatment, and education processes. Have a positive attitude. Be sure the parents understand the abilities and assets of their child. Emphasize the things the child can do rather than those he or she cannot do. Help the parents learn how they can influence their child to think positively about himself or herself. Parents can also help others who might be working with the child to focus on the child's strengths and assets.

    For years we have been aware of the value of involving parents of students at all stages, but recently we discovered the advantages of drawing students into the planning of their own educational experiences. Now we have the opportunity (and responsibility) to involve both parties in planning, administering, and evaluating these special programs. While the paperwork may be a hassle, there is no doubt that we shall learn a great deal about individualizing instruction as we participate in IEPs. Most teachers will want to do whatever is necessary to help handicapped students profit from their instruction.

TEACHER REACTIONS TO PUBLIC LAW 94-142

Although several years have passed since Public Law 94-142 was first introduced, many teachers are uncomfortable with this additional responsibility that has been placed on regular classroom teachers. A major concern is teachers' lack of faith in their ability to help handicapped students. Stephens and Braun (1981) attribute the reluctance of teachers to integrate special students into regular classes to the teachers' lack of knowledge of special students. At Michigan State University a three-credit-hour course on mainstreaming was used to measure the effect that increased knowledge about handicapped students has on teacher confidence about putting these students into regular classes (Pernell et al., 1985). The 28 participants in the course had an average of six years teaching experience. Initially, the attitudes toward mainstreaming were in the negative to neutral ranges, but at the last session the attitudes were all in the high-positive range. The conclusions were that "the results of the findings support the importance of increased experience, knowledge attainment and skill acquisition as a catalyst in the formation of positive attitudes towards mainstreaming students" (Pernell et al., 1985, p. 136).

As a beginning teacher, you will have help from experienced personnel when you do your first IEPs. This book gives you a good introduction, but it will be your responsibility to learn as much as you can about Public Law 94-142 during your clinical experiences and once you begin teaching. You will continue learning about this law and similar laws as they emerge and change.

TEACHING THE GIFTED AND TALENTED

Some of the most neglected students in American schools today are students whose abilities are unusually high—gifted and talented students. According to the U.S. Commissioner of Education, "Gifted children are frequently overlooked in our schools. A review of current educational practices shows that the majority of public schools need to do more to meet the needs of this special group of children. The average classroom of 35 students has two gifted students (Alvins & Gourly, 1977), but very little money is spent to provide programs for them. During the 1970s, some $6.5 million was alloted to gifted students annually, compared with the $600 million alloted to the handicapped and the staggering $2 billion alloted to the economically disadvantaged (Stevens, 1977, p. 32). The gifted have been ignored in recent years, and their unique needs have not been attended to by any of the many new programs that have emerged to provide for other groups of needy students.

While we would like to believe that ignoring the gifted has not been intentional, there is evidence that the neglect was purposeful. Working against programs for the gifted are the following attitudes (L'Abate & Curtis, 1975):

1. The programs are undemocratic.
2. They are unpopular with parents of children who are not identified as being gifted and who always compose the majority of the school population.
3. There is fear that special provision for the gifted will hamper improvement of general education for all.
4. The gifted already have many advantages, and this will enable them to outdistance the average child further and to obtain a number of exclusive opportunities.
5. Some feel that any extra effort and money should be used for the benefit of those who are handicapped.
6. The gifted are able to take care of themselves without any extra assistance.

There are still more reasons for opposition to programs for the gifted (Kaplan, 1974, pp. 7–8):

1. Programs for the gifted and talented reinforce the segregation of students.
2. The utilization of individualized instruction abolishes the need for separate programs for the gifted and talented.
3. Overemphasizing the gifted and talented through a special program creates an elitist population.
4. What is good for the gifted and talented is good for all children.
5. If classroom teachers were doing their job, there would be no need to offer a special program for the gifted.
6. What is offered to the gifted should be commensurate with what is offered to the students in other special education programs.

Some teachers and administrators believe it is undemocratic to give bright students special attention; other teachers, resenting the superior student's competency, enforce egalitarianism as a sort of equalizer (Cutts & Moseley, 1952).

Teachers of gifted and talended students have more positive attitudes toward these students than do regular teachers, and schools that have gifted programs have less-positive attitudes toward gifted students (Ferrante, 1983). The prevailing negative attitudes in schools with gifted programs can be attributed to the disruption of classes when these students are pulled out periodically to attend the special programs. Nicely (1980) found that teachers are more willing to have this occur when they know more about gifted children. But some educators are questioning purposeful neglect of this group of special students and point out that there is historical precedent in Thomas Jefferson's advocacy of special education provisions and settings for students of more able learning capacity (Durr, 1964). During the nineteenth century, private schools for the intellectually elite proliferated in New England and in the South. The first systematic provision of special programs for the gifted in the public school setting was in the St. Louis school system in 1868 (Witty, 1951). The first federal legislation for the gifted student was the 1958 National Defense Education Act, which provided loans for the gifted to pursue higher education (Johnson, 1976). Only two years later the U.S. Office of Education began operating "Project Talent" programs to stimulate discovery and development of national human resources. In 1969, Public Law 91-230 mandated a report to Congress on the education of the gifted and talented from the U.S. Office of Education. During the mid-1980s many states created combinations of loans and grants to attract gifted students into math and science teacher education programs.

WHO ARE THE GIFTED?

In the past there was a tendency to use IQ scores to identify the gifted, but recent studies suggest that this method overlooks some gifted students who do not have the aspiration or motivation needed to score highly on these tests. Unfortunately there are few other measuring devices, so most schools and researchers continue to use standardized intelligence tests.

Some authors insist that the term *gifted* be reserved for students who are highly motivated as well as capable. Another author provides the following definition: "The gifted student is likely to have above-average language development, persistence in attacking difficult mental tasks, the ability to generalize and see relationships, unusual curiosity, and a wide variety of deep interests" (Durr, 1964). Other authors who accept a broad definition of *gifted* still consider only the high performers on intelligence tests in their programs for the gifted (DeHann & Havinghurst, 1961). Whatever the current status of the definition, the best method for identifying the gifted is, at least at this time, the individual intelligence test (Gallagher, 1975).

Over the years the gifted have been victimized by such false stereotypes as "social misfits," "weird," or "mad scientists." Like all other people, the gifted feel a need to utilize their talents. When the teacher does not challenge students or provide opportunities for them to use their abilities, like all other students they are apt to become frustrated.

As a teacher, you will want to find different materials and assign different tasks to challenge these students. Education programs for the gifted "must deal with their subject matter profoundly" (Bull, 1986, p. 42). The traditional practices of giving the gifted the same assignments—and, perhaps even worse, assigning more of the same problems—must be replaced by activities that will hold their interest and challenge their minds. Many school systems have specially trained professionals to work in programs for the gifted. Find out if your school or school system has such a person, and inquire about testing programs for identifying gifted students. The first responsibility you have to these students is to identify them. Then you must either try to provide adequate challenges or see that someone else does.

TEACHING THE UNDERACHIEVER

Underachievers are students with high intellectual or academic potential whose performance falls in the middle third in scholastic achievement—or worse, in the lowest third (Gowan, 1957). Few educators realize how serious this problem is. First, the percentage of gifted students who are achieving far below their abilities is staggering. One study found that more than half the highly gifted students work well below their abilities (Milner, 1957). The tremendous waste in potential is enough to prompt serious concern.

A second reason for concern is that these gifted students who are achieving below their abilities academically are also contributing socially below their abilities (Newland, 1976). Thus, there is a further waste of human resources. Still another reason for concern about underachievers is that once gifted students begin to perform below their ability, the trend is difficult to reverse. It quickly becomes accepted as a way of life (Heinemann, 1977).

Identifying the Underachiever

Underachievers, like all special students, must first be identified by the teacher before they can get help. You may find it more difficult to recognize underachievers because they are frequently mistaken for low-ability students. One teacher in-service program lists the following characteristics of underachievers (Heinemann, 1977):

1. Belligerent toward classmates and others.
2. Extremely defensive (given to rationalizing, ad-libing, excusing failures, lying).
3. Fearful of failure and of attempting new tasks because of the likelihood of failure.
4. Resentful of criticism, yet likely to be highly critical of others.
5. Prone to habitual procrastination, dawdling, daydreaming, sulking, brooding.
6. Frequently absent.
7. Inattentive—wriggling, doodling, whispering.
8. Suspicious, distrustful of overtures of affection.
9. Rebellious.
10. Negative about own abilities.

No student would display all these characteristics simultaneously, but one who shows several at once should be investigated.

Some of the likely causes of underachievement are physical limitations (such as poor vision or hearing), learning disabilities, and even social maladjustments. Often low performance is a result of low expectations at home and school, which eventually lead to low expectations by the student. But to be sure that a particular student is indeed performing well below ability, you must check previous performance records or report cards and standardized tests. For example, a student who is making Cs but has stanine scores of 8s and 9s, is clearly performing far below ability.

Helping the Underachiever

Once you have identified the underachievers in your classes, you may have many approaches to helping them to improve their performance, academically and socially. You may want to consider using some of the following:

1. Special guidance to develop positive self-concepts.
2. Extensive use of films and captioned filmstrips instead of textbooks; use of taped lessons to improve listening, thinking, reading skills.
3. Firsthand experiences to stimulate and motivate, especially for students from disadvantaged backgrounds (remember, middle-class Anglo students, as well as the poor and some minority students, may come from such backgrounds).
4. Assignments and teaching methods adjusted to the individual interests and abilities of students and relating to hoped-for or established goals, whether personal or academic.

5. Teacher-student sessions for planning work to be covered.
6. Tutoring by willing and able senior citizens who can provide the warmth and understanding, kind encouragement, and praise often missing at home.
7. A special opportunity class for underachievers of mixed ages with similar problems working out of the regular class, even out of the regular school where possible, for at least part of the day.
8. Group therapy with a warm, understanding counselor or teacher to discuss freely any fears, frustrations, angers.
9. A team approach to working with underachievers who are gifted/talented, including the teacher(s), parent(s), a counselor, and perhaps at times the student.
10. Use of grades and tests *only* as measures of progress and thus as indicators of areas needing additional work.
11. Instruction in how to learn—how to concentrate, remember, understand and follow directions, use key words, etc.
12. Instruction in problem-solving techniques and the inquiry method.

Many contemporary programs for the gifted and talented students include nontraditional content and skills. Research shows that basic research skills can be taught to gifted children of middle school level and even younger (Kent & Esgar, 1983). Scientific research methodology has been taught successfully in science classes (Riner, 1983). There are numerous reports of junior high students being employed by school districts to conduct workshops for teachers on the use of computers (Torrence, 1986, p. 640). Other common trends include teaching gifted students inventing (Hoffman, 1982), debating (Lengel, 1983), logical reasoning (Weinstein & Laughman, 1980), creative writing (Stoddard & Renzulli, 1983), thinking (Cinquino, 1980), and forecasting (Crabbe, 1982). Whatever method(s) you choose, it is important to remember that no one type of program will meet all the needs of all gifted and talented students (Stewart, 1982).

RECAP OF MAJOR IDEAS

1. There is a strong trend toward keeping handicapped students in classes with nonhandicapped peers whenever possible.
2. Nonhandicapped people have a tendency to underestimate the mental ability of physically handicapped students.
3. Federal law requires teachers to design a special learning program for each handicapped student.
4. In working with handicapped students, teachers should always consider how severe the handicap is, how long the student has had it, and how stable the condition is.
5. Emotionally disturbed students too need to experience success and should not be subjected to threats or ridicule.

6. Parents of handicapped children have a right to help plan the program for their children and a right to evaluate it and even insist on changes to improve it.
7. The percentage of gifted students whose performance is substandard is very high.
8. There are ways to identify underachievers and help them.

POSTTEST

Now that you have read the chapter, take a moment to respond to the following statements again:

	Agree	Disagree	Uncertain
1. Most needs of handicapped students can best be met in an environment where the student is with others who have similar handicaps.	___	___	___
2. Federal law requires that individualized programs be offered to each handicapped student.	___	___	___
3. The length of time a student has had a handicap is irrelevant, because the handicap itself is what must be worked with.	___	___	___
4. People who are not handicapped tend to overestimate the mental abilities of physically handicapped students.	___	___	___
5. Except for certain physical or mental limitations, handicapped students behave no differently from nonhandicapped students.	___	___	___
6. Emotionally disturbed students tend to be either hostile or apathetic.	___	___	___
7. Some traumatic experiences are actually good for emotionally disturbed students.	___	___	___
8. The teacher of students with a sensory handicap should help them learn to ignore their handicap.	___	___	___
9. Students who have learning disabilities are usually below average in mental ability.	___	___	___
10. Mainstreaming is nothing more than moving handicapped students from special classes back into the regular classroom.	___	___	___
11. The mainstreaming movement will probably remove the need for special-education teachers.	___	___	___

CASES

Case 1: An Explosive Experience

Shirley Norton was excited about her new teaching assignment. She had edged out 40 other applicants for the one vacancy in the physical education department at Sherwood High. Her first day started off with a rush. By noon she was so tired she hardly tasted the cafeteria food she was consuming all too rapidly. But according to the many complaints from the more established teachers, she wasn't missing much. Shirley quickly swallowed the last bite, bussed her tray to the long conveyor belt, and walked back toward the gym.

When Shirley entered the gym she found one of her seniors, Debbie, breaking out the windows. Debbie was running, screaming, and crying hysterically as she punched out the panes with a broom handle. Shirley knew that Debbie had been in her class playing volleyball just before lunch and had become very upset. Approaching Debbie, Shirley asked her to hand over the broom. This was a mistake. Debbie whirled around and began hitting Shirley, swearing each time. Just as Shirley was about to collapse, Debbie dropped the broom and herself collapsed on the floor, sobbing.

As perplexed as she was shocked, Shirley was relieved to see one of the senior physical education teachers enter the room and take over the situation as though it were just another part of the job.

Discussion

1. How should a teacher approach a student who is behaving frantically and irrationally? Very carefully. When people are in such a state, their behavior is unpredictable. This was evidenced by Debbie's attacking a new teacher, whom she hardly knew.
2. What should Shirley do about this incident? Debbie clearly needs help. She might begin by checking Debbie's record for previous similar incidents. The school (or school system) psychologist should be apprised of the incident. If no psychologist is available, the school counselor should be informed. If the school has neither a psychologist nor a counselor, the principal should be alerted. Otherwise, Debbie will be a threat to herself and to her classmates and teachers.

Case 2: An Introduction to Mainstreaming

After teaching social studies for three years, Dave no longer thought of himself as a novice teacher, and he had experienced some unusual and challenging encounters with parents. At the beginning of Dave's fourth year, a student named Arnold Swartz transferred to Edison High and was assigned to one of Dave's classes. Arnold was classified as mildly retarded, and from the very beginning it was obvious that he could not meet the demands Dave made of all his students. Dave asked that Arnold be removed from the class, but the principal refused to transfer Arnold. Dave decided to ignore Arnold—after all, the education of the other 28 students should not be sacrificed. Arnold seemed content, and everything was working well until the first report cards were sent home.

That evening Arnold's mother telephoned Dave very upset. Arnold had received a D− in social studies and there was no explanation of why he had done so poorly. Dave wanted to tell her that Arnold was not capable of doing any better, but he knew that Mrs. Swartz was already aware of her son's limitations. Before the conversation ended, Dave and Mrs. Swartz agreed to meet with the principal, at which time Dave would then explain exactly what he was doing (or not doing) to help Arnold. As he went to bed, Dave was wondering how the principal would react and what he could do to help a boy like Arnold.

Discussion

1. Was Dave wrong in wanting to give his time and energy to the students who could benefit most?
   A teacher's desire to experience success with students is admirable, but each teacher is responsible for the intellectual growth of *all* his or her students. Dave was wrong to neglect a student who found learning more difficult.
2. What alternative does Dave have if Mrs. Swartz insists on meeting with him periodically to discuss the progress of her son?
   Legally, Dave has no alternative. Professionally, he should welcome such visits.
3. What if Mrs. Swartz demands special attention for her son? Will Dave have to make exceptions for Arnold just because he is different?
   Because this difference threatens Arnold's learning, Dave will have to develop an Individualized Education Program and implement and coordinate the design and utilization of the plan.

ACTIVITIES

All teachers should seek to learn more about students who differ significantly from most of their classmates. Some may be brighter, some may be slower. Some may be physically handicapped, others emotionally handicapped. All teachers now deal with students in each of these categories. Instead of ignoring them or separating them from their "normal" peers, teachers will alter the classroom to accommodate these individuals.

The following activities will help you begin to answer this question: How will *you* provide for the special students in your classes?

1. Because most classes have students whose IQs range from considerably below average to well above average, how will you attempt to meet the needs of the students on both ends of this continuum? Include a few strategies for simplifying content and making it more accurate. Also include techniques for challenging the bright students.
2. Suppose you recognize a handicapped student in your class. Describe the steps you will use to go about getting information about this student.

SUGGESTED READINGS

Althoff, R. H. (1981). *The effects of an inservice training procedure on the attitudes of regular education teachers toward mainstreaming of handicapped students.* Ed.D. dissertation, Wayne State University.

Alvins, J. J., & Gourly, T. J. (1977). The challenge of our gifted children. *Teacher, 96,* 45.

Barbe, W. B., & Renzulli, J. S. (Eds.). (1981). *Psychology and education of the gifted.* New York: Irvington.

Beasley, W. A. (1984). *Microcomputer applications in the education of the gifted.* Doctoral dissertation, University of Georgia.

Bogdan, R. (1983). "Does mainstreaming work?" is a silly question. *Phi Delta Kappan, 64,* 427–428.

Boyer, E. L. (1978). What's right with our schools? *Ohio Schools, 41,* 15.

Bull, B. L. (1986). Education for gifts and talents: A change in emphasis. *Education Digest, 51,* 40.

Cinquino, D. (1980). An evaluation of a philosophy program with fifth and sixth grade academically talented students. *Thinking, 2, 3, 4,* 79–83.

Clark, B. (1983). *Growing up gifted* (2nd ed.). Columbus, Ohio: Merrill.

Crabbe, A. B. (1982). Creating a brighter future: An update on the future problem solving problem. *Journal for the Education of the Gifted, 5,* 2–11.

Cutts, N., & Moseley, N. (1952). *Teaching the bright and gifted.* Englewood Cliffs, N.J.: Prentice-Hall.

DeHann, R., & Havinghurst, R. (1961). *Educating gifted children.* Chicago: University of Chicago Press.

Doubrave-Harris, M. J. (1982). *The relationship of inservice training to the attitudes toward, and knowledge of, mainstreaming of three groups of educators.* Ph.D. dissertation, Bowling Green State University.

Durr, W. K. (1964). *The gifted student.* New York: Oxford University Press.

Enoch, M. M. (1979). *Relationship of teacher attitudes toward mainstreaming with respect to previous special education training, teaching level, and experience with exceptional children.* Ph.D. dissertation, George Peabody College for Teachers.

Ferrante, R. A. (1983). *Survey of attitudes of regular teachers, teachers of the gifted and talented, and administrators toward gifted education.* Ed.D. dissertation, University of South Carolina.

Gallagher, J. J. (1975). *Teaching the gifted child.* Boston: Allyn & Bacon.

Gold, S. (1984). Sixty years of programming for the gifted in Cleveland. *Phi Delta Kappan, 65,* 497–499.

Gowan, J. C. (1957). Dynamics of the underachievement of gifted children. *Exceptional Children, 24,* 98–101.

Hanline, J. F., & Murray, C. (1984). Integrating severely handicapped children into regular public schools. *Educational Leadership, 66,* 273–276.

Heinemann, A. (1977). Module 6: Underachievers among the gifted/talented—Star power: Providing for the gifted, p. 4. Austin, Tex.: Educational Service Center, Region XIII.

Hoffman, J. G. (1982). Inventions. *G/C/T, 24,* 54–55.

Hurtado-Portillo, J. L. (1980). *Effects of an inservice program on the attitudes of regular classroom teachers toward mainstreaming mildly handicapped students.* Ph.D. dissertation, University of North Carolina at Chapel Hill.

Johnson, B. (Ed.). (1976). Federal legislative history on gifted and talented, Bulletin 2.

Kaplan, S. (1974). *Providing programs for the gifted and talented: A handbook,* pp. 93–123. Ventura, Calif.: Office of Ventura Co. Superintendent of Schools.

Kent, S., & Esgar, L. V. (1983, May-June). Research techniques for gifted primary students. *G/C/T,* 28–29.

Khatena, J. (1982). *Educational psychology of the gifted.* New York: Wiley.

Kirk, S. A. (1972). *Educating exceptional children.* Boston: Houghton Mifflin.

Koci, J. I. L. (1980). *A study of the needs of regular classroom teachers in implementing Public Law 94-142.* Ed.D. dissertation, University of Houston.

L'Abate, L., & Curtis, L. T. (1975). *Teaching the exceptional child.* Philadelphia: Saunders.

Lengel, A. L. (1983). Classroom debating in the elementary school. *G/C/T, 28,* 57–60.

Love, H. D. (1974). *Educating exceptional children in a changing society.* Springfield, Ill.: Thomas.

McNamara, B. E. (1986). Parents as partners in the I.E.P. process. *Academic Therapy, 21,* 3.

McRainey, G. (1981). *Teacher-pupil contact as a factor in the development of positive attitudes toward handicapped students.* Ph.D. dissertation, George Peabody College for Teachers.

Marston, R., & Leslie, D. (1983). Teacher perceptions from mainstreamed versus non-mainstreamed teaching environments. *Physical Educator, 40,* 8–15.

Milner, J. B. (1957). *Intelligence in the United States.* New York: Springer.

Morbeck, J. U. (1980). *In-service education needs of senior high school regular classroom teachers relative to mainstreaming learning disabled students.* Ed.D. dissertation, University of Idaho.

Newland, T. E. (1976). *The gifted in socio-educational perspective.* Englewood Cliffs, N.J.: Prentice-Hall.

Nicely, R. F., Jr. (1980). Teachers' attitudes toward gifted children and programs: Implication for instructional leadership. *Education, 101,* 12–15.

Pernell, E., McIntyre, L., & Bader, L. A. (1985, Winter). Mainstreaming: A continuing concern for teachers. *Education, 106,* 131–137.

Pietroski, M. S. (1979). *An analysis of background variables associated with classroom teachers' attitudes toward mainstreaming.* Ed.D. dissertation, Boston University.

Powell, M., & Bearad, J. W. (1986). *Teacher attitudes: An annotated bibliography and guide to research.* New York: Garland.

Reynolds, M. C., & Birch, J. W. (1977). *Teaching exceptional children in all America's schools,* Chapter 4. Reston, Va.: Council for Exceptional Children.

Riner, P. S. (1983). Establishing scientific methodology with elementary gifted children through field biology. *G/C/T, 28,* 46–49.

Seidman, S., & Spain, M. (1983). A gifted approach to the development of a social studies unit. *Roeper Review, 5,* 29–30.

Stephens, T. M., & Braun, B. L. (1981). Measures of regular classroom teachers' attitudes toward handicapped children. *Exceptional Children, 46,* 4.

Stevens, B. J. (1977). What about that other special education? *Pennsylvania School Journal, 126,* 32.

Stewart, E. (1982). Myth: One program, indivisible for all. *Gifted Child Quarterly, 26,* 27–29.

Stoddard, E. P., & Renzulli, J. S. (1983). Improving the writing skills of talent pool students. *Gifted Child Quarterly, 27,* 21–27.

Tannenbaum, A. J. (1983). *Gifted children: Psychological and educational prospectus*. New York: Macmillan.

Torrence, E. P. (1986). Teaching creative and gifted learners. In M. C. Whittrock (Ed.), *Handbook of research on teaching* (3rd ed.). New York: Macmillan.

Ungerleider, D. E. (1986). The organic curriculum. *Academic Therapy, 21,* 465–466.

Weinstein, J., & Laughman, L. (1980). Teaching logical reasoning to gifted students. *Gifted Child Quarterly, 24,* 186–190.

Witty, P. (Ed.) (1951). *The gifted child*. Boston: D. C. Heath.

C H A P T E R **9**

Teaching in Multicultural Settings

Objectives

- Name three qualities of American high schools that inhibit success for minority students.
- Give two approaches for helping minority students build positive self-images.
- Write a daily lesson plan that will exalt unique characteristics of several cultures.
- Explain the significance of the 1975 *Lau v. Nichols* decision by the U.S. Supreme Court.
- List 10 things a teacher of a multicultural group should do to adjust to the students, then list 10 things the teacher should avoid doing.
- Create a one-hour simulation activity that will enable all students in a class to experience different cultural roles.
- Name five principles of multicultural education.

PRETEST

	Agree	Disagree	Uncertain
1. There is little a teacher can do to meet the needs of students from other cultures unless the teacher has special training.	____	____	____
2. Teachers should not concern themselves with different cultures because all students are Americans and need to learn the American way of life.	____	____	____
3. Schools do not have to provide instruction in other languages just because some students speak first languages other than English.	____	____	____
4. Students who belong to other cultures should be grouped with like students throughout the school day.	____	____	____
5. To avoid embarrassment, teachers should refrain from discussing the backgrounds of students from minority cultures.	____	____	____
6. It is dangerous to generalize about cultures other than your own.	____	____	____

Middle-Level Message

You have often heard of people with a reputation for turning liabilities into assets. Middle-level teachers who teach in multicultural settings have the opportunity to do this. They can view the situation either as a handicap or as a unique opportunity. The results usually parallel the teacher's view.

If you choose to turn your pluralistic classes into an asset, you can do so by identifying the unique contributions each ethnic group has made to our society. Then you should find ways to amplify these contributions. In this chapter you will learn how to make members of each ethnic group more aware of and proud of their heritage. You will also learn how to select textbooks and other materials that will facilitate attainment of this goal.

Finding appropriate supplementary materials for use in multicultural middle-level classes can be difficult. Appendix F includes an annotated list of centers and agencies that provide schools with extensive reading lists, many of which are free.

Unfortunately, many stereotypes of other cultures have their origins in ethnic jokes. Although the majority of these jokes are loaded with inaccurate stereotypes, each cultural group does have unique characteristics. The differences in language and custom often form barriers to learning in American classrooms. Millions have been spent on programs to raise the academic performance of children who come from minority groups, yet there has been no effective reversal of the disappointing results (Stewart, 1975). But, as Fantini (1986, p. 12) states, "The school curriculum has to reflect multicultural understandings. Multilingual and multicultural educations are no longer frills but major necessities."

How much, and exactly what, can the teacher do? Teachers may be the only people who can significantly improve the education minorities receive. American schools have several features that make success difficult for multicultural students (Henson, 1975). First, they are so large that they appear impersonal to immigrants. Second, teachers tend to be overly concerned with tests, grades, and competition. Furthermore, teachers tend to sell minority students short and underestimate their ability to succeed and to contribute.

TAKING A POSITIVE APPROACH

To many students and teachers, the term *multicultural* has negative connotations. It brings to mind problems, which is unfortunate because this in itself may cause problems. In other words, if teachers interpret multicultural settings as being prone to problems, they may approach multicultural classes with skepticism. Students sense this and will not trust the teacher. But if teachers view the multicultural setting as an opportunity to increase their own knowledge and enrich their own sense of values, the classroom experience is more likely to prove rewarding for everyone. According to McCormick (1984, p. 94), "a cornerstone of multiculturalism in education is cultural pluralism, an ideology of cultural diversity, which celebrates the differences among groups of people." The following principles of multiculturalism in education show some reasons for meeting the needs of all students (Garcia, 1984, p. 108).

PRINCIPLES OF MULTICULTURALISM IN EDUCATION

1. In the classroom, as in society at large, cultural diversity should be considered a cause for celebration.
2. Cultural diversity is a valuable asset for society to preserve and enhance.
3. Teachers should strive to provide educational equity for all students.
4. Multicultural education directly counters elitism, sexism, and racism in American public school teaching and learning.
5. Schools should not place too many minority students in classes for the learning disabled or emotionally impaired.
6. Emancipation of minority students from inequitable treatment serves society.

PERSONALIZING TEACHING

The population in the United States has become very mobile. With one family in five moving each year, even many of our smallest schools have student populations from different cultural backgrounds. In every situation it is important for teachers to recognize cultural differences and exalt them to make students feel proud of their cultures and capable of applying their uniqueness to strengthen our nation.

No matter where you teach, cultural differences will abound. This is true in affluent suburbs, working-class urban areas, and rural areas. Even among students with similar ethnic backgrounds and economic classes, there will be pronounced differences in religious backgrounds. As long as there is one student whose background is different, the need for skills in working with culturally mixed classrooms will be there—even in the smallest communities and schools.

The problems often seem greater in larger schools, where there are so many students that even getting to know them all is difficult. But in this setting the challenge and the need to personalize is even greater, because there is a tendency for members of similar cultural backgrounds to form cliques. Cultural cliques can be hotbeds of prejudice. This, of course, refers not to organized clubs but to the informal gatherings in parking lots, hallways, and cafeterias with no constructive purpose. Every teacher can contribute to dissolving such groups by getting to know each student on a more personal level and by volunteering to sponsor clubs for students of similar cultural backgrounds. International clubs are excellent for acquainting students with other cultures.

But such techniques are applicable in all classes, multicultural or not. Most students, irrespective of cultural background, would profit more if classes were personalized, if competition among students were reduced, and if realistic demands were made of everyone. The self-concepts of all students will be enhanced when teachers assign tasks that are within students' ability and provide encouragement and rewards. However, students from other cultures are different in several specific ways, and it is essential to be aware of these differences when learning how to teach them.

A group of teachers interested in discovering the strengths of various minority and ethnic students surveyed teachers throughout much of southern Florida, identifying 2,000 such strengths (Cheyney, 1976, pp. 41–42). The survey showed that the children were generally:

highly responsive to affection	independent
physically dexterous	imitative
protective of siblings	uninhibited
academically persevering	emotionally cool
musically oriented	monetarily proficient
artistic	rich in humor
authority minded	competitive
resourceful	forgiving

While awareness of these qualities can help in the designing of learning experiences for multicultural classes, we must resist the temptation to build yet another stereotype for all multicultural children. Each student is an individual, and as such may possess all or none of these traits. This list is included because it provides teachers of multicultural classes with a point to begin analyzing their students. And this is how teachers should begin—by analyzing the *strengths* of each student.

A REASON FOR OPTIMISM

In 1975, in *Lau v. Nichols* (U.S. 563, 18. ct. 786), the Supreme Court mandated that all schools in the United States with 20 or more students who speak a common first language other than English are to provide systematic instruction in that language. This emphasis has had a great impact on many schools, but this or any other federal mandate alone is inadequate. If we are to meet the needs of minority students, it will be through the concerns, skills, and efforts of teachers.

Another reason for optimism is the emphasis that professional associations are giving multicultural education. For more than a decade, the Association for Supervision and Curriculum Development has given high priority to multicultural education in its publications and meetings. In 1979 the National Council for the Accreditation of Teacher Education (NCATE) added a multicultural standard that colleges of teacher education must meet if they are to attain and retain accreditation. This means that, in the future, colleges of teacher education must provide students opportunities to enable them to "understand the unique contributions, needs, similarities, differences and interdependencies of students from varying racial, cultural, linguistic, religious and socio-economic backgrounds" (NCATE, 1985, p. 5). The 1986 revision of NCATE standards continues to stress multicultural education.

THE TEACHER'S DECISION

We are fortunate to have multicultural classes. Schooling involves learning about life, and life in the late twentieth century is multicultural. While all multicultural classes will have some unique problems, they also offer students a chance to learn about contemporary life. And in order to accept themselves and others, students should have an understanding and appreciation of cultural diversity (Fantini, 1986, p. 123). Yet these advantages do not come to our attention as quickly as the problems do. If the advantages are to be realized, teachers must make a commitment to enjoy and capitalize upon cultural differences in their classes (Henson & Henry, 1976). It is a matter of teacher attitude.

In-service education and other information-gathering methods can help improve teacher attitudes toward multicultural education. Although some such programs have not been able to do this (Cathey, 1980), other programs have left participants feeling more positive about multicultural education (Nussel & Weirsma, ERIC ED 227 200). Dandridge (1980) found that the more teachers know about multicultural education, and the more professional preparation they have, the more positive their attitudes will be. Knowledge and preparation can prevent resentful and negative attitudes toward multicultural education.

Let's Ponder

Assumptions of Cultural Pluralism

After reading the following assumptions (Tesconi, 1984, p. 88), respond to the questions below.

1. An individual's membership in . . . a cultural group life . . . promotes . . . self-esteem, sense of belonging, respect for others, purposefulness, and critical thinking.
2. [The development of] tolerance and openness to different others . . . is dependent upon the opportunity of individuals to encounter and interact with a variety of culturally different others.
3. No one way of life can be said to be better than any other, and to be humane, a society must afford room for many competing and oftentimes conflicting ways of life.
4. It is valuable to have many ways of life in competition. . . . Such competition leads to a balance or equilibrium in the social order.
5. Loyalty to a larger society—a nation—is a function of, and dependent on, socially sanctioned loyalties rooted in a multiplicity of diverse ethnic and cultural groups.

Respond to the following questions.

1. With which of these assumptions do you agree? Disagree? What are the bases for your disagreement?
2. Do you believe loyalty to a single ethnic group, as opposed to loyalty to a multiplicity of ethnic groups, facilitates or impedes loyalty to the nation? Assumption 3 says that no one way of life is superior to all others; therefore all groups must have some advantages.
3. Name some ethnic groups in the United States, and list at least one advantage of membership in each group. List one contribution each group has made to the United States.

All students are members of some culture. We should not think that only the minority students are culturally disadvantaged. Every group is rich in heritage. If the Anglo fails to understand the richness of a minority student's background, is not the Anglo culturally disadvantaged? We think so. The teacher who views a multicultural classroom as a positive climate for overall student learning will help erase some of each student's cultural ignorance. We tend to fear and distrust what we do not understand, and the teacher can do much to alleviate this lack of understanding.

In working with the multiculturals, the teacher cannot help but know that there are differences, but the effective teacher will also realize that, basically, children are children (Cheyney, 1976, p. 111). If you question that time spent preparing to teach minorities is economically spent, remember that lessons and methods that work effectively with these students will also work well with the other students.

THE TEACHER'S ROLE

"The courts can grant equal opportunity, but they cannot give equal chance" (Payne, 1984). The history of treatment of minorities in the United States tells us that whether multicultural students receive a quality education will depend on teachers' actions. Although this book makes a conscious attempt to avoid long lists, one list is essential at this point. Read and consider each of the following (from Dawson, 1974, pp. 53–54). Collectively, these dos and don'ts provide an excellent guide for teachers in multicultural classrooms.*

DOS FOR TEACHERS IN MULTICULTURAL CLASSROOMS

1. Do use the same scientific approach to gain background information on multicultural groups you would use to tackle a course in science, mathematics, or any subject area in which you might be deficient.
2. Do engage in systematic study of the disciplines that provide insight into the cultural heritage, political struggle, contributions, and present-day problems of minority groups.
3. Do try to develop sincere personal relationships with minorities. You can't teach strangers! Don't give up because one black or other minority person rejects your efforts. All groups have sincere individuals who welcome honest, warm relationships with members of another race. Seek out those who will accept or at least tolerate you.
4. Do recognize that there are often more differences within one group than between two groups. If we recognize diversity among races, we must also recognize diversity within groups.
5. Do remember that there are many ways to gain insight into a group. Visit their churches, homes, communities; read widely and listen to various segments of the group.
6. Do remember that no one approach and no one answer will help you meet the educational needs of all children in a multicultural society.
7. Do select instructional materials that are accurate and free from stereotypes.
8. Do remember that there is a positive relationship between teacher expectation and academic progress.
9. Do provide an opportunity for minority students and students from the

---

* Helpful suggestions of "Dos and Don'ts" were made by Delores Fitsgerald and Robin Kovats of St. Paul the Apostle School, and by Rven Oas Burvard of St. Columbia School, both in New York City.

mainstream to interact in a positive intellectual setting on a continuous basis.

10. Do use a variety of materials, especially those that utilize positive, real-life experiences.
11. Do provide some structure and direction to children who have unstructured lives, primarily children of the poor.
12. Do expose all students to a wide variety of literature as a part of your cultural sensitivity program.
13. Do remember that even though ethnic groups often share many common problems their needs are diverse.
14. Do utilize the rich resources within your own classroom among various cultural groups.
15. Do remember that human understanding is a lifetime endeavor. You must continue to study and provide meaningful experiences for your students.
16. Do remember to be honest with yourself. If you can't adjust to children from multicultural homes, get out of the classroom.

DON'TS FOR TEACHERS IN MULTICULTURAL CLASSROOMS

1. Don't rely on textbooks, teachers guides, and brief essays to become informed about minorities. Research and resources will be needed.
2. Don't use ignorance as an excuse for not having any insight into the problems and culture of blacks, Chicanos, Native Americans, Puerto Ricans, Asian Americans, and other minorities.
3. Don't rely on the "expert" judgment of one minority person for the answer to all the complicated racial and social problems of his or her people. For example, blacks, Mexicans, Indians, and Puerto Ricans have various political views on all issues.
4. Don't be fooled by popular slogans and propaganda intended to raise the national consciousness of an oppressed people.
5. Don't get carried away with the "save the world concept." Most minorities have their own savior.
6. Don't be afraid to learn from those who are more familiar with the mores and cultures than you.
7. Don't assume that you have all the answers for solving the other person's problems. It is almost impossible for an outsider to be an expert on the culture of another group.
8. Don't assume that all minority group students are culturally deprived.
9. Don't develop a fatalistic attitude about the progress of minority students.
10. Don't resegregate students through tracking and ability grouping gimmicks.
11. Don't give up when minority students seem to hate school.
12. Don't assume that minorities are the only students who should have multicultural instructional materials. Students in the mainstream can be

culturally deprived in terms of their knowledge and understanding of other people and of their own heritage.

13. Don't ask parents and students personal questions in the name of research. Why should they divulge their suffering?
14. Don't get hung up on grade designations when sharing literature that provides insight into the cultural heritage of a people.
15. Don't try to be cool by using the vernacular of a particular racial group.
16. Don't make minority students feel ashamed of their language, dress, or traditions.

Let's Ponder

The following statement was made by a minority ethnic group member who has become a recognized national leader in the study of multicultural education (Garcia, 1984, p. 104). Consider his comments as you respond to the questions below.

Correcting Classroom Discrimination

"I remember well my eighth-grade English teacher who made me write a letter to the school newspaper ten times before submission. The fact that my father was an unemployed coal miner, that my parents had seven years of schooling between them, and that English was spoken minimally in our house did not impede her from making a positive difference in my life. Not only did I learn to write a letter well, but I learned the importance of discipline, perseverance, and mentorship—all very important outcomes of schooling."

1. Some teachers overlook minority group students whose level of success is minimal. Do you think the person who made this statement condones this practice? Can you give one reason teachers should or should not hold high expectations for members of minority groups?
2. As a teacher, what can you do to win the confidence and respect of minority students? Would you agree that respect is usually a reciprocal process?
3. Assuming that all people have some degree of prejudice toward members of certain minority groups, how can you elevate your appreciation for minorities?

These dos and don'ts are presented as general guidelines for teachers who have members of one or more minority ethnic groups in their classes. Because all teachers have some representatives of other cultures in their classes from time to time, these guidelines should be appropriate for all of us. One additional suggestion—which is so obvious that it may be overlooked—is that the teacher should not give in to the temptation to make quick, automatic generalizations about any culture.

These guidelines are based on volumes of data, but even when using scientifically derived suggestions teachers should remember, that regardless of culture, all students are individuals and their individuality should be respected.

SELECTING ETHNIC MATERIALS

Because more than half the states in the nation require multi-ethnic programs and development of multi-ethnic materials special materials for multi-ethnic groups should not be difficult to find (Klassen & Gollnick, 1977, p. 137). As noted by Bishop (1986, p. 23), "It is promising to realize that efforts to include books that reflect all ethnic backgrounds not only enable minority students to identify more closely with the school while improving their reading ability, but also enable nonminority students to broaden their understanding of other peoples and cultures." In selecting materials for teaching about ethnicity—and in selecting all materials to be used in multicultural settings—it is important that the teacher not automatically assume that different ethnic groups need elementary or remedial materials. The following classification system was designed to help teachers select multi-ethnic materials at the appropriate levels of complexity, depending on the objectives of the unit.*

Level I materials are low in complexity, designed to highlight the achievements of all ethnic groups. Such material includes biographies and success stories of ethnic Americans. These materials are usually highly complimentary—so much that they often exaggerate. They are usually attractive and conspicuously displayed in the classroom by teachers. They should be used sparingly and selectively.

Level II materials depict "true/real" experiences of ethnic groups. Problems of the group are shown in a way that suggests that members of other groups, such as the majority ethnic group, are responsible for bad experience, but without specifying who the others are. The use of these materials should be limited.

Level III materials show the historical experiences of more than one ethnic group. Portrayals are limited to racial groups (blacks, hispanics, Native Americans) or white groups (Irish Americans, Italian Americans, or Polish Americans), but not both. A common approach is to select a major theme, such as "metropolitan/urban life," and present the unique experiences of each group. Such material purposefully accentuates the differences between minority groups or white ethnic groups, and fails to show the experiences and behaviors common to all groups. If misused, this material could widen existing gaps between classmates of differing ethnic groups.

Level IV materials, the most complex materials, are designed around broad content generalizations. They chronicle experiences common to all groups and identify common characteristics. They provide students with a multi-ethnic perspective on the American experience. Because these materials require critical analysis, they should be used with groups that are capable of conducting sophisticated discussions and critical, objective analysis. The following list of sources

---

* Special credit and thanks is given to Dr. Jesus Garcia and Dr. Ricardo Garcia for the use of this classification system, which was taken from their article "Selecting Ethnic Materials," *Social Studies, 44,* 1980.

shows where materials at each of the levels listed above can be obtained (Garcia & Garcia, 1980).

Sources for Materials on Ethnic Groups

Level I. Materials in Level I can be ordered through major and minor publishing houses and are often packaged as multimedia. Examples of such sources are:

Multicultural Multimedia Services
P.O. Box 669
1603 Hope Street
South Pasadena, CA 91030

Social Studies School Service
P.O. Box 802
1000 Culver Boulevard
Culver City, CA 90230

Level II. Materials in Level II chronicle the experiences of minority groups. Materials on Chicanos and Chinese Americans can be obtained from:

Handel Film Corporation
8730 Sunset Boulevard
West Hollywood, CA 90060

Level III. Bi-ethnic materials can be obtained from:

Children's Book and Music Center
5373 West Pico Boulevard
Los Angeles, CA 90019

Level IV. Multi-ethnic materials can be obtained from:

Social Studies School Service
P.O. Box 802
1000 Culver Boulevard
Culver City, CA 90230

EMF
P.O. Box 4272
Madison, WI 53711

As you approach your first teaching position, you may want to develop a portfolio of materials to use with multicultural groups. But whether you do this or not, it is imperative that you view multicultural experiences as a challenge and an opportunity—not as an opportunity to "save" minority students from their own ethnic group, and not to shape them into the "ideal" mold, but to help them learn to appreciate and respect the culture of the majority group and those of other minority ethnic groups. A sensible, if not the best, approach to selecting materials for multicultural groups is to achieve some balance of materials from the varying levels of complexity. But the most important criterion for selecting materials is the degree to which each source is useful in attaining the objectives of the unit or lesson.

Because cultural diversity has made this nation strong, it does not make sense to try to melt down the cultures into one. On the contrary, the schools should help preserve many of the characteristics that make each culture unique. In the past, teachers have made some common mistakes in working with multicultural groups. Often they made such a fuss over the differences between and among groups that they spread the gap that exists in the students' minds about differing characteristics among the groups. On the opposite end of the continuum, teachers have tried to blend all cultures into one. For 200 years the United States has been considered a melting pot. The concept was first created by a French-born writer, Crevecoeur, in 1782 (Ramirez & Castaneda, 1974, pp. 5–6).

ACADEMIC ACHIEVEMENT FROM EVERYONE

Too often teachers accept low performance from minority students—"That's just the way they are"—but this is a cop-out. By making an exception for minority students and letting them go along without experiencing maximum success, teachers deny them their right to develop to their maximum potential—a goal that we should hold up for *all* students.

THE TEACHER'S WIDER ROLE

We have been examining the teacher's role in working with multicultural classes with respect to instruction, but the teacher has a much broader role. Because teaching involves more than mere instruction, we should see just where the teacher can find opportunities to fulfill the goals of multicultural education.

A Teacher Corps/Association of Teacher Educators project resulted in a book titled *In Praise of Diversity: A Resource Book for Multicultural Education.** The book concludes with an article that identifies a number of implications for teachers of multicultural groups that extend beyond the classroom into all areas of the teacher's work.† Two avenues teachers can use to praise diversity are identified. These avenues are *process* and *content*. Now we turn to some ways to use process to praise diversity.

---

* See Suggested Readings section at the end of this chapter for complete bibliographical information.
† Appreciation is extended to Carl A. Grant, Susan L. Melnich, and H. N. Riven, to the Teacher Corps, and to the Association of Teacher Educators for permission to use abstracts from the article "In Praise of Diversity: Some Implications."

USING PROCESS TO PRAISE DIVERSITY

Have you ever considered that as a teacher you will be positioned in a prominent (highly visible) position in the community? This will enable you significantly to affect and shape the community's atmosphere and the general attitudes toward different cultures. Your behavior both inside and outside the classroom is important. According to Grant, Melnich, and Riven (1977), teachers have at least the following functions:

1. Director of learning
2. Counselor and guidance worker
3. Mediator of culture
4. Link with the community
5. Member of the school staff
6. Member of the profession

Director of Learning
Much of this chapter has focused on the teacher's instructional role. Since suggestions were provided to show how teachers should "gear up" their instruction to allow for, praise, and promote the cultural differences in the classroom, we need not discuss this dimension again.

Counselor and Guidance Worker
Since the philosophy of this book is personalizing education, each chapter emphasizes the need for working with each student in a way that extends beyond the academics. Only one further comment seems warranted. Each teacher in the school has responsibility for vocational guidance. The best vocational guidance programs are interdisciplinary and run throughout the grades. Each teacher should help students become aware of possible vocational potentials. Do not assume that members from all cultures feel an equal need for long-range planning; you will need to introduce some students to this concept and its advantages.

Mediator of Culture
Earlier in this chapter we discussed a need for stressing the contributions of all cultures represented in the classroom to "our culture" and to humanity at large. This should not preclude emphasis on the democratic processes and the rights and responsibilities of American citizens; rather, it should complement this goal. One way to do this is to teach problem-solving skills for coping with potential conflict areas. Simulations can be used to develop these skills. (See the simulations listed in Chapter 2.)

Link with the Community
In the 1970s the LINKS Project was established at Indiana State University. Written by a science educator, Chris Buethe, this project helped nonscience teachers develop science materials to use in their classes. For example, English

teachers were able to link the high-interest area of science to their classes by assigning students essays or other projects that would link the otherwise seemingly unrelated subjects. This strategy can also be used to link the multicultural class to the community. Cultural diversity should be exalted in the community at large. Since most teachers sooner or later accept leadership roles in the community, they can use these positions toward these ends. Perhaps most important of all, teachers can demonstrate their own commitment by praising diversity and affirming pluralism as they work and live in the community.

Member of the School Staff

Since teachers' roles within the school extend beyond the classroom and involve fellow teachers, administrators, and auxiliary personnel, they can find many opportunities to influence their colleagues. In their article "Organizing for Innovation," Huckins and Bernard stress the importance of informal systems upon organizations and upon their constituents. They warn that substantial parts of the informal system operate below levels of awareness. In most schools an important location for informal influence is the teachers' lounge, but, of course, not all influence there is positive. In a supervision text, Henry and Beasley (1982) use the phrase *lounge lizards* to caution teachers of the potential damage that can inadvertently result from careless comments in informal climates. But if such informal settings do affect the behavior of their participants, it seems that the lounge would be an ideal place for teachers who are dedicated to multicultural education to demonstrate their concerns, not in negative ways but in positive, constructive behaviors.

Member of the Profession

As members of a profession, teachers are expected to use their influence and skills to improve themselves and the profession. One major responsibility is to communicate the positive dimensions of education to all members of society. The previous decade brought criticism and scorn to American schools. Individual teachers can communicate the roles and achievements of their schools through conversations, discussions, and the written word. Professional meetings offer excellent opportunities for communication, and professional journals offer similar opportunities. Teachers who are committed to furthering multicultural education will find that many education and teacher associations give top priority to these ends.

RECAP OF MAJOR IDEAS

1. Several qualities of American schools militate against efforts of minority group students to succeed academically and socially.
2. Having students of several cultural backgrounds adds strength to a class and to a school.
3. By assigning tasks within the ability range of students, by providing

encouragement, and by giving rewards, teachers can help minority and other students build their self-concepts.

4. Federal law requires schools to teach in the national language of students when 20 or more students share a common first language.

5. The contributions of minority groups to society should be discussed in classes.

6. Teachers should select and use textbooks that portray cultures in positive and realistic ways.

7. There are more differences within cultures than among cultures.

8. Some of the professional education associations make concentrated efforts to assure proper education for minority groups and development of positive attitudes toward multicultural education.

9. Teachers should demand continuous academic growth from minority students.

10. Teachers should strive to build a positive attitude toward cultural diversity in their classrooms.

POSTTEST

Now that you have read the chapter, take a moment to respond to the following statements again:

	Agree	Disagree	Uncertain
1. There is little a teacher can do to meet the needs of students from other cultures unless the teacher has special training.	____	____	____
2. Teachers should not concern themselves with different cultures because all students are Americans and need to learn the American way of life.	____	____	____
3. Schools do not have to provide instruction in other languages just because some students speak first languages other than English.	____	____	____
4. Students who belong to other cultures should be grouped with like students throughout the school day.	____	____	____
5. To avoid embarrassment, teachers should refrain from discussing the backgrounds of students from minority cultures.	____	____	____
6. It is dangerous to generalize about cultures other than your own.	____	____	____

CASES

Case 1: A Student Is Hooked on Drugs

When the supervisor of student teachers came to visit Debbie Wright, she found her on the school's front step. At first Debbie could not explain what was wrong because she was crying too much. Finally she explained she had a student in one class who was addicted to heroin. Because the school was located in one of the city's lowest socioeconomic areas, most of the students had experience with some form of drugs, and many were undoubtedly addicted.

What was so special about this student? He was a likeable guy and seemed to like this student teacher. Debbie said, "I feel so sorry for him I just want to reach out and hug him. What can I do?"

Discussion

1. **How can a teacher help a student who is on drugs?**
   Teachers can and should discuss the dangers of drug use, but this will probably not help the student who has a drug problem. Debbie must realize that she can have an influence on many students, but her ability to help them with psychological and emotional adjustments is limited. People who are hooked on drugs experience psychological, emotional, and physical disorders. Debbie should refer all drug cases to the counselor or, if available, a school psychologist or psychiatrist.

2. **Why should Debbie refrain from expressing the pity she feels for the student?**
   This only encourages the student to feel sorry for himself, and when in this mental state the student will do little to improve or attempt to overcome the undesirable conditions. The teacher who is really concerned about a student who is underprivileged or in trouble should put the concern into action. She should be willing to give some time and energy to the student instead of showing pity.

3. **How can a teacher who feels as Debbie did show concern without showing pity?**
   Usually the teacher who shows pity for a student is really anxious to talk to the student about his problems because she wants to express her own feelings to the student. But it may not be the best thing for the student to discuss his problems. He may be ashamed of them. To push him into discussing them might intensify the problem. It could also produce new emotional problems.

Case 2: A Teacher Belittles a Slow Student

In terms of performance quality, Jerry Simms was one of the poorest students Shelly had ever had. At first she tried to encourage Jerry to listen, then she tried to force him to do his daily home assignments. Nothing seemed to help. Finally, Shelly made an inexcusable response to his indifferent behavior. She remarked in front of his peers, "Jerry, you don't have one iota of understanding about the subject we are studying, do you?"

Later, after relating the incident to some other teachers, she learned that Jerry had almost no home life. She began to regret what she had said and decided to drive by and see where he lived. The temperature was below freezing, and cracks in the walls let the lights show through. She learned later that the building had once been a storehouse for grain and had dirt floors. A student told her that there were only two chairs and a table inside.

Shelly's experience with Jerry began to haunt her. She began to ask herself, How can I help him?

Discussion

1. **How can the teacher learn about a student's home life?**
   An experience like Shelly's makes the teacher want to see the student's home and family. But this is not always practical and is not necessarily a wise method. It is not practical because there are too many students in similar circumstances. It is not wise because the student may be embarrassed to have his family and home exposed for observation.
   As a beginning teacher, you will be amazed at how much other teachers know about the students in your class—even the teachers who have never taught your students. Do

not hesitate to ask other teachers about your students. It is perfectly professional so long as the discussion is directed to understanding the student better and does not degenerate into a gossip session. Your school will keep a cumulative record on each student. This record will contain comments made by students' previous teachers. Here you can learn about a student's general behavior and academic potential.

2. Why might a dedicated teacher lose her temper with a low-performing student like Jerry?

Most classes have students whose performance is low because they are too lazy to improve. The teacher cannot always know which students are lazy and which are handicapped by a disadvantaged home life. Therefore, instead of becoming irritated with students who are not attentive, the teacher should try to determine the cause of their apathy.

3. To what ethnic group would you guess Jerry belongs? Shelly?

Shelly and Jerry are both Anglo-Americans.

Case 3: A Poor School Has a Good Atmosphere

When Bob, a supervisor of student teachers, first saw Rio Grande, an inner-city school, his first reaction was disbelief that such a school could exist in the twentieth century—the buildings should have been condemned decades ago because they were firetraps. Placing two beginning teachers in this environment went against Bob's better judgment, but he took a deep breath and went in to meet the principal.

Mr. Lopez was a delightful middle-aged man, gregarious and energetic. He introduced Bob to his secretaries and to several members of his large faculty, which was 95 percent Latin American. Each teacher had the same spark of enthusiasm and pleasantness.

Bob was still suspicious because he had been inside many dilapidated inner-city schools. He was keenly aware that in schools like this the students were often discourteous, rude, disrespectful, and difficult to control. Nevertheless, his responsibility was to assign two student teachers to this staff for the next term, so he promised himself he would visit frequently and provide encouragement and reassurance to make the experience tolerable for them.

When Bob visited, both student teachers assured him they were getting along well. There were apparently no major discipline problems in their classes. Both worked hard and enjoyed teaching in this school. From talking with the principal, some of the faculty members, and these two student teachers, Bob found three elements that seemed to be working together to produce the wholesome, optimistic atmosphere in a physical environment that had initially seemed so depressing. First, the principal stressed the importance of total involvement of everyone, including faculty and students, on both academic and extracurricular matters. These student teachers were immediately involved in evening and weekend school activities. The principal considered them important members of the faculty.

Second, the principal's enthusiasm was reflected in every faculty member and classroom. Most of the students were very poor readers, which severely limited the rate of learning, but the teachers were patient and continually encouraged their students.

Bob discovered the third element contributing to this school's wholesome atmosphere when he expressed his concern at the slow rate at which material was being covered. A faculty member responded that because many of the students were academically slow and had poor home lives that destroyed their concern and respect for others, one of the most important objectives was to teach the students to cooperate with others. The faculty members at Rio Grande certainly set good examples for their students.

Discussion

1. Teaching respect for others should be an important objective in any deprived community, but exactly what can the teacher do to teach students to respect others?
   Before learning to respect others, one must first learn to associate with others. Believe it or not, many students who attend ghetto schools have a keen sense of individual pride, and they resent working with others because they think cooperative efforts show that they cannot complete a task alone. This feeling can be avoided by carefully assigning students with similar characteristics to the same groups. For example, timid students may be assigned to the same group, students with strong leadership potential may be assigned to another group, and aggressive students may be assigned to another group. This provides all students with opportunities to contribute.
   A second technique for teaching students to respect each other is to assign individuals to help a classmate who is having difficulty with the lesson. This gives students opportunities to feel responsible for others, which is basic to learning to respect others.
2. Some student teachers never intend to teach in rundown buildings located in inner-city ghettos, so why do they need the experience of teaching in such schools?
   One does not have to go to a ghetto to find deprived students. Many teachers will never teach in ghettos, but they will have to teach deprived students, for there are many ways in which students are deprived. By teaching in ghetto schools, student teachers learn to become aware of many of the barriers that must be overcome before they can work effectively with deprived students. Many psychological and social needs must be met before students are in a state of readiness to approach the academic tasks demanded of them.
3. Could the fact that this faculty was almost entirely composed of Latin Americans explain the unexpected open climate in this school?
   This probably did have some effect on the climate at Rio Grande, because Latin Americans do tend to express themselves openly and enthusiastically, using a high degree of both verbal and nonverbal communications—an observation based on three years' experience living and working in a Latin community.

ACTIVITIES

At one time or another, all of us will teach classes that represent different cultures, so we will need strategies for working with cultural differences. In fact, even in a class whose ethnic composition is similar, there is often a diversity of cultural backgrounds. The following activities will help you work with multicultural groups.

1. Most of us are biased toward our own ethnic group. Make a list of your own biases.

  2. All ethnic groups have some cultural qualities that can make a contribution to American society. Name some ethnic groups, and identify one such quality of each.

  3. Describe a strategy that would be appropriate in your subject and grade level for breaking down cultural prejudices. Consider including techniques for showing the attributes of different classes and groups.

SUGGESTED READINGS

Amos, O. E., & Landers, M. F. (1984). Special education and multicultural education: A compatible marriage. *Theory into Practice, 23,* 144–150.

Bishop, G. R. (1986). The identification of multicultural materials for the middle school library: Annotations and sources. *American Middle School Education, 9,* 23–27.

Cathey, F. M. (1980). *Teacher perceptions of multicultural education in comparison with their previous multicultural education preparation.* Ph.D. dissertation, George Peabody College for Teachers.

Cheyney, A. B. (1976). *Teaching children of different cultures in the classroom* (2nd ed.). Columbus, Ohio: Merrill.

Cole, D. J. (1984). Multicultural education and global education: A possible merger. *Theory into Practice, 23,* 151–154.

Coles, R. (1970). *Uprooted children.* New York: Harper & Row.

Dandridge, J. A. (1980). *The attitudes, knowledge of subject matter, and classroom behaviors of teachers using multicultural/multiethnic programs.* Ed.D. dissertation, University of Southern California.

Dawson, M. E. (Ed.) (1974). *Are there unwelcome guests in your classroom?* Washington, D.C.: Association for Childhood Education International.

Fantini, M. D. (1986). *Regaining excellence in education.* Columbus, Ohio: Merrill.

Garcia, J., & Garcia, R. (1980). Selecting ethnic materials. *Social Studies, 44,* 232–234.

Garcia, R. L. (1984). Countering classroom discrimination. *Theory into Practice, 23,* 104–108.

Grant, C. A., Melnich, S. L., & Riven, H. N. (1977). *In praise of diversity: A resource book for multicultural education.* Washington, D.C.: Association of Teacher Educators.

Henson, K. T. (1975). American schools vs. cultural pluralism. *Educational Leadership, 32,* 405–408.

Henson, K. T., & Henry, M. A. (1976). *Becoming involved in teaching,* Chapter 9. Terre Haute, Ind.: Sycamore.

Irving, K. J. (1980). Cross-cultural awareness and the English-as-a-second-language classroom. *Theory into Practice, 23,* 138–143.

Klassen, F., & Gollnick, D. (1977). *Pluralism and the American teacher.* Washington, D.C.: American Association of Colleges of Teacher Education.

McCormick, T. E. (1984). Multiculturalism: Some principles and issues. *Theory into Practice, 23,* 93–97.

National Council for the Accreditation of Teacher Education (1985). *Standards for the accreditation of basic and advanced preparation programs for professional school personnel.* Washington, D.C.: NCATE, p. 5.

Nussel, E. J., & Wiersma, W. (ERIC ED 227 200). *Inservice education and its effects on teacher attitudes.*

O'Reilly, P., & Borman, K. (1984). Sexism and sex discrimination in education. *Theory into Practice, 23,* 110–116.

Payne, C. (1984). Multicultural education and racism in American schools. *Theory into Practice, 23,* 124.

Powell, M., & Beard, J. W. (1986). *Teacher attitudes: An annotated bibliography and guide to research.* New York: Garland.

Ramirez, M., & Castaneda, A. (1974). *Cultural democracy.* New York: Academic Press.

Smith, F. R., & Cox, C. B. (1976). *Secondary schools in a changing society.* New York: Holt, Rinehart & Winston.

Stewart, I. S. (1975). Cultural differences between Anglos and Chicanos. *Integration, 8,* 21–23.

Teacher Corps (1977). *In praise of diversity: A resource book for multicultural education.* Edited by M. J. Gold, C. A. Grant, & H. N. Rivlin. Washington, D.C.: Association of Teacher Educators.

Tesconi, C. A. (1984). Multicultural education: A valued but problematic ideal. *Theory into Practice, 23,* 88.

Van Til, W. (1978). *Secondary education: School and community.* Boston: Houghton Mifflin.

PART IV

APPLYING TECHNOLOGY TO TEACHING

Today's teachers have at their fingertips a variety of technologies with potentials as broad as the teacher's background and perspective. Chapter 10 will make you aware of the wide range of commercially produced media and prepare you to make your own materials. Chapter 11 explains the status of the microcomputer in the schools and discusses ways to use the microcomputer to elevate the level of thinking in the classroom. As you read these two chapters, think about the subjects and the grade levels you plan to teach. Think also about your own strengths and preferences, and as you learn about new technological developments, think of ways you can adjust the old and new developments to increase their effectiveness in your future classes.

Using Media

Objectives _____

- Name two widely used forms of media in middle and secondary schools.
- Give two guidelines for using the bulletin board.
- Give one guideline for introducing any audio or visual presentation, and two guidelines for concluding a presentation.
- Name two types of teacher- or pupil-made media.
- Name two newer types of media and explain an advantage of each over its predecessors.
- Name and explain a common misuse of media.
- Name two content areas in which teachers today perceive a need for more instruction.
- Provide a theoretical rationale supporting the use of media in instruction.

PRETEST

	Agree	Disagree	Uncertain
1. Films should be used only when they have instructional value.	——	——	——
2. Audiovisual equipment is most effective when kept separate. Therefore the teacher should use only one machine for each lesson.	——	——	——
3. Films that contain professional introductions need no further introduction by the teacher.	——	——	——
4. Generally, the best bulletin boards are those designed by students.	——	——	——
5. By consulting the research data, teachers can determine the type of media that is best for each purpose.	——	——	——
6. Middle and secondary school students spend more time watching television than they spend in the classroom.	——	——	——
7. Symbolism, such as that provided through the media, is an essential part of the learning process.	——	——	——

Middle-Level Message

Transescence is an age of activity and excitement. Instead of fighting these natural behaviors, middle-level teachers should learn to channel the abundance of energy and enthusiasm of students at this stage into productive activities. Media is especially important to this age-group—their world is one of radios, tape recorders, and televisions. The students' love for media frequently conflicts with academic expectations that teachers hold for this age-group, but this need not be a problem if you can use media constructively in your lessons. Even higher levels of success can be attained if you learn to involve your students in the development of media-based presentations. The level to which your students will benefit from media will depend upon your skills in clarifying the relationships between the media and the academic objectives of each lesson. Remember that in a recent national survey, half the middle-level teachers reported that they have inadequate knowledge of media and how to apply it in their classrooms.

For several decades, the rate of technological developments in the United States has greatly exceeded educators' ability to determine the impact the various media have on American youth. It has also exceeded the schools' ability to integrate media into the classroom. As a result, most teachers do not have the knowledge and skills they need to use media in ways that would fully utilize the potential of media in the education process. In one study, 49 percent of a random national sample of middle school teachers reported that their background in instructional media was insufficient to prepare them for their instructional responsibilities (Henson, Chissom, & Buttery, 1986).

Why do so many of our teacher education programs fail to prepare teachers to use media effectively in their instruction? The answer may be no more than conjecture, but this is an important question. Perhaps few educators understand the role that media and the symbols they produce play in learning.

Much of our contemporary understanding of the learning process has its roots in the work of John Locke. During the last half of the seventeenth century, Locke postulated that the mind is like a blank slate (*tabula rasa*) that remains empty until something is placed on it. He believed that the only way to fill this slate is through experience. Most current educators recognize that much of what we know comes through indirect or vicarious experiences, and the history and practice of education in the United States supports Locke's emphasis on experience.

During the last quarter of the nineteenth century, John Dewey and Colonel Francis Parker introduced child-centered education into American schools. Lecture and recitation were replaced with student activities. This child-centered education, called the Progressive Movement, dominated the curricula from the early 1920s to the early 1940s, and Harvard University was commissioned to study its effectiveness. The study ran from 1933 to 1941 and was named the Eight-Year Study. It found that students who graduated from the child-centered schools equaled their counterparts in traditional schools in the attainment of subject matter, and they outperformed them in attaining academic honors and grades. Furthermore, the graduates of the progressive curricula were significantly superior in intellectual curiosity, creativity, drive, leadership, and intraclass activities. They were also more objective and more aware of world events. Heinich, Molenda, and Russell (1985) remind us of Jerome Bruner's (1966) advice that instruction should proceed from direct experiences through iconic representations of experience—that is, through symbolic representation, such as pictures, films, and other media.

The exact roles that media play in learning are complex and not fully understood at this time. Some studies suggest that different types of images produce varying influences on memory (Kosslyn, 1981, p. 469). Other research suggests that images are coded into abstractions, stored in memory, and later reconstructed as they are recalled (Gagne, 1970). The following conclusions by Clark and Salomon (1986, p. 474) summarize the latest understandings of how media should be used in instruction. First, "It appears that media do not affect learning in and of themselves," and second, "Past research on media has shown quite clearly that no medium enhances learning more than any other medium regardless of learning task, learner traits, symbolic elements, curriculum content, or setting."

This does not suggest that the use of media in instructional planning should be minimized. Rather, it reflects the complexity involved in learning and the premature stage of educational research on media instruction. It does suggest that, in planning to use media in curricula, teachers should not attempt to locate research that shows what particular medium is best for each lesson. Clark and Salomon (1986, p. 474) hasten to add that "newer media also afford convenient and often novel ways to shape instructional presentations."

This chapter introduces a wide variety of media available in most schools and gives suggestions for using each medium. Become familiar with these media so you will be prepared to use a variety of media during student teaching and other clinical experience opportunities. The "Activities" section at the end of this chapter suggests other ways you can prepare to make full use of media to enrich your future teaching.

THE MEDIA IN YOUR OWN SCHOOL

Most teachers have access to many teaching aids—for example, projectors, films, posters, and records. Most larger schools have a media center; other schools provide media through the school library. Some school districts keep all their media in one location and make it available to each teacher on one or two day's notice. Teachers who avoid using media may shortchange their students by omitting an additional learning experience that might reach some students better than any other strategy. As you examine some of the media available, decide what will be worthwhile for you and your future students.

THE 16MM PROJECTOR

To many students, viewing a film is the same as seeing a movie, if the film is entertaining. From a teacher's perspective, a film should be both entertaining and educational. Above all, it should help students attain some specific course objectives. The teacher can help by introducing the film before showing it, giving pupils a few specifics to look for and pursue. After the film is over, involving students in a discussion of those key points is a good way to review the film. Whether note taking should be required depends on how quickly the material is introduced, the purpose of the film, and whether there is adequate light for writing. Identifying appropriate films and preparing the necessary instructions require that teachers preview films before showing them in class.

Some teachers choose to show a film to fill in time, such as on a Friday afternoon before a lengthy vacation. This practice is questionable because it encourages students to think of films purely as sources of entertainment. Films should be a planned part of the instructional program and coordinated with the rest of the unit.

A good film can be an excellent way to introduce a topic. It can help students build a mental framework by giving them an understanding of unfamiliar material.

A quality film can also create enthusiasm for the topic being studied. Many teachers also find films useful for reviewing a topic or a unit, because films can summarize a lot of information quickly. Films that are technical in nature are excellent for teaching highly technical processes. For example, a physical education teacher may use films on bowling, golfing, swimming, and other sports to show the necessary skills and techniques. Whatever the purposes for using a film, those purposes are more likely to be attained if they guide the selection of the film and if the purposes are communicated to the students.

Before graduation you will probably take courses that provide opportunities to work with various equipment found in a media center. Should you fail to apply yourself in this setting and remain unable to operate the projector correctly, you will introduce confusion when you later attempt to use this machine in your own classroom.

FILMSTRIP AND FILM LOOP PROJECTORS

Like the 16mm film, a good filmstrip or film loop (a miniature motion film that runs for only a few minutes and then repeats itself) is an excellent addition to a unit of study. These too should be previewed and planned into the lesson. The approach for showing a 16mm film can also be highly effective when used with these media. The sequence of events is to alert students to a few key concepts to pursue and to see that this is achieved by holding a discussion or question-and-answer session at the end of the film loop or filmstrip. The advantage the filmstrip and the film loop offer over the 16mm projector is that they allow for discussion during the film, which can add motivation and depth of understanding.

THE OVERHEAD PROJECTOR

Aside from the chalkboard, the most commonly used audio or visual medium in the classroom is the overhead projector. It offers two distinct advantages over most other types of audiovisual equipment. First, it is available and versatile. You can make transparencies easily with a few sheets of inexpensive clear acetate and a grease pencil, or you can use colored felt-tip pens made for writing on the acetate. The color will add interest to the lesson. A second advantage of the overhead projector is that it allows you to face the class at all times, seeing hands as they are raised, watching facial expressions, and retaining good control. The chalkboard does not provide these opportunities.

Success with the overhead projector depends on whether there are appropriate quality materials and whether the machine is used correctly.

Securing Materials
The quality of overhead projectors in the United States is high. Most machines have a standard-size surface and produce a clear image. Their 500-watt intensity can produce a clear image without having to darken the room or even turn off the

lights. These machines are durable and, unless abused, seldom require maintenance. A major concern, then, is how to get good transparencies to use on the
projector.

There are two ways to acquire good transparencies: Teachers can persuade
the school to purchase them, or teachers can produce their own materials. The
most commonly purchased material for the overhead projector is the simple transparency. Commercial publishers offer a wide range of transparencies in most
subjects for use at different grade levels. Most of the transparencies sold today are
multicolored and designed to capture students' attention. Many communicate
major concepts simply and clearly.

Check with your department head and your school's learning center and/or
media center to see what supplies and catalogs for ordering these materials are
available. When ordering transparencies, check the age-group (or range of ages)
for which the transparencies are designed. Following is a list of sources for transparencies:

> Audio Visual Communications, Inc., 159 Verdi Street, Farmingdale, NY
>   01135
> AeVac Educational Publishers, 1604 Park Avenue, South Plainfield, NJ 07018
> Encyclopedia Britannica Film, Inc., 425 Michigan Avenue, Chicago, IL
>   60611
> ESSCO Educational Supply Co., Inc., 2825 East Gage Avenue, Huntington
>   Park, CA 90255
> Johnson Plastic, Inc., 526 Pine Street, Elizabeth, NJ 07206
> Miliken Publishing Company, 611 Olive Street, St. Louis, MO 63101
> Scott Reprographs Division, Holyoke, MA 01040
> Lansford Publishing Company, 2516 Lansford Avenue, San Jose, CA 95125
> Valiant Industries, 172 Walker Lane, Englewood, NJ 07631

Producing Materials

Because of cost, convenience, and suitability for lesson plans, many teachers
make their own overhead transparencies. There are several processes for doing
this, but because some are quite elaborate and require machinery not available to
most teachers, only the easiest and fastest methods will be discussed.

If your school has a thermal copying machine (most schools do), you can
place a sheet of special transparency film over the sheet you want to copy and run
it through the machine. This method, which takes about 10 seconds, can be used
to copy pictures or print with a carbon base. Because most printed materials do
use carbon, they can be reproduced quickly. Even pencil drawings, theme papers,
problems, and the like usually work well. Copyright laws forbid reproducing
copyrighted material for profit. In the past, teachers were permitted to copy
materials for use in their classes, but because of abuse and because copyright laws

are changing, you should check with your administrators to see that your projects do not violate the law.

A second method of producing transparencies is equally inexpensive, easy, and fast. Just run a sheet of frosted acetate through the spirit duplicator as you would a piece of paper. The image will be printed on the sheet. For further details on the production of transparencies, see this chapter's "Suggested Readings," especially the entries for Kemp (1975) and for Haney and Ullmer (1975).

Using the Overhead Projector

As mentioned earlier, effective results with the overhead projector depend on good materials and good utilization. The following list provides guidelines for using the overhead projector.

1. Use a good transparency pencil or pen (not an ordinary felt-tip pen).
2. Select the best classroom position for projection so that all students can see the projection clearly.
3. Face students when speaking to them—you don't have to turn around every time, as you would when using a chalkboard.
4. Any transparent models or objects, such as plastic rulers, protractors, ripple tanks, and test tubes, can be projected vividly.
5. Tracing charts or drawings on construction paper or on chalkboards can be easily accomplished by simply projecting the original transparency.
6. When you do not want to show the entire transparency, cover up the portion of the contents with paper (masking technique).
7. When you want to add or correlate the contents simultaneously, simply add on another transparency (overlay technique).

Once you have the materials, concentrate on the next important step—the actual positioning and focusing of the machine. Before attempting to focus it, determine how far from the screen the machine will be. This is easy: Direct the light onto the screen and move the projector away from the screen until the light fits just immediately within the boundaries of the screen. Then the image can be brought into focus simply by changing the distance between the lens and the machine's surface. Most machines have a knob that can be turned to achieve focus.

There is one more matter to consider when you use the overhead projector. You may prepare the transparency in advance, or you may write, sketch, or draw on a clear sheet of acetate during the lesson. Bringing the transparency to class already prepared offers an advantage over using the chalkboard. The teacher does not have to take time from the lesson and attention from the students to write the paragraphs, make the lists, or draw the diagrams. But there is also an advantage to developing the visual material during the lesson: You can stop and involve students at strategic points. Perhaps the best method is to prepare transparencies in advance, leaving some empty spaces for the teacher and students to complete as the lesson progresses.

Overlays

Transparencies are clear, so they can be stacked on top of each other to add dimensions or details to the image. Because such superimposure requires accuracy in placing each transparency exactly over the one underneath, you will find it helpful to make a cardboard frame for the first transparency, then tape one side of the second transparency to the left side of the frame. If yet another superimposure is desired, tape the top of the next transparency to the top of the frame. Continuing to tape one side of each transparency at a 90-degree angle to the previous one, you can stack up as many transparencies as you want.

During education courses that provide opportunities to teach peer lessons, and during your student-teaching internship, you will have opportunities to experiment with making your own transparencies, with using prepared materials, and with preparing materials during the lesson. Experiment with all these approaches.

THE OPAQUE PROJECTOR

Before the thermal copy machine and the overhead projector were available, the opaque projector was frequently used in classroom instruction, and it does have some advantages. It can project an image on a screen directly from the book, saving the time and expense of making a permanent copy of the material. Also, there is no question of copyright infringement.

Its greatest problem is its bulky size, blocking the image from the view of many students and becoming a major barrier between the teacher and some students. A second design problem is the weakness of the image. A good image often requires total darkness in the room, leaving students unable to take notes or work problems but free to engage in other less academic pursuits of their own choosing. Other disadvantages are that it is noisy and that its opening, although adjustable, prevents the use of very thick books. In addition, if a book is left too long on the projector, the intense heat will damage the page.

With so many disadvantages, you may never choose to use this machine in teaching a lesson, yet you may find it useful for projecting very large images on the wall for the purpose of tracing.

THE SLIDE PROJECTOR

Like the overhead projector, the slide projector projects an image so intense that it can be seen in most lighted classrooms. One advantage of slides is that they can capture real scenery, people, and events that are relevant to the subject under study. Just think how much more interesting a Spanish class can be if the teacher shows a collection of slides taken on a vacation to Mexico. Or the social studies teacher can intensify interest by showing slides of people at work in different countries. The biology teacher can produce a similar effect with slides of plants and animals taken on a visit to the desert, mountains, plains, and seashore.

Although 110 cameras produce a slide that is too small to be clear in most classrooms, 126 cameras work well. The 35mm cameras, which are more expensive, produce even better slides. When taking pictures for slides, take more than one of each promising subject to increase the likelihood of getting quality results. If people are being photographed at close range, be sure to get their permission. Encourage students to take slides to share with the class. Field trips should always have follow-up discussions, and good slides will enhance the discussion.

THE RECORD PLAYER

Even though you may associate the record player with music and dancing, you should not limit its use to these alone. A story or poem read by Orson Welles, or a ballad sung by Burl Ives, can communicate in special ways. As with other media, the purpose should be made clear from the beginning and reemphasized at the end, and the students should have assigned tasks that will involve them with the content portrayed through the media. The record player can have good application in the area of language arts, most specifically in developing listening skills. Good questions during the discussion after the record are a means of positively reinforcing students who did listen attentively.

TELEVISION

No discussion of the role of media in education would be complete without including television. The effect of television on today's youth is reflected in statistics that show that Americans spend between 23 hours a week (for children under five) and 44 hours a week (for adults) watching television (Miller 1977). American students spend more time watching television than they spend in school (Morriset, 1984). In the classroom, televisions have become a common medium for instruction. Today, more than half of all teachers in the United States use television material in their classes (Riccobono, 1984).

In the future, television will play an important role in the education of our children. You can help by holding discussions about quality programs in your classroom. Teachers' professional associations and unions can lobby for more quality programs designed for adolescents at each age level. And of course you can support the educational networks and encourage others to do likewise.

THE BULLETIN BOARD

Good media are not always purchased—they can be made by teacher or students. The bulletin board (or cork board or felt board) can be an excellent way to stimulate thinking. The board should never be allowed to become dated, and the contents should revolve around a central theme.

A bulletin board can help make subjects come alive. Posters and pictures depicting one aspect of a unit under study give all students a similar opportunity to learn, regardless of their home situation or background. Consider, for example, a teacher who is starting a unit on Africa. On the bulletin board that teacher places a map of Africa with a photograph of the leader of each country pasted in the respective country. During discussions of leaders, countries, and events, each student can identify the leaders and locate the events. Without this visual aid, students who do not watch the news regularly and who have never visited Africa would be at a disadvantage. Although a picture cannot replace personal experience, it does narrow the gap between the students who have some awareness of the country and those who do not.

Bulletin boards have other uses. Placing a "Problem of the Week" in one corner of the board and encouraging students to attempt solutions any time their other work is completed can be motivating. In a week's time, all students will have had the opportunity to solve it and will be eager to compare their answers with the teacher's. One teacher uses the bulletin board to make a time line for social studies. Each day a few students are responsible for "bringing it up to date," based on the material covered that day.

Many teachers are concerned less with how a bulletin board looks than with what it says or does. They let the students be solely responsible for it, so that everything on it represents their efforts. Throughout the year, the board is constantly changing, because the world is always changing. Some teachers believe that an attractive, neat bulletin board is the mark of a good teacher. They will spend hours cutting out letters and making an eye-catching display, especially before an open house or parent-teacher meeting, and definitely during American Education Week. As long as it looks good and visitors will be impressed, they think, it doesn't matter that the bulletin board lacks function—that students actually learn nothing from it. Unfortunately, some principals, wanting to see such neatness, encourage teachers in this direction.

THE CHALKBOARD

The chalkboard has value beyond its most common use. The students' attention should focus on it automatically, without a request from the teacher. Some teachers achieve this by placing a "thought for the day" at the top of the chalkboard and leaving it there all day. Graffiti can also get students' attention. For example, imagine students entering a room to see the message HELP ME! I'M TRAPPED BACK HERE! written backward on the board.

Colored chalk can be stimulating, but check with the custodian before you use it. Some colored chalk is difficult to remove from certain surfaces, even with soap and water. Chalkboards have been permanently damaged by nonstandard white or colored chalk.

SOME NEWER TYPES OF MEDIA

In recent years, audiovisual equipment has become more attractive and effective. The dimension of sound has been added to filmstrip and slide projectors. Some schools even have facilities for teachers to make their own sound slides. This could be an interesting project for you and your classes, regardless of subject content. Check out the audiovisual facilities and possibilities your school offers.

The videocassette recorder (VCR) has great potential for use in secondary and middle school classrooms. It is unique in that it makes possible the viewing of television programs aired at times other than class time.

Before copying a program, always get permission from the network showing the program. This should not be a problem if the request is made on the school's letterhead stationery and is co-signed by an administrator. Wait for permission to be granted. One network filed a lawsuit against a university that used its newscasts regularly without network permission.

The VCR can also be useful for capturing students' behavior as they perform psychomotor skills—for example, a student bowling or a drama class acting—permitting students to study their technique. This makes it possible for them to see their mistakes either in isolation (by freezing the picture) or as a part of the total process.

MEDIA COMBINATIONS

Media combinations can enhance almost any lesson. For example, before showing a film, filmstrip, or videotape, you can outline the objectives of the lesson on the chalkboard or overhead projector. These lesson objectives may be used again for review at the end of the period. Or, as a tape recorder or record plays a new dance, you could outline the steps on the overhead projector. Some teachers become very sophisticated with the way they develop and use audiovisual equipment. Others use media only in simple ways, which still can be quite effective.

RECAP OF MAJOR IDEAS

1. Media decisions should be based on how much a particular type of media facilitates and enhances the effectiveness of a particular lesson.
2. Films, tapes, and records should always be previewed before use in the classroom.
3. The use of such media as tapes, films, filmstrips, and records should be prefaced by an introduction that instructs students to look for particular objectives and should be followed by a review of these objectives.
4. Media should be used to its maximum advantage.

5. Transparencies for the overhead projector are versatile and easily prepared by the teacher.
6. Whenever feasible, middle and high school students should be involved in the preparation and use of media for instructional purposes.
7. Such media as bulletin boards, photography, slides, and videotapes offer excellent opportunities for students to use their creative abilities.
8. While neatness is always desirable, the value of bulletin boards is determined more by their function than by their beauty.

POSTTEST

Now that you have read the chapter, take a moment to respond to the following statements again:

	Agree	Disagree	Uncertain
1. Films should be used only when they have instructional value.	____	____	____
2. Audiovisual equipment is most effective when kept separate. Therefore the teacher should use only one machine for each lesson.	____	____	____
3. Films that contain professional introductions need no further introduction by the teacher.	____	____	____
4. Generally, the best bulletin boards are those designed by students.	____	____	____
5. By consulting the research data, teachers can determine the type of media that is best for each purpose.	____	____	____
6. Middle and secondary school students spend more time watching television than they spend in the classroom.	____	____	____
7. Symbolism, such as that provided through the media, is an essential part of the learning process.	____	____	____

CASES

The following cases show several mistakes that teachers make when using media. For each misuse, you can make your own mental corrections to reverse the effects of these media on the students.

Case 1: Too Much Research Is Conducted in the Teachers' Lounge

Mark found his first two weeks of teaching to be a variety of everything but teaching. He called rolls, made seating charts, made entries in a state attendance record book, and distributed textbooks—although he wasn't sure why because there seemed to be no time to use them. By the beginning of his third week he overheard some colleagues expressing his exact sentiments in the teachers' lounge.

MR. MILLER: Mary, I don't know how you do it. You seem to

MRS. JENKINS: have your classes running so smoothly, yet you are acting chairperson of the Social Studies Department and sponsor of the Teachers of Social Studies Club. What is your secret?

MRS. JENKINS: Tom, you're flattering, but I'm sure your classes are well organized too.

MR. MILLER: No, I'm dead serious. I seem to work harder and get further behind. You know the old adage "The harder I work etc., etc." I just barely have time to put one foot in front of the other. I mean, having to lecture for five hours daily with only one planning period is more than a full-time job. Then we have all the paperwork and the ballgames. I really mean it. I'd like to know how you manage everything.

MRS. JENKINS: Well, I may not know what I do, but I know one thing I don't do, and that's lecture all day. I order a number of good films during the summer and have them coming in all during the year.

With this news in mind, Mark went to the resource center. Within the next 20 minutes he had found dozens of films that seemed appropriate for his classes. He chose only those that ran for one or two full periods and that could be used in both his history and government classes. With this accomplished, he felt he could relax a little.

Indeed, the coming weeks saw a new Mark with a fresh, new style. With films on Tuesdays and Thursdays, he could relax and plan for every other day. This was much less demanding than the old style of planning new lessons for each day. The students welcomed it too. The first few films provided great entertainment. Mark's classes soon earned the reputation and title "Mark's Cinema." He enjoyed the joke and laughed when a colleague kiddingly accused him of serving popcorn and soft drinks.

But all good things must come to an end, and this magic system was no different. As strange as it sounds, the students were the first to tire of the films. When the class turned into chaos, Mark was astounded and perplexed. How could such a neat system turn so sour?

Discussion

1. Was Mark wrong to select films several months in advance?
No. This is a good practice, because it ensures that the popular films will be available and it enables the teacher to coordinate the films with the lessons. Good films can complement even the most interesting lessons. A good film is often an excellent way to introduce a new study unit because of the vast amount of material a film can cover in a short period of time.

2. Why did Mark's students come to dislike the new system?
Because of the way Mark used the films, all they offered his students was a change from the old routine. Soon the films became an old routine, equally as boring as the lectures.

3. What was wrong with Mark's system?

First, Mark chose films that took up the whole period, leaving no time to introduce or summarize the main concepts in each film. Second, Mark tried to substitute the films for lessons instead of using them to enrich each lesson. Finally, Mark used each film in both his history classes and his government classes, but it is unlikely that even one film was appropriate for both subjects. Mark apparently did not even bother to preview any of the films, but this essential step must precede the showing of any film.

Case 2: A Bulletin Board Is Misused

During her second full week of student teaching in ninth-grade English, Carla Cromwell was assigned to take over composition writing. Carla was aware that students who do good work need to be positively reinforced, so she included in her plans a way to give those students a feeling of success. On Friday, after giving a special writing assignment, she posted the 6 best papers from the group of 23. The caption at the top of the bulletin board in large, colorful letters read "We Have Some Good Writers." In the same class, six other students had papers with A grades, and only three had made below a C.

Discussion

1. Should a teacher post student papers on bulletin boards?
   The answer to this question depends on the circumstances. In general, putting the "good" papers on the board will positively reinforce the owners of those papers, but the teacher needs to consider the effects on the other students too. It is possible that other papers should have been posted, especially the six with grades of A. By ignoring these, the teacher implies that they are less than good. More often than not, a student whose paper is displayed because of its quality is the student who already has high self-esteem. The students who seldom do good work also need positive reinforcement but are not likely to see their papers posted.
   There are also nonacademic talents and behaviors that are worth promoting. The teacher who looks for promptness, cooperation, creativity, decision-making ability, communication skills, or other desirable traits will be able to recognize every student for being good at something. This is the time to make it known to all by placing the actual work, or a note describing it, on the bulletin board. The following list is only a sample of what could be displayed.

   Paula was the first to complete the term project.
   Did you see the paintings that Carol and Susan entered in the school exhibit?
   John and Dave really make a smooth team in tennis doubles.

   The point is that when only good work in a single subject is posted, some students will become discouraged. They will think they have no chance to be recognized. On the other hand, never giving reinforcement this way can be detrimental to the motivation of the higher-achieving students. Therefore, it is a good idea to mix up the routine, making sure that each student is positively recognized from time to time.
2. How could Carla have been more humane in dealing with the compositions?
   Although there are many alternatives, some stand out. First, why post them at all? Instead, write words such as "Good work" or "Way to go!" Carla could talk individually with the few who did poorly and encourage them to improve their work.
   Another approach would be to establish standards for each student. For instance,

Jack, a poor speller, has fewer spelling errors on a new paper than on a previous paper. That should be considered progress—indeed, even success—regardless of the number of errors on the latest paper. Carla can enter into a contract with him to get a score commensurate with his abilities. She could do the same for each of Jack's classmates. All students who fulfill the contract would get their names entered on the board under the heading "Writers of the Week."

Case 3: A Teacher Has Problems with a Film

Sharon Croft was in her first month of teaching in a twelfth-grade Spanish class. In the film catalog she located a 12-minute color film that was appropriate for her class. She ordered it from the school system's central media library, but instead of receiving it on the day she requested, she received it the day she planned to show it.

Having taken a course in college dealing with the use of multimedia, Sharon felt confident about using the projector. Getting ready to show the film proved to be no problem, but during the actual presentation Sharon noticed something was wrong. The takeup reel was spilling film onto the floor, and by the time she realized it, much of the film lay in disarray next to the projector stand. Although she was alarmed, Sharon decided to finish the film rather than turn off the machine.

Discussion

1. Was Sharon's decision a wise one?
   Sharon probably did what was best. Had she noticed the spillage as soon as it began, she would have needed only a little time to turn off the machine and correct the problem. However, since so much film was on the floor, the educational benefit of the film may have been lost by stopping it and rewinding. Any action Sharon might have taken, other than what she did, would have disrupted the class.
2. What harm can be done to film when it spills onto the floor?
   The major harm is scratches that may result from the film rubbing against furniture or dirt on the floor. If the teacher is careful when rewinding, the film may not be too damaged. Other damage that may occur during the rewinding process is breaking or "crimping" of the film itself.

Case 4: Dated Material Decorates the Room

Ms. Jefferson's room in Public School No. 128 had a bulletin board running the entire length of the wall from the front of the room to the back, ending at the doorway. Having taught in this room for more years than she cared to admit, Ms. Jefferson was constantly faced with finding a use for the bulletin board. Out of frustration she had decided to caption it "What's happening now" and began gathering newspaper and magazine articles about developments in the Spanish-speaking countries of the world. When completed, it was a colorful collage, a mixed bag of names, places, faces, and events. All visitors to the room noticed it immediately, but on closer inspection they realized the material was all at least a year old.

Discussion

1. What effect might the display of old news have on students?
   Consciously or unconsciously, students may view the teacher as outdated. As teachers get older, they do not necessarily become outdated. In fact, most retain a youthful exuberance—probably the result of continuous association with younger people. Although students do notice age, that does not usually affect their judgment of a teacher. It is the manner in which the teacher operates that affects the students. In Ms. Jefferson's classroom, she was about a year behind.
2. How can the problem of bulletin board obsolescence be avoided?
   Whatever the alternatives, they should involve the students. With as much bulletin board space as Ms. Jefferson had, no wonder she had difficulty keeping up with it. Having students maintain a bulletin board relieves the teacher from this chore while giving students opportunities to become further involved with the lessons. Committees could be chosen for the purpose of changing the display at given intervals. This would provide students needed responsibilities and opportunities to learn to work cooperatively with others. Although the most attractive bulletin board displays may be the work of teachers, the best displays are often made by students.

ACTIVITIES

Because you have grown up in a world of multimedia, you probably know a lot about media and have many ideas about applying it to instruction that were not addressed in this chapter. The following activities will give you an opportunity to relate the material in this chapter and your previous knowledge about media to improve the teaching of your own subjects.

1. Make a list of anecdotes you can use to communicate to your students. Explain the media you will use for each. For example, will you post these on the bulletin board, write them on the chalkboard or overhead transparency, or distribute them on mimeograph handouts?
2. Select an important theme or concept in your field of study and devise several ways to introduce it using a different form of media with each.
3. Devise one good multimedia presentation to introduce a topic in your major field. If you have skills in photography, art, music, or drama, consider using these in your presentation.
4. Visit your university's media center. Ask about new or recent media developments. Select one of these new developments and research the literature to determine its potential for classroom use.

SUGGESTED READINGS

Adams, R. S., & Biddle, B. J. (1970). *Realities of teaching with video tape*. New York: Holt, Rinehart & Winston.

Bosco, J. W. (1984). Interactive video: Educational tool or tray? *Educational Technology, 24,* 13–19.

Bruner, J. C. (1966). *Toward a theory of instruction*. Cambridge: Harvard University Press.

Cassidy, M. F., & Knowlton, J. Q. (1983). Visual literacy: A failed metaphor? *Educational Communications Technology, 31,* 67–90.

Cheatwood, D., & Benokraitis, N. (1983, April 10). Making the most of bad times: Integrating the media, funding, and teaching. *Teaching Sociology,* pp. 337–351.

Clark, L. H., & Starr, I. S. (1976). *Secondary school teaching methods,* Chapter 14. New York: Macmillan.

Clark, R. E., & Salomon, G. (1986). Media in teaching. In M. C. Wittrock (Ed.), *Handbook of research on teaching* (3rd ed.). New York: Macmillan.

Dick, W., & Carey, L. (1985). *Systematic design of instruction.* Glenview, Ill.: Scott, Foresman.

Erickson, C. W. H., & Curl, D. H. (1972). *Fundamentals of teaching with audiovisual technology* (2nd ed.). New York: Macmillan.

Gagne, R. N. (1970). *The conditions of learning.* New York: Holt, Rinehart & Winston.

Gleaves, K. S. (1978). School media center: The changing scene. *Peabody Journal of Education, 55,* 169–204.

Haney, J. B., & Ullmer, E. J. (1975). *Educational communications and technology.* Dubuque, Iowa: Brown.

Hanks, W. (1983). Using cable access channel increases student motivation. *Journalism Education, 38,* 33–34.

Heinich, R., Molenda, M., & Russell, J. D. (1985). *Instructional media and the new technologies of instruction* (2nd ed.). New York: Macmillan.

Henry, M. A., & Beasley, W. (1982). *Supervising student teachers the professional way: A guide for cooperating teachers* (3rd ed.). Terre Haute, Ind.: Sycamore Press.

Henson, K. T., Chissom, B., & Buttery, T. J. (1986). Improving instruction in middle schools by attending to teachers' needs. *American Middle School Education, 2,* 2–7.

Hoover, K. A. (1976). *The professional teacher's handbook* (2nd ed.), Chapter 18. Boston: Allyn & Bacon.

Kemp, G. E. (1975). *Planning and producing audio-visual materials* (2nd ed.). New York: Crowell.

Kim, E. C., & Kellough, R. D. (1978). *A resource guide for secondary school teaching* (2nd ed.). New York: Macmillan.

Klein, G., & Swinton, G. (1972). *Television teaching techniques.* Sydney, Australia: Angus & Robertson.

Kosslyn, S. M. (1981). The medium and the message in mental imagery: A theory. *Psychological Review, 88,* 44–66.

Miller, M. S. (1977, June). The Farrah factor. *Ladies Home Journal,* p. 34.

Morrisett, L. (1984). Forward to J. Murray and G. Salomon (Eds.), *The future of children's television.* Boys Town, Neb.: Boys Town Center.

Morsy, Z. (Ed.) (1984). *Media education.* Paris: UNESCO.

Riccobono, J. A. (1984). Availability, use, and support of instructional media, 1982–1983. In *Corporation for public broadcasting.* Washington, D.C.: National Center for Educational Statistics.

Rowntree, D. (1982). *Educational technology in curriculum development* (2nd ed.). Bath, Eng.: Pitman.

Travers, R. M. W., & Dillon, J. (1974). *The making of a teacher.* New York: Macmillan.

Wegner, H. (1978). *Teaching with film.* Fastback No. 103. Bloomington, Ind.: Phi Delta Kappa.

Yannone, D. S. (1984). Videotaping to improve classroom management. *Media Methods, 21,* 21–23.

C H A P T E R **11**

Using Microcomputers in Education

Objectives

- Name and discuss axioms that teachers can use as guidelines for selecting computer knowledge and skills to improve their teaching.
- List some common misconceptions that pre-service and in-service teachers have about microcomputers.
- Make a list of attitudes that facilitate mastery of computer skills and a corresponding list of impeding attitudes.
- Define computer literacy and contrast it with computer awareness.
- Differentiate between computer managed instruction and computer assisted instruction.
- Name at least three levels at which computers can be applied to teaching.
- Explain how the computer can be used to help teach both slow students and advanced students.
- Design a system for evaluating computer software for classroom use.

PRETEST

	Agree	Disagree	Uncertain
1. All teachers need to develop some proficiency with computers.	____	____	____
2. People who are not quantitatively inclined usually find the computer difficult to understand and master.	____	____	____
3. In selecting a computer, individuals or schools should begin by asking "What can I afford?" and "What brand is best?"	____	____	____
4. Like many people who purchase computers for personal use, many school systems have rushed into buying computers without understanding the unique capabilities and limitations of the computer.	____	____	____
5. A computer should be selected according to how the purchaser intends to use it.	____	____	____
6. The major instructional advantage that computers offer is their ability to improve drill-and-practice type instruction.	____	____	____
7. Anyone who is capable of meeting all other teaching certification requirements should be able to master the computer at the level needed to improve teaching responsibilities.	____	____	____
8. Some of the newest microcomputers have creative abilities of their own.	____	____	____
9. Eventually, all teachers will need to become experts at designing new programs.	____	____	____
10. A high level of confidence is helpful for teachers who are beginning to develop their computer skills.	____	____	____

Middle-Level Message

The rapid expansion of microcomputers into the schools has had an important impact on middle-level teachers in two ways. First, it made them realize that they must learn to use this tool if they are to be effective teachers in today's society. Second, the speed with which computers appeared in schools produced fear in many teachers. When the telephone and the automobile were invented, they produced a similar fear in people. As a result, many Americans avoided these new inventions and never learned to use them. As with the telephone and the automobile, the best way to become competent and comfortable with the computer is to have direct contact with it.

As you read this chapter, note the many advantages that the computer offers for your classes. If you have not taken courses in computer education, locate a microcomputer on your campus and spend some time learning everything you can about it. If your college or department of education has a computer lab, ask to see a demonstration of software that is appropriate for middle-level classrooms.

The United States is experiencing a computer revolution that is having a profound effect on all its institutions. The business world was among the first to realize that the computer would have such a dramatic effect that any company from the major industries down to small family businesses would lose their ability to compete unless they learned to apply the computer to increase their efficiency. Hospital managers were quick to see the advantage this innovation offered in keeping track of thousands of patients, diseases, and drugs. Attorneys realize a similar advantage as they attempt to keep thousands of court cases at their fingertips. Law enforcement officers take advantage of the computer to run an identification search on any one of 200 million U.S. citizens plus thousands of aliens, not to mention to determine immediately the authenticity of millions of driver's licenses and automobile registrations. The agricultural industry uses the computer to produce better hybrids of plants and animals, reducing tasks that once took years of experimentation to a few hours or even a few minutes.

This revolution has filtered down into the homes of millions of Americans. It is no wonder that educators are also examining the vast opportunities this innovation offers the field of education. This chapter will help you appreciate what the computer has to offer education by providing the basics for understanding the history and nature of today's computers. We will also focus on computer literacy and then look at some changes that have occurred as a result of the computer. Finally, you will have an opportunity to explore your own role with the computer and see how you can plan to use it to your advantage.

HISTORY OF THE MICROCOMPUTER

Perhaps you have heard parents or grandparents describe the first computer they ever saw. If not, you have surely seen these computers in science fiction movies. You enter a large room that is literally congested with enormous machines; your immediate reaction is one of awe; you may be overwhelmed by the size and complexity of the operation. On the other hand, your reaction and that of your future students may be far more casual—"So what?" or even "Wow! What dinosaurs we have here!" Whatever your reaction, you should realize that in their heyday these machines represented a significant breakthrough in technology, a breakthrough that is now revolutionizing the lives of everyone.

The early computers had to be so huge because information storage room was needed. Information was stored on keypunch cards, and machines had to sort and house thousands of these cards. While there remains a need for such giant computers, a single invention enabled the development of the microcomputer. This invention, which revolutionized computer technology, was a small improved memory unit called a microprocessor unit (MPU). This newer unit is a tiny rectangular integrated circuit, called a chip, that is smaller than a dime, yet it contains the equivalent of 20,000 different components, such as transistors, capacitors, and diodes. The chip is very similar to the human brain, which has trillions of small electrical circuits (called neurons).

The invention of the microcircuit reduced the size of the computer so much that the jobs formerly performed by units weighing a few tons can now be performed by what are now called microcomputers, some of which can even be carried in one hand like a briefcase. The cost has been reduced a thousandfold so that the earlier computer that cost more than a million dollars can now be bought for a thousand dollars. Furthermore, the microprocessor unit can do the job much faster. A job that once required hours of typing on keypunch cards can now be done in seconds, or at most in minutes. A microcomputer can fetch or store a word in one-millionth of a second (one microsecond).

This introduction to the history of the microcomputer has admittedly been cursory. The special glossary at the end of this chapter will give you the opportunity to become further acquainted with this exciting field of study. We now turn to the problem of just how much—and, more important, what types of—computer information tomorrow's teachers need to be effective in their profession.

USING COMPUTERS IN TEACHING

The popularity of microcomputers in education has had an irreversible impact on schools. Today's teachers must be prepared to use computers in the classroom. Computers are changing our lives, and because a major purpose of schools is to prepare future citizens, school programs would be grossly inadequate if they failed to prepare graduates to function productively in the society at large.

But teachers and schools have another equally important need for computers, a need relates to the computer's increasing potential. Computers have become less expensive and more versatile. The range of computer use in all fields, including education, is limited only by the creative limitations of the mind. Teachers can use computers to manage instruction, or they can use computers as tutors. For example, the computer can be used for drill and practice, simulation, problem solving, and creating. In other words, the computer can be used to expand the types of instruction students receive, and they can be used to improve a teacher's current mode of instruction. A less-recognized advantage is the computer's ability to free the teacher to give more personal attention to students. But are teachers ready for this role? Do they have the expertise required to provide quality individualized counseling? Too often the answer is no.

This chapter will help the teacher or prospective teacher develop positive attitudes toward the use of computers in schools and will cover ways of using computers to manage, improve, and test instruction. Suggestions for evaluating programs will be provided.

COMPUTER MANAGED INSTRUCTION (CMI)

Resulting largely from external accountability programs (often at the state level), many schools have adopted massive programs to improve the quality of instruction and ultimately increase the standardized test scores of large numbers of students. The mastery learning program and interclass grouping mentioned in Chapter 7 are examples. Such programs require extensive record keeping. Some of the programs are district-wide and involve thousands of students, so large that they could not be managed at all without computers. Using computers, schools and school systems can provide individualized education plans for thousands of students.

The managing of student records, diagnosing and prescribing material, monitoring progress, and testing are collectively called computer managed instruction (CMI). By definition, computer managed instruction does just as the name implies and no more—it manages the records. It does not provide instruction, although it may contain instructional programs. But the value of CMI should not be underestimated. Some CMI programs are packages or systems that include course objectives and corresponding test items.

Because CMI programs are usually quite expensive, selection should be made carefully. If your future school(s) offer the opportunity, try to provide input into this selection process. Preview CMI programs to see whether they are easy to operate—"user friendly." Determine whether a program is capable of keeping the types of information you would want for your classes. If at this time you are not sure what kind of information you will need the computer to manage for you, examine the lesson plans and learning units in Chapters 3 and 4. Another factor to consider when providing input into the selection of CMI programs is the degree to which the program involves students.

Some of the most effective CMI programs have been developed for particular school districts or states. Personnel in local school district offices will often design a program to match the district's objectives, curricula, and schedules. In many instances, outside entrepreneurs have learned about state-wide instructional management accountability requirements and developed programs for individual schools or districts.

Ideally, your school should have a committee to select CMI programs. Express your desire to be a member of that committee. When the committee selects a few programs, ask the vendor for names of other schools who have used the programs and contact them for their input.

COMPUTER ASSISTED INSTRUCTION (CAI)

Unlike computer managed instruction, which in its purest form is limited to testing and record keeping, computer assisted instruction (CAI) links the student directly to the material to be learned via the computer. The student is actively involved in the learning process. The involvement itself has a motivating effect. There are various levels of involvement, depending upon the type of CAI program used.

Drill and Practice

At the lowest level, the computer behaves much like the early teacher, who lectured and then had students recite the material in the same form. In all secondary and middle-level subjects at all grade levels there seems to be some information that is basic to the mastery of each discipline. For example, at the entry middle school level, students need to know their multiplication tables to be successful in their math classes. In beginning chemistry, high school students are often required to memorize the Periodic Table of Elements. Drill and practice is an effective approach for learning at this level of knowledge. The computer can give questions, score the answers, and give immediate feedback.

Tutorial

The drill-and-practice application just mentioned describes the computer in the role of the teacher, tutoring the student, but not all tutorial application of computers is limited to this simple recall or knowledge level. In fact, one of the first applications of computers to education was a tutorial program that used simulations. Project PLATO, funded by the National Science Foundation, began in the 1950s at the University of Illinois. This program has several thousand students at elementary through college levels. Other PLATO projects have sprung up throughout the United States. Preceding the development of BASIC language, PLATO uses a higher-level language. Some CAI programs that use BASIC include a project at the Minnesota Educational Computing Consortium in Minnesota and the Chicago City Schools Project, which provides several thousand fourth- through eighth-grade students with tutorial lessons in mathematics and reading.

How effective are CAI programs, compared with traditional instruction? Chambers and Sprecher (1980) reviewed the literature to determine what research studies have found about the effectiveness of CAI. They cited eight separate studies which found that CAI either improved learning or showed no difference when compared with traditional instruction, seven studies which found that CAI reduced learning time compared to the regular classroom, and six studies which found that CAI improved student attitudes about using computers for instruction. These studies included a variety of CAI programs (e.g., drill and practice, tutorial, and simulations). But the reader should not judge the success of CAI as compared with teacher instruction, for in most of these studies (as in most studies in general) these programs had teachers present who participated in the instruction.

Simulation

As you have already seen, using computers for helping with instruction usually involves varying degrees of combinations of different types of instruction. This makes it impossible to put programs into completely separate categories. For instance, tutorial programs can involve drill and practice or simulations, making what are really combination programs—tutorial–drill-and-practice or tutorial-simulation combinations. This is also true of simulation programs. While simulations can be used simply to provide examples to reinforce memorization, most simulations involve the learner in problem solving. Students have the opportunity to live out roles and find solutions to often complex problems.

SOME MISCONCEPTIONS

The most obvious and common misconception since the development of the early "teaching machines" of the 1940s is that the machine will replace the person. So it has been in education—many still fear that computers will replace teachers. But this can never happen. Although the popular microcomputers dazzle the mind with their speed and ability to store large quantities of information that can be recalled and assembled in millionths of a second, the microcomputer, like all other computers, has no imagination. It is not creative. It does not have the ability to appreciate or love. Therefore, it cannot attend to the many human needs that all students have.

In essence, by itself, the computer cannot teach at all. Students cannot be made to learn, but sometimes they can be encouraged, enticed, and led to learn. The computer cannot provide the role model that students need to encourage them to learn, keep them on a steady track, and occasionally put them back on track when they go astray. Ironically, the nonhuman qualities that give the computer its advantages (vast speed, capacity, and the ability to work endlessly without getting tired or making errors) are also the qualities that make the computer dependent on the teacher. More helpless than the students themselves, the computer cannot do anything but follow commands.

A second misconception that impedes computer application in instruction is the tendency of many to think of the computer as a simple drill-and-practice machine. Future teachers should strive to use the computer in a variety of ways. Special attention should be given to using computers to promote higher levels of thinking and even creativity. Students should be taught to use the computer to solve problems. Correctly utilized, the computer even has the ability to expand the creative abilities of students. Teachers should search for ways to require students to develop problems to be solved. The more advanced students can learn to write programs to solve these problems.

In future classrooms there must be a concern for the impact the computer will have on society. Students at all levels should be encouraged to look at ways computers threaten to diminish the quality of human life in modern societies. Advanced students can learn to write programs that will counteract these negative effects. Generally, the emphasis of computer assisted instruction has shifted from drill and practice to tutorial to simulations. The age levels using computers for instruction have shifted from university to high school to elementary school.

Henson (1984) found that teacher education programs in major American universities are lagging behind other American institutions in their application of microcomputers and that as late as the mid-1980s universities were not giving adequate attention to preparing future teachers to select computer hardware and software. The findings of this study were reinforced by another study, which showed that teachers have concerns about using computers in the classroom and about the inadequacy of teachers' training (Berg, 1983).

TEACHERS' FEAR OF COMPUTERS

Some of the miconceptions about computers are the basis for much of the fear of computers that many teachers share. By counteracting these false beliefs, teachers can lower their anxiety levels. In retrospect, some of the dominating fears of a few years ago now seem totally irrational, and others seem inane. For example, when teaching machines were introduced, many teachers were afraid that they would be replaced by a machine. For years many teachers refused to use television in the classroom for fear television would replace the teacher. The same fear resurfaced again recently when teachers began using microcomputers.

Many find the computer threatening because of the many things it can do so well, but they fail to realize that without an operator the computer can do nothing. There is a direct correlation between the microcomputer's ability to contribute to teaching and the degree to which the developers of software and the users understand the learning process. Put simply, there is no danger that teachers will ever become subservient to computers.

The degree to which microcomputers can improve learning without teachers being involved is inversely proportional to the level of learning produced. For example, although the computer can be programmed to help students memorize facts, the teacher must become involved with higher-level educational opportunities, such as problem solving, weighing values, and making complex decisions based on logical reasoning. The teacher must first identify the higher-level goals and objectives and then be able to select the appropriate software to achieve these objectives. The teacher's mental powers are always needed in the use of computers.

The common fear of microcomputers among many teachers should not be interpreted as dislike or disapproval of the use of computers in the classroom. On the contrary, Floyd (1983) found that even teachers in rural schools who have limited knowledge about microcomputers have positive attitudes toward their use. Fear of computers does not appear to be associated with the teachers' demographic characteristics (such as sex or age). But the extent to which teachers have had positive experiences with computers does affect their attitudes toward computers (Placke, 1983). Positive experiences can come from meaningful interactions with computers in professional methods courses, especially when students learn concepts concurrently with the application of those concepts—that is, with "hands on" experience. Muller (1978) found that teachers acquired more-positive attitudes when they learned concepts and their applications concurrently, instead of first learning the concepts and then later learning how to apply them.

EDUCATIONAL SOFTWARE
AND CURRICULUM PLANNING

The level of development of educational software is still very low. Much of the software is designed to be glamorous but lacks a sound theoretical base—in other words, it is not instructionally sound. Since 1950 there has been considerable progress in the United States toward teacher-developed curricula, following a period of having curricula developed by federal, state, and local agencies. This was a positive shift, but the current trend toward using more prepackaged computer programs threatens to reverse the trend toward teacher-developed curricula.

As early as the late nineteenth century, student participation in the development of curricula was being encouraged. This was continued in the Progressive Education Era, from World War I to World War II, when student involvement was determined to have more advantages than disadvantages. Students who were involved learned more, were more motivated, developed more self-reliance, and were more creative than their traditional counterparts. Will tomorrow's students be encouraged to improve their curricula? Will they be taught to evaluate their CAI programs and modify them to produce better curricula? Not necessarily.

The 1960s and 1970s brought increased interest in humanizing the curriculum and in values clarification. Many educators considered these to be positive directions. But will developers of educational software continue to produce programs of second-wave mentality—programs that lack imagination and variety? According to Siegel and Davis (1986), there is reason to believe so, as reflected in the great number of computer books written to teach amateurs to program and the very few books that tell how to select educationally sound software.

In the past, curriculum guides tied daily instruction to overall aims. Do we have any assurance that computer programs will do this, or that, even if they do, students and teachers will see the relationships between the two? These are a few of the author's concerns about the direction and effects of the computer movement on education. The following is a list that includes these and other concerns.

SOME PROBLEMS AND LIMITATIONS OF COMPUTERS IN EDUCATION

A tendency to overuse drill and practice at the expense of ignoring higher levels of application, such as simulation and problem solving

A belief that computers can replace teachers

Dehumanizing effects of CAI

Limited availability of good educational software

Lack of student involvement in program design

Lack of teacher involvement in curriculum development

Use of programs unrelated to educational aims

Emphasis on narrow facts rather than on broad generalizations

Limited opportunities for students to express their ideas orally and in writing

Lack of necessary counseling skills

Lack of opportunities to apply new knowledge

An instructional process so complex that attempts to compare CAI with traditional teaching methods are almost impossible

Uncertainty about the teacher's role

You can probably double the number of entries on this list. Yet teachers should consider CAI as a tool that has the potential to become more important as new and better ways to apply it are discovered. Instead of dwelling on the limitations and problems of computers in education, take a few minutes to list some advantages computers can bring to education. For each advantage, list ways to increase the likelihood that the potential will actually be realized.

WHAT IS COMPUTER LITERACY?

The term *computer awareness* means knowing about computers. In contrast, *computer literacy* is often thought to mean knowing enough about computers to function competently in society today. Tomorrow it will mean even more—perhaps including being able to use the computer to counteract its negative effects in our classrooms and in society at large. Even with its current definition, computer literacy means different things to different people. To the professional programmer it means being able to design programs, but to the secondary and middle-level teacher its meaning is not so specific.

By now, most teachers recognize the need to know more about computers. Current concerns have two major dimensions. First, teachers want to know more about computers so they can use them in their teaching and improve learning in the classroom. Second, teachers want to help students acquire the understandings and skills they need to perform effectively in their future chosen occupations, where computer knowledge will undoubtedly be needed. In other words, today's teachers want to be computer literate themselves, and they want to be able to help their students become computer literate too.

Because these two goals are different—one is practical and teacher oriented, the other is student and future oriented—the exact computer knowledge and skills needed by one teacher or student may differ from what others need. For this reason we cannot identify a specific set of computer knowledge and skills that can meet the needs of all teachers. But teachers do share certain basic needs. Through its elementary and secondary schools committee, the Association for Computing Machinery recommends that all teachers be able to *understand* computing (Schall, Leake, & Whitaker, 1986, p. v) and lists the following essential competencies: All teachers should—

1. Be able to read and write simple programs that work correctly and understand how programs and subprograms fit together into systems
2. Have experience using educational application software and documentation
3. Have a working knowledge of computer terminology, particularly as it relates to hardware
4. Know by example, particularly in using computers in education, types of problems that *are* and some general types of problems that *are not* currently amenable to computer solution
5. Be able to identify and use alternate sources of current information on computing as it relates to education
6. Be able to discuss at the level of an intelligent layperson some of the history of computing, particularly as it relates to education
7. Be able to discuss moral or human-impact issues of computing as they relate to societal use of computers generally and educational use particularly

---

Let's Ponder

Identifying Your Own Computer Needs

As you begin to sort out the facts, principles, and skills you will need to work with computers, it is important to take an inventory of your needs at this time. Begin with yourself, because your needs may be quite different from those of your classmates. Think about your own attitudes toward the computer and the subject(s) you will be teaching and respond to the following questions.

1. How enthusiastic are you about the microcomputer itself?
2. How threatened do you feel by the task of operating machines and equipment such as telephones, televisions, recorders, and typewriters?

3. What special opportunities does your subject offer for students to be creative?
4. Are there certain aspects of your subject that are especially boring?
5. Do you enjoy simulations and games? If so, what about them do you find satisfying?
6. In what type of school system do you plan to seek employment? Urban? rural? affluent? impoverished? conservative? progressive?

BASIC AXIOMS ON COMPUTER USE FOR TEACHERS

Many prospective teachers, like many teachers who are now teaching in our classrooms, have uncertainties and fears about computers. The following basic content generalizations, in the form of axioms about the application of computers to education, will help you sort out your emotional reactions to or doubts about computers as you begin to fill this broad gap in your knowledge and skills. They also give you an opportunity to begin preparing yourself in this area. Computers will be an important part of your future teaching responsibilities.

Application Axioms

The following axioms address the body of computer knowledge you will need to carry out your teaching responsibilities.

Axiom No. 1: *There is a definable body of computer knowledge that is indispensable for all teachers.* While computer needs vary from teacher to teacher, there is certain basic information that all teachers need. Included is a minimum vocabulary, set out in the Glossary at the end of this chapter. Another category of indispensable information is an awareness of the broader generalizations in the field. This information can be acquired by studying the following axioms.

Axiom No. 2: *The computer needs of teachers vary from one teacher to another and from one location to another.* Some individuals have a natural affinity for computer knowledge—to the point that they become engulfed with, even obsessed by, computers. You will notice among your own future students that this natural liking for computers is not limited to adults. Teachers and students who experience this level of excitement about computers should be encouraged to pursue the area of study as much as they desire. For some teachers, computers will never have this level of fascination. Teachers who are not inclined in this direction should not be required to make a lifetime study of computers.

The level to which a particular school system is involved in computers also influences the degree to which teachers will need to pursue study of computers. Teachers who have computers in their classrooms have greater immediate need for knowledge about computers and their application than do teachers whose school has no computers.

Axiom No. 3: *Teachers should first learn to operate the brand(s) of computers that are in their schools.* As teachers begin preparing for their future computer responsibilities, one of the first questions is "How many computers should I learn to operate?" Another common remark is, "Once you learn to operate one microcomputer, it is no problem to transfer this knowledge to another brand.'' The latter statement is not without its limitations. It may be true that someone who has mastered a certain brand of computer and who thoroughly understands how it operates may have little difficulty using other computers. However, although many teachers have become quite adept at writing their own programs, most teachers will not attempt to reach a high level of computer mastery. As teachers become involved with computers, they would be wise to limit the number of brands they work with. An attempt to learn to operate several types of computers at once may lead to confusion, frustration, and discouragement. As we shall see, a positive, confident attitude is important to success.

Axiom No. 4: *Selection of one brand of computer over others should begin with an examination of the teacher's philosophy*. An important criterion for selecting a computer is the nature of the intended use of the computer. But the answer to this question depends on you. By itself, the computer can do nothing. Your own enthusiasm, interest, and priorities will determine the degree to which computers can improve your effectiveness.

Two questions should be foremost in your mind as you begin the process of selecting a computer. What can I do with this computer that I could not do without it? And what noninstructional responsibilities that take away from my teaching time can a computer perform for me? In addition, the quality of software each brand offers must be considered, because it may place serious restrictions on a computer's ability to deliver these goals.

Most teachers would like to have exciting and challenging lessons, but teachers—even the most effective ones—are limited. We are limited by our own abilities to be creative and to develop creative assignments, and we are limited by the many nonteaching chores that befall all teachers. An analysis of our own goals and our own limitations should precede selection of a computer brand.

Axiom No. 5: *Teachers should use computers toward the attainment of higher-order goals*. Those whose familiarity with computers is limited often also have a limited view of what the computer is capable. They are apt to associate computers with the old teaching machines, whose primary objectives were aimed at facilitating rote memorization. Today's teachers must realize that the potential of the microcomputer greatly exceeds drill-and-practice functions. When used for instructional purposes, teachers should use the computer to attain higher goals. For example, many commercial programs require problem solving, and in doing so they help students develop problem-solving skills. Some teachers write their own programs to add new challenges for their students. Indeed, many students are writing their own programs and are learning ways to use the computer to solve a multitude of real, practical problems. Software for instructional goals falls into four general categories: drill and practice, tutorial, simulation, and administrative.

Attitudinal Axioms

A teacher's attitudes and feelings influence the level of proficiency with the computer that the teacher will develop. As you examine the next set of axioms, carefully analyze your own attitudes and feelings. Realize that almost everyone has some suspicions and reservations about the abilities of the computer to improve learning and that most of us have fears about our own ability to become proficient with the computer.

Axiom No. 6: *A confident posture is essential for teacher success with computers*. The immediate appearance and rapid distribution of microcomputers, intensified by the thrusting of new computer requirements on teachers (many of whom have had no former contact with computers), has caused a great amount of fear in many teachers throughout the United States. The ultimate question is: What if I can't master the computer? This is unfortunate and tragic, because confidence is a prerequisite to optimal success with the computer.

Axiom No. 7: *All teachers are capable of learning to use computers effectively to improve learning in their classrooms*. All teachers and prospective teachers who can meet all other certification requirements are also capable of learning to use the computer effectively in their teaching roles. Because confidence is essential for learning to use the computer, you must take a determined stance and view the computer as the tool it is—a tool you can use to help students attain your course objectives.

Axiom No. 8: *A proactive posture is essential for teacher success with computers*. While confidence is probably 90 percent of the task of learning to use conventional software, without action you will fall short of your goal. Your efforts should begin now, while you are still taking this course. Once you start learning to program, your logical-thinking skills will improve. When this happens, you will probably find that your initial fears will be replaced by enthusiasm and eagerness in your lessons and in other aspects of your teaching role.

Let's Ponder

Analyzing Your Own Attitudes

Read the following paragraph and respond to the questions below.

Most of us have reservations about the potential of the computer to make substantial improvements in our classrooms. We also have reservations about our own abilities to learn to master the computer. Because these reservations place severe limits on your future ability to use the computer effectively, you must search out your own feelings and begin to develop the confident and assertive posture that will help you attain the proficiency you will need to improve your teaching.

1. How responsible do you feel for promoting problem-solving skills in your students?
2. Do you believe the microcomputer offers much potential for promoting creative thinking?
3. How would you feel if you were asked to attend a computer in-service program or workshop?
4. What evidence is there that the computer will become a permanent fixture in most American schools?
5. How do you feel about teachers having so many nonteaching responsibilities, which include such clerical tasks as issuing textbooks, maintaining daily attendance records,

and collecting money for various projects? Would you be able to use this time more constructively if these tasks could be performed by computers?

6. How do you feel about test-item banks? Do you think it is always better to start from scratch each time you begin developing a test, or do you believe there is an advantage in using questions again and again, perfecting them as needed.

7. What aspects of the computer movement do you like best? least? For example, where do you see its greatest potential? its greatest limitations?

8. As you look 10 years into the future, do you believe teaching will be improved because of the computer?

COCURRICULAR AND EXTRACURRICULAR COMPUTER APPLICATIONS

The potential unlimited use of the microcomputer to improve instruction in the classroom is perhaps the greatest area of promise that the computer offers teachers, but it is not the only important area of contribution. What follows are two real-life examples of different, yet important, noninstructional applications of the computer. Although neither brought about a direct change in instruction, each had dramatic positive effects on increasing learner attainment.

Improving a Local School Program

A school district in suburban Indianapolis developed a successful computer application to improve the academic performance of lower-achieving students. teachers had become concerned that many students were not being challenged to improve their academic performance. The mediocre and poor students received little recognition, no matter how hard they worked. What these students needed was a motivator, an incentive, some kind of recognition. Thus the idea for the "Roaring 500 Club" was born.

Membership in this club was reserved for the 500 students throughout the whole district who had the greatest improvement in each six-week grading period. The computer facilities in the school system were such that a computer program was quickly written to select those 500 students at the end of each grading period. The names of the 500 students who had improved the most during each grading period were incorporated into a large attractive display in a glassed-in case located right inside the main entrance of each school. The display was titled in bold lettering "The Roaring 500 Club." It is the first thing everyone who enters sees.

The advantages are obvious. First, students who had little or no chance of attaining academic recognition under the previous system could now earn recognition. Second, in this program the low achievers had a greater opportunity to succeed than did the straight-A students, who had little margin for improvement.

Improving District and State-wide School Programs

When we think of using the microcomputer to improve instruction, our first thoughts may be limited to unique ways of applying the microcomputer in the classroom. Some fantastic programs are being, and will continue to be, developed at this level, but we should not overlook the broader possibilities that the computer offers school systems.

Consider the potential for improvement of educational programs at state and district levels. State accountability programs continue to grow. By the early 1980s, more than 75 percent of the states had already developed their own accountability programs. For example, one state developed a state-wide accountability program known as AIM (Accountability in Instructional Management). This program requires each of the state's 150 school districts to develop a unified curriculum from grade 1 through grade 12. Each program must have objectives, teacher and student activities, and resources for each lesson throughout the year. Furthermore, each objective must have some test items. These curricula must be developed by the teachers working together in their own areas to develop systematic, sequenced lessons. Because each teacher must write objectives and then select activities to teach these objectives, the ultimate benefit of this program will be that each teacher will be more aware of the objectives of each course and how they are to be attained. Furthermore, the testing program will measure and reinforce the objectives.

But imagine the logistical chore of having to keep up with hundreds of objectives and thousands of test items. The answer to this complicated problem for many school systems will be the microcomputer. Programs that require a computer to store all the test items and objectives are already available, and upon the command of any teacher the computer will randomly select test items and make up a test to match the objectives of a grading period. In fact, because each objective is keyed according to its level in its respective taxonomy domain, the teacher can request a tailor-made test of items designed to fit the capabilities of each group of students. Without the aid of the computer, these improvements would be too time-consuming to implement.

RECAP OF MAJOR IDEAS

1. The development of an advanced microprocessor unit in the mid-1970s revolutionized the computer industry, making computers smaller, faster, and cheaper.
2. Other institutions and professions in our society have been quick to take advantage of the microcomputer to improve their operations.
3. The rapidity with which school systems are purchasing computers may result in the procurement of millions of dollars worth of machines that will not be effectively utilized.
4. At this time, *computer literacy* is an ill-defined term. What is needed to make one teacher computer literate may be quite different from what is needed to make another teacher computer literate.
5. While some may believe that the overall advantages of the computer movement are exceeded by its detriments, it cannot be denied that the microcomputer will have dramatic effects on education in our schools.

   6. Computer selection should be based on intended use and the characteristics of the local school setting.
   7. Many teachers and prospective teachers doubt their ability to master the computer at a level necessary to improve their teaching. Yet most, if not all, are capable of attaining these skills and understandings.
   8. Effective application of the computer to teaching requires using the computer in ways other than mere drill and practice. The microcomputer should also be used to teach problem solving and to develop creative thinking.
   9. Computers can be used to take over many nonteaching responsibilities that currently befall teachers, thus freeing the teacher for several hours each week. This time can be used to plan lessons, design programs, examine software, or otherwise improve instruction.
   10. As individuals first begin learning to operate microcomputers, the process can be simplified by limiting the number of brands of computers they attempt to learn to operate to one or two.

POSTTEST

Now that you have read the chapter, take a moment to respond to the following statements again:

	Agree	Disagree	Uncertain
1. All teachers need to develop some proficiency with computers.	____	____	____
2. People who are not quantitatively inclined usually find the computer difficult to understand and master.	____	____	____
3. In selecting a computer, individuals or schools should begin by asking "What can I afford?" and "What brand is best?"	____	____	____
4. Like many people who purchase computers for personal use, many school systems have rushed into buying computers without understanding the unique capabilities and limitations of the computer.	____	____	____
5. A computer should be selected according to how the purchaser intends to use it.	____	____	____
6. The major instructional advantage that computers offer is their ability to improve drill-and-practice type instruction.	____	____	____
7. Anyone who is capable of meeting all other teaching certification requirements should be able to master the computer at the level needed to improve teaching responsibilities.	____	____	____
8. Some of the newest microcomputers have creative abilities of their own.	____	____	____
9. Eventually, all teachers will need to become experts at designing new programs.	____	____	____
10. A high level of confidence is helpful for teachers who are beginning to develop their computer skills.	____	____	____

CASES

The success of computer use in any school depends largely on the enthusiasm and determination of the teachers. As you read the following cases, consider how you would handle each predicament if you were one of the people involved.

Case 1: A Faculty Resists Microcomputers

The members of the Parent-Teacher Association at Eastside Middle School decided that their major project for the year would be to purchase three microcomputers—one to be used by the school's administrator and two to be available for students and faculty. A first-year teacher, Larry Worley, was excited when he learned he might have the opportunity to apply his knowledge of computers, but he was shocked to learn later that the majority of the faculty opposed the purchase. In the teacher's lounge he heard two senior faculty members discuss plans to express their concern at the next faculty meeting. They wanted to ask their colleagues to support them in openly opposing the computer purchase. The reasons they gave for their opposition were:

1. Microcomputer use in schools is a fad that will soon pass, leaving thousands of dollars of hardware and software to gather dust in storage.
2. Eastside Middle School serves the town's lower-socioeconomic residents. Student performance on standardized tests is consistently below that of other schools in town. Concern for improving the general level of basic skills should take precedence over beginning a new project.
3. Few, if any, teachers at Eastside have any computer expertise.

Larry wants to stifle these plans to abort the purchase of microcomputers, but he realizes that as a first-year teacher he may not have any influence with the faculty.

Discussion

1. What could a faculty do to ensure the longevity of their computer programs?
   The most obvious method might be for each teacher to learn more about microcomputers, but this is not likely to occur on an individual basis. Frequently, a group of teachers take the initiative to seek help from outside consultants. Local universities, community colleges, and business and technical colleges are usually eager to develop a special course to teach computer awareness and computer literacy when enough teachers are interested. Should such an approach be chosen, these teachers should involve the school's administrator(s), since the teachers will ultimately need financial support and perhaps time off for the courses.
2. How could one respond to the claim that schools should first do a good job with basic skills before buying computers?
   First, there is a tendency to associate computers with gifted students. While it may be true that more gifted students than slower students take advantage of computers, this need not happen. Microcomputers offer tremendous potential for the attainment of

basic skills. Drill-and-practice computer programs can be more motivating than teacher-directed drill and practice.

As a future teacher, you should try to find ways to use the computer to benefit all students, regardless of academic ability and interests. In this respect, teaching with the microcomputer is as different as traditional teaching. Finding ways to challenge all students has always been difficult, but it has been and continues to be an important responsibility of all teachers.

Case 2: A Problem of Morale

Microcomputers are no novelty at Brookwood High, which for the past five years has served as a testing ground for a privately funded project. By graduation, most Brookwood students have written their own programs, which range from farm management projects that 4-H club members have designed to perform mundane chores, to more sophisticated but less practical individual programs, such as chess and other games designed for amusement.

At the beginning of the school year, each junior and senior student is assigned a microcomputer. Centrally located, these microcomputers are available to students throughout the day. It has been five years since microcomputers were introduced at Brookwood. Student enthusiasm has not diminished, and every day some students continue to forfeit part of their lunch periods for increased time on the computer.

Unfortunately, the computers have failed to bring equal stimulation to the Brookwood faculty. On the contrary, the experiment initially aroused fears in some faculty members that computers might someday reduce the number of teachers needed. A good publicity program that praises the success of the project keeps this concern alive. Although the teachers seldom discuss the effects of the program, their concerns are manifested in their general behavior toward the students and even toward one another. Sarcasm has become commonplace in Brookwood classrooms, and teachers seldom congregate socially.

Discussion

1. Was the Brookwood teachers' fear of possible replacement rational?
   Although the likelihood of this occurring was remote, it is natural for teachers to feel threatened by this unfamiliar change. The popularity of computers among the students increased the threat.
2. How can you avoid computer-based fear?
   Although you may never completely avoid all computer-related fear, you can minimize it by learning more about them.

ACTIVITIES

1. Consider the direction that the definition of computer literacy has taken. Now try to extend this definition into the future. (Hint: Look at the major

trends in our society today, such as increased population, the faster pace of life, and transportation, then consider the effects these will have on numerous lifestyles. Now redefine computer literacy.)

2. Make a list of the advantages the microcomputer offers to secondary and middle schools. Make a corresponding list of disadvantages. Now see if you can find ways to convert any of the disadvantages to advantages. (Hint: Consider the effects on the levels of student involvement and on levels of thinking.)

3. Suppose you have accepted a teaching position in a school that has never used microcomputers. The administration has agreed to purchase a computer for each department, but your department opposes the purchase. Devise a rationale to convince your colleagues that the department needs a microcomputer.

FINAL NOTE

The manuscript for this book was printed out by a microcomputer. The computer operator was a high school English teacher who mastered the microcomputer on her own without any formal instruction.

GLOSSARY

BASIC (Beginner's All-Purpose Symbolic Instruction Code) A versatile and popular computer language used extensively by educators.

Binary digits (one and zero) Used to code information and store it electronically in a computer.

CAI (Computer Assisted Instruction) The application of computers to help individuals learn.

Chip An integrated circuit.

COBOL (Common Business Oriented Language) A higher-level programming language developed for use in business.

Computer An electronic machine that performs rapid, complex calculations or compiles and correlates data.

Database A file containing information in a format that makes it applicable and available to a user's needs.

Debugging The process of locating and removing errors from a program.

Diskette See *floppy disc*.

Downtime A period of time when a computer is not functioning properly.

EPROM Erasable Programmable Read Only Memory.

Execute To perform the operations specified by a computer instruction or program.

Floppy disc A flexible disc used widely by microcomputers.

FORTRAN   (FORmula TRANslation) A high-level programming language designed for scientific studies.

GIGO   (Garbage In, Garbage Out) Bad or faulty input leads to bad results.

Hardware   The machines or equipment of a computer system.

High-level language   A language that, when translated into machine language, produces many machine language instructions. A language that is more English-like than machine-like.

Instruction   A statement that specifies an operation.

Integrated circuit   A solid-state electronic circuit on a single layer of silicon.

Interface   An electronic go-between used to connect the computer to another device, such as a disk drive.

Interpreter   A computer program that translates and executes expressions one at a time.

Keyboard   A typewriter-like instrument for putting information into a computer; replaced the earlier keypunch machine.

Line printer   An instrument that prints computer output in the form of letters, numbers, and other symbols.

Load   To enter data into a program or to enter a stored program into memory.

Loop   A sequence of program instructions that are repeated until an exit command is given or a predetermined completion is reached.

Low-level language   Computer-programming language that is closely related to machine language.

Machine language   The instructions that a computer can recognize and execute without translation, usually expressed in ones and zeros.

Microcomputer   Microprocessor, memory, and auxiliary hardware, such as video units and printers, connected together in a single unit.

Microprocessor   The memory unit of a computer, often called a chip.

Microsecond   One-millionth of a second.

Minicomputer   A small computer that has peripheral equipment attached to it. Together with its equipment, it is larger than the microcomputer but smaller than the general-purpose computer.

Pascal   A relatively new higher-level language used extensively with microcomputers.

Personal computer   An inexpensive microcomputer designed for the home or small business.

PROM   (Programmable Read Only Memory) ROM that is programmed by the user, not the manufacturer.

RAM   (Random Access Memory, also called read-write memory) A high-speed memory to which the user can have access in about one-millionth of a second.

ROM   (Read Only Memory) Memory produced by the manufacturer to which the user cannot store or write additional information.

Software   Computer programs.

Solid state   Electronic components, such as diodes, resistors, and transistors, that are made of solid materials, as opposed to tube-type components.

Time-sharing   The distribution of computer-processing time among many users simultaneously.

SUGGESTED READINGS

Adams, J. (1983, March). How one computer science program grew. *Classroom Computer News*, pp. 74–75.

Bardige, A. (1983, March). The problem solving revolution. *Classroom Computer News*, pp. 44–46.

Barstow, D. (1979, February). Computers and education: Some questions and values. *Creative Computing*, pp. 116–120.

Berg, R. (1983). Resisting changes: What the literature says about computers in the social studies classroom. *Social Education, 47*, 314–316.

Bitter, G. G. (1984). *Computers in today's world.* New York: Wiley.

Bork, A., & Chambers, J. A. (1981, September). Computer assisted learning in the U.S. secondary/elementary schools. *Computing Teacher, 8*, 50–51.

Burke, M. W. (1986). *The effects of inservice in computer training on teachers' attitudes toward educational computing.* Doctoral dissertation, University of Alabama.

Callison, W. L. (1985). *Using computers in the classroom.* Englewood Cliffs, N.J.: Prentice-Hall.

Carrozzo, G. (1983, September). Teaching the basics with basic computers. *Educational Computing Magazine, 3*, 54–57.

Chambers, J. A., & Sprecher, J. W. (1980). Computer assisted instruction: Current trends and critical issues. In *Communications of the ACM.* Association for Computing Machinery.

Colburn, P., Kelman, P., Roberts, N., Snyder, T., Watt, D., & Weiger, C. (1985). *Practical guide to computers in education* (2nd ed.). Reading, Mass.: Addison-Wesley.

Dennis, R. J., & Kanksky, R. J. (1985). *Instructional computing: An action guide for educators.* Glenview, Ill.: Scott, Foresman.

Floyd, M. A. (1983). *An investigation of public school teachers: Knowledge about, attitude toward and willingness to use microcomputers as instructional tools.* Ph.D. dissertation, Pennsylvania State University.

Forbis, S. (1983, October). Designing educational computer games. *Health Education, 14*, 15–18.

Harper, D. O., & Stewart, J. H. (1983). *RUN: Computer education.* Monterey, Calif.: Brooks/Cole.

Henson, K. T. (1984). *The status of microcomputers in colleges of education in major American universities.* Unpublished manuscript.

Kulik, J. A. (1983). Synthesis of research on computer-based education. *Educational Leadership, 41*, 19–21.

Leausis, E. (1983, November–December). Computers in education: A bit of rationale. *Educational Computing Magazine, 3*, 10–11.

Luehrmann, A., & Peckham, H. (1984). *Computer literacy: A hands-on approach.* New York: McGraw-Hill.

Maples, M. D. (1983, September). The social and ethical implications of integrating computers in education. *Educational Computing Magazine, 3*, 24.

McIsaac, D. N., & Baker, F. B. (1981, October). Computer managed instruction system on a microcomputer. *Educational Technology, 21,* 50–59.

Muller, G. E. (1978). *The effects on teacher knowledge, attitude, and classroom behavior of simulated practice versus application of behavior management techniques during in-service instruction.* Ph.D. dissertation, University of Texas at Austin.

Papert, S. (1980). *Mindstorms: Children, computers, and powerful ideas.* New York: Basic Books.

Peterson, D. (1984). *Intelligent schoolhouse: Readings on computers and learning.* Reston, Va.: Reston.

Picket, S. M., & Hunter, B. (1983, September). Redefining literacy. *Momentum, 14,* 7–9.

Placke, J. E. (1983). *A study of the relationship between teacher attitude toward computers and leadership styles.* Ed.D. dissertation, University of Tulsa.

Riedesel, C. A., & Clements, D. H. (1985). *Coping with computers in the elementary and middle schools.* Englewood Cliffs, N.J.: Prentice-Hall.

Roberts, L. G. (1983). The computer age comes to our nation's classrooms. *Theory into Practice, 22,* 308–312.

Schall, W. E., Leake, L., Jr., & Whitaker, D. R. (1986). *Computer education: Literacy and beyond.* Monterey, Calif.: Brooks/Cole.

Schimizzi, N. V. (1983). Microcomputers in schools. Buffalo: State University of New York College at Buffalo. ERIC document reproduction source number ED 247-904.

Schmidt, G. (1983, October). Teachers learn about computers and learn about learning. *Learning, 12,* 36–37.

Siegel, M. A., & Davis, D. M. (1986). *Understanding computer-based education.* New York: Random House.

Syllabuses for the future. (1979). *AEDS Monitor.* Washington: Association for Educational Data Systems.

PART V

CLASSROOM MANAGEMENT

By this time you are probably wondering when we are going to get to the heart of the matter and discuss the teacher's role in the classroom. After all, such topics as discipline, classroom management, and motivation are the survival skills—without them, everything else you might learn about teaching becomes insignificant. This observation is correct. Without good discipline, management, and motivation skills, today's teacher will have a short career. These skills are not merely desirable or important—they are indispensable.

As you read, think beyond the survival point. Interaction with students is essential for effective instruction. The higher levels of thinking are best achieved through dialectic teaching, where the teacher and students share ideas. It is the teacher's responsibility to establish a climate where interaction among students and between the teacher and students occurs freely.

C H A P T E R *12*

Motivation

Objectives

- List 10 techniques for stimulating student interest.
- Explain the role of competition in motivating students.
- Name two ways a teacher can solicit the cooperation of parents.
- Explain Piaget's concept of "equilibrium."
- Role-play a teacher being confronted by an angry parent.
- State the relationship between self-concept and motivation.
- Describe the teacher's main responsibility in development of students' self-concepts.
- Explain the teacher's role in the use of humor in the classroom.
- Give three guidelines for using grade contracts.
- List five guidelines for using reinforcement in the classroom.

PRETEST

	Agree	Disagree	Uncertain
1. The more reinforcement the better.	____	____	____
2. Teacher enthusiasm cannot be planned.	____	____	____
3. Teachers are expected to tell students how to apply knowledge that is highly theoretical.	____	____	____
4. All teachers should *give* their students some success every day.	____	____	____
5. Humor is most successfully used in the classroom when it is systematically planned to fit the lesson.	____	____	____
6. Behavior modification is an example of internal motivation.	____	____	____

Middle-Level Message

William Alexander, the father of the middle school, advised that the middle school should serve not just the intellect but the whole child. This chapter will show you how to relate better to the whole child. This is essential for motivating the transescent. For example, you will learn to use humor and enthusiasm to stimulate student interest. You will also learn how to protect the students' self-concepts and nurture them toward positive growth.

As you read this chapter, think about the relationship between the emotional self and cognitive development and how you can apply the understandings shared through Piaget's work to your own future teaching in the classroom. Remember that although you cannot give success to your students, you are responsible for creating a climate that encourages and facilitates achievement. This means that you must motivate your students.

The world is a busy one, full of people who are competing for attention. Others try desperately to get our attention so they can sell us both material goods and ideals. There are many strategies for capturing our attention. Industries plan advertising campaigns that use a variety of media—television, radio, newspapers, magazines, and even the telephone—to enter our homes and make an imprint on our minds.

Everyone wants to sell something. Whether we need it does not matter so long as we buy it. After falling victim to this a few times, we become defensive and skeptical and feel that we must protect ourselves. We do this in several ways. For example, an artist may keep a few paintings at home to defend against salespeople. When asked at his front door to purchase a thousand-dollar set of encyclopedias, the artist invites the salesperson inside and offers to trade a thousand-dollar painting for the encyclopedias. Others defend themselves by becoming aggressive and forcing the salesperson to leave. But many are too polite for that, and not having a stock of thousand-dollar items to trade, they have learned to stand or sit patiently, pretending to hear while completely tuning out. They become quite skilled in pretending to listen. But as a college student you don't have to be told that!

So it is with secondary and middle school students, who day after day are forced to hear sales pitches by teachers who are often overloaded with knowledge that seems to be of questionable value. Like the ill-tempered adult, some youths speak up and criticize the product that they perceive to be irrelevant. But like most adults, many adolescents are too polite to do that, so for their own defense they shut us out and merely pretend to listen. Like any uninterested client or customer, they are good at faking their interest. They learn to watch for cues that tell them when to laugh and when not to. Some even fake it further by asking questions and then only pretend to listen to the answers.

Teachers daily face uninterested students who, skeptical of the teacher's wares, feel that their time and energy could be spent more wisely elsewhere. The teacher is largely responsible for changing these attitudes. Effective teachers exert much control over learning. Brophy and Good (1986) say that measures of teacher control typically relate either positively or curvilinearly to achievement. Effective teachers use praise frequently, ask more questions, and move their classes at a brisk pace.

Having just spent four years studying a particular subject, like other enthusiastic young teachers, you may assume that others share at least some of this interest. But to *assume* is dangerous. Instead, you would be wiser to analyze students and identify any existing interests about the subject. Once identified, you may kindle even a spark of interest into a more serious commitment.

But can a teacher really make all the students like a particular subject and every lesson? This is an excellent question, to which the answer is no. You can no more make students interested against their will than you can force students to learn. Your best strategy is to entice students, but before you can do this successfully your students must have an appropriate mind-set toward the subject, toward themselves, and toward you, the teacher.

STUDENT ATTITUDES TOWARD THE SUBJECT

While many students are turned off by studying, others are equally interested in learning. If members from both groups described the subjects they were taking in school, the adjectives they chose would differ drastically. And this is true for every subject—some students actually love it, others hate it. Most who hate it find it either boring or difficult or both. Let us first look at the students who find your subject boring, and then learn what you can do about it.

Students are concerned with relevance. They are confronted with so much knowledge that they must be highly selective, choosing what can be useful to them. Therefore teachers must show students how to apply what they are learning to practical problems, preferably in their own lives. For example, math ratios may be boring to some students until they learn to use them to determine the power and economy of their automobile. One major make of a full-size station wagon retained the same size engine and relatively the same carburetor from 1971 to 1973, but the manufacturer changed the ratio in the transmission, resulting in a gas-mileage loss of more than 33 percent. Other students may find ratios useless until they realize that they use them daily in cooking.

The wise teacher prepares a response to the age-old question "Why do we have to study this stuff?" After all, it does seem unfair to force students to listen to something they perceive as useless. It is impossible for a textbook to provide this answer. It must come from you. You might begin by analyzing your own reasons for enjoying the subject. Take a moment now and list a few reasons why you chose your subject for a major. Now look at your list of reasons and determine what potential each has for convincing an uninterested student that your subject is worth studying. If your explanations seem ineffective, consider other ways you might convince students of the worth of your subject. Try to recall successful efforts of your teachers. Perhaps they used demonstrations, anecdotes, or personal examples to awaken your interest. Can you think of a few techniques to stimulate your students? Imagine you are introducing a new unit of study. How might you use each of the following approaches to gain everyone's attention?

Demonstration	Questioning session
Problem	Debate
Personal experience	Joke
Group assignment	Discussion

Remember that students always see things in terms of *their* prior experiences, not yours. Can you alter each of your ideas to fit the age-group of your class?

Learning flourishes when students are involved vigorously, so see if you can think of ways to increase the level of student involvement within each approach. For example, you could have students help with the demonstration. Remember, though, that involvement is a better motivator when it is meaningful. Students should also be allowed to participate in the demonstration itself. With the problems approach, you might introduce a puzzle for everyone to work. When you use personal experiences, you could ask for volunteers to share their own experiences.

Were you able to think of ways to increase student involvement in the other areas? If not, give it another try. Once you begin to think of classrooms as places where students are always active, it becomes easier to plan meaningful experiences.

Let's Ponder

Abraham Maslow Speaks about Intrinsic Learning

Read the following paragraph and respond to the questions below.

> To understand the breadth of the role of the teacher, a differentiation has to be made between extrinsic learning and intrinsic learning. Extrinsic learning is based on the goals of the teacher, not on the values of the learner. Intrinsic learning, on the other hand, is learning to be and to become a human being, and a particular human being. It is the learning that accompanies the profound personal experiences in our lives. . . . As I go back in my own life, I find my greatest education experiences, the ones I value most in retrospect, were highly personal, highly subjective, very poignant combinations of the emotional and the cognitive. Some insight was accompanied by all sorts of autonomic nervous system fireworks that felt very good at the time and which left as a residue the insight that has remained with me forever. (Maslow, 1973, p. 159)

Such personal relationships with students affect the learning that occurs in classrooms. Brophy and Evertson (1976) found that more achievement occurs in classrooms where teachers take a teacher-student approach. This reinforces the need for teachers to involve students in the planning and execution of lessons. Student suggestions about content selection and classroom activities should be solicited, and those student-generated suggestions that are reasonable should be used.

1. What does Maslow mean by intrinsic learning?
2. What is the teacher's role in promoting intrinsic learning?
3. How would you explain intrinsic learning in terms of the domains of the educational taxonomies? More exactly, which two of the domains does Maslow address? What does he say about the relationship between these two domains?

STUDENT ATTITUDES TOWARD THEMSELVES

Motivation depends on self-perception. Each student comes to your room with a definite picture of himself or herself as a person and as a student. If either image is negative, it will act as a strong barrier to learning. Your job is to recognize these attitudes so that you can help the student change a negative self-concept. The task may seem monumental, but one of the greatest rewards of teaching is knowing that for some students you will be the person that helps them find themselves and helps them discover their own potentials. Unfortunately, not all students have this experience—some drop out of school before making that discovery. Others seem just to putter along, somehow managing to get through high school or complete a high school equivalency program. Some of those who go to college come to realize that they are infinitely more capable than even they ever believed.

You may hear a teacher say, "It's not my fault if they bring these attitudes to my class." This may be true. The fault may belong to previous teachers, parents, friends, or to the student. But that is not the point. Teachers must know that they can become powerful negative motivators simply by the way they relate to students. Therefore, you should avoid negative comments *to* the student or *about* the student, such as "You know him—he's a hopeless case" or "Her entire family is that way—dumb." Another common remark of teachers is "You can't make a sculpture out of mud." But remember that, at first, all clay looks a great deal like mud!

Not everyone is an Einstein, and we cannot always mold people into the patterns we design, but that is not the teacher's role. The teacher is there to provide a climate in which students can see their own strengths, believe in themselves, and become what they want to become (Combs, 1962). The students must perceive that there is at least a possibility they will succeed before they will attempt something. Once they experience success again and again, they have a good chance of becoming successful in whatever field of endeavor they are in—school or otherwise. It is worth repeating: Students who perceive themselves as good students will work hard to protect that image, just as athletes who have good reputations are willing to give it their very best.

The old cliché "Success breeds success" is very true, but it does not explain how the teacher can provide success experiences for students who are not usually successful. Actually, no teacher can *provide* success for anyone. All you can do is to create a climate conducive to learning, experimenting, and even failing. Because some failure is inevitable, it must be expected. What is important is how your students perceive and respond to failure, not the failure itself. If they see failure as defeat it can be devastating, but if you teach them to see failure as stumbling blocks for growth, they can learn and grow from their mistakes.

STUDENT ATTITUDES TOWARD THE TEACHER

What teacher qualities are important to you? Close your eyes for a moment and think of the best teacher you ever had. Can you remember and list the five most important qualities that made you like that teacher?

Now compare your list with the results of a survey taken to determine what teacher characteristics students prefer most. Did you include a statement that tells how the teacher felt about you? The students in the survey did. In fact, the most frequently mentioned quality was that the "favorite" teacher was concerned about the student—and in a very special way. The ideal teacher was determined to see that the student achieved in the subject and took whatever time necessary, in class or out, to explain the subject. An expert in the subject, this teacher knew how to get things across and was even willing to help students in areas other than academics.

The profile of a good teacher is beginning to emerge, and this profile extends beyond knowledge and teaching skills—it includes how the teacher actually *feels* about the subject and about the students. Few students will get excited over any subject about which the teacher appears to be bored. A teacher who shows excite-

THIS CHAPTER IS
DEDICATED
TO ALL
OF THOSE
WHO DIED
WHILE WAITING FOR
THE BELL TO RING

Figure 12.1 An Epitaph for Student Victims

ment or a serious love for the subject entices students to seek the reason for that excitement. Students develop positive attitudes toward teachers who are enthusiastic, task oriented, and present the material clearly (McConnell, 1977).

Another teacher quality that rated high in the survey was humor. Educators are just beginning to learn about the role humor plays in motivation. Described as a social lubricant (Lemke, 1982), humor can relax the class in tense moments. For the prospective teacher, many questions quickly emerge: "How can I use humor when I can't even tell a joke? How much humor should I allow? And by encouraging humor, am I not inviting discipline problems?"

Baughman's Handbook of Humor in Education (Baughman, 1974) answers these questions. Not always planned, humor is better described as an attitude or philosophy. In other words, the role of the teacher is to be merely accepting of humor. The students themselves will provide the creativity and the delivery skills if you provide a climate for its development. As Weber and Roff (1985, p. 38) note, "[Humor] can be used to remove tension." It should be gentle, because "Sarcasm endangers student-teacher relationships and student feelings of self worth" (Weber & Roff, 1985, p. 39). The current literature will help you learn new ways to use humor in your classes.

The concern about discipline is justified. You do not want your classroom to turn into a circus. Achievement is higher where serious misbehavior is minimal (Evertson, Emmer, & Brophy, 1980). You can control the humor by establishing an understanding that it must be kept clean in content and vocabulary and that rudeness is not permitted. Sarcasm and ridicule endanger both the teacher-student relationship and the students' feelings of self-worth (Charles, 1981; Gnagey, 1981). Short interruptions in a serious lesson might provide needed relaxation, for humor is psychologically relaxing. But it is the teacher's responsibility to see that such interruptions are short.

It is easy to return to the lesson if the lesson itself is interesting and well structured. For this reason, a good lesson plan with clear objectives and adequate student involvement is indispensable to classroom motivation. The pace should be crisp, and students should remain challenged. For learning to occur in an informal setting, however, you must have a well-structured lesson planned. A balance must be achieved. Teachers should not become so enslaved to a lesson plan that they lose the students along the way.

How informal should a class be? A good rule of thumb is to make each class as informal as possible, retaining only enough structure to move through the lesson systematically, according to the plan. When the students become especially interested in a part of the lesson, allow time for discussing that part, but always return to the lesson plan.

Let's Ponder

Read the following excerpt and respond to the questions below.

John Steinbeck (1959) describes how his biology teacher motivated him—for life:

> My eleven-year-old son came to me recently and, in a tone of patient suffering, asked, "How much longer do I have to go to school?"
>
> "About fifteen years," I said.
>
> "Oh! Lord," he said despondently. "Do I have to?"
>
> "I'm afraid so. It's terrible and I'm not going to try to tell you it isn't. But I can tell you this—if you are very lucky, you may find a teacher and that is a wonderful thing."
>
> "Did you find one?"
>
> "I found three," I said. . . .
>
> My three had these things in common—they all loved what they were doing. They did not tell—they catalyzed a burning desire to know. . . .
>
> I shall speak only of my first teacher because, in addition to other things, she was very precious.
>
> She aroused us to shouting, bookwaving discussion. She had the noisiest class in school and didn't even seem to know it. We could never stick to the subject, geometry or the chanted recitation of the memorized phyla.
>
> Our speculation ranged the world. She breathed curiosity into us so that we brought in facts or truths shielded in our hands like captured fireflies.
>
> She was fired and perhaps rightly so . . . for failing to teach the fundamentals. . . . She left her signature on us, the signature of the teacher who writes on minds. I suppose that, to a large extent, I am the unsigned manuscript of that high school teacher. What deathless power lies in the hands of such a person.
>
> I can tell my son who looks forward with horror to fifteen years of drudgery that somewhere in the dusty dark a magic may happen that will light up the years . . . if he is very lucky. . . .
>
> I have come to believe that a great teacher is a great artist and there are as few as there are any other great artists. It might even be the greatest of the arts since the medium is the human mind and spirit.

1. What techniques did Steinbeck's teacher use to motivate her students?
2. Steinbeck suggests that, in addition to her techniques for motivating students, this teacher had a special quality. Can you identify that quality? Can it be learned?
3. Defend or challenge Steinbeck's assertion that teaching is an art (as opposed to a science).

ENTHUSIASM

You can talk at length about the importance of learning a particular subject or about certain information being essential to future learning, but unless you yourself appear to be interested in a lesson, your words will probably go unheard. On the other hand, if each day you are excited about the lesson, students will wonder what you find so interesting.

To behave enthusiastically does not mean becoming overly emotional, yet you cannot afford to be nonchalant or just mildly interested. You need not compete with the entertainment world, for what you have to offer—useful knowledge and leadership—is better than entertainment. When you explain why the lesson is being pursued and how it can be applied, you want to be taken seriously.

How can you appear both serious and excited? Think for a moment about the college courses you are taking now, and select a class you really enjoy. How would you describe the teacher? Does the teacher speak in a monotone? Does the teacher read a lecture to the class each day? Is the teacher afraid to let the class laugh a little when a humorous incident occurs? Does the teacher always sit behind a desk and require you to sit at your desk? Probably not. Most teachers we enjoy are neither foolishly funny nor extremely straightlaced, but they probably are intensely interested in the subject. For most teachers this is not a problem so long as their lesson has been well planned.

KEEPING STUDENTS CHALLENGED

The most important type of motivator is the one that comes from within. It often follows success. According to Jean Piaget, each individual strives to achieve and maintain a state of equilibrium (Evans, 1973). In other words, when students see inconsistency in information, they are internally motivated to remove that inconsistency. Figure 12.2 shows how a student's learning progresses in steps or plateaus. The distance from A_1 to A_2 represents a quest for learning as it is being satisfied. When satisfaction is reached at A_2, the student is in a state of equilibrium and remains there until another contradiction arises at B_1 (Evans, 1973, p. 141). Each time students satisfy the reason for an apparent inconsistency in information, they gain a higher plateau and reach a state of equilibrium in their thinking.

The teacher should not allow students to become idle when they level off, but should always be prepared to present the students with further contradictions to their knowledge. Does this suggest that the teacher's role is to introduce problems or contradictions purposely to *puzzle* students instead of helping students find answers? To this Piaget would answer yes.

In simple terms, a contradiction occurs when students discover that understandings they hold contradict or appear to contradict each other. The teacher guides students to realize that they lack certain knowledge, and then provides one or more learning experiences to help them gain the understanding they need. There is no force-feeding. Students must internally feel the need to erase this

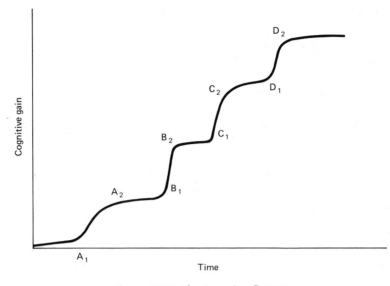

Figure 12.2 The Learning Pattern

contradiction. Once learning has occurred, those students are at peace, resting on a plateau. It is then that the teacher must make them aware of another contradiction, and the whole process repeats itself. This is motivation by keeping the student challenged—the author's interpretation of Piaget's theory of equilibrium.

But presenting too many contradictions at one time can have a nonmotivating effect. When faced with what seems to be an impossible task, students will tend to give up, feeling that success is out of their reach.

Student interest can also be increased dramatically by simply increasing the academic demands in the classroom: "Today, students want to be challenged more. Most teachers don't realize it, but many students are bored because teachers are not adequately challenging them (Frymier, 1979). A recent Gallup Poll supports this claim. Approximately half the teenagers contacted throughout the nation said that students do not have to work hard enough in school or on homework (Gallup, 1985, p. 42). Even the learning materials in most schools are not interesting. According to Frymier (1979), 70 percent to 90 percent of the curriculum materials are low in their ability to motivate, to stimulate creativity, and to challenge the intellect of students. Therefore, it will probably be left up to the teacher to initiate the challenge by introducing more rigorous, yet relevant, knowledge and activities.

CLARIFYING GOALS AND PROCEDURES

As we saw in Chapters 2, 3, and 4, students will work more intensely when they know where they are headed and how to get there. Unfortunately, teachers and students do not talk much about the meaning and purposes of content. In fact, teachers seldom give feedback, even when students make mistakes (Anderson, 1983; Cornbleth & Korth, 1983). When students lose sight of the goals, they often lose interest. When they do not understand how to do assigned tasks, they become frustrated and discouraged. In both cases poor work is usually the result.

Each task should begin with a clarification of the expected outcome. In other words, show your students how to recognize the answer, or a concept or principle, when they find it. To be sure that students understand the proper procedures, you might begin each assignment by working a sample problem and then having the students work another problem collectively. Encourage questions and have students help one another with the sample problem.

Once the assignment is given, however, the teacher's job is far from over. Some students will still have questions about goals and procedures. Now you can help by circulating among the students and answering individual questions as they arise. Knowing that the teacher is available and therefore concerned with their learning will motivate students who need help to ask questions.

USING THE OPINIONS OF STUDENTS

Make a special effort to seek the opinions of students, letting them know that you value their suggestions, their likes and their dislikes, and, above all, their judgment. Giving them an opportunity to voice their ideas can help identify misconceptions. Until people have had an opportunity to express their opinions, they are not apt to consider the opinions of others. In addition, just knowing that their questions and opinions are valued is great motivation. Consider one or more teachers you had who appeared to be intolerant of your questions or concerns. You probably soon lost the desire to ask about anything, and you probably also lost some respect for yourself and for those teachers.

STUDENT CONTRACTS

There are basically two kinds of student contracts: behavior contracts and grade contracts. Both types are contingency contracts, and both types affect behavior.

Behavior Contracts
A behavior contract is an agreement between the student and the teacher that if a student behaves in a specified manner the teacher will reward that behavior in a certain way. The reward for good behavior might range from a piece of candy for young children to free time for older students. Several authors have reported successful contingency contracting (Pinsker, M., Porter, S., Seaton, C., Beasley, R., Legg, P., & Tester, C., 1985; Redmon, W. K., & Farris, H. E., 1985; Salend, S. J., 1987).

Grade Contracts

Competition among students can have serious side effects—such as making the less capable feel inept, alienating students from their peers, and encouraging snobbishness in high achievers—but competition can be a strong motivator too. Americans are a competitive people, and the competitive attitude has been largely responsible for this nation's rapid development.

One way to retain the motivation and avoid the undesirable side effects is to encourage students to compete with themselves. Many of the best athletes do this. In fact, once golfers or bowlers become too interested in the performance of others, their own performance often fails. Like bowling and golf, learning is in certain respects an individual activity in which learners compete with themselves. They are always challenged, yet they find that success is possible.

You can use student contracts to encourage students to compete with themselves. Unlike most teacher-made tests, which are norm-referenced and force students to compete with their classmates, student contracts are criterion-referenced and set the student only against the tasks at hand. Most contracts run for the duration of a grading term. Following is an example of a contract for a unit on art history.

STUDENT CONTRACT FOR ART HISTORY

Grade	Requirements
A	Meet the requirements for the grade of B plus visit a local art gallery. Sketch an example of a gothic painting. Visit a carpenter-gothic style house and sketch the house. Show at least three similarities in the two products.
B	Meet the requirements for the grade of C plus name and draw an example of each of the major classes of columns used in buildings.
C	Meet the requirements for the grade of D plus submit a notebook record of the major developments in art since 1900, naming at least six major painting styles and two authors of each style.
D	Attend class regularly and participate in all classroom activities.

I _____ agree to work for the grade of _____ as de-
   (Student's name)   (specify grade)
scribed in this contract.

To encourage students to be realistic in their expectations, you may stipulate that students can lower their expectations at any time, but the contract may contain a built-in penalty for any alterations. Most contracts do not permit students to raise their grade expectation, but in designing your contracts, try to fit them to the needs of your particular students. The major disadvantage of using contracts is that you will need additional time to design, complete, and keep up with a large number of contracts.

GRADES AND TESTS

Many teachers believe that unannounced tests and threats of assigning low grades can be effective motivators, but the research does not support this. When tests and threats are used in the traditional manner, the downgraded students continue to fail. Low test scores can also be discouraging, especially if the teacher does nothing to help the student acquire the missed knowledge and skills. Unfortunately, teachers and students spend very little effort on reviewing and building skills that have not been learned (Chansky, 1962). Another study found that anxiety produced by grades actually lowered the grades of middle-ability students (Phillips, 1962). So it appears that, while tests themselves can be sources of learning when time is spent going over the material covered, the use of tests or grades (or threats of either) to motivate is a serious misuse of tests that will not significantly increase the motivational level.

TERM PROJECTS

Individual or group term projects can be a highly motivating device in secondary and middle schools when correctly used. First, they must be truly term projects—lasting for the duration of the term. This gives students time to select and research their chosen area of study. A list of topics provided by you can be helpful in suggesting ideas and boundaries, but it is important to let students be free to choose their particular project.

To increase motivation, find ways to display the projects. A science fair, art exhibit, or similar event is an excellent means of exposure. Occasional attention given to these projects during the term by parents and relatives can spur on the investigators and whet their enthusiasm for their projects.

ASSIGNMENTS FOR EXTRA CREDIT

Assignments for extra credit are common in many classrooms, yet their power to stimulate interest is very limited. In fact, they often produce the opposite effect. If extra credit assignments are to motivate positively, the task must be meaningful and must be selected far in advance of the end of the term, preferably at the beginning of the term or study unit. Giving a student an opportunity to copy a 10,000-word report from an encyclopedia at the end of a semester is likely to produce a negative attitude toward learning rather than increase the student's motivation.

REWARD AND REINFORCEMENT

Rewards can be an important motivator or stimulator of student interest. Substantial use of corrective feedback in the academic areas, praise for correct or proper behavior, and making use of students' ideas to let them know that their contributions are valued all have a positive relationship to achievement and attitudes (Gage & Berliner, 1984). Some students work to please their teachers; others watch their teachers closely for feedback that assures them they are achieving at an acceptable rate. Your use of rewards can bring reinforcement to both types of students. Clark and Starr (1976, p. 55) offer the following suggestions for teachers who want to improve their skills using rewards:

TECHNIQUES FOR IMPROVING THE USE OF REWARDS

1. Reward new [good] behavior everytime it occurs.
2. Once a student becomes established, gradually reduce the frequency of reinforcement until the reinforcement comes at occasional and haphazard intervals.
3. At first, reward the behavior as soon as it occurs. Then, as students become more confident, delay the reward somewhat.
4. Select rewards that are suitable for the individual pupils.
5. With recalcitrant or resistive pupils, begin by giving small rewards.
6. Use contingency contracts.

BEHAVIOR MODIFICATION

In education, behavior modification, like contingency contracts, is an agreement. Instead of earning grades, however, the student earns certain stated rewards for displaying specified types of behavior or for completing certain tasks. Behavior modification is more popular in middle schools; it is much more difficult to find adequate reinforcers for high school students (Warshaw, 1975). One reinforcer that has proven effective for secondary school classes is free time earned by the student through certain specified performance. For example, in one English grammar class a 75 percent level of bad behavior was reduced to 15 percent by a contract that rewarded proper behavior by giving free time (Sapp, 1973).

In one program for a predominantly black inner-city class of underachievers that provided the opportunity to earn free time, to listen to records, to read comic books, to play games, to receive candy bars and bubble gum, and to participate in planning class activities, the average student grades rose from D level to B level and class attendance rose from 50 percent to 80 percent (Sapp, 1973). While one would not expect to produce such dramatic effects in every case, these results are encouraging for the use of behavior modification programs in secondary and middle schools.

A SUMMARY OF MOTIVATION STRATEGIES

Because any one technique for motivation is apt to produce different results with each application and each group of students, you will probably profit more if you concentrate less on specific techniques and more on the general strategies for motivating students that have already been discussed. Here is a summary of these strategies.

1. *Be honest with students*. Don't pretend to know everything. It is far more important to be a teacher who is approachable than a teacher who is impeccable.
2. *Use the subject to motivate*. Emphasize the areas of knowledge that have special appeal to the particular age-group of each class.
3. *Be pragmatic*. Show the students how they can use the knowledge in their daily lives.
4. *Use a variety of approaches*. For each topic of study, select the approach(es) you believe will best stimulate student interest.
5. *Involve all students*. All students should be actively involved in each lesson. Remember that in a sense all individuals are motivated. The teacher's challenge is to provide meaningful activities for students to pursue—activities that lead to the discovery of knowledge and relationships pertinent to the lesson.
6. *Be positive*. Students work harder and achieve more when they feel competent in what they are doing. Serious use of reinforcement can lead to improving the self-confidence of students.
7. *Be personal*. Don't be afraid to relate to students on a personal basis. Teachers who remain formal at all times build barriers between themselves and their students.
8. *Use humor*. Don't be afraid to enjoy your students. There's no time when student attention is more completely captured than when humor is occurring. Relax occasionally and let it happen.
9. *Be enthusiastic*. Plan into the lesson events that you will enjoy. Enthusiasm is highly contagious.
10. *Challenge your students*. Nothing is more boring than a lesson that fails to challenge the learners. Keep the pace brisk yet within the reach of the students.

RECAP OF MAJOR IDEAS

1. It is the teacher's responsibility to convince students that the topics under study are worthwhile to the student. This requires basing motivational efforts on the students' perspectives, which may differ from the teacher's.
2. Teachers need not try to compete with the entertainment world. Teachers offer leadership, a quality that middle school and high school students need in their often unstructured lives.
3. Teachers cannot force students to become interested in a lesson. At best, the teacher can only entice student interest.
4. Application is an important avenue to motivation. Teachers should strive to show students how they can apply the content being taught to their daily lives.
5. Involving all students in lessons is a great motivation technique, yet teachers and students seldom discuss the purpose of a lesson.

6. Positive student self-concepts are strong motivators, whereas negative concepts work against the teacher's efforts to motivate.

7. Humor holds much potential for motivation. Successful use of humor does not require the teacher to entertain students constantly. By relaxing the classroom atmosphere, the teacher can allow natural humor to develop among the students.

8. Thorough planning and a well-structured lesson will enable teachers to be less formal. A controlled degree of informality can contribute to the motivational level in the classroom.

9. Teacher enthusiasm is an indispensable element in motivation. Teachers can ensure their own excitement by planning into each lesson activities both they and the students will enjoy.

10. Class tempo is important to the motivational level. Students tend to be more highly motivated when the pace of the lesson is fast enough to challenge them but not so fast that it keeps them confused.

11. Goal clarification is essential to motivation. It is only natural that students are more interested when they know what they are doing.

12. Rewards and reinforcement should occur only following success. Therefore, teachers should assign tasks the students can perform well.

13. Reinforcement should be spaced at varying intervals.

14. Personal teacher-student relationships add to the level of student interest.

POSTTEST

Now that you have read the chapter, take a moment to respond to the following statements again:

	Agree	*Disagree*	*Uncertain*
1. The more reinforcement the better.	____	____	____
2. Teacher enthusiasm cannot be planned.	____	____	____
3. Teachers are expected to tell students how to apply knowledge that is highly theoretical.	____	____	____
4. All teachers should *give* their students some success every day.	____	____	____
5. Humor is most successfully used in the classroom when it is systematically planned to fit the lesson.	____	____	____
6. Behavior modification is an example of internal motivation.	____	____	____

CASES

The teacher must include motivation strategies in each daily lesson plan. As you read the following cases, begin making a list of strategies that you will use each day and throughout the year to elevate your own level of enthusiasm as well as that of your students.

Case 1: A Student Is Labeled a Failure

Mike Creswell was a quiet boy, although a bit mischievous at times. He often blushed and bowed his head whenever Jane, his teacher, spoke his name in the classroom. Jane's heart poured out to Mike because he reminded her of an animal that had been kicked around so much it never knew when more punishment was coming. Mike appeared to distrust everyone, which probably explains why he had no close friends.

Jane met Mike's parents at a social affair and noticed that his father avoided mentioning Mike was in her class. When she became convinced that he was not going to bring it up, Jane simply stated that she was pleased to have Mike in her class. Mr. Creswell immediately apologized for the inadequacies of his son and then quickly changed the subject to another son, who was more academically inclined. Jane could see that Mr. Creswell was ashamed of Mike and that he did not really like the boy.

Through talking with other teachers, Jane learned that Mike's father constantly yelled at him at home, and some past incidents showed that Mike was actually beaten when he failed to live up to his father's expectations. Jane guessed that Mike preferred the beatings to the verbal downgrading, because the pain of physical punishment is temporary but the pain of being told you are unable to measure up never ends.

Some students never get over the damage their parents and teachers do by measuring them against a brother or sister who performed better in school. Most youths do not have the insight to see that what they can and do achieve is important, regardless of how much more or less someone else achieves. Unfortunately, many adults tend to lead students to think this way.

Jane began encouraging Mike and verbally rewarding him for each task he performed successfully. By the end of the year, she could see improvement in the quality of Mike's work, and he had begun to relate better to her and to some of his classmates.

Discussion

1. If a parent of one of your students seems ashamed of the child, how should you react?
   The parent who is ashamed of a son or daughter will probably try to avoid discussing the child. Many teachers feel obligated to talk about the student at every opportunity without being obvious about it. The parent who reacts to an apparent weakness by ignoring the child is not behaving in an acceptable way. The teacher can encourage discussion of the child's weakness with the parent if the weakness does exist. The teacher can always offer to help the parent help the child correct it. You may be able to think of other approaches that suit your personality more.

2. How could the teacher make Mr. Creswell proud of his son?
   The teacher could initiate discussions about the areas in which Mike is most capable, which may or may not be academic. By checking Mike's cumulative records, standardized examination scores, and previous grades, and by talking with other teachers, the teacher could identify Mike's strong areas. This would provide topics for discussion with Mr. Creswell.

3. How can you encourage other students to associate with a lonely child?
   By assigning the student tasks that are within the student's capabilities, the teacher can allow the student to experience some success, and peers will begin to take notice. The teacher can also assign group projects, making sure that the particular student's group has a task to which that student can contribute.

4. How can the teacher convince a parent that one sibling should not be compared with another?
   The teacher should emphasize that individuals excel in different areas. Furthermore, the teacher might remind the parent that a child's failure to achieve does not always indicate lack of ability, but could indicate a failure of teacher and parents to motivate the student.

Case 2: A Student Teacher Uses Threats to Motivate

Bob Wright was eager to begin student teaching. On the first day that Ms. Lee, his supervisor, visited, Bob was presenting a well-organized lesson. He had a beautiful outline on the board and was discussing some interesting topics. However, the students were complacent and appeared to be unconcerned. The supervisor did not mention this to Bob, leaving him unaware of the students' response, or lack of it. During later observations, it was obvious that Bob had noticed something was wrong and was becoming upset with the students because they seemed so uninterested. Throughout the period he would remark, ''You had better pay attention because this will be on our next test.'' Some of the few who initially were interested began to lose interest.

Ms. Lee sugggested to Bob that instead of threatening to give a test he try actually giving the test, that each time he caught himself on the verge of saying ''You had better . . . or else'' he should go ahead and administer the ''or else.'' By the end of the semester Bob's class was having healthy discussions. The students began listening to Bob and interacting with him.

Discussion

1. Is the teacher justified in giving a pop quiz when students fail to complete homework assignments?
   Probably not, unless the teacher believes that the failure is the result of laziness and the quiz will motivate. The teacher's energy would be better spent improving lessons. Using pop quizzes can even lead to punishing students for what is really the teacher's inadequacy. An announced quiz set at a specific time each week would probably be a stronger motivator than an unannounced quiz. How do you feel about the use of pop quizzes to motivate? Can you defend your position?
2. How was the idea of a test used by Bob?
   Bob used tests as a force to coerce students to study. The success of his students was probably a result of his involving students in discussions and not a product of the unannounced tests. Students can be led to understand the worthwhile uses of test results. By using a test as a weapon against student misbehavior, the idea of testing becomes negative. Threatening students in any way is poor teaching practice.

Case 3: A Teacher Runs Out of Material

The day had finally arrived for Mrs. King to begin teaching her own classes. It was exciting just to hear her describe the experience in the teacher's lounge later than morning. All had not gone well, however, and some teachers recalled similar experiences early in their own careers.

Mrs. King's first class started well. She had a well-structured lesson that immediately captured the attention of the class. When after a few moments she realized that the students were more interested in the lesson than in her, she felt relieved, and the first half of the hour went well. Time passed quickly and so did the lesson, and suddenly it was all over. The material was covered, but there were a good 15 minutes left in the period. What could she do?

Mrs. King did not have much experience, but she did not lack creativity. She immediately decided to review the lesson, but when this was accomplished in five minutes she was again at the point of panic. Then one student asked a question. From Mrs. King's report, the question was apparently answered thoroughly, since all 10 remaining minutes were used in answering that one question. It was not an experience Mrs. King wanted to repeat. She began thinking of ways to avoid the task of stalling and ad-libbing to kill time.

Discussion

1. What can a teacher do to prevent running out of planned lesson material?
Instead of planning only one lesson in advance, a teacher should always come to school with at least two days' plans. Then if one lesson ends sooner than expected, the teacher can begin another. Can you think of other such planned ways to cope with this emergency?

Lesson plans that surprise a teacher and are completed sooner than expected are usually plans that do not involve the students. As we have already stressed, the teacher should plan student involvement into every lesson. Often, student involvement will increase a one-day lesson to more than a single class period, but this should be cause for celebration rather than concern. Both the teacher and the students should ask questions throughout the period. Teachers who feel that they do not have time for questions might be the same teachers who find themselves having completed the lesson with 15 minutes remaining in the period.

When a lesson ends early, teachers have numerous alternatives. Not long ago, many school systems required each teacher to post a daily schedule on the classroom door and that schedule was to be followed precisely. Except for a very few cases, today's teachers have more freedom.

2. If there are no questions, how can a teacher fill the remainder of a class period?
Most teachers find this an opportune time for student involvement. If the students have been passive during most of the period, they will be physically and psychologically ready for some action. To ease this tension, the teacher might try changing the routine. For instance, the students could come to the board to work problems, or the teacher could divide the class into small groups to formulate questions for discussion. The important thing is to enable each student to become active in working with the lesson. (Does this suggest another answer to the first question?)

ACTIVITIES

The following activities will help you plan for a more stimulating climate in the classroom.

1. Examine your own personal traits. For each adjective you would use to describe yourself, describe at least one way you can use this trait to make your class environments more interesting.

2. A degree of informality seems essential for maximum motivation in the classroom. Student teachers often ask, "How informal can I or should I be with my students without having them taking advantage of my friendship?" Make a list of ways you can show your concern for your students. For each of these, explain how you can prepare to prevent their taking unfair advantage. It may be helpful if you decide at this time exactly where you will draw the line.

SUGGESTED READINGS

Anderson, L. (1983, April). *Achievement-related differences in students' responses to seatwork.* Paper presented at the annual conference of the American Educational Research Association, Montreal.

Baughman, M. D. (1974). *Baughman's handbook of humor in education.* New York: Parker.

Brophy, J. E. (1985). Teacher-student interaction. In Jerome B. Dusek (Ed.), *Teacher expectancies.* Hillsdale, N.J.: Erlbaum.

Brophy, J., & Evertson, C. (1976). *Learning from teaching: A developmental perspective.* Boston: Allyn & Bacon.

Brophy, J., & Good, T. L. (1986). Teacher behavior and student achievement. In Merlin C. Whittrock (Ed.), *Handbook of research on teaching* (3rd ed.). New York: Macmillan, p. 337.

Chansky, N. M. (1962). The X-ray of the school mark. *Educational Forum, 12,* 347–352.

Charles, C. (1981). *Building classroom discipline: From models to practice.* New York: Longman.

Clark, L. H., & Starr, I. S. (1976). *Secondary school teaching methods.* New York: Macmillan.

Combs, A. (Ed.) (1962). *Perceiving, behaving, becoming.* Washington, D.C.: Association for Supervision and Curriculum Development.

Cornbleth, C., & Korth, W. (1983, April). *Doing the work: Teacher prospectus and meanings of responsibility.* Paper presented at the annual meeting of the American Educational Research Association, Montreal.

Evans, R. I. (1973). *Jean Piaget: The man and his ideas* (3rd ed.). New York: Dutton, p. 141.

Evertson, C., Emmer, E., & Brophy, J. (1980). Predictors of effective teaching in junior high mathematics classrooms. *Journal for Research in Mathematics Education, 11,* 167–168.

Frymier, J. (1979, February). Keynote speech at Southwest Educational Research Association, Houston, Texas.

Gage, N. L. (1978, March). Bored students. *School and Community, 64,* 29.

Gage, N. L., & Berliner, D. C. (1984). *Educational psychology* (3rd ed.). Boston: Houghton Mifflin.

Gallup, A. M. (1985). The seventeenth annual Gallup poll of the public's attitudes toward the public schools. *Phi Delta Kappan, 67,* 35–47.

Gnagey, W. J. (1981). *Motivating classroom discipline.* New York: Longman.

Hoover, K. A. (1976). *The professional teacher's handbook* (2nd ed.). Boston: Allyn & Bacon.

Keller, F. S. (1968). *Learning reinforcement theory.* New York: Random House.

Lemke, J. L. (1982, April). *Classroom communication of science.* Final report to National Science Foundation/Rising to Individual Scholastic Excellence NSF/RISE.

Maslow, A. (1973). What is a taoistic teacher? In L. J. Rubin (Ed.), *Facts and feelings in the classroom.* New York: Walker.

McConnell, J. (1977). *Relationships between selected teacher behaviors and attitudes/achievements of algebra classes.* Paper presented at the annual meeting of the American Educational Research Association.

Phillips, B. (1962). Sex, social class, and anxiety as sources of variation in school activity. *Journal of Educational Psychology, 53,* 361–362.

Pinsker, M., Porter, S., Seaton, C., Beasley, R., Legg, P., & Tester, C. (Sept. 1985). Project success: A contingency model for ninth grade. *National Association of Secondary School Principals Bulletin, 69,* 127–129.

Redman, W. K., & Farris, H. E. (Jan., 1985). Improving the academic productivity of high school students through behavior contracting: A model project. *Journal of Instructional Psychology, 12,* 46–58.

Salend, S. J. (1987). Contingency management systems. *Academic Therapy, 22,* 245–253.

Sapp, G. L. (1973). Classroom management and student involvement. *High School Journal, 56,* 276–283.

Steinbeck, J. (1959). The education of teachers. *Curriculum Programs.* Washington D.C.: National Education Association, p. 71.

Symonds, P. M. (1968). *What education has to learn from psychology* (3rd ed.). New York: Teachers College Press.

Warshaw, M. (1975, August). Behavior modification in secondary schools. *Educational Technology,* 25–52.

Weber, W. A., & Roff, L. A. (1983). "A review of the teacher education literature on classroom management." In W. A. Weber, L. A. Roff, J. Crawford, & C. Robinson (Eds.), *Classroom management: Reviews of the teacher education and research literature.* Princeton: Educational Testing Service.

From Discipline to Self-Discipline

Objectives

- Give two reasons why teachers must not rely on power and punishment for discipline.
- Contrast two different approaches to classroom discipline.
- Describe the public's attitude toward discipline in today's secondary and middle schools.
- Define *discipline* in terms of order and control.
- Explain the relationship between quietness and discipline.
- List three guidelines for conducting a private talk with a student who has misbehaved.
- Tell what is wrong with the adage "Be tough at first and relax the rules as time passes."

PRETEST

	Agree	Disagree	Uncertain
1. Truly effective *discipline* and *classroom management* are inseparable terms.	____	____	____
2. As perceived by the American public, discipline is the greatest problem in our schools today.	____	____	____
3. Discipline is the same as restraint.	____	____	____
4. There are times when physical punishment is the best approach to resolving a discipline problem.	____	____	____
5. A quiet class is usually a well-disciplined one, and a noisy class is usually undisciplined.	____	____	____
6. At the beginning of the year, the teacher should be strict, since it is always easy to loosen the rules but difficult to strengthen them.	____	____	____
7. Discipline models should be consistent with accepted learning theories and with management theories in other fields.	____	____	____
8. The ultimate goal should be to get students to discipline themselves.	____	____	____

Middle-Level Message

Discipline presents a special challenge for the middle-level teacher. A recent survey shows that most middle-level teachers feel a strong need for more classroom management skills. The best approach is a preventive one. Use this chapter to learn how to prevent discipline problems. Avoid relying on your position of authority, or worse, corporal punishment, to achieve discipline in your classes.

Your position as teacher should get you through the first five minutes of your career. From then on, you will need the knowledge and skills offered in this chapter. To survive, you must master them. As the teacher, you must learn how to earn the respect and cooperation of your students. Only then can you lead them to a state of self-discipline. Don't settle for anything else.

Following a brief period of secondary and middle school classroom observations for a seminar, a group of pre-service college students gave the following reports.

REPORT 1

The eighth-grade English class was a farce. Chaos prevailed. At any one time it was impossible to tell who had the floor. In spite of the teacher's efforts to gain control and focus the students' attention on the lesson, the discussion resembled a racquetball, forever bouncing in undetermined directions. The teacher's repeated reprimands and threats to the reluctant learners were evidence that the teacher did want to gain control of the situation, but each lesson was like all others—the teacher simply had no control. Each day little if any cognitive gain was being made throughout the entire period.

REPORT 2

The junior biology class was all business. When the teacher looked over his pair of narrow bifocals a deadly silence fell over the room. There was never a question of who had control. When each daily lecture began, students sat upright and took notes. When seats were assigned, there were no disruptions, no discussion, no questions. Even to think about getting off task in this class was out of the question. When the bell rang at the beginning of the period, it signaled the end of all social interaction. Even such nonverbal communications as smiles and nods of approval were seldom seen.

REPORT 3

Sixth grade was a time for enjoying learning. Each day the students arrived alive with curiosity. Students brought with them truths captured as insects, rocks, leaves, and other treasures they often carried in their hands and pockets. When the class began, they always knew the daily objectives and how each activity led to one or more of those objectives. Almost every student felt capable of mastering the goals of the class. But the organization and structure that were present in this classroom did not get in the way of learning or of enjoying each lesson. They also did not cause unnecessary quiet. In fact, this sixth-grade class was usually quite noisy. Somehow even private conversations seemed to focus at least to some degree on the topics being studied. Although a constant chattering and buzzing characterized the class, the teacher seemed able to get the students' attention.

Many variables affect classroom climates. The differences in the three classes described above can be attributed largely to one factor—the classroom management skills of the teachers. In essence, good management skills are a prerequisite to good discipline. A 1985 Gallup Poll cited discipline as the number-one concern of the public over the schools (Gallup, 1985). In fact, discipline has held this dubious honor for 15 out of the past 16 years.

DISCIPLINE: A DEFINITION

Discipline is defined in many ways. In the past, the term was associated with such concepts as punishment, restraint, and forced behavior, but many educators now reject such negative interpretations. A more contemporary view of discipline involves such concepts as order and control. Because order implies direction, discipline might be defined as a climate that is controlled with the purpose of providing order. Even the manner in which the control is introduced varies.

Let's Ponder

Some, possibly most, contemporary educators reject the use of excessive force and constraint in the name of discipline. Yet some insist that such measures as force and even punishment are essential for disciplining certain students who, they maintain, do not understand anything else. These educators say that the teacher is justified, even obligated, to use whatever measures are necessary to discipline their students. What is your position on this issue? Do you agree with either of these extremes?

DESIRABLE TEACHER ATTITUDES
TOWARD DISCIPLINE

Discipline Is a Must

Discipline, defined as order and control, is essential. Because each teacher is responsible for ensuring that maximum learning occurs in the classroom, each teacher is responsible for maintaining the discipline necessary to meet this goal. Teachers must know and accept their responsibility to establish and maintain discipline, because that is a prerequisite to achieving good behavior in most classrooms. Good discipline does not just happen; it begins with certain teacher attitudes. Acceptance of responsibility for classroom discipline is an important and basic teacher attitude. And "each teacher must find the discipline techniques most congruent with his or her educational philosophy and individual student needs" (Bell & Stefanich, 1984, p. 134).

Teacher Efficacy

Some teachers have a tremendous influence on the behavior of students in their classrooms, and all teachers have the potential for exercising this influence. It is important that teachers realize they have this capacity. A desirable attitude is: As the teacher, I must and will establish and maintain in my classroom the climate necessary for maximum learning. Such an attitude makes students feel secure and is apt to earn more respect for a teacher than an attitude of doubt and insecurity.

A Focus on Learning

There have been some major shifts in the ways *discipline* has been defined over the years. Paramount among these is a recent tendency to substitute the term *classroom management* for discipline. The major difference is that classroom management is generally more positive. It connotes skills and leadership, but more important, it implies a specific purpose—which is to develop and maintain a classroom climate that maximizes learning. This placing of learning as the basis for decision-making is another important teacher attitude.

Teaching and Discipline Are Inseparable

It does not matter whether a teacher chooses to use the term *discipline* or the term *classroom management,* so long as the teacher realizes that these cannot be separated from the act of teaching. Nothing works better for establishing and maintaining discipline in a classroom than planning and executing a good lesson. This idea was developed in Chapter 3 on planning daily lessons.

The Cooperative Approach

Thus far, we have described discipline as the teacher's sole responsibility. Teacher efficacy can contribute to establishing a desirable classroom climate. But teachers should not be alone in their concern for maintaining a well-disciplined class. After all, if chaos prevails it is the students who suffer most. Therefore, many teachers choose to involve their students in maintaining discipline in their classrooms. This makes the job easier, and it also promotes a very important student attitude toward discipline. That attitude is self-discipline.

DISCIPLINE: A CONTINUUM OF VIEWS

The wide range of views about discipline can be seen by placing them on a continuum (see Figure 13.1). Clearly, some teachers remain at the far left side of the continuum. Other teachers (such as the sixth-grade teacher at the beginning of the chapter) have moved to the opposite extreme. Teachers at the right side of the continuum often appear to have few or no discipline problems. In fact, they often seem to ignore the topic altogether, whereas teachers on the left side of the continuum may seem obsessed with the idea.

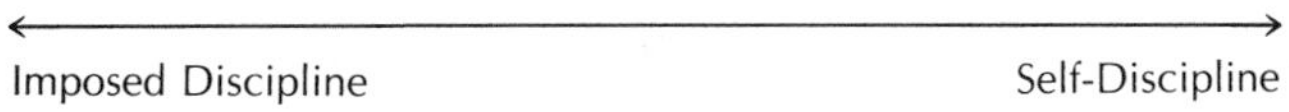

<img src="" alt="A horizontal double-headed arrow with Imposed Discipline on the left and Self-Discipline on the right." />

Imposed Discipline   Self-Discipline

Figure 13.1 Discipline Continuum

Let's Ponder

Make a list of objectives or statements to describe teachers who fall on the left side of the Discipline Continuum, then make a corresponding list to describe teachers who belong on the right side.

Perhaps you have already surmised that your next task will be to determine where you belong on this continuum. This may not be easy, but it is very important because you will need to know where you stand on this question so you can act accordingly in the future.

LEARNING THEORIES AND EDUCATION

Teachers are not alone in their tendency to span the spectrum with their perceptions of discipline. Management practices should be consistent with our knowledge and theories of learning, and even these range from one end of the spectrum to the other. The following is a review of some major learning theories. As you recognize each of these from your earlier courses in educational psychology, see if you can accurately place each theory on the Discipline Continuum.

Faculty Psychology

Before the twentieth century there was little effort to understand the process of learning. The first collective beliefs that were actually written down and accepted by a significant number of psychologists (perhaps the vast majority) became known as faculty psychology. Perceiving the brain as a muscle that had special capacities (faculties), these theorists believed that further development of the brain hinged on certain conditions. They believed that, like any muscle, the brain must have plenty of exercise in order to grow. This exercise should be difficult and boring, not enjoyable, and therefore lectures and recitation should be the major teaching methods.

Although faculty psychology seems absurd to many contemporary educators, this theory still plays a role in modern education. A visit to almost any school will reveal that faculty psychology continues to shape the climate in many classrooms. Some recent reports on education have given renewed life to these theories. Many private schools that are designed according to the faculty psychology theory have been established and are experiencing rapid growth in popularity and number.

Stimulus-Response Psychology

By the turn of the century, a new school of thought had become influential in shaping American education. The stimulus-response (S→R) psychologists perceived all behavior as responses to stimuli. To effect learning, the teacher merely needed to change the classroom stimuli. This school of thought has some validity, because student behavior is indeed shaped to some degree by the total stimuli in the classroom environment. By removing undesirable stimuli, the teacher can remove much of the undesirable behavior. By adding other stimuli (rewards), new behavior could be added. But recognizing that the degree to which a stimulus shapes behavior is determined somewhat by the individual (organism) who is responding, the S→R symbol that represented the stimulus-response theory was changed to (S→O→R).

Behavioral Psychology

Some psychologists disagree with the stimulus-response psychologists, maintaining that only a small portion of human behaviors are responses to stimuli. Behavioral psychologists believe that most human behavior is overt—that is, purposive and self-initiated. They recognize that repetition, rewards, and reinforcements play important roles in shaping behavior. Some of the major education programs that emerged out of this school of thought are programmed instruction, behavior modification, and computer assisted instruction.

Phenomenology

By the middle of the twentieth century, some psychologists began paying more attention to the individual. Rogerian psychologists listened carefully to their clients and considered the individual's own perceptions. From this concern grew a new psychological theory called phenomenology. Unlike earlier psychologists, who focused their energy on finding more effective ways of forcing or persuading students to change their behavior, phenomenologists studied ways of getting students to change their own behavior.

From this school of thought came the idea of the self-concept. These psychologists realized that students will work diligently to protect their self-image. By helping their students develop a positive image of themselves as competent students, a teacher could indirectly cause students to channel their own behavior in more positive directions.

Let's Ponder

Now see where you would place each of the above learning theories on the discipline continuum. Clearly, they belong somewhere left of center because each uses external stimuli. In effect, each perceives the role of the teacher to be one of using a combination of repetition, rewards, reinforcements, and punishments to alter student behavior.

Reality Therapy

Reality therapy is an approach to behavior management that has been modified for classroom use by Dr. William Glasser, who contends that misbehavior is a result of a lack of involvement in the school process. Failure and lack of a sense of students' responsibility for the outcomes of their behavior causes misbehavior. Conversely, success begets success. According to this theory, teachers should (1) display strong positive emotional characters, (2) state rules clearly so they are understood, (3) spend some time each day with each student, (4) focus on present behavior and avoid references to past behavior, and (5) require students to evaluate their own behavior. In addition, teacher and student(s) should (6) develop together a corrective plan that is simple, short, and success oriented. It should have only a few rules, but they must be obeyed. Finally, (7) the teacher should obtain a verbal or written commitment from the student(s) (Curwin & Mendler, 1980).

The philosophical basis for Glasser's theory is that society as a whole has shifted from socially sanctioned goals to personal goals—know yourself and know what you want. The result has been the emergence of an "identity society." For this reason, schools should shift from an external focus of control—do what the teacher says—to an internal focus of control, whereby students are involved in planning and directing the school activities.

Group Management Theory

In contrast to Glasser, who perceives discipline as a one-on-one cooperative endeavor between the teacher and each student, Fritz Redl and William W. Wattenberg (1975) believe that discipline problems are a product of group behavior and should be approached accordingly. As early as 300 B.C., Plato warned about the negative influence urbanization can have on a culture. In his *Republic,* he predicted that as cities grow the behavior of the inhabitants changes, and often for the worse. Group management theory recognizes that when people are in groups they behave differently from when they are alone. Furthermore, as groups grow in number they also develop definite characteristics.

Teachers must recognize the effects groups have on the behavior of the total classroom or on groups within the classroom. The teacher can exert influence either directly or indirectly in two major directions. First, the teacher gives support to the group—for example, provides encouragement while standing ready to help the group achieve its goals. This requires guiding the class carefully toward the goals. Suppose one of the behavioral goals of the class is for each student to remain at his or her desk. The teacher's role is to monitor the group and, when signs of restlessness appear, to alter the situation to provide for more movement. Or suppose near the end of the period students may be getting off-target and wandering—mentally if not physically. Recognizing the situation, the teacher introduces an assignment, summarizes the day's lesson, or uses a similar technique to pull the students back to the lesson.

Group management techniques are not concerned with blaming either the group or the individual for misbehaving. The perspective is more one of being alert at all times, managing the environment to reduce the number of problems and problem-causing elements, and helping the group and individuals overcome hurdles and reach their goals.

Group management discipline is based on the philosophy that neither individuals nor groups want to misbehave, that misbehavior is the result of barriers. When individuals or groups fail to make progress toward their goals, it is because the goals are unclear or too demanding, or because there are elements in the environment, or some other interference, that prevent their attainment—and not because the individual or group wants to be difficult.

Redl and Wattenberg (1959) endorsed the use of punishment, but only under certain conditions. Punishment should never be the teacher's first attempted solution to a problem, and when it is used it should be administered in an objective manner. The individual or groups being punished must clearly understand the reason, and the teacher must remain calm. It is important to recognize that punishment can easily become a trap for teachers if they make it too harsh, get others to administer it, overuse it, or use it to make impossible demands of students. The ultimate goal of group management discipline is, by helping students analyze their own behavior, to lead them to a state of self-control—that is, self-discipline.

Maslow's Hierarchy of Needs

Abraham Maslow developed a theory based on clinical observation and logic. According to Maslow, all human beings have some common needs, which fall into five clusters that can be arranged in the following hierarchy:

	Low
Self-actualization needs	↑
Esteem needs	Frequency
Social needs	of
Safety needs	encounters
Physiological needs	↓
	High

The needs at the lower levels of the hierarchy are the more frequently experienced needs. Furthermore, each level of needs must be satisfied before the higher levels can be met. Maslow's Hierarchy of Needs has been used extensively by management in business and industry for several decades.

McGregor's Theories X and Y

Douglas McGregor noticed that in a large national chain of department stores many of the stores were highly successful while many of their counterparts were financial failures. Upon closer inspection he noted that the successful stores and the unsuccessful stores were managed under very different types of management. He named the successful management style Theory Y and the unsuccessful management style Theory X. The unsuccessful Theory X managers were the traditional type of managers. They all shared the following perceptions:

Most people are inherently lazy.

People must be closely supervised.

People tend to shun responsibility.

People like to be directed.

Getting people to attain objectives requires the use of coercion, control, and threats of punishment.

In contrast, the highly successful Theory Y managers espoused the following beliefs:

The expenditure of mental and physical effort is natural.

If the conditions are right, people will not only accept responsibility but also seek it.

If people become committed to objectives, they will exercise self-direction and self-control.

Most people have a high degree of imagination, ingenuity, and creativity.

This more positive approach to management has become identified as modern management theory. However, some contemporary management theorists reject this theory as too idealistic. In all fairness, the accuracy of the theory depends on the particular environment.

Let's Ponder

Consider Maslow's Hierarchy of Needs, McGregor's Theory X, and McGregor's Theory Y. Where would you place each of these on the Discipline Continuum? Can you see a relationship between Maslow's Hierarchy of Needs and student behavior in the classroom? For example, can you name some physiological needs that must be met before students improve their self-esteem? Can you name any social needs that must be met before students can improve their self-images as competent students? Have you known teachers whom you would label Theory X managers? Theory Y managers? What traits did each exhibit?

CLASSROOM MANAGEMENT DISCIPLINE MODELS

Being aware of learning theories and management theories from disciplines outside education will help us relate education discipline and management theories to the Discipline Continuum in Figure 13.1. Following are a few of the many discipline and management theories in use in education today. Weber, Roff, Crawford, and Robinson (1983) reviewed the literature on classroom management and grouped the strategies into the following eight categories: authoritarian, behavior modification, group process, instructional, intimidation, permissive, sociomotional climate, and cookbook. Because these groups are both numerous and self-descriptive, only selective examples will be given.

Authoritarian Strategies

The authoritarian approach to classroom management places the teacher in control from the very beginning. Using nonpunitive measures, the teacher establishes and enforces rules, issues commands, and uses mild desists (explains privately why the student is being asked to discontinue the behavior), proximity control (stays near the misbehaving student), and isolation. Jacob Kounin (1977) introduced the mild-desists strategy because he found that teachers seldom tell students why certain behaviors are considered bad. He further noticed that when teachers use strong reprimands they often do so publicly, making other students feel anxious.

Group Process Strategies

Group process strategies are based on a belief that classroom behavior occurs in a social or group context. The teacher's role is to set reasonable expectations, stay alert to the classroom group interactions (exhibit withitness), foster group cohesiveness, involve students in decision making, and resolve conflicts through discussion, role playing, and negotiation.

Instructional Strategies

The instructional approach to classroom management utilizes the belief that the teacher's time is better spent preventing problems than solving problems. This approach is discussed in detail in Chapter 12.

Intimidation Strategies

Intimidation strategies put the teacher in charge. The teacher uses harsh reprimands, threats, physical restraint, and corporal punishment. These teachers do not tolerate any foolishness. Classes managed by this style may or may not be characterized by a high degree of learning.

MODELS DEVELOPED SPECIFICALLY FOR EDUCATION

The learning and management theories presented thus far in this chapter are adopted from other disciplines, and their relevance to the secondary and middle school classroom varies from theory to theory. This has prompted development of models designed specifically for classroom use. Following are descriptions of some more popular ones. As you read about each model, see if you can place it on the Discipline Continuum (Figure 13.1).

The techniques presented thus far in this chapter should not be used in isolation, but should be incorporated into an overall consistent pattern. Several models showing examples of such structured approaches to discipline are available. In her book *Classroom Discipline*, Laurel Tanner (1978, p. 6) introduces the following models.

1. Training model
2. Behavior modification model
3. Psychodynamic model
4. Group dynamics model
5. Personal-social growth model

Training Model

Discipline is always concerned with regulating or changing behavior. This may be achieved either externally or internally—that is, change can be effected by means of external stimuli, or it can be the result of the subject's own purposive behavior. The training model is concerned totally with the former category, since any training program for classroom behavior is almost certain to result from the teacher's effort rather than the students'.

Although the effectiveness of the training model has been demonstrated by police officers, soldiers, and firefighters (to name only a few professions), who must learn to respond immediately and automatically to certain stimuli, most educators believe that this model is less desirable than the others for use with middle school and high school students. Their attitude is understandable, because the purpose of schooling is to prepare students to think for themselves rather than always to respond to the desires or demands of others.

Even in the high school classroom, though, some degree of training is helpful. For example, students can learn to stop talking when the class is being addressed, to remain seated when they complete an assignment, or to raise their hands when they want to speak. Most of these patterns, though, are holdovers from the earlier grades. High school discipline programs should not overemphasize or overuse the training model.

Behavior Modification Model

Like the training model, behavior modification depends on external stimuli to effect the desired changes in behavior. But unlike the training model—which does not require its subjects to think, just respond automatically—behavior modification does require students to change their behavior in order to receive definite rewards.

Neither the training model nor the behavior modification model requires students to think through their behavior at a very high level; instead, the subjects are conditioned to behave the way the teacher wants them to. Still, behavior modification strategies do work at the high school level. Behavior modification programs have been known to reduce the amount of inappropriate behavior in secondary school classrooms by as much as 75 percent (Sapp, Clough, Pittman, & Toben, 1973). This method is used extensively with mentally and emotionally handicapped students.

Psychodynamic Model

Unlike the training model and the behavior modification model, the psychodynamic model requires that the teacher know and understand each student. As an outgrowth of Freudian psychology, the model is based on the belief that knowing and understanding a student's behavior will lead to improvement in that behavior. This model is more advanced than the previous models in that it involves a search for the cause of misbehavior. But some educators are critical of this model because it stops at this point, without offering suggestions for correcting the behavior.

Group Dynamics Model

The group dynamics model recognizes the importance of social interactions and social pressures on students. Instead of focusing on an individual student in isolation, it looks at the individual in relation to the total group behavior. The focus is on the teacher, and the goal is to design good working conditions for the total group.

This model differs further from the models previously discussed in that it ties discipline to instruction. To avoid (or in response to) a behavior problem, the teacher would design a learning activity to divert students' attention from the problem to learning the lesson at hand. Utilization of this model requires an awareness of student behavior to the degree that problems can be nipped in the bud as soon as they begin to develop.

Like the psychodynamic model, this model recognizes that learning is a group activity, but it goes one important step further. Whereas the psychodynamic model depends solely on the teacher's understanding the students, this model requires the teacher to take action. In this sense it is far more practical.

Personal-Social Growth Model

Contemporary educators recognize that merely being able to regulate student behavior and suppress undesirable behavior is not enough. The title of this chapter reflects this concern. To become good citizens in a democratic society, students must ultimately learn to discipline themselves, to manage their own behavior. This requires experience—which means that you, the teacher, must be willing to share your power and responsibility for discipline with your students. Indeed, the students must feel that they are in control. They must also understand the purpose(s) behind desired behavioral patterns. Ideally, they should see the desired goals of the class and choose the ways they are to behave in order to attain these goals.

TRENDS IN DISCIPLINE TODAY

The order of strategies and models discussed above reflects the chronological pattern of metamorphosis of discipline in American education. At one time the school assumed total authority to define good discipline. Explains one educator, "With evangelic fervor . . . teachers have taught, indoctrinated, and compelled students to whom and what they were to comply with and become the ideal model that the school mystically judged as being desirable" (Hansen, 1974).

Today, good discipline is not considered synonymous with total, blind conformity. Students are involved with deciding what type of discipline is best for doing the job in their particular setting. Plymouth Junior High School's program for discipline is reflective of many current programs. It strives to put the responsibility on the student whenever possible, be consistent but flexible in enforcing the basic rules, and find alternatives for classroom activities, rewards, and consequences so the student does not force himself into a corner (Shook, 1975).

A school in Houston, Texas, developed a disciplinary system that reduced the frequency of corporal punishment to 7 percent and suspensions to 20 percent (Sanders & Yarbrough, 1976). The program's strategies were to provide a personal atmosphere, to help students clarify their values, to provide a crisis-intervention center for students with serious problems, and to provide an ever-changing set of clear objectives relating to real-life needs of students.

One reason that schools are turning to less-authoritative means for disciplining is that teachers today realize that power does not bring student cooperation, that, on the contrary, it stimulates more resistance. A second and equally important reason is that it would be inconsistent to use force. The aim is to produce students who approach the challenges of life courageously because they are able to relate to others, are resourceful in problem solving, and are responsible in their behavior (Dinkmeyer & Dinkmeyer, 1976).

THE CASCADE MODEL FOR CLASSROOM DISCIPLINE

Another modern classroom discipline model is the Cascade Model. This model presents a systematic plan for maintaining classroom discipline. Like a waterfall, it involves stages arranged in a particular sequence. By following the sequence, the teacher can approach classroom management logically. The early stages are preventive.

Preventive Discipline
Basic to the Cascade Model is a set of premises that includes certain attitudes. For example, there is the belief that a good, positive climate will prevent discipline problems. This climate includes both the physical environment and a positive attitude toward students. Expectations are made clear to students. The teacher is encouraged to involve students in developing rules at the beginning of each year. Even the rules are stated in positive terms: "If you need to say something, raise your hand" or "Have your homework completely finished, neat, and in on time." Consequences for violating the rules are also developed with student input. These consequences come in a certain order—for example (1) warning, (2) detention, (3) time-out, (4) in-school suspension, and (5) immediate removal from the classroom. If because of the nature of a particular student's history this sequence must be altered, the reason for the inconsistency should be made clear to the student.

Supportive Discipline
A second group of stages involves supportive discipline, or reinforcing desired behaviors. These reinforcers may be verbal or nonverbal, written or nonwritten. Praise is given in specific terms, telling why it has been earned. Parents are often told about the accomplishments of students and are encouraged to help by giving praise at home for achievements at school.

Corrective Discipline
The next tier of steps in the Cascade Model is labeled corrective discipline. At this level the teacher approaches the students with the problem using the "I" approach—for example, "I can't start the class until the room is quieter. We waste several minutes at the beginning of each hour. Have you any suggestions how we might solve this problem?" Each suggestion is discussed, the class votes, and their choice is tried for a period of time.

Adaptive Discipline

The fourth and final tier of the Cascade Model, adaptive discipline, is used when all else fails. Here, a private conference takes place. The teacher tries to remain positive, to avoid damaging the student's self-image. A satisfactory or acceptable behavior is identified, and both parties sign a contract. If the plan fails, it is altered again until it works. (For further references, see Rutter, Maughan, Mortimore, & Duston, 1979.)

Let's Ponder

Now add to your Discipline Continuum all the rest of these classroom management models. Examine your final map. Where would your own philosophy of discipline be located on this continuum? When you have finished this task, compare your chart with the sample in Figure 13.2. The exact position of any of these theories on the continuum would be somewhat subjective and therefore could vary as the perceptions of the individual placing them might vary. Figure 13.2 shows the general locations of these theories as perceived by the author. Study this chart and see if your own judgment for the position of any of these theories differs. Be prepared to defend your perception.

AVOIDING DISCIPLINE PROBLEMS

Control: Getting Off to a Good Start

Control is best achieved by cooperation between teacher and students, but it is your responsibility as teacher to have control from the first minute—before a cooperative arrangement can be discussed. Begin each year by being especially alert to the needs and desires of students. In this context, *needs* refers not so

Externally Imposed Discipline	LEARNING THEORIES				Self-Controlled Discipline
	Faculty Psychology	Stimulus-Response Psychology	Behavioral Psychology	Phenomenology	
	NONEDUCATION MANAGEMENT THEORIES				
	McGregor X Theory	Maslow's Needs Theory		McGregor Y Theory	
	CLASSROOM MANAGEMENT THEORIES				
	Training Model	Behavior Modification Model	Psychodynamic Model	Group Dynamics Model	Personal-Social Growth Model
				Group Management Theory	Reality Therapy

Figure 13.2 Discipline Continuum Showing General Locations of Major Learning Theories, Management Theories, and Discipline Theories

much to present whims but to serious needs of the present and the future. Some of these may be the adolescent's needs for approval, success, and independence and social needs. As the students show that they can handle freedom, you can gradually remove restrictions. Each time you feel that the class has progressed beyond the need for a rule, you can suggest that it be removed. This lets them know that the class has *earned* the prerogative of canceling the rule if they so wish, that you are not just being inconsistent with the rules.

It is easier for the firm teacher to become less strict than for the casual teacher to become more strict, but there is danger in beginning the year with too many rules. Only essential rules and restrictions should be established. In the 1950s a principal made a rule that all boys must wear belts. This was in reaction to jeans worn so low on the hips that the navel showed through the often unbuttoned shirt. But the boys noticed that the principal did not define "belt." The rule was obeyed—the boys wore short ropes through belt loops, they wore ropes eight feet long (dragging on the floor), they wore string belts, they wore leather belts, but belts they did wear. The principal was also a learner, and the rule was rescinded promptly.

One common mistake teachers make is to establish unnecessary and unenforceable rules.

Using Enthusiasm

The best single diversion from behavior problems is a well-planned and well-executed lesson that involves all students, especially if a teacher shows enthusiasm for the subject. The lesson will be even more successful if the objectives are clear and frequent feedback is given to show students how well they are progressing. In addition to adding clarity to the lesson, increasing student involvement, and giving frequent feedback, teachers can further raise their level of enthusiasm by planning some content and activities in each lesson that they know that they and the students will enjoy.

Using Names

The teacher who knows a student's name has more influence over that student—if that teacher uses the name appropriately. For example, suppose you are teaching a lesson the first day of school and a boy sitting in the back row begins to attract the attention of others while you are talking. It would be awkward to have to stop, look at the seating chart, and count seats in order to direct your reprimand to the right person. To say "You in the red-and-black-striped shirt" would get him the attention of the entire class and could lead to a repetition of the disruption to regain that attention. But to reprimand without designating the individual might alienate other class members. Simply walking near the disruptive student is often all that is needed to alleviate the problem. This technique is known as proximity control.

If you knew the boy's name, you could drop his name in the middle of a sentence as you were presenting the lesson, without even looking at him and without breaking the pace of the lesson. Such action on your part tells him and the rest of the class that you are very much aware of his attempts to disrupt the class but that the lesson is too important to be impeded by anyone's selfish attempt to gain attention.

Helping Students Learn Self-Respect
Students who perceive themselves as troublemakers make trouble. Those who perceive themselves as good students or good guys are obligated to live up to this image. Avoid saying and doing things that tend to downgrade students, and take any opportunity to say and do things that will improve a student's self-image.

Avoiding Threats
Some teachers threaten groups of students and individuals, not realizing that a threatened person is challenged to misbehave. It is not uncommon for a teacher to remark "All right, class, I am not going to tell you again to be quiet," implying "I can make you wish you had behaved." Such a statement usually promotes misbehavior and diminishes learning. As Hart (1983) explains, "the brain tends to 'downshift' under threat." Avoid threats you never intend to carry out—better yet, avoid threats completely.

Avoid Public Reprimand
Any serious problem you have with an individual student should be dealt with privately. Reprimanding a student in the presence of peers will damage peer relationships, which are important to people of all ages, and it forces the student either to rebut or concede. A rebuttal damages the student's relationship with the teacher; a concession causes the student to lose face with peers. Public reprimand is also a threat to the rest of the class. Believing that they could receive the same treatment, they may lose confidence and trust in the teacher.

Avoiding Ridicule
When students misbehave, you should try to change their future behavior patterns. That is all. Never ridicule a student, whether in public or in private. Ridicule is directed at a person, not at correcting behavior.

DEALING WITH PROBLEMS

Be Prepared to Handle Problems When They Do Develop
The best way to avoid problems in the classroom is to be well prepared each day and to have interesting experiences for each class. However, even the most effective teachers have discipline problems, so it is good to be prepared, to think ahead to a time when a discipline problem might develop in your class. What will you do?

Always Ask Yourself Why
No student wants to misbehave, so why do they? There is a cause for all behavior. Classical psychologists say that all behavior is a reaction to a stimulus—that is, everything we do is in reaction to other people or other things. Phenomenologists

believe that every misbehavior is an expression of a need, that therefore each time a student misbehaves we should ask ourselves "What need is that student trying to satisfy?"

The need may be for more attention, or perhaps for approval of peers if a student does not get adequate reinforcement from family and teachers. If the misbehavior is hostile, it may be an attempt to alleviate frustration because of some perceived injustice. Sometimes the need or the cause of the behavior cannot be determined. To ask misbehaving students what the need is would not help, because they probably do not know.

The creative teacher is often able to provide acceptable avenues for students to express themselves. When a student causes serious disruptions, you should study that student's cumulative record and discuss the problem with the school counselor. Learning more about the student may give you ideas about how to work more effectively with that student. Become more tolerant when you see that the student is attempting to alter previous unsatisfactory behavior for the better.

Avoiding Confrontations

Because misbehavior is often an attempt to get attention or to express discontent, the person who misbehaves may seek to create a scene in order to confront the person who could draw the most attention to the disruption—the teacher. Sometimes you may be tempted to engage in emotionally charged disputes with students. Remember, though, that an emotional person does not seek reasonable or rational answers, but instead seeks to justify the behavior. Any argument will only result in the student's becoming more defensive. You may be able to help students realize that their misbehavior is disruptive and provide opportunities for them to express their opinions, but you can do so only after they have calmed down and become less emotional.

The Private Talk

Avoiding a serious confrontation does not necessarily mean ignoring the student. If you do not ask a student to refrain from the undesirable behavior, that student and other class members may assume that the teacher does not really care whether a rule is broken. The difference between noting a disruption and engaging in a confrontation is in the manner in which the action is taken, which should be as quietly and uneventfully as possible. If the student responds negatively, ignoring the student is appropriate, but if the disruption continues the student should be asked to leave the room and wait outside until the end of the period, when you are free to arrange for a private talk. Private conferences can be effective if they place part of the responsibility for correcting the student's behavior on both the teacher and the student and if the teacher looks for the cause of the misbehavior.

If you must ask a student to leave the classroom, you must have a private talk with the student before he or she is allowed to reenter. During the private talk you should keep your emotions under cover. You can express disappointment with the student's behavior, but make certain that the student does not interpret this as a personal dislike. In an extreme case, where the student continues to misbehave after the private talk, you should call for the principal's assistance. Your mission, after all, is to provide a classroom environment conducive to learning and you cannot afford to allow one student to continue disrupting it.

Using Firmness and Consistency

All teachers should assert themselves. Whatever tactics you use to maintain discipline should be applied consistently with all students every day. Firmness does not imply harshness and constant sternness. If you are firm but calm, your students will appreciate it and your health will be better (Elrod, 1976).

RECAP OF MAJOR IDEAS

1. All teachers experience discipline problems.
2. Good classroom discipline is essential for maximum learning. Because the teacher is in charge of instruction, discipline is the teacher's responsibility.
3. Good discipline implies order and control. Quiet is important to the extent that it is essential for order and control and for effective communication.
4. Teachers should begin each year by being firm yet friendly. Classroom humor is desirable, but it must not lead to excessive disruptions.
5. Too many rules can cause added problems. Students should be told why each rule is necessary. Whenever feasible, it is good practice to involve students in setting classroom rules.
6. Consistency and fairness are essential to establishing and maintaining good discipline.
7. The best deterrent to discipline problems is a well-planned and well-executed lesson, with clear goals, that involves all students. Teacher enthusiasm for the lesson contributes to student motivation.
8. Effort is better spent preventing problems than trying to learn how to manage disasters. Although the latter skill may be helpful, few teachers feel they are experts in that area.
9. Teachers should avoid making threats and using sarcasm and public reprimands, because these tend to lower students' self-esteem and self-respect. Instead, teachers should look for opportunities to compliment students, thus helping build positive self-images.
10. When planned and executed correctly private conferences can be an effective means of handling disruptive students. When private conferences fail, the teacher should arrange a joint conference with the principal, counselor, and parents or guardians.

POSTTEST

Now that you have read the chapter, take a moment to respond to the following statements again:

	Agree	Disagree	Uncertain
1. Truly effective *discipline* and *classroom management* are inseparable terms.	____	____	____
2. As perceived by the American public, discipline is the greatest problem in our schools today.	____	____	____
3. Discipline is the same as restraint.	____	____	____
4. There are times when physical punishment is the best approach to resolving a discipline problem.	____	____	____
5. A quiet class is usually a well-disciplined one, and a noisy class is usually undisciplined.	____	____	____
6. At the beginning of the year, the teacher should be strict, since it is always easy to loosen the rules but difficult to strengthen them.	____	____	____
7. Discipline models should be consistent with accepted learning theories and with management theories in other fields.	____	____	____
8. The ultimate goal should be to get students to discipline themselves.	____	____	____

CASES

Discipline is a problem in our schools, and it is the teacher's responsibility to maintain discipline in the classroom. The following cases will help you develop your own ability to discipline your future students. They show some of the real dilemmas in which teachers often find themselves. As you read each case, imagine yourself in the situation and decide how you would handle it.

Case 1: A Principal Has Too Many Discipline Problems

Middletown School was divided into a junior and senior high with the lower grades in one building, the upper grades in another, and the principal's office in a breezeway connecting the two buildings. The windows in Jan's classroom faced the breezeway. Jan had taught for only a few weeks at Middle-town. Each time a discipline problem developed, she immediately referred the offender to the principal's office.

One day Jan was amused to see another teacher leading a student to the principal's office. Later that day she saw a replay of the event. After that, Jan began counting the number of times teachers marched offenders to the princi-pal's office. The record for one day was nine trips; the record for one teacher in one day was three trips.

Jan began to realize that this principal was spending a large amount of time disciplining the students of teachers who could not or would not assume the responsibility. She resolved to handle all future discipline problems her-self, except in an emergency.

Discussion

1. How are the student's impressions of a teacher affected when the teacher takes disci-pline problems to the principal?
    The first time this occurs it may go unnoticed by the students, but if it is repeated again and again, the students will soon realize that the teacher is weak and unable to handle problems. Troubles in this teacher's class will increase.
2. Does the number of discipline problems reflect the quality of that teacher's teaching?
    Yes. The teacher who has planned an interesting lesson that involves the students will have fewer discipline problems than the teacher who is dull, boring, and poorly pre-pared.

Case 2: A First Telephone Call from a Parent

Don Harrader was a quiet member of the ninth-grade science class that John taught. In fact, it was difficult for John to think of Don as a member of the class because Don was so withdrawn. Don was making above-average grades until a unit on simple machines began. He received an F at the end of the unit when an exam was administered. When John talked to Don about the grade, he replied that he just did not care for that part of the course.

The next day John was having lunch when the message arrived that Mr. Harrader had called and asked that he call back. John recalled Don's recent decline in grades and suspected this was why his father had called. John left the lunchroom and went directly to the telephone. Mr. Harrader immediately asked why Don had an F in John's class. Trying to be objective and honest, John answered that Don claimed to have no interest in simple machines. Don's father replied, "I understand, but I want to know if Don has been misbehaving in class." John assured him the answer was no, and the conver-sation ended.

In the days following, John did a lot of thinking about Don, Don's rela-tionship with his father, and Don's lack of real friends among his peers. One weekend John parked by the tennis courts and was watching a match when Don walked by and saw him. He asked if John played tennis and would play a set with him. John agreed. He found that Don was certainly not the same boy he saw each day in science class. There was never a happier person. From that day on, John had no trouble stimulating Don's interest in class. When Don learned that his teacher was interested in rocks, he brought his rock collection to share with the rest of the class.

A simple telephone call had stimulated John's interest in Don. An unplanned tennis match had removed Don's apathy. Together these two events had resulted indirectly in motivating a shy student.

Discussion

1. If an angry parent telephones, how should the teacher respond?
   First, the teacher must refrain from showing his or her emotions, so the parent can see that the teacher is being objective regarding the student. This is the best way to show the irate parent that the parent is the one who is being unreasonable. Second, the teacher must be honest with the parent. If the student is failing to do satisfactory work, the teacher must say so. Frankness and honesty must prevail before the teacher and parent can begin working together to motivate the student, and it is the teacher who must initiate this honesty.
2. Parental neglect is the cause of many discipline problems at school. How can the teacher provide attention for the neglected child?
   You can probably think of many ways to show interest in a student who is neglected at home. Most students have an area in which they have a strong interest, although they may never reveal it in the classroom. The teacher can often identify a student's interests by observing the student's activities outside the classroom. A teacher who shows an interest in a student's nonacademic activities may find that the student pays more attention to the teacher in class and to school assignments.

Case 3: A Student Conquers Her Parents

School had been in session for only two weeks when we had the first PTA meeting of the year. Mrs. Snyder came by and told me, "Our daughter Sandy is in your class. Do what you can with her. Just because we have little control over her doesn't mean we approve of her behavior. Do what you can to discipline her. If it means beating her, that's okay too." I shuddered, because I knew this parent actually meant it. The only Sandy I could recall was a neat and attractive girl—I remembered seeing her the first day and thinking she might become a top student.

One of the greatest values of PTA meetings is that they stimulate teachers to become personally interested in their students. This happened here, for Mrs. Snyder's words led me to learn more about Sandy. I found out that Sandy was indeed the neat, attractive, pleasant girl in my eighth-grade class, but it soon became obvious that she was not living up to my hopes for her. She was dating juniors and seniors, staying out past midnight during the week, and never completing homework assignments, if she even tried.

I still do not know how Sandy conquered her parents and took away all their control, but by admitting to her that they could no longer control her, they made it impossible for her teachers to motivate her to learn. A person's behavioral patterns do not change much when he or she walks into a classroom. It is not realistic to expect the teacher to make dramatic progress with a student at school when the parents cannot make any progress at home. Fortunately, there is always a chance that together parents and teachers can stimulate the student to change behavior patterns and direct energy toward academic achievement—but only if the parents and teacher openly discuss the student's problem. Although Mrs. Snyder had made the mistake of giving up, she was closer to helping Sandy than she knew, because she had admitted that Sandy needed help.

I began to watch Sandy each day. When she began to goof off, I was there to offer help. Sandy soon learned that, unlike her parents, I expected quality work from her—in fact, that I insisted on it. Sandy became more responsible. By the end of the year she was enjoying the class and doing the assignments. Her parents soon learned that punishment, which would not help anyway, was not necessary.

Discussion

1. Should you defend a student against her parents if they are clearly mistreating her?
Respecting the close ties between the parent and the student, you must not do anything that will destroy whatever positive feelings apparently unconcerned parents have for their child. Instead, try to improve the situation by helping parents and child learn to respect each other. Avoid downgrading either the student or the parents in the presence of the other. If the conditions are really serious, you can consult the school counselor for advice and assistance.

2. What precautions can you take against losing control of an unrestrained student like Sandy?
How much control you will have over students like Sandy is determined during the first few class periods. Begin by showing a keen interest and a determination to help all students—even those who appear hopelessly unmanageable. Above all, let them know you expect the highest quality work that each student can provide, and improvement from day to day.

Case 4: Poor Management Results in a Near Catastrophe

Of the students in my five sections of eighth-grade science, Tim Walker was the most easygoing, quiet, and pleasant. Tim was a model student—that is why I was surprised when the accident occurred.

I had stepped outside the room to help patrol the hallway traffic between periods. Tim and another boy were the first students to enter the classroom. Because they were alone for a minute before the rest of the class arrived, they began horsing around. Tim tripped. As he fell, he grabbed for a desk, and one of his fingers caught in the corner of the metal desk frame. The finger was almost entirely cut off. Tim was rushed to a hospital, where the finger was sewn back in place. The doctors advised him that the finger had been saved and could be rehabilitated.

This was a close call for Tim and for me. I was excused because I had been responsible for hall duty at the time of the accident, but for weeks I shuddered when I thought of the many times I had left my room for brief intervals. Since this accident occurred, I have not permitted roughhousing in my classroom.

Discussion

1. Should you ever leave a student in charge of a class?
    Even if you have placed a student in charge, you are responsible and legally liable for the welfare of every student in your classroom. When you go out, do not leave a student in charge unless you are willing to accept the legal blame and pay the penalty for whatever may happen during your absence.
2. If a parent comes to your room to talk to you while your class is in session, what should you do?
    Do not leave the room to go elsewhere and talk to the parent. Tell the parent that you are sorry you cannot talk now, and make an appointment to see the parent during your next planning period.
3. What are your legal responsibilities for being in the classroom at specified times?
    As the teacher, you are responsible for the safety of students in your classroom at the times you are scheduled to be there. An exception can be made when an emergency requires you to leave your room—for example, if the principal calls for you or if you must take a student to the principal's office for discipline.

Case 5: A Real Pro Goes into Action

Randy Graham, a bright and witty student, was especially troublesome in Mr. Hall's junior history class. One day, to show the spirit of a certain age, Mr. Hall read a few verses of poetry while the students followed along in their books. At the end of the first verse, Randy applauded Mr. Hall. Because Mr. Hall was large, solemn, and stern-looking, the other class members were shocked. Looking directly at Randy, Mr. Hall said solemnly, "Thank you, Mr. Graham," and continued reading. Randy never again misbehaved in that class.

Discussion

1. Should a teacher ever attempt to control misbehavior by applying humor to the event, as Mr. Hall did?
    Humor is always appreciated by adolescents, but it must be used judiciously in the classroom. It can backfire unless the teacher retains a degree of seriousness, even while using humor.
2. If Randy had caused trouble later during the hour, should Mr. Hall again have used humor?
    One of the greatest dangers of humor in the classroom is overuse. If Mr. Hall had continued responding humorously, Randy could have started a game that many students might quickly learn to prefer over studying history.

Case 6: An Experiment with Oral Reprimand

In my first teaching position my homeroom consisted of 47 seventh-graders— who were also my first-period math class. There were so many rows that they seemed to merge at the back of the room. From my desk I could see only about two-thirds of the faces at any time. Disruptions were common in the hidden areas of the back rows.

I talked with the class about it, but each day was a little worse than the day before. I did not want to use derogatory comments, but I finally ran out of options. When two boys in the back row kept jabbing each other, I asked them to come with me out into the hall. The other class members were silent. They could hear the reprimands I directed to each boy in the hall. The boys were embarrassed, and there were no more disturbances for the rest of the week.

The following week, when things again appeared to be getting out of hand, I repeated the verbal reprimands. As we left the room this time, the class was not silent, and several giggles could be heard. During my second month I was reprimanding one student or another almost every day. It was difficult to believe that such corrective measures were having so little effect in curbing the problems. On the contrary, my reprimands seemed to be promoting more problems. I was baffled.

I vowed to stop using reprimands. Each time a problem developed, I stopped the lesson, walked over near the troubled area, and silently and unsmilingly stared for a moment, then continued with the lesson. The effect was tremendous. I kept verbal reprimands to a minimum because the few positive results were surely outweighed by the trouble that they caused me.

Discussion

1. When reprimand or verbal attack is used, what effect does it have on the rest of the class?

   The use of verbal reprimand almost always has a damaging effect on the teacher's rapport with students who are not receiving the reprimand. The teacher should remember that a learning environment must be appealing, free from threat and resentment. Verbal reprimand can destroy that kind of atmosphere because it introduces fear and resentment.

2. Why was verbal reprimand more effective at first than later on?

   A methodology that is directed only toward restraining or penalizing a student, rather than toward helping the student, always becomes less effective as it is repeated. Verbal reprimand can restrain students only so long as it frightens them. At first they were afraid of the reprimand because it was unfamiliar to them, but as they experienced the behavior again and again, they became less afraid of it and the reprimand ceased to be effective.

3. Can the teacher make verbal reprimand more effective by being increasingly stern?

   This is doubtful, because any degree of sternness that is familiar to students fails to intimidate them. Also, increasing sternness is a challenge to the student to misbehave even more. In a sense, the teacher is saying that if the previous verbal punishment was not sufficient, the teacher is capable of conquering the students by becoming sterner. Therefore, students are challenged to continue misbehaving to test the teacher's assertion.

ACTIVITIES

The following activities will help you deal with all these discipline concerns.

1. You have undoubtedly heard or read statements about school discipline that you do not agree with. Explain one way in which your idea of how students should behave differs from the ideas of others.
2. Describe a problem that the schools in your community are facing. Explain how you would work to eliminate that problem if you were teaching in a local school.
3. Develop a discipline strategy building on one of your personal strengths.
4. What would you do if a student became enraged and refused to be quiet? The other students are waiting to see your reaction. How will you handle the situation?

SUGGESTED READINGS

Alschuler, S. (1980). *School discipline*. New York: McGraw-Hill.

Bell, L. C., & Stefanich, G. P. (1984). Building effective discipline using the Cascade Model. *Clearing House, 58*, 134–137.

Bersani, H., Jr. (1985). How to fail at classroom management. *Academic Therapy, 20*, 357–359.

Broadbelt, S. (1973). Teachers' mental health: Whose responsibility? *Phi Delta Kappan, 55*, 268–269.

Curwin, R. L., & Mendler, A. N. (1984, May). High standards for effective discipline. *Educational Leadership, 41*, 75–76.

――― (1980). *The discipline book*. Reston, Va.: Reston.

Davis, E. D. (1984). Should the public schools teach values? *Phi Delta Kappan, 65*, 358–360.

Dinkmeyer, D., & Dinkmeyer, D., Jr. (1976). Logical consequences: A key to the reduction of disciplinary problems. *Phi Delta Kappan, 57*, 664–666.

Duke, D. L. (1980). *Managing student behavior problems*. New York: Teachers College Press.

Elrod, W. (1976). Don't get tangled in discipline problems. *Music Educator's Journal, 63*, 47–50.

Gallup, A. M. (1985). The seventeenth annual Gallup Poll of the public's attitudes toward the public schools. *Phi Delta Kappan, 67*, 35–47.

Glaser, R. (Ed.) (1971). *Nature of Reinforcement*. N.Y.: Academic Press.

――― (1986). *Advances in Instructional Psychology*. Vol. 3. Hillsdale, N.J.: Erlbaum Associates.

Glasser, W. (1985). *Control theory in the classroom*. New York: Harper & Row.

Hamilton, S. F. (1983). Socialization for learning: Insights from ecological research in the classrooms. *The Reading Teacher, 37*, 150–156.

Hansen, J. M. (1974). Discipline: A whole new bag. *High School Journal, 57*, 172–181.

Hart, L. A. (1983). *Human brain and human learning*. New York: Longman.

Helge, E. E. (1978). Good discipline: Yours for the asking. *Lutheran Education, 113*, 181–185.

Henson, K. T. (1977). A new concept of discipline. *Clearing House, 41*, 89–91.

Jessup, M. H., & Kiley, M. A. (1971). *Discipline: Positive attitudes for learning*. Englewood Cliffs, N.J.: Prentice-Hall.

Jones, V. (1983). Current trends in classroom management: Implications for gifted students. *Roeper Review, 6*, 26–30.

Kearney, P. (1985). Power in the classroom: Teacher communication techniques and messages. *Communication Education, 34*, 19–20.

Kounin, J. S. (1977). *Discipline and group management in classrooms*. Melbourne, Fla.: Krieger.

Long, J. D., & Frye, V. H. (1981). *Making it till Friday* (2nd ed.). Princeton: Princeton Book Co.

Madsen, C. H., Jr., & Madsen, C. K. (1974). *Teaching/Discipline* (2nd ed.). Boston: Allyn & Bacon.

McDaniel, T. R. (1984). Developing the skills of humanistic discipline. *Educational Leadership, 41*, 71–74.

McGregor, D. (1967). *The Professional Manager*. C. McGregor & W. G. Bennis (Eds.). New York: McGraw-Hill.

Maslow, A. (1968). *Toward a Psychology of Being*. 2nd ed. New York: Van Nostrand.

Redl, F. (1975). Disruptive behavior in the classroom. *School Review, 83*, 569–594.

Redl, F., & Wattenberg, W. W. (1959). Mental hygiene in teaching (2nd ed.). Orlando, Fla.: Harcourt Brace Jovanovich.

Rutter, M., Maughan, B., Mortimore, P., & Duston, J. (1979). *Fifteen thousand hours*. Cambridge: Harvard University Press.

Sanders, S. G., & Yarbrough, J. S. (1976). Achieving a learning environment with order. *Clearing House, 50*, 100–102.

Sapp, G. L., Clough, J. D., Pittman, B., & Toben, C. (1973). Classroom management and student involvement. *High School Journal, 56*, 276–283.

Shook, J. (1975). Alternatives for managing disruptive classroom behaviors. *School and Community, 61*, 28–29.

Spaulding, R. L. (1983a). A systematic approach to classroom discipline, Part I. *Phi Delta Kappan, 65*, 48–51.

—— (1983b). A systematic approach to classroom discipline, Part II. *Phi Delta Kappan, 65*, 132–136.

Tanner, L. (1978). *Classroom discipline for effective teaching and learning*. New York: Holt, Rinehart & Winston.

Thompson, G. H. (1976). Discipline and the high school teacher. *Education Digest, 42*, 20–22.

Wattenberg, W. W. (1977). Ecology of classroom behavior. *Theory into Practice, 16*, 256–261.

Wayson, W. W., DeVoss, G. G., Kaeser, S. C., Lasley, T., Pinnell, G. S., and the Phi Delta Kappa Commission on Discipline. (1982). *Handbook for developing good discipline*. Bloomington, Ind.: Phi Delta Kappa, 1982.

Wayson, W. W., & Lasley, T. J. (1984). Climates for excellence: Schools that foster self-discipline. *Phi Delta Kappan, 65*, 419–421.

Weber, W., Roff, L. A., Crawford, J., & Robinson, C. (1983). *Classroom management:*

Reviews of the teacher education and research literature. Princeton, N.J.: Educational Testing Service.

Wegmann, R. G. (1976). Classroom discipline: A negotiable item. *Today's Education, 65,* 92–93.

Whiteside, M. (1975). School discipline: The ongoing crisis. *Clearing House, 49,* 160–162.

Wilde, J. W., & Summers, P. (1978). Teaching disruptive adolescents: A game worth winning. *Phi Delta Kappan, 59,* 342–343.

Young, J. W. (1975). Maintaining classroom control. *School and Community, 61,* 13.

PART VI

TESTS AND EVALUATION

Every teacher is responsible for testing and evaluation, terms that are frequently confused and misunderstood. This part will help you understand the many uses of tests and evaluations in the classroom. Most secondary and middle schools in the United States require grades, so you must learn all you can about constructing, administering, and scoring tests and about converting these results, along with other criteria, into grades. Because most teachers have been underusing formative evaluation and criterion-based evaluation, Chapter 15 explains their advantages for secondary and middle school teachers.

C H A P T E R *14*

Test Construction, Administration, and Scoring

Objectives

- List two advantages of objective test questions and two of essay questions.
- Develop an objective test that measures different levels of the cognitive domain.
- Describe a minimum and a maximum standard teachers can use to determine the appropriate level of difficulty for writing test questions.
- List five guidelines for administering a test.
- Construct a discussion-type test that will measure the students' ability to judge or evaluate.
- State two practices that ensure fairness on a discussion-type exam.
- Design a system for scoring an essay exam that will justify assigning more value to some questions than to others.
- Write a general essay-type question that promotes divergent thinking. Then rewrite the same question, making it more specific.
- Write a multiple-choice question with five choices, two of which are viable distracters.
- Write a question for each level of the affective and cognitive domains.

PRETEST

	Agree	Disagree	Uncertain
1. Objective questions test only the student's ability to retain facts.	____	____	____
2. Competition among all students is good.	____	____	____
3. Essay questions must be scored subjectively.	____	____	____
4. Essay questions tend to measure what students know, whereas objective questions measure what they do not know—that is, their learning gaps.	____	____	____
5. Beginning teachers tend to make tests too difficult.	____	____	____
6. Tests should contain both objective questions and essay questions.	____	____	____
7. Most teachers have an adequate background in testing.	____	____	____
8. Essay tests reveal students' thought processes.	____	____	____
9. Most American students are capable of supporting their opinions.	____	____	____
10. Multiple-choice test items should have only one plausible answer.	____	____	____
11. The more specifically essay questions are worded, the better they are.	____	____	____
12. Application level test items require the use of principles.	____	____	____

Middle-Level Message

Teachers often view testing as their most unpleasant responsibility. This occurs when teachers fail to understand how to use tests appropriately. Middle level teachers often express a need to know more about classroom management and motivation strategies. Perhaps this accounts for much of their misuse of tests. Middle level teachers and high school teachers desperately need to learn more about the use of tests and their effects on students. In this chapter you will learn how you can use a variety of tests to assess student performance. You will also learn the major advantages and limitations of each type of test and how to construct, administer, and score tests to increase achievement in your classes. Help your students realize that test scores are not important terminal goals but they are important indicators of success.

As a teacher, you will be responsible for the testing program in your classes. Even teachers who teach in secondary schools that give departmental tests will have to contribute to the construction, administering, and scoring of the tests. Therefore, the bulk of this chapter focuses on helping prospective or beginning teachers improve their skills in these areas. This chapter is concerned with teacher-made tests; Chapter 15 covers standardized tests.

TYPES OF TESTS

Before you begin constructing tests, you should be aware that there are many types of tests and that you have a number of options when it comes to designing tests. For many years American educators have been predisposed to written tests. The practice of using written tests may have been so strongly embedded in your own teachers that when you hear the word *test* you think of a pencil-and-paper exercise.

But there are alternatives. Teachers can choose simply to ask questions orally to solicit oral responses, or they can give a performance test that requires students to perform exercises, such as role playing in a drama class, assembling an engine in an auto mechanics class, or responding in dialogue in a foreign language class. Concern that written tests too frequently measure only the recall of knowledge, ignoring the student's ability to apply it, have prompted greater use of oral and performance options. Most teacher-made tests are of the pencil-and-paper variety. As we examine several types of written tests, keep in mind their potentials and limitations for measuring different student competencies.

ESSAY VS. OBJECTIVE TESTS

When choosing to use a written test, the teacher must decide whether it will be an objective test or an essay-type test, or possibly a combination. The two types differ drastically in many ways. First, the essay test can be said to measure what students know, whereas the objective test is often accused of measuring what students do *not* know. The essay test does permit students to select from and use their own knowledge storehouse in the response. By contrast, the objective test (true-false, matching, and multiple choice) does not provide this freedom. In fact, the objective test can also leave students thinking that they understand the lesson but that the test questions just happened to be from less familiar areas.

Most important, the essay test is flexible enough to give students opportunities to express their own views—to reach beyond the recall level into the application, analysis, synthesis, and evaluation levels, and even into the affective domain. In addition, essay questions enable teachers to determine a student's thought processes. As Quellmaiz (1985, p. 32) puts it, "The essay format is especially useful for assessing how students reach and explain their conclusions." The National Assessment (1981) exam, which asked students to interpret or evaluate literary selections in essay form, found that few students could offer even rudimentary support for their opinions. This attests to the need for using essay items in assignments and on tests.

ESSAY TEST ITEMS

Discussion

Of all types of test items, the essay question is perhaps the most misused. When questions are stated broadly, such as "Discuss Shakespeare's work" or "Discuss the Industrial Revolution," students wonder, "Where should I begin?" and "What issues am I supposed to address?" By carefully restricting the question, you can reduce the ambiguity—for example, "Discuss the types of humor in Shakespeare's *Twelfth Night*" or "Discuss the role of Eli Whitney's cotton gin in the Industrial Revolution." By sharpening the focus of essay questions, you will also simplify your scoring. The more exactly you state your expectations, the more accountable your students become for including the expected content in their answers. By giving an example, you can further clarify your expectations—for example, the question "Discuss the role of Eli Whitney's cotton gin in the Industrial Revolution" could be followed by "Address its effect on the labor market."

Explanation

Good questions on explanation tests focus on a certain *process*—for example, "Explain the water cycle." Because the water cycle involves a definite sequence of activities (e.g., rain → runoff → evaporation → condensation), students can be held accountable for a specific body of knowledge, plus the sequences involved in the process. When using explanation questions, avoid general questions like "Explain the Civil Rights movement of the sixties." Stated that way, the question is at best just a discussion and would be better worded as such.

Situation

Situation test items measure a student's response to a certain situation. Students are asked to apply their knowledge, values, and judgment to decide how they would respond to a given set of circumstances. For example, the teacher of a first-aid course might ask, "If you were driving down the road and came upon an accident that had left a person lying in the road unconscious and breathing heavily, what would you do?" Like other types of essay questions, situation questions are at their best when they request a definite body of knowledge. They have the further advantage of requiring students to apply that knowledge.

Compare or Contrast

Questions that ask students to compare and/or contrast force them to sharpen their understanding about similar or dissimilar concepts. In other words, they require students to differentiate between two or more concepts by focusing on particular similar or dissimilar qualities—for example, "Compare and contrast World War I with World War II." You can get more-specific answers by adding limits to the question—"Compare and contrast World War I with World War II according to their ground strategies, air strategies, number of casualties, and the number of countries involved."

OBJECTIVE TEST ITEMS

Some popular types of questions found on objective tests include true-false, multiple choice, and matching. Less common is the fill-in-the-blank question. Each type calls for a specific, predetermined answer. Objective test items are often criticized for testing what students do not know rather than what they do know. Furthermore, they tend to encourage guessing.

But objective tests have certain advantages over essay tests. First, they are more quickly scored. This is important to today's teachers, who would better invest time in preparing lessons than in scoring tests. Furthermore, objective questions are likely to be more fairly scored because there is no doubt about whether an answer is correct. This too is an important advantage, since most teachers want their students to perceive them as fair and impartial.

THE PURPOSE OF TESTING

Is testing necessary? What is the advantage of testing? Could the purpose not be achieved some other way? How does testing assist the instructional program? How can I improve my own testing program? When we think of testing we think of grades. But if we say that the purposes of testing is to determine grades, another good question might be Why do we need grades? Justifying tests merely as grade determiners is not sufficient; many educators are not at all convinced that grades are necessary.

Testing helps your students determine their general rate of progress in a specific subject. This information is important both to you and to the student. And to report a grade—which is required by most school systems and is expected, if not demanded, by most parents—you must know the student's general rate of progress. Chapter 12 showed that if students know their rate of achievement they can be motivated or encouraged to achieve even more.

Testing also helps the teacher determine the progress of the class as a whole.

The rate of progress in teaching is always proportional to the learning rate of the class. In other words, your teaching cannot be better than your students' learning. Test results can help you identify areas where you need to improve your methodology and clarify misunderstandings in the classroom—that is, where to slow down, where to repeat more, or where to use different methods. Testing also provides a way to diagnose individual strengths and weaknesses of both students and teacher. Through testing, you can help a student identify areas in which he or she should spend more effort.

Recognize the test as a tool for helping you improve your methodology and for helping your students improve listening and study habits. Then construct, administer, and evaluate tests with these purposes in mind.

TEST CONSTRUCTION

If you experience mild shock when grading your first set of test papers, do not immediately question your teaching ability. "Many teachers argue that the topic of test construction has not been addressed sufficiently in undergraduate teacher training programs" (Carter, 1983) and that "programs are needed to help them develop, manage, and provide practice for evaluation" (Fluitt & Gifford, 1980). Carter (1984) found that many teachers are unable to recognize what skill a particular test item was testing. Pre-service teacher training often fails to include a course on testing (Coffman, 1983), and assessment is rarely a topic for in-service training (Stiggins, 1985). Realizing that most of the fault is not in the teaching but in the testing, you may ask, How can I construct good tests?

Stating the Directions
Each test should begin with a written statement explaining how to complete the test. Like all assignments, the directions should be in specific terms. For example:

> Each item on this test is worth one point. Select the single choice you believe is best. Do not leave questions blank and do not mark more than one choice. If you have questions, please raise your hand and I will come to your desk. When you finish, please turn your paper face down on your desk and begin working quietly on the assignment now written on the board.

Once the test is written, the teacher should check it for any ambiguity or possible misinterpretations, making changes and clarifying accordingly. The directions should always state the maximum time allotted for taking the test. Clear directions will prevent unnecessary interruptions during the testing period and will prevent the discomfort students feel when they are not sure what is being asked of them.

State the Value of Each Question
Most teachers find it convenient to specify or assign values to questions in terms of percentages. Assign relative values, asking yourself how much each question is worth in relation to the other questions. The value of each question should be

proportional to the amount of time spent on that topic in class and the amount of time required to answer the question.

Often a test will consist of several short-answer questions or short problems that carry equal value. On such tests, the teacher need not specify separate values, but merely state in the directions that each question has equal value. On tests that do have questions of varying values, the value of each question should appear in the margin alongside the question.

Select a Variety of Questions

Which type of question is best—objective or subjective? Actually, each type offers advantages that the other does not, so most tests should contain both objective *and* subjective questions. Objective questions require more time to construct, but they require less time to answer and to score, so many objective questions can be included on each test. Subjective questions can measure creativity and allow students to express their feelings and attitudes; they also show how well students can organize their thoughts.

Many testing experts believe multiple-choice questions are the best type of objective questions. True-false questions are seen to be of average value, and fill-in-the-blank questions the least valuable. It is agreed, though, that several types of objective questions should be used. An advantage of variety is that students who find one type of question especially difficult to answer will not be penalized by having an entire test of that type. Multiple-choice and other types of test questions will be discussed later in this chapter.

Include Both Easy and Difficult Questions

Every test should have some questions so easy that almost every student in class can answer them correctly. The test should begin with the less-difficult questions, so that each student will be encouraged to go on to the following question. Placing easy questions at the beginning of multiple-choice exams has increased test scores significantly—almost 10 percent (Savitz, 1985). Remember that the purpose of the test is to measure ability, not tolerance. Avoid placing a 40-point question at the end of the test. Slower students will think it is unfair if they fail the test because the time ran out just as they began answering a last question that is worth that many points.

If every question on a test were so easy that every student could answer it correctly, the test would be of little use. A test should have some questions that challenge even the most capable students. Each question should be a little more difficult than the preceding question, but never try to make the question difficult by wording it so it is vague, too general, or tricky. The difficult questions should be difficult because they are especially challenging and involve a complex process, and they should measure the attainment of important concepts.

Cover Important Material

Most teachers believe it is necessary to test at least once every two weeks. From the large volume of material covered in this time span, what should be selected for inclusion on the test? A good rule is that any test should contain questions about information covered each day of the testing period. In other words, it should begin testing where the previous test stopped and should test right up through the day preceding the test date.

Ideally, the time spent studying various areas of content should be in proportion to the importance of this content. Therefore, the percentage of time studying an area should be proportional to the percentage of the test that the particular area comprises. For example, if in a unit on astronomy a week was spent studying the sun and only one day was spent studying the moon, the total value of test questions about the sun should be about five times as great as the total value assigned to questions about the moon.

Testing the Test

Many teachers insist on taking a test themselves before administering it. Besides catching typographical errors and ambiguously worded questions, the teacher can at the same time develop a master answer sheet. Without a list of answers when beginning to score a test, a teacher has a tendency to accept the first student answers and use these as a standard for judging the accuracy of the answers on the other students' papers.

WRITING TEST QUESTIONS

Selecting the Type of Test

Upon completing a unit of study—or, as we shall see, even during a unit—the teacher must decide when to give an examination and then either design the right type of questions or select the right type of ready-made exam. Both decisions—when to measure and what type of test to use—should be based on the purpose of the test. Essay questions measure some skills best, while objective questions are more suitable for measuring other skills. Let us look at the more commonly used types of test questions and some advantages and limitations of each. The suggestions for improving the questions should be of particular interest.

Essay Questions

While all tests questions fall into two categories—subjective or objective—the subjective, or essay, question is a type of its own. Essay questions have some important limitations. First, they are difficult to control. Actually, they require the teacher to relinquish some control, for the student is free to answer (and actually *must* do so) in terms of his own perspective. This leads to another problem—the scoring. You must decide whether to count such variables as—

1. Ability to focus on the teacher's perspective
2. Writing and spelling skills
3. General neatness
4. Comprehensiveness
5. Specific facts and concepts

6. Broad generalizations
7. Creativity
8. Attitudes
9. Logical reasoning
10. Other skills outside the knowledge category, such as the ability to synthe-size or evaluate

These uncertainties must be resolved before you give the test so disagreements will not arise between you and your students. To avoid this risk, you may want to avoid essay or discussion tests in favor of more specific, objective tests. But first consider the advantages of essay questions.

Essay-type questions excel in their ability to let students express themselves. In responding to an essay question, students can be as creative, imaginative, and expressive as they wish; furthermore, they can state and evaluate their own beliefs and values. This is especially important for two reasons. First, evaluation is the highest known level of thinking (according to Bloom's Taxonomy of Educational Objectives, as seen in Chapter 2.) Second, when responding to test questions, students often have a strong desire to express their own beliefs and to justify their responses.

Writing Essay Questions. A teacher who chooses to use essay questions should structure each question to emphasize the ideas the student should address. This will minimize the difference between teacher and student perceptions of expectations. Following are examples of good and bad essay test items.

A. Discuss the causes of the Revolutionary War.

How would you respond to this question? What is wrong with it? You probably wouldn't know where to begin, because the question is far too general. Suppose it were rewritten to read:

B. Name and discuss three main causes of the Revolutionary War.

Now the question lets you know you are expected to cover three main causes, but it is still a monumental and time-consuming task. You could not ask more than two or three questions of this type on any test. A test should reflect the complete range of material covered in class since the previous test. Suppose the question is altered further, as seen in sample C:

C. Name and discuss three economic factors that contributed to the development of the Revolutionary War.

Now the scope of the question has been limited drastically. The student can immediately eliminate the many political and social factors. By making the question more specific, you are reducing its ambiguity and limiting the scope of responses the question will elicit. But because discussion questions offer the teacher a unique opportunity to stimulate students to think independently and creatively, you probably will want to include at least one question designed for that purpose. An example of such a question is sample D:

D. Suppose England had won the war. What changes would have occurred in the American lifestyle?

This question gives students the opportunity to use divergent thinking—that is, it requires them to expand their thoughts by using their imagination. Therefore it is of a higher order than the previous questions. Notice, though, that it requires you as teacher to give up much of your ability to regulate or restrict the area of student responses. In a class of 30 students, this question would probably elicit 30 different responses and create problems in scoring the answer. For this reason, before asking such a question you should be sure that the purpose for selecting the question was to measure imagination and creativity; these would be two considerations that would count heavily in determining a grade for this question.

It is worth taking the time to word the questions very carefully so they will achieve their objectives. And you will save time in scoring essay answers if you structure questions unambiguously. To be sure, the wording and scoring of good essay questions is not easy; it requires time and thought. The quality of the responses you get will probably correlate highly with the amount of time you spend on the questions.

Scoring Essay Questions. A good approach to assigning values to each part of a response is to take the test yourself before administering it. Then you can assign credit for each part of the expected response according to their respective values. For example, take sample question D: "Suppose England had won the war. What changes would have occurred in the American lifestyle?" Assume that the classroom discussion and/or textbooks and other materials included such concepts as more rigid tariffs, lower prices, and worsening labor conditions. Each concept could receive 2 points credit. Other reasonable responses could receive 1 point each, making the total value of the question 9 or 10 points.

Multiple-Choice Questions

Multiple-choice questions are popular today, partly because of the increasing availability of machine scoring but also because the questions themselves have merit. Like the true-false and fill-in-the-blank test, a multiple-choice test enables the teacher to ask many questions and thus cover many topics on the same test. Unlike true-false and fill-in-the-blank tests, however, the multiple-choice test restricts the amount of success derived by guessing. "The multiple-choice item seems best suited to bring out the finer distinctions between what is good, what is best, and what represents loose thinking, if not downright error" (Mouly, 1970).

But this advantage is realized only when the teacher designs each test question appropriately. Keep in mind also that tests should be used to help students learn. When correctly written, the multiple-choice test can become an excellent learning device.

Like all other types of tests, the multiple-choice test should be selected on its merits—that is, on its ability to achieve specific goals. Then it should be designed to achieve those goals. If its purpose is formative (to promote learning), it should be designed one way; if its purpose is to determine student success (summative), it should be designed differently. We shall look at specific designs for specific purposes, but first let us answer some general questions that you might have about developing multiple-choice tests.

How Many Alternatives Should I Include? It is wise to include at least four choices, and five may be desirable if a purpose of the test is to promote learning. Should I include among my alternatives *all of the above* and *none of the above?* Because *all of the above* enables one to measure knowledge about the question, it is a legitimate option. Because *none of the above* does not enable the student to relate specifically to the question, it should be avoided. The bottom space could be more wisely used to include a concept related to the material being tested.

How Should I Phrase the Stem of a Multiple-Choice Question? First, keep it brief. Avoid using more than one sentence, lest a student trip on the question itself. Second, avoid negatives in the stem. Both unnecessary length and negatives tend to confuse and interrupt the thought process. A test question should always be written so that it communicates as clearly as possible. See the following examples.

E. All isosceles triangles
   a. have at least two equal sides
   b. have at least two unequal angles
   c. have at least three equal sides
   d. have at least three equal angles

Item E could be simplified as follows:

E. All isosceles triangles have at least
   a. two equal sides
   b. two unequal angles
   c. three equal sides
   d. three equal angles
F. Which of the following is *not* an example of sedimentary rock?
   a. limestone
   b. sandstone
   c. chert
   d. all of the above

Item F should be changed to read as follows:

F. An example of igneous rock is
   a. limestone
   b. sandstone
   c. chert
   d. all of the above

How Should I Select the Alternatives? If you are designing the test to promote learning, you should purposely include several alternatives that are closely related. If the purpose of the test is grading, the number of near-correct answers should be reduced to only one or two. To have all answers almost acceptable would be unduly taxing and might result in teacher preference as opposed to student preference. A question with only one attractive answer would be equally poor design. It would not promote learning or thinking and therefore would not discriminate between those who have mastered the material and those who have not. Examine items G, H, and I and for each question identify at least one major flaw. Then rewrite each to eliminate those flaws.

> G. Alexander Graham Bell invented the
>   a. cotton gin
>   b. telegraph
>   c. radio
>   d. all of the above
>   e. none of the above
> H. Water is not an example of a
>   a. liquid
>   b. solution
>   c. fluid
>   d. compound
>   e. base
> I. The pilgrims began arriving in America in the early 1630s. Some came via Holland; others came directly from the port of Southampton in England. The real reason for their coming was to
>   a. escape persecution
>   b. seek freedom of religion for all
>   c. form a new denomination
>   d. all of the above

The obvious error in item G is the alternative "none of the above." The question could be corrected simply by eliminating the fifth choice. The stem of question H contains a negative. The question could be corrected by deleting the *not* and changing the choices. The stem of item I is unnecessarily long. It could be corrected by eliminating the first two sentences.

What Other Common Errors Can I Avoid? Some multiple-choice questions give the correct answer unintentionally. Items J and K contain questions that make this mistake. See if you can identify which part leads the student to the correct answer. Then rewrite the question to avoid the error.

> J. A well-known French psychologist is
>   a. Wilburn Smith
>   b. Robert O. Williams
>   c. Jean Piaget
>   d. Warner Hayes
>   e. Sam Jones

K. The nickel is an example of an
   a. alloy
   b. solution
   c. compound
   d. metal
L. The speed of light is
   a. 100 feet/sec
   b. 100 miles/hr
   c. 120 miles/hr
   d. 186,000 miles/sec

Item J leads the student to select an alternative based on grounds other than knowledge about psychologists. In item K, the use of the word *an* suggests the correct answer; incidentally, the alternative being sought in item K is not the only correct alternative provided. In summative tests, take care not to include more than one correct answer. Test item L is poor because it fails to include a strong distracter (a plausible or near-correct choice).

Fill-in-the-Blank Questions

Although the fill-in-the-blank question can boast of no real strengths at all, it has managed to survive throughout the history of our schools. Not only does this type of question limit the teacher to measuring only knowledge (or recall) level information, but it seldom achieves this with any degree of accuracy. The fill-in-the-blank question often puts the student in the impossible position of trying to guess what the teacher wants. Mastering the material does not guarantee success on this type of test.

Nevertheless, the fill-in-the-blank test appeals to many teachers because it can be developed quickly and effortlessly. (This does not reflect the way it *should* be developed, but merely the way it is often developed.) Some teachers lift sentences right out of the text and print them verbatim on the test, substituting a blank for one or more words. Item M is an example of a typical fill-in-the-blank question. How would you answer it? Can you modify it to eliminate its ambiguity?

M. The Battle of New Orleans was fought in _____ .

This type of question unintentionally invites the imagination to run wild. A creative student might respond with New Orleans, the rain, winter, anger, or mud, blood, and beer. An infinite number of correct answers are possible and should be given full credit, but the student need not know anything about the Battle of New Orleans to respond correctly. Other students may become discouraged over the ambiguity and leave the space blank, therefore getting penalized for the teacher's failure to communicate clearly.

While you would usually be wise to choose another type of question, suppose you want to test for highly technical or specific factual information. When correctly written, the fill-in-the-blank test can achieve this. A teacher writing item M to test for the date of the beginning of the battle need only insert *the year of*—that is, "The Battle of New Orleans was fought in the year of _____ ." The wording of fill-in-the-blank items must be very specific.

Another common mistake with fill-in-the-blank questions is including blanks throughout the sentence. Item N is an example of this error.

N.   _____ tests are more _____ _____ than are _____ _____ tests.

This kind of question can be even more frustrating to students than single completion items.

In conclusion, avoid fill-in-the-blank tests when other types of tests will achieve your objectives. If you do use them, remember that being specific is the key to designing good questions.

Matching Test Items

Most teachers use matching tests at some time or another. This type of test enables the teacher to measure the students' ability to make important associations. Its value is apparent from the number of national standardized tests that test for the examinee's ability to make associations, ranging from the picture association game on *Sesame Street* to the Miller Analogy Test used in many college graduate programs.

Matching tests are not easy to construct. Care must be taken to avoid using a stimulus that matches with more than one response (Oliva, 1972, p. 523). An examiner wishing to have students use a stimulus more than once should inform them that they may use the same number or letter in their answers repeatedly. For example, in item O, stimulus number 1 would fit in both responses A and D.

O.   Stimulus   Response
  1.   Noun   ____A.   Water   ____E.   Slowly
  2.   Verb   ____B.   Blue   ____F.   Her
  3.   Adjective   ____C.   Fishing   ____G.   Into
  4.   Pronoun   ____D.   Moon
  5.   Adverb

Notice also that in item O the number of responses exceeds the number of stimuli. This is to discourage guessing. Another important precaution in writing multiple-choice items is to avoid giving hints. Item P illustrates such carelessness in item writing.

P.   Match the dates with the corresponding events.
  1.   1861   A.   Signing of the Magna Charta
  2.   1812   B.   Beginning of the Civil War
  3.   1776   C.   Storming of the Bastille
  4.   1215   D.   Signing of the Declaration of Independence
  5.   1918   E.   War of 1812
                 F.   Cardinal Principles of Secondary Education

Obviously, "War of 1812" is a dead giveaway. Such matches should be avoided on matching tests because they fail to measure any level of understanding.

HIGHER-LEVEL QUESTIONS: COGNITIVE DOMAIN

Returning to Bloom's Taxonomy of Educational Objectives discussed in Chapter 2, we find that the major areas in the cognitive domain are:

Level 1. Knowledge
Level 2. Comprehension
Level 3. Application
Level 4. Analysis
Level 5. Synthesis
Level 6. Evaluation

Most types of objective questions discussed so far have been limited to measuring the retention of information, but this does not mean such test items as multiple-choice and matching cannot be designed to test for higher levels of understanding. It is erroneous to conclude that only discussion-type questions can measure higher levels of understanding. Each type of question can be used to measure different levels of all three learning domains. The following examples show prospective teachers, student teachers, and novice teachers at least one way of designing questions to measure understanding at each level.

Level 1: Knowledge
Since we are all familiar with questions that test *only* one's ability to recall facts, this first level need not be discussed.

Level 2: Comprehension
Charts, maps, graphs, and tables lend themselves well to measuring learning mastery at the comprehension level. Questions at this level should require the student to translate, interpret, or predict a continuation of trends (Bloom, Hastings, & Madaus, 1971). For example, Figure 14.1 shows the general sales ratio of a book during its first three years of publication. If a certain book has sold 10,000 copies in the first year and 30,000 copies by the end of a second year, how many copies can we estimate it will have sold by the end of a third year? Of course, a multiple-choice question could be written to use with this graph—for example:

The total accumulated sales projected by the end of the third year is:
a. 10,000
b. 20,000
c. 30,000
d. 40,000

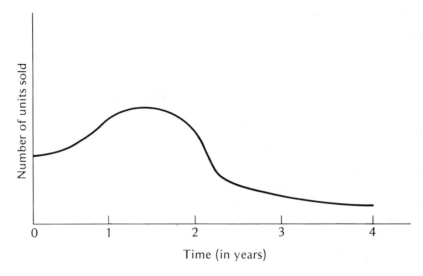

Figure 14.1 Sales Ratio of Textbooks.

Level 3: Application

Questions measuring the ability to think at the application level must require students to apply abstractions—such as general ideas, rules, and methods—to concrete situations. In other words, the student must use a principle or generalization to solve a new problem. The following example is offered to clarify the process of generalizing.

> You enter the old kitchen, in which there is a blazing hearthfire complete with bubbling, boiling teakettle. Oh, it's always there anyway; you've seen it before. Besides, your mind is on something else. Your quaint kitchen is pretty well tuned out by you, or you only perceive it at the (blob) level. Wait, something focuses your attention on the event system that is the boiling kettle. You've noticed. Now you're beginning to operate. You've noticed something, and something is happening. The lid jumps up and down. You wonder why. Ah, cause, the why sets you to scrutinizing relationships. First you attend, focus, observe, isolate. Next you want the cause of something. Establishing tentative cause gets you to infer a low-level generalization. 'That lid will move because steam is pushing it up and down. If that particular kettle is put on that fire and it boils, then its lid will jump up and down' a relatively low level of abstraction because the particulars of the scene are still involved. The next level of abstraction, of generalizations, will take you to a point of thinking, 'When a kettle is placed on a fire, the water will boil and cause a loose lid to move' (Ward, 1969).

You have gone from the particular to the general, although you are still involved with the category of tea kettles. Several levels of application are possible here. First, the student can match a principle with its correct corresponding situation, as in item Q.

Q. Match each situation with the principle at play. Each stimulus may be
used repeatedly.

1.	Radiation	A.	A sea breeze
2.	Convection	B.	An air conditioner
3.	Conduction	C.	A kite
		D.	A heater
		E.	A hot coffee cup

A second level of application requires the student to restate a problem. For
example, in the story of the teakettle you might say that the problem at hand is to
determine why the lid is moving. Given this situation and problem, the students
can be asked to state the problem without using the word *steam*. Still another level
of application would require the student to use a generalization to predict what
will happen in a different situation where the same principles are involved. You
might ask the student a question like "Suppose the kettle lid were held fast and the
spout were stopped up. What would happen when the kettle was placed on the
stove?" (Caution: Don't try this experiment!)

While there are other levels of application, these examples show how you can
arrange experiences or tasks that force students to perform at the application
stage.

Level 4: Analysis

The analysis level requires breaking down generalizations, concepts, and principles in order to clarify the ideas or understand them better. A common type of
question for measuring at the analysis level gives the student one or more paragraphs to read and then a list of questions. These questions do not simply ask for
retention (knowledge level) and the ability to predict patterns or trends (comprehension level); they require the student to identify underlying assumptions of the
author. For example, the students might be asked to read the following parable on
education taken from Plato's *Republic*. In the seventh book, which opens with a
beautiful description of the nature of man confined in a dark cave, Plato proceeds
to show the means and plan for learning true philosophy and how we may attain
the serious and sober practice of social life and politics.

Behold men, as it were, in an underground cave-like dwelling, having its entrance open toward the light and extending through the whole cave, and within it
persons, who from childhood upwards have had chains on their legs and their
necks, so as, while abiding there, to have the power of looking forward only, but
not to turn round their heads by reason of their chains, their light coming from a
fire that burns above and afar off.

Let us inquire then, said I, as to their liberation from captivity . . . and their
cure for insanity, such as it may be, and whether such will naturally fall to their
lot; were a person let loose and obliged immediately to rise up, and turn round his
neck and walk, and look upwards to the light, and doing all this still feel pained,
and be disabled by the dazzling from seeing those things of which he formerly
saw the shadows; what would he say, think you, if any one were to tell him that
he formerly saw mere empty visions, but now saw more correctly, as being

nearer to the real thing, and turned toward what was more real, and then, specially pointing out to him every individual passing thing, should question him and oblige him to answer respecting its nature; think you not he would be embarrassed, and consider that what he before saw was truer than what was just exhibited?

. . . But if, said I, a person should forcibly drag him thence through a rugged and steep ascent without stopping, till he dragged him to the light of the sun, would he not while thus drawn be in pain and indignation, and when he came to the light, having his eyes dazzled with the splendor, be unable to behold even any one thing of what he had just alleged as true?

And consider this, said I, whether, in the case of such as one going down and again sitting in the same place, his eyes would not be blinded in consequence of coming so suddenly from the sun? Quite so, replied he . . . and as for any one that attempted to liberate him and lead him up, they ought to put him to death, if they could get him into their hands? Especially so, said he. (Davis & Burges, 1901)

The teacher might follow this passage with a series of questions, such as the following:

1. Why does Plato select an underground cave for his location for "mankind"?
2. Why does Plato have his released prisoner look at the *blinding* firelight and then the *blinding* sun?
3. Why did Plato choose to have the released prisoner *dragged* to the outside rather than merely led?
4. Upon his return to the cave, why might the released prisoner be put to death for telling the truth?

Notice that each question focuses on a specific part of the parable. This is important to the analytical process. Notice also that the student is required to *use* the particular passage to solve a problem. If this assignment seems difficult or bizarre, remember the assignments you as a high school student had in poetry classes. You probably have had extensive contact with analysis assignments and analysis level test questions. This is only one of several types of analysis questions, but it should help prepare you to introduce your students to analysis tasks.

Level 5: Synthesis

In recent years, students and teachers have come to hold in high esteem assignments that have no single, predetermined, "correct" answer but that require students to apply their unique talents and perceptions to arrive at an acceptable answer. Unfortunately, today's teachers are feeling pressure from members of the community who want the schools to reject these exercises in divergent thinking and return to the traditional approach to teaching the "Three R's."

The value of such synthesis tasks is summed up in the concept of Gestaltism—that is, "The whole is greater than the sum of its parts." The student is given the task of putting together a number of concepts to communicate a uniquely different idea, one that is his or her own. This is the essence of creativity itself, which is known by the artist, painter, songwriter, movie producer, dancer, architect, and others who use their minds, bodies, and talents to express themselves. Rich in aesthetic qualities, it also has practical value, because the synthesis process requires perceiving problems from different perspectives, leading to inventions and to "building a better mousetrap."

Instead of trying to satisfy the demand for exercises that require "the" correct answer, students could better spend the time seeking out relationships that will guide their actions. If this sounds unscientific, today's scientists would not agree that such open-ended exercises requiring divergent, creative thinking are at all unscientific.

> For example, if a layman were to ask a physicist for a definition of light, he would likely be told that light may be considered a wave phenomenon (wave theory) or it may be thought of as having particles (corpuscular theory). If the layman insisted on *the* correct definition of light, the physicist would probably respond "That isn't a useful question; physicists have stopped asking it" (Conant, 1952). The reason that physicists no longer pursue a "correct" definition of light is that it is irrelevant. One definition, within a limited situation, enables scientists to account for certain phenomena; the other definition, in another set of circumstances, is more useful (Zais, 1976, p. 14).

We should recognize the value of lower levels of thinking and their importance in the curriculum. What better way is there to master the multiplication tables than by rote memorization? Yet to limit classroom tasks only to those that require memorization would be to keep students from experiencing the types of problems they must be prepared to solve in future life. Such a restriction also robs them of the ability to form new perceptions and express new conceptualizations.

In synthesis tasks, students are asked to take certain material, reorganize it, and assemble it in a new way to give it new meaning. The problem must be new to the students and, when possible, of special interest to them. For this reason, the students should be involved in identifying the problem. This does not preclude assigning a particular problem to a group of students or to the entire class.

The teacher is responsible for either providing problems for the students or leading them in the selection process. Since there is no single, correct answer, care should be taken to stipulate exactly what criteria to use in evaluating the work. For example, consider the following problem.

> In many American communities, interest and participation in high school sports is so intense, and the financial support for athletics is so great, that many complain that academic subjects are neglected. Suppose you are captain of the football team at such a school. Furthermore, suppose the classrooms have deteriorated and the school does not have the funds to restore the buildings. To make things worse, suppose your team has just ended another losing season. Prepare a statement to justify continuation of an interscholastic sports program in face of these critical circumstances. Devise a plan that will enable the school to finance the necessary building restorations and still finance the team for coming years.

Or the geology teacher may present a rock for students to examine. Giving each student, or group of students, the materials needed to run tests for color, hardness, and acidity, the students would tell where the rock originated and substantiate this conclusion with logic. The main objective is that the student *design a plan* for locating the derivative of particular rocks. The location itself is irrelevant. Another example of a synthesis task would be to give each student a box of assorted materials with which to devise a container that will support the fall of a raw egg when dropped from a two-story window.

Studies on creativity (Torrance, 1967) indicate that the mind is usually more creative when the student—

1. Is encouraged to pursue a direction that seems right for him or her even when to others it may seem disorderly
2. Is given the opportunity to work alone, yet allowed (not forced) to share his or her work with others
3. Works in a pressure-free environment
4. Is protected from peer pressure to conform
5. Works within areas of his special interests

When you develop tasks at the synthesis level, consider these conditions and try to provide an atmosphere that is most conducive to creative thinking.

Level 6: Evaluation

Tasks at the evaluation level require students to make judgments based on logical accuracy, consistency, and other given criteria, in addition to remembered criteria. An example of a task at this level would be to present students with a politician's election platform and ask them to examine it for accuracy, logic, and consistency. Students would also be expected to compare it with the politician's previous political behavior or support or rejection of bills involving similar issues—in other words, does he practice what he preaches?

Other levels of evaluation tasks require students to identify values or assumptions on which judgments are made. For example, in your methods classes you may be asked to write a critique of your peers while they teach a mini-lesson. Suppose you were asked to respond to the following questions:

1. The critic found the lesson organized so that the concepts
   a. flowed smoothly
   b. were illogically presented
   c. were arranged in chronological order
   d. both a and b
   e. both b and c
2. According to the critic, the delivery of the lesson was
   a. enhanced by the teacher's poise and self-confidence
   b. strengthened by the use of good visual aids
   c. augmented by the absence of unnecessary jargon and technical terms
   d. all of the above

Other types of evaluation questions require the student to make judgments about a particular work based on similar works. The students may even be given an opportunity to form their own list of criteria to use to evaluate.

Space limitations do not allow discussion and samples of test items in all the sublevels of the six categories of Bloom's taxonomy, but you can explore further by examining the sources listed at the end of this chapter. Of special help are the Bloom books, the Mager book, and the Stiggins book.

AFFECTIVE DOMAIN

The attainment of knowledge and of the skills needed to apply that knowledge is what school is all about, but unless the students elect to *use* that knowledge and those skills, a great deal has been wasted. For example, although the ability to read has some intrinsic value, suppose students choose not to read because they do not like to read. Suppose other students master just enough skills in math to pass the required courses, but in the meantime develop such fear or contempt toward mathematics that they refuse even to try to keep an accurate checkbook. In a sense the efforts of those students and their teachers have failed, for learning itself is defined as a somewhat permanent change in behavior. Exactly what have these students failed to learn? They have failed to learn to appreciate the potential that is embedded in the ability to read; they have failed to realize their own potential in the area of mathematics.

Experience with people who have chosen not to use the knowledge and skills they have shows how important *attitude* toward knowledge is. The proper attitudes are indispensable for successful, happy living, as the cases of learned people who have become destructive to society or to themselves demonstrate. The greatest lists of aims for American education contain aims that are dependent on certain attitudes. For example, examine the Seven Cardinal Principles of Secondary Education:

1. Health
2. Command of the fundamental processes
3. Worthy home membership
4. Vocational efficiency
5. Civic participation
6. Worthy use of leisure time
7. Ethical character

Does not success in any of these areas depend on the development of certain attitudes? Even in the aim that may seem to be most separated from attitudes—vocational efficiency—certain attitudes are necessary for success. More than 85 percent of all jobs lost are lost because of an inability of workers to get along with their supervisors and co-workers.

In a national poll of attitudes toward education, 80 percent of the responses listed extracurricular activities as important, while 43 percent listed "To get along better with people at all levels of society'' (Gallup, 1985). It is clear that teachers must help students develop both necessary skills and certain attitudes.

QUESTIONING TECHNIQUES

In their *Taxonomy of Educational Objectives, Handbook II: Affective Domain,* Krathwohl, Bloom, and Masia (1964) give five levels of internalization of values:

1. Receiving—a willingness to tolerate a phenomenon
2. Responding—voluntarily using the phenomenon
3. Valuing—prizing and acting on the phenomenon
4. Organizing—using values to determine interrelationships between the phenomena
5. Characterizing—organizing values, beliefs, ideas, and attitudes into an internally consistent system

As you consider what expectations you will have of students in your future classes, take time now to list two attitudes you want them to have toward the subject you will teach. Now, using the following examples as models, write a question that will measure student attitudes at each of the first four levels: receiving, responding, valuing, and organizing.

Example 1: A math teacher uses the following questions to measure attitudes at each level.

1. Receiving: Would you like to join the math club?
2. Responding: When you play games that involve scorekeeping, do you ever volunteer to keep score?
3. Valuing: Do you plan to take math next year when it becomes an elective?
4. Organizing: Have you ever thought of math as an art?

Example 2: A history teacher covering the Civil War asks the following questions.

1. Receiving: Would you like to own Confederate relics?
2. Responding: If your family or friends planned a vacation that had Vicksburg, Mississippi, on its route, would you suggest visiting the battleground?
3. Valuing: Do you feel excited when seeing a movie on the Civil War?
4. Organizing: While studying this unit on the Civil War, have you ever tried to decide for yourself ways in which each side was wrong?

Using the definition of each level of internalization, and using these examples as models, write a question to test each level of your two statements about attitudes that you want your future students to have.

The teacher's role in development of attitudes will extend into other areas. First, you must help students learn to examine their current attitudes, particularly their values (values clarification) and to understand the basis for their values—

that is, the process they use to develop values. To achieve this, you can give students tasks requiring them to analyze their values. Second, you can help students develop their moral values by assessing the level of their moral maturity and then giving them problem situations requiring them to perform at a level slightly above their current level of maturation.

Lawrence Kohlberg (1976), a former professor at Harvard University, developed a hierarchy of three major stages through which each person must pass in the development of ethical awareness. These are:

Level 1. Preconventional—behavior is determined by rewards and punishment. (What's best for me?)

Level 2. Conventional—behavior is controlled by anticipation of praise or blame. (What will others think?)

Level 3. Postconventional—behavior is regulated by principles embodying generality and comprehensiveness. (What's the right thing to do?)

A familiar example would be why a person obeys a stop sign:

To avoid getting a fine. (Level 1)
To avoid criticism from others and to avoid breaking a law. (Level 2)
To avoid hurting others. (Level 3)

A different version of the same problem might be as follows. In one of our major cities, the fine for violating a stop sign was increased overnight from about $20.00 to $87.50. Many police officers refused to enforce the law, which they perceived as unreasonable; others enforced it because they had taken an oath to enforce all the laws. At what level did each group of police officers behave?

Not all attitudes are limited to moral behavior. Other important behaviors that the school should foster include learning to appreciate, desire, find interesting, enjoy, and empathize.

TEST ADMINISTRATION

Preliminary Arrangements

If your test is to be valid, you must make certain preliminary arrangements. First, see that all students are physically prepared—that they have the necessary materials, such as sharp pencils, paper, reference sources, and measuring instruments. If not, allot time before the test for each student to make these preparations.

Second, be sure everyone is comfortable. The room should not be hot or cold or noisy. Merely closing windows facing a noisy highway or closing the door to a noisy hall can help. Adjusting a room thermostat or radiator controls can help. Each student should have enough room to avoid being cramped. Remind everyone to remove unnecessary books and papers from desktops, lest some students try to balance their paper on top of a stack of books or support books or purses in their laps.

Finally, if test results are to reflect true abilities, students should be mentally relaxed. Many students become so tense during tests that they are unable to show that they know the material. You can help relieve tension by telling a joke, relating a humorous personal experience, or simply talking for a moment about a ball game, a party, the weather, or another activity unrelated to the test.

Before the test begins, specify how the students should ask questions, if they have any. Do you want them to raise their hands and direct their questions to you at once? Or do you want to go to the student to answer a question? Usually it is better if the students do not ask questions so the whole class can hear, because it disrupts others. Also, tell students in advance what to do when they finish the test. Should they bring it to you? Then should they study another subject, read a library book, or just relax?

Taking the Test

Begin each test by reading the instructions aloud and allowing time for questions. All students should begin at the same time. This provides structure. Also, students should not be permitted to talk or otherwise disrupt others. Test administration should be conducted comfortably but uniformly.

Once the test has begun, do not interrupt. If there are questions, answer the individuals who ask the questions and make a note of each necessary clarification or correction. To avoid interruptions, near the end of the testing period you can inform the entire class of all these corrections at one time. Avoid making disturbing noises during the test, such as rattling papers, talking, or walking around the classroom. Remain in the room at all times during the test.

To end the test in an organized way, take up all remaining papers when time is called. Students who feel pressured and do hand in their papers, and then see that a few persistent students are allowed additional time to finish, will feel cheated.

Test Scoring

Whether the test questions are objective, subjective, or both, the scoring should always be as objective as possible. Otherwise your judgment will be affected by your likes and dislikes for the students, by the general appearance of the paper, and by a force that all teachers experience—a tendency to equalize the scores by subconsciously accepting poor responses from the poorer papers and being overly critical and deducting credit from respectable responses on the better papers. Because this is common among beginning teachers, test scoring leaves them feeling guilty and many develop a real dislike for testing.

Testing is as much a part of the teacher's role and responsibility as preparing and executing lessons. How, then, can you avoid developing the common distaste for testing? Learning and using the following principles should be of some help.

Specify the Answers before the Scoring Begins. Before you begin scoring, write out the answer to each question on the test. As already mentioned, teachers should always be the first to take their own test. By establishing some correct responses, you will have a guideline for accepting and rejecting the students' answers. This does not mean, however, that all other answers are wrong. Inevitably you will find some student answers that are as accurate and desirable as your own predetermined ones. When this occurs, accept these answers as correct and add them to your master sheet. This practice encourages creativity, which should be a part of all school activities—including tests.

Sometimes an unusually large portion of the class misses a relatively easy question. When this happens, you should be suspicious of the question. By examining the responses of five or six of the top-scoring papers, you can check the validity of the question and determine whether you failed to cover the material in class or whether the wording of the question was misleading. Whatever the problem, it should be eliminated.

Subjective questions invariably draw responses that are not exactly right and not exactly wrong. When this occurs, partial credit should be given, reserving full credit for answers that reflect the major points made in class. But be sure that this test is not a measure of the student's ability to guess what the teacher wants and give that response.

Conceal All Names. To protect your students from possible unfair scoring caused by your personal feelings, conceal the names before you begin scoring. There is no advantage in knowing whose paper you are scoring, but there are the previously mentioned disadvantages.

RECAP OF MAJOR IDEAS

1. Because both objective-type and subjective-type questions have unique advantages and disadvantages, it is usually best to include questions of both types on a test.
2. Objective questions are easily scored and permit the teacher to cover much material by including many questions on a test, but they do not enable the student to be self-expressive or creative.
3. Subjective items permit students to show their knowledge and state their feelings, and they enhance writing and synthesizing skill development; however, they restrict the teacher's ability to test all material covered. Subjective questions are also difficult to score.
4. All tests, including essay-type tests, should be graded as objectively as possible.
5. Each test should measure everything covered since the previous test.
6. Credit should be assigned to each item according to the time and emphasis it received in class.
7. On discussion-type tests, teachers should give partial credit for accurate answers, even though they were unanticipated.
8. Multiple-choice items should contain four or five choices, one or two of which should be strong distracters.
9. To pilot the test, the teacher should take it before administering it to students.

POSTTEST

Now that you have read the chapter, take a moment to respond to the following statements again:

	Agree	Disagree	Uncertain
1. Objective questions test only the student's ability to retain facts.	____	____	____
2. Competition among all students is good.	____	____	____
3. Essay questions must be scored subjectively.	____	____	____
4. Essay questions tend to measure what students know, whereas objective questions measure what they do not know—that is, their learning gaps.	____	____	____
5. Beginning teachers tend to make tests too difficult.	____	____	____
6. Tests should contain both objective questions and essay questions.	____	____	____
7. Most teachers have an adequate background in testing.	____	____	____
8. Essay tests reveal students' thought processes.	____	____	____
9. Most American students are capable of supporting their opinions.	____	____	____
10. Multiple-choice test items should have only one plausible answer.	____	____	____
11. The more specifically essay questions are worded, the better they are.	____	____	____
12. Application level test items require the use of principles.	____	____	____

CASE

The development, administration, and scoring of teacher-made tests are major responsibilities of all teachers. Failure to develop expertise in any of these dimensions of testing can lead to serious problems. The following case shows a common problem situation in which teachers find themselves.

Case: A Twelfth-Grade Class Wants Information about an Upcoming Test

Ms. Wheeler had been teaching physical education for about five years when she noticed a sudden change in student attitudes toward tests. Up until that time she had considered that discussing tests before giving them was unethical and absurd. If an exam was going to be a fair measure of students' knowledge about the subject, would not a previous discussion destroy the test's validity and purpose? The only information she ever gave about a test was when it would be given. Although previous classes had teased, asking questions about what would be on the test, Ms. Wheeler knew that they never expected her to answer their questions.

But this twelfth-grade class was different. When they asked for information about the upcoming test, they expected her to provide it. They never asked about specific content, but they did ask such questions as "How many questions will the test have?" "How much will each question count?" and "How many are true-false questions?" Taking these questions as good-natured teasing, Ms. Wheeler ignored them and went on with the lesson. But it became clear that the students were serious. They became upset when they had no advance notice about how long a test would be and the type of questions it would contain.

Soon after having been confronted with these disgruntled students, Ms. Wheeler changed her policy and began holding a discussion about each test a few days before giving it. This practice was successful. First, the students no longer felt she was trying to trick them with an unfamiliar test, and they could study according to the type of test they were to take. Second, she came to see that answering certain questions about a test did not suggest what content to study as much as it suggested the correct *method* of study.

Discussion

1. If you reveal the number and type of questions to be included on a upcoming test, will the test be less valid and less reliable?
   No, not if all the students in your class have this information. It may help them identify the important ideas in the unit. It may improve the scores of students who use the information to study for the test, but these students will probably learn more in accordance with their increased scores. If you are afraid to provide information about an objective, factual test you are planning to administer, you can increase the length of the test. It will then be so comprehensive that the student who scores high on it will have to know a majority of the content studied during the unit.

2. Do today's students view tests as less important than did the students of a few years ago?
   Today's students feel tests are important. The main difference is that yesterday's students saw tests as important for one reason only—to determine grades. Today's students see an additional purpose in tests: They want to score well because they know that test scores reflect the quality of their learning. This is why they want to know how to study for each test. They realize that a test that tricks them is not an accurate instrument for measuring their learning progress.

3. How can you make testing more palatable?

By removing fear from testing, you can make it less distasteful to yourself and your students. Develop a routine for test administration and return, and always be as pleasant as you can. Your manner will help the students relax, and if you follow the same routine each time you give a test, you can ease feelings of insecurity.

When returning tests, always go over each question and explain the correct answers. Partial credit should always be given when it is earned.

ACTIVITIES

In this chapter you have read about good practices for constructing, administering, and scoring tests and examined questions written at different levels of the cognitive and affective domains. Now you have an opportunity to assemble and apply your knowledge and skills on testing.

1. In your major teaching field, develop an objective test containing a combination of true-false, matching, and multiple-choice items. Include questions that measure the higher cognitive levels as well as some that measure in the affective domain.

2. Construct an essay test, then rewrite each question to make it more precise and manageable.

3. Decide exactly how you would prefer to administer a test. Then write a set of instructions to guide student behavior during and immediately following the test. Ask some of your classmates to interpret your instructions. Look for discrepancies in the interpretations and rewrite items that had multiple interpretations.

4. Write a subjective test item. Identify and list the most important points that students should include in their responses. Now identify and make a list of secondary points that are important, but less so than the primary points. Assign 2 points each to the primary points and 1 point each to the secondary points.

5. For the preceding test item, develop three alternative ways of testing that do not use pencil and paper. Try to make each of these alternative tests discriminate between those who understand the primary and secondary points and those who do not.

6. Make a list of unique advantages offered by essay questions and a list of unique advantages offered by objective questions.

SUGGESTED READINGS

Bloom, B. S. (1956). *Taxonomy of educational objectives: The classification of educational goals, Handbook I: Cognitive domain*. New York: McKay.

Bloom, B. S., Hastings, J., & Madaus, G. F. (1971). *Handbook on formative and summative evaluation of student learning*. New York: McGraw-Hill.

Bloom, B. S., Madaus, G. F., & Hastings, J. T. (1981). *Evaluation to improve learning.* New York: McGraw-Hill.

Carter, K. (1983). *Tackling the testing issue: Testwiseness for teachers and students.* Paper presented at the annual meeting of the American Educational Research Association, Montreal.

Carter, K. (1984). Do teachers understand principles for writing tests? *Journal of Teacher Education, 35,* 59.

Coffman, W. E. (1983). *Testing in the schools: A historical perspective.* Paper presented at the UCLA Center for the Study of Evaluation Conference on Paths to Excellence: Testing and Technology, Los Angeles.

Conant, J. B. (1952). *Modern science and modern men.* Garden City, N.Y.: Doubleday/Anchor.

Davis, H. & Burgess, G. (Trans.). (1901). *The republic: The statesman of Plato.* New York: Dunne.

Fluitt, J., & Gifford, C. (1980). Who's teaching teachers how to teach test-wiseness? *Contemporary Education, 51,* 152–154.

Gallup, A. M. (1985). The 17th Gallup Poll of the public's attitudes toward the public schools. *Phi Delta Kappan, 67,* 35–47.

Girod, G. R. (1973). *Writing and assessing attitudinal objectives.* Columbus, Ohio: Merrill.

Good, T. L. (1982). How teachers' expectations affect results. *American Education, 18,* 25–32.

Johnson, J. A., Collins, H. W., Dupis, V. A., & Johanson, J. H. (1985). *Introduction to the foundations of American education* (6th ed.). Boston: Allyn & Bacon.

Kohlberg, L. (1976). Moral stages and moralization: The cognitive developmental approach. In T. Lickona (Ed.), *Moral development and behavior: Theory, research, and social issues,* pp. 31–53. New York: Holt, Rinehart and Winston.

Krathwohl, D. R., Bloom, B., & Masia, B. (1964). *Taxonomy of educational objectives: The classification of educational goals, Handbook II: Affective domain.* New York: McKay.

Mager, R. F. (1962). *Preparing instructional objectives.* Palo Alto, Calif.: Fearon.

Mosston, M. (1972). *Teaching: From command to discovery.* Belmont, Calif.: Wadsworth.

Mouly, G. J. (1970). *The science of educational research* (2nd ed.). New York: Van Nostrand Reinhold.

National Assessment of Educational Progress (1951). Reading, thinking, and writing: Results from the 1970–1980 National Assessment of Reading and Literature, Denver, Colorado.

Oliva, P. F. (1972). *The secondary school today* (2nd ed.), Chapter 18. New York: Harper & Row.

Popham, J. (1981). *Modern educational measurement.* Englewood Cliffs, N.J.: Prentice-Hall.

Quellmaiz, E. S. (1985). Needed: Better methods for testing higher-order thinking skills. *Educational Leadership, 43,* 29–35.

Renner, J. W., Bibens, R. F., & Shepherd, G. D. (1972). *Guiding learning in the secondary school,* Chapter 10. New York: Harper & Row.

Rosenfield, P., & Anderson, D. D. (1985). The effects of humorous multiple-choice alternatives on test performance. *Journal of Instructional Psychology, 12,* 3–5.

Savitz, F. R. (1985). Effects of easy questions placed at the beginning of science multiple-choice examinations. *Journal of Instructional Psychology, 12,* 6–10.

Simon, S. B., Howe, L. W., & Kirschenbaum, H. (1972). *Values clarification.* New York: Hart.

Stiggins, R. J. (1985). Improving assessment where it means the most: In the classroom. *Educational Leadership, 43,* 69–74.

Torrance, E. P. (1967). Creative teaching makes a difference. In John C. Gowan (Ed.), *Creativity: Its educational implications.* New York: Wiley.

Ward, M. W. (1969). Learning to generalize. *Science Education, 53,* 423–424.

Williams, R. H. (1975). How to improve professor made tests. *Improving college and university teaching yearbook.* Corvallis: Oregon State University Press.

Wulf, K., & Schave, B. (1984). *Curriculum design: A handbook for educators.* Glenview, Ill.: Scott, Foresman.

Zais, R. S. (1976). *Curriculum principles and foundations.* New York: Crowell.

C H A P T E R **15**

Evaluation

Objectives _____

- Define *evaluation*.
- Differentiate between testing and evaluation.
- List three factors a term grade should reflect.
- Justify the practice of using assignments for extra credit and justify rejection of the practice.
- Describe one major limitation of using the bell curve in assigning high school grades.
- Determine the stanine scores for a class of students, and transfer stanines into percentages.
- Differentiate between formative evaluation and summative evaluation.

PRETEST

	Agree	Disagree	Uncertain
1. Evaluation is the same as the sum of all test scores of an individual.	_____	_____	_____
2. A student's grades should be based only on what the student has learned.	_____	_____	_____
3. The bell curve is appropriate for use in assigning letter grades in most secondary and middle-level classes.	_____	_____	_____
4. For a group of secondary school students, final course grades should parallel their respective IQs.	_____	_____	_____
5. The teacher's judgment should not enter into the grading process.	_____	_____	_____
6. Evaluation is frequently used in secondary and middle schools to promote learning.	_____	_____	_____
7. A student's effort should determine that student's success in class.	_____	_____	_____

Middle-Level Message

Testing is one thing, evaluation is another. Be careful if you don't know the difference. You may be like the dog that chased the skunk—when he caught it, he didn't know what to do with it. Before giving your first tests, consider what you will do with the results. This process of deciding what to do with the results is called evaluation. Middle level learners need organization in their lives. You can help provide organization for your students by mastering the concepts in this chapter and coordinating your tests with your more comprehensive evaluation program. Most teachers fail to use the most valuable type of evaluation—formative evaluation. Formative evaluation has strong potential for helping you to promote learning. A second important type of evaluation is criterion-referenced evaluation. Most teachers fail to use this type of evaluation too.

It is time to begin thinking of evaluation as an important instructional tool. It can even be used to diagnose your own teaching weaknesses. Use this chapter to learn how to use evaluation positively to raise the achievement levels of your classes.

Evaluation is different from testing. Testing should be conducted objectively and apart from the teacher's own values. Evaluation demands that you make a qualitative judgment, or set values, on what you measure. As Bloom, Hastings, and Madaus (1981, p. 105) state: "There is no statistical or completely objective method that can be used to assign grades to a student's score or a student's product. Ultimately a judgment of the worth or value of that score or product must be made by the teacher." Evaluation is also different from testing in that it is much broader. Testing requires such tasks as selecting or constructing the appropriate exams, administering them, and scoring the responses, but all this is merely a prerequisite to evaluation.

Evaluation begins where testing ends. Once the results are determined and the tests are returned, you must make use of these results if the testing is to be worthwhile. The use that you make of test results is evaluation. The list below shows the relationship between measurement and evaluation and their parts.

RELATIONSHIP BETWEEN MEASUREMENT AND EVALUATION

Measurement
1. Deciding on type of test
2. Selecting a ready-made test or constructing a teacher-made test
3. Administering the test
4. Scoring the test

Evaluation
1. Formative: Using the test to promote learning
2. Summative: Using the test (and possibly other criteria) to grade the student, teacher, or program

Notice that evaluation is divided into two main categories—formative evaluation and summative evaluation. As you read the following paragraphs, note that there is a sharp distinction between the two. Your effective use of evaluation depends upon your ability to separate the two basic types.

FORMATIVE EVALUATION

Comparatively little use has been made of formative evaluation. Formative evaluation can be defined as the designing and using of tests for only one specific purpose—to *promote* learning. Formative evaluation enables teachers to monitor their instruction so they can keep it on course (Oliva, 1982, p. 411). Also, "If any student cannot learn excellently from the original instruction, the student can learn excellently from one or more correctives" (Block & Henson, 1986, p. 24). While most teachers agree that going over test answers in class can help some students learn more about the material, they are aware that this is not likely to result in total mastery of the material. It is essential that there be a much more systematic use of evaluation, separate from grading and aimed only at promoting learning.

Successful use of formative evaluation requires a change in attitude of both teachers and students, who have for too long equated tests with grades. When using tests for formative purposes, you should—

1. Avoid recording individual scores.
2. Be concerned only with whether the student has mastered the material at an acceptable level.
3. Involve each student in keeping a continuing record of individual progress.
4. Avoid mentioning grades.
5. Assume that, when properly motivated, all students are capable of mastering the material.
6. Avoid pushing students so fast that they become confused and discouraged.
7. Reassure students that the results of these tests will not count toward their grades.

Since this is the opposite of the way both students and teachers have usually perceived evaluation, you will need to be patient and reassuring if you elect to use tests to help students learn.

SUMMATIVE EVALUATION

Since teachers have been using tests almost exclusively for determining student grades, you may assume that with all that practice teachers are systematic in the way they convert raw scores into letter grades. But this is not so. Each teacher seems to have an individual system, and many teachers use a different system each grading period. Why? Because most teachers never find a system with which they are satisfied. There is no single system that is right for all classes. When you become aware of the strengths and weaknesses of various grading systems, you will be in a better position to choose wisely.

COMPETITIVE EVALUATION

All evaluation systems can be grouped into two categories: those that force a student to compete with other students (norm-referenced) and those that do not require interstudent competition but instead are based on a set of standards of mastery (criterion-referenced). Traditionally our schools have required competition among students and many teachers believe that competition among students is necessary for motivating. Many also believe that competition is needed to prepare students for adulthood in a competitive world, especially for getting ahead in their future employment.

Standardized Tests
An example of tests that force students to compete among themselves is the standardized test, which is very popular in our schools today. Standardized tests have several features in common. First, they are based on norms derived from the

average scores of thousands of students who have taken the test. Usually these scores come from students throughout the nation, so each student's performance is compared with that of thousands of other students.

Standardized tests are usually used to measure or grade a school's curriculum. Seeking to make teachers more accountable, state officials have forced schools to use standardized tests, given to students to measure teacher success— and yes, they are even used to measure student success. For example, for decades the state of New York administered its Regents exams to determine student success. By the early 1980s almost all states had legislated minimal learning standards, and tests are presently being developed to determine the level of attainment of each student and each school. Florida, which in July 1980 began testing its teachers for 23 generic competencies (Oliva & Henson, 1980), and Oklahoma are examples of the many states that use standardized tests to make their students, teachers, and colleges of education accountable.

The Normal Curve

A second use of tests that requires students to compete with others is the normal curve, or probability curve. The curve could well be called the natural curve or chance curve, because it reflects the distribution of all sorts of things in nature. This distribution is shown in Figure 15.1.

The normal curve is divided into equal segments. The vertical line through the center (the mean) represents the average of a whole population. Each mark to the *right* of the mean represents one average, or standard deviation, above the average. Each vertical line to the *left* of the center represents one standard unit of deviation below the mean. As the figure shows, about 34 percent of the population is within the one standard deviation unit above the mean, and about 34 percent of the population is within the one standard deviation below the mean. Only about 14 percent of the population is in the second deviation range above the mean, and

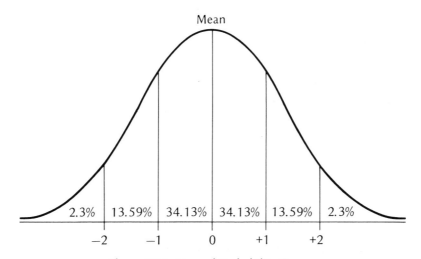

Figure 15.1 Normal Probability Curve

about 14 percent is in the second deviation range below the mean. A very small portion of the population (approximately 2.3 percent) deviates enough from the mean to fall within the third unit of deviation above the mean; an equal portion deviates three standard units below the mean.

To give another example, if the temperature is taken every day at 3:00 P.M. from June 15 until August 15 for 10 years, and if a mean or average is taken, the individual temperatures are listed vertically from hottest to coldest, and the line is divided into six equal parts, then 34 percent of the temperatures would fall in the section just above the middle, 34 percent would fall within the section just below the middle, 14 percent would fall in the second section above the mean, and 14 percent in the second section below the mean. Only 2.3 percent of the temperature readings would fall in the third section *above* the mean, and 2.3 percent would fall in the lowest section *below* the mean.

Some of the many things that are subject to this type of distribution are the weight and height of animals and plants, the margin of error of both man and machine, and, of course, the IQs of human beings. Not all phenomena are distributed in the ratios represented by the normal curve. For example, the chronological ages of the human population do not follow this pattern.

The normal curve, as it is often applied to the assigning of grades in a school classroom, makes several bold assumptions. First, like other evaluation schemes that are based on competition among students, it assumes that the level of a particular student's performance compared with the average of a group of students (usually the student's classmates) is important. Second, it assumes that all students have an equal opportunity to succeed—as though all have equal potential, which is extremely unlikely unless the class has been homogeneously grouped. Third, it assumes that the number of students used as a norm is large enough to reflect the characteristics of all students at the particular grade level. Unless the class size exceeds 100 students, this is a bold assumption indeed. The use of the normal curve assumes that 68 percent of the students will earn Cs, 13.5 percent will earn Bs, and another 13.5 percent Ds, and that 2.5 percent will earn As and 2.5 percent will fail.

Stanine Scores

Many schools use stanine ("standard nine") scores to determine student performance. This method uses the normal distribution curve to group test scores into nine categories (see Figure 15.2). This modification of the bell curve evaluation gets rid of the As, Bs, Cs, Ds, and Fs. Many feel that the psychological advantage of escaping the letter grade stigma is important. Also, having nine categories gives the teacher more groups in which to place projects that must be arbitrarily evaluated.

School-wide Standards

Even more popular than the standard curve is the practice of schools setting their own standards. You are undoubtedly familiar with the following system:

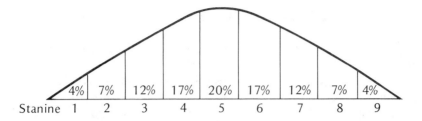

Figure 15.2 Normal Distribution Curve to Determine Stanine Scores

90 percent and above   = A
80–89 percent   = B
70–79 percent   = C
60–69 percent   = D
Below 60 percent   = Failure

This type of evaluation makes an important, and often false, assumption. It assumes that the test's level of difficulty fits the abilities of the students exactly. Student teachers usually realize this error as they begin marking their first set of papers and find that almost everyone failed the test. Although the exact percentage requirements may vary from school to school, the system remains a common method of evaluation.

Let's Ponder

The following passage illustrates the magnitude of the standard of error in geology and demonstrates why standardized test scores often have an equally alarming high standard error.* Read the passage, then think about this as you respond to the questions below.

A Very Standard Error

My friend was a geologist. We were in his backyard, awed by the majesty of the Rocky Mountains. The monstrous flat sloping rocks that are the hallmark of Boulder, Colorado, were the subject of our conversation.

"Do you know how old those rocks are?" my friend inquired.

"I have no idea at all," I replied.

"They are about four hundred million years old," he said, "give or take a hundred million years."

1. Do you think the general public is aware of the large standard of error common to many standardized test scores? What evidence can you offer to support your answer?
2. What do educators do that suggests that they do not consider the fallibility of standardized test scores?
3. Realizing that standardized tests frequently have large standards of error, how do you think this should affect a teacher's use of standardized test scores? Why?

---

* The passage is from J. Frymier, On the way to the Forum: It's a very standard error, *Educational Forum, 36,* (1979): 388–391.

NONCOMPETITIVE EVALUATION

Researchers and educators have recently come up with much evidence that shows that grading in the high school should be strictly an individual concern—involving the teacher and the student. "Criterion-referenced tests (which do not force competition among students) contribute more to student . . . progress than [do] norm-referenced tests" (Fantini, 1986, p. 132). Once it was thought that competition for grades was necessary because it motivated students to do their best. This is certainly true for students who have the most ability, but forcing the less-capable students to compete with their classmates can discourage them and force them to concentrate on their inadequacies. Competition can also be bad for the more-capable student. The teacher can reduce this damage by refraining from making test scores and grades public.

Many contemporary educators feel that grades should reflect the student's effort, that no one should receive an A without really trying, and that no students who are exerting themselves to their full potential should receive an F. These teachers hold that the purpose of grading is not to acknowledge high IQs and to punish those who do not have high ability, but that each grade should reflect the *degree of progress* a student makes relative to that student's ability.

Students should be required to keep a record of their progress in class. According to Pratt (1980, p. 258), "Many schools allow students to write their own self-appraisal. . . . This encourages students to reflect on their own learning." Students' judgment should be sought and used in determining their grades. A relevant question may be "How do you believe the quality of your work now compares with your previous work? Do you believe this is the best you can do?" Of course this approach requires that the teacher know each student—and not as a face but as a developing, growing person.

Grading Involves More than Testing

While the terms *grading* and *testing* are often used synonymously, this is a mistake. And most teachers believe that a student's grade should reflect more than test scores. Fantini (1986, p. 112) states, "No test reveals all there is to know about the learner, and no test should be used as an exclusive measure for any student's capacity." Neither can a single test measure all a student knows about any topic. Some things other than the acquisition of knowledge are important in school. For example, as a teacher you will be responsible for seeing that each student develops certain behavioral patterns and attitudes, such as honesty, promptness with assignments, the ability to work with others, and respect for others. Therefore each of these traits should be reflected in a student's grade. Evaluation of these qualities is essentially subjective, and to avoid becoming prejudiced you should decide at the beginning of the year just how much weight this part of the total evaluation carries and take care not to exceed the limits.

Grades should represent all the major activities a student engages in while in your classroom. Daily work and possibly term projects should perhaps carry as much weight toward the final grade for the term as the tests. If you use several tests (weekly or bi-weekly), daily assignments, term projects, and daily discussions, you will have more satisfactory material on which to base the final grade.

Begin with Much Understanding

As a beginning teacher recently exposed to college tests, you will probably grade too firmly. To avoid alienating and discouraging your students, be a little lenient at first. This does not mean you should be quick to change a grade when a student is unhappy with it, for this often results in reinforcing complaints. Being lenient at first means you should not expect only one particular answer on most types of questions and that you should not expect everyone to score 70 and above. It means that if you believe Jimmy is trying, even though he scores 55 instead of the 60 set as passing, he may receive a C or D rather than an F. Discussions with Jimmy throughout the year will let you assess the degree to which he is applying himself.

Assignments for Extra Credit

To challenge the most capable students, some teachers include a bonus question on every major test. This is fine if those who do not answer it correctly are not penalized. Some teachers offer extra credit to students who come to special sessions and complete extra assignments on problems with which they are having difficulties. This procedure also can be helpful in motivating students.

When a student asks for an assignment for extra credit at the end of the grading period, however, the student may be less interested in learning than in raising a grade. The student may really be asking, "Will you assign me some extra punishment so that my grade can be elevated?" The teacher may respond by assigning the student 40 problems the student already knows how to work, or by assigning the task of copying 2,000 words from an encyclopedia, library book, or magazine without having to learn the content. This practice is most undesirable, for it encourages some students to procrastinate until the last minute and then to subject themselves to x amount of punishment rather than attaining x amount of understanding. They also learn to dislike the subject that produces the pain.

When students ask to do extra work for credit, base your decision on whether you believe they will learn from the task. You may ask the students what type of assignment they propose to do and what they expect to learn from it. If they can convince you that they can and will learn as a result of the task, the assignment may be warranted.

GRADING SYSTEMS

The decision on a specific grade is essentially a subjective one. There is one question that may be helpful to you each time you assign a grade: What grade will be the best for this student? The answer you will give will be determined by that student's ability and application. To assign a grade that is higher than deserved is certainly not good for the student, and neither is assigning a grade lower than what the student has earned.

But having a philosophy of grading is not enough. As a teacher, you will be making decisions based on the information you have at hand. And the task is a serious and often thankless one. Pratt (1980, p. 259) explains, "[Grading] is a sensitive area, one in which the teacher can feel uncomfortably exposed and can be subject to powerful pressures to make decisions that are in conflict with the educator's professional judgment."

So let's begin preparing for that day by examining a typical situation at the end of a grading period. Ideally you will have a variety of feedback upon which to base each grade—for example, there should be some class projects, presentations, classwork, homework, and tests. Following is a list of such feedback that you might have on each of your students at the end of a six-week grading period.

Six weekly tests
One final exam
One term paper
One oral presentation or term project
One group project
Thirty homework assignments
Twenty classroom assignments

In order to arrive at a grade for the six-weeks period, assign relative values to each item on your list. Be sure to consider the amount of time the student has spent on each activity. You may want to begin by rank-ordering these elements according to the time invested in each—for example—

Activity	Time Required
Homework 30 × 40 min.	20 hours
Classwork 20 × 30 min.	10 hours
Group project	6 hours
Six weekly tests at 50 min.	5 hours
One term paper	4 hours
Oral presentation of project (including preparation)	3 hours
One final exam	1 hour

When totaled, these activities are found to have required 49 hours of student time. To simplify the process, you might simply assign an additional hour's credit to class participation. With a new total of 50 points, you may choose to assign 2 percent of the total grade to each hour spent in each activity. Thus the following system would emerge:

Homework	= 40 percent
Classwork	= 20 percent
Group project	= 12 percent

Weekly tests	=	10	percent
Term paper	=	8	percent
Oral presentation	=	6	percent
Final exam	=	2	percent
Classroom presentation	=	10	percent

But suppose you as the teacher of this class are not happy to have the final exam count only 2 percent against 10 percent for classroom participation. This is no problem, for you can now distribute 6 percent to the final exam and 6 percent to participation or 7 percent and 5 percent, and so on. Suppose you discover an error in addition; these percents total more than 100 percent. You should reduce the other percents in proportion to their size, taking off about 10 percent of each of the 8 items.

The distribution in your particular system will not be identical to this one. That does not matter, so long as you assign each grade based on your chosen system. But on what criteria other than the time spent on each activity could you base your grading system? How about the degree of emphasis given each topic in class? What about the degree of cooperation with other students, and so on?

Your school may require a certain percentage for an A, B, C, or D. But if you are free to design your own requirements, do not forget to ask yourself, What grade will be most appropriate for and most helpful to this student?

RECAP OF MAJOR IDEAS

1. Report-card grades should reflect a variety of types of student performance, including classwork, homework, reports, projects, and tests.
2. Few secondary or middle-level classes are large enough to support using the bell curve to determine grade distribution.
3. Formative evaluation can be used by secondary and middle-level teachers to promote learning.
4. Criterion-referenced tests offer the advantages of letting students compete only with themselves and of clearly informing students what is expected of them before they take each test.
5. Competition among students of varying capabilities is often damaging to the less capable students and can also be damaging to the more capable students.
6. The final decision about what grade should be assigned to a student should always consider what is best for that student.
7. Unlike the act of measurement, grading and evaluation cannot be performed in the absence of the teacher's own values.

POSTTEST

Now that you have read the chapter, take a moment to respond to the following statements again:

	Agree	Disagree	Uncertain
1. Evaluation is the same as the sum of all test scores of an individual.	____	____	____
2. A student's grades should be based only on what the student has learned.	____	____	____
3. The bell curve is appropriate for use in assigning letter grades in most secondary and middle-level classes.	____	____	____
4. For a group of secondary school students, final course grades should parallel their respective IQs.	____	____	____
5. The teacher's judgment should not enter into the grading process.	____	____	____
6. Evaluation is frequently used in secondary and middle schools to promote learning.	____	____	____
7. A student's effort should determine that student's success in class.	____	____	____

CASES

As in other aspects of teaching, you will daily encounter new challenges related to evaluation. No list of principles can be comprehensive enough to guide your behavior in all circumstances. The following cases show the complexity of such a seemingly simple task as assigning a student a grade or convincing others of the limitations and functions of grades.

Case 1: A Parent Confuses Grades with Success

Susie Bates was in the eighth grade when her schoolwork took a rapid decline. From one six-week grading period to the next, her grades fell from B to F. Susie's father, a high school principal, telephoned Susie's principal to discuss the matter—after report cards were passed out. Susie's principal called Susie's homeroom teacher to the telephone. Mr. Bates began with the usual question: "Can you tell me why Susie's grades have fallen so much?" The teacher responded "No." Mr. Bates mentioned that Susie had started playing in a pop band a couple of nights a week and had suddenly become especially interested in boys. Did the teacher think this could have any connection with her low grades? As difficult as it may be to believe, this was how a high school principal responded to the failure of his own child.

The Bates case was typical in that the parent called after the grading period was over to ask what could be done about Susie's low grade. He was really asking, "What are you going to do about it?" but the teacher can do very little after the fact, except help Susie and her father realize that Susie's problem is not that she received an F but that she did not learn enough in a given period of time and that little can be done to correct the past. We can only try to avoid repeating the mistake. Teachers who are serious about helping students learn to be suspicious of a Bates-type call as much as they learn to appreciate a sign of parent interest that comes early enough to help a child.

The teacher explained to Mr. Bates that he wanted to help Susie achieve and learn, not just get higher grades, and that perhaps together they could do this by encouraging Susie and then rewarding her achievements by letting her know how proud they were of her.

Discussion

1. Should a teacher change a grade at the request of a parent?
   Generally not, unless there has been a mistake. To yield to the pressure of a parent will teach the student that force is a satisfactory method for achieving success.
2. Students often come to teachers near the end of a grading period and ask for an extra assignment to pull up a grade. Should this be permitted?
   Only if the student can learn from the assignment—and even then the teacher should avoid allowing this too often. Extra assignments to increase a grade can teach students to procrastinate during the term because they expect they will be allowed to increase their grade at the last moment.

Case 2: A Student Is Given a Break

Linda Eliot was in Mrs. Rolando's ninth-grade math class. She was a delightful girl, always bubbling and happy. Perhaps her lack of seriousness explained the Ds and Fs in all her subjects, or perhaps her Ds and Fs had caused her to become less serious about her schoolwork. At the end of the school year Linda had a D+ average. The fact that she had performed higher than usual tempted Mrs. Rolando to give her a C rather than the earned D+, but she decided to talk with Linda before assigning a grade.

Mrs. Rolando began by asking if Linda was aware that she was on the C and D border. Linda responded with enthusiasm. Mrs. Rolando told Linda that the grade was unclear but that she believed Linda was a C student rather than a D student and that if she really wanted to know which she was there was a plan for finding this out. Linda listened eagerly while her teacher explained that she would assign her a C for the semester if Linda agreed to bring her report card at the end of the first grading period of the next year. At that point they would check her math grade to see if the assumption was correct. Linda happily agreed to these terms. Mrs. Rolando thought the possibility of Linda's remembering the plan throughout the summer vacation and into another school year was remote, but no harm could come of the ploy.

Following a pleasant summer, a new school year began. Mrs. Rolando had a total of 180 new faces to remember and get to know. At the end of the first grading period she was handing out report cards when two girls came rushing through the doorway. Without saying a word, Linda handed over her report card. Mrs. Rolando recalled the agreement they had and scanned the card. She found not only that Linda had a B— in math but also that in all her subjects the lowest grade was a C—. Linda explained that she was now eligible to try out to be a cheerleader. This was obviously an important moment and a triumph for Linda.

Discussion

1. Was the teacher justified in giving Linda a higher grade than she earned?
   The teacher should feel free to experiment if and when an unusual circumstance warrants it, but she should be discreet and caution the student against publicizing the event. She should always make the student understand that she is not giving the student anything except an opportunity to prove her ability.
2. What potential damage is there in telling a student you are assigning a grade that is above his or her average earned grade?
   It could encourage the student to be lazy. Also, an unearned grade does not have the motivating power that an earned grade has. If you believe a student deserves a break, you may decide to assign her a slightly higher grade without telling the student, leaving the student to think she had scored slightly higher than she thought on the final test for the term.

Case 3: Parents' Attempt to Motivate Their Child Backfires

Dr. Bough was a reputable physician whose daughter was in Mr. Hammonds's eighth-grade science class. Mr. Hammonds hardly noticed Ann for the first few weeks of the term. She was very quiet, and she never volunteered to answer questions. When asked to respond, she would wait, hoping he would call on another student.

One day Mr. Hammonds received a note from the counselor to return a call to Mrs. Bough. They scheduled an appointment to discuss Ann's performance in school. When the time came, Mr. Hammonds was ready. He had studied Ann's cumulative records and her schoolwork over previous years. He found that the three IQ scores on file were 99, 101, and 102—remarkably consistent and also remarkably average. Ann's grades had consistently been Bs, indicating that she had been performing high in relation to her ability. Ann was currently taking five academic subjects and band, with no study period. Her test scores in Mr. Hammonds' room had steadily declined from B to D—.

Both parents came to the session. As usual, Mr. Hammonds began by letting the parents talk while he listened. Right away he saw that they had two things to say, politely but firmly: Ann was capable of making top grades and she was doing her best. In fact, often after she had scored a D or an F on Mr. Hammonds's test, her mother would quiz her orally and she would score 100. After the next test, Mr. Hammonds gave Ann an oral exam, asking the same questions. She had failed the written test, but scored 90 percent on the oral repeat. Ann studied hard, learned the material, then failed the tests. Why?

Ann's parents saw themselves in her. Both of them had been A students, so why shouldn't Ann make As? They had considered each of Ann's Bs failures. By pressuring her to get As, Ann's parents had turned each test into a trauma that produced mental barriers. The problem carried over into each daily lesson—when a teacher looked at Ann, she froze. Ann had developed real emotional problems. No parents are more interested in their child's success in school, and no parents are more willing to express their concern to the teacher, but one could argue that the Boughs were not trying to help Ann. They were trying to get her to make higher grades, not because they wanted to help her but because they saw themselves in Ann. By making straight As she would reflect the "Bough image" to her teacher and classmates. Perhaps this conclusion is unfairly harsh, but it does point out a common tendency that parents have to lose objectivity when trying to help their children.

Mr. Hammonds suggested to Ann's parents that they not discuss grades with her until he could experiment with an idea. He promised that he would call them when the experiment was over, and they agreed to cooperate. For the next few weeks Mr. Hammonds observed Ann, searching for an answer. Several times he caught himself on the verge of reminding the class that they would be held accountable for the material on the next test, but each time he refrained. He soon noticed that Ann and the rest of the class became more confident.

Discussion

1. How could the teacher make Ann's parents understand that the ultimate goal should be to have Ann learn, not merely to get a high grade?

The teacher should not stress grades in his discussion with parents or students. The conference should recognize her progress. Even when discussing the student's successes, the teacher should avoid using percentages and letter grades. Eventually students should learn that grades are important only when they reflect the students' effort and accomplishments.

ACTIVITIES

As you read this chapter, your mind probably leaped forward to the time when you will be teaching and grading your own classes and the types of activities that would become your criteria for grading. You had an opportunity to examine a grading system for a hypothetical class. Here you have an opportunity to design a system of your own.

1. Suppose you have complete autonomy with regard to grading. (This is very rare in secondary and middle schools.) Decide whether you would use a norm-referenced or criterion-referenced system, and defend your choice.

2. Suppose you are forced to use the A B C D system with 90, 80, 70, and 60 percent intervals. List the criteria you would use for grading, and assign a relative value (percent) to each.
3. Because formative evaluation is seldom used in secondary and middle schools, research the literature and prepare a report on formative evaluation. Discuss with your professor and/or classmates the relevance of each characteristic to secondary and middle school classes.
4. Arrange a debate between one team that defends grade competition among classmates and a team that opposes such competition. Ask both teams to limit their remarks to those they can substantiate with a written article. During the debate, have a judge (perhaps the professor) throw out any comments that students cannot defend with written support. Make a list for each point earned by each team. Then, with all the points listed on the board, hold a general discussion (not a debate) on whether and when student competition should be held.

SUGGESTED READINGS

Aspy, D. N., & Roebuck, F. N. (1977). *Kids don't learn from people they don't like.* Amherst, Mass.: Human Resources Development Press.

Block, J. H., & Henson, K. T. (1986). Mastery learning and middle school instruction. *American Middle School Education, 9,* 21–29.

Bloom, B. S., Hastings, J. T., & Madaus, G. F. (1981). *Evaluation to improve learning.* New York: McGraw-Hill.

Brightman, H. J. (1984). Constructing and using computer-based formative tests. *Educational Technology, 24,* 36–38.

Butts, R. F., Peckenpaugh, D. H., & Kirschenbaum, H. (Eds.) (1977). *The school's role as moral authority.* Washington, D.C.: Association for Supervision and Curriculum Development.

Conner, K., Hairston, J., Hill, I., Kopple, H., Marshall, J., Scholnick, K., & Shulman, M. (1985). Using formative testing at the classroom, school, and district levels. *Educational Leadership, 43,* 63–68.

Fantini, M. D. (1986). *Regaining excellence in education.* Columbus, Ohio: Merrill.

Kim, E. C., & Kellough, R. D. (1978). *A resource guide for secondary school teaching* (2nd ed.). New York: Macmillan.

Miller, J. P., & Seller, W. (1986). *Curriculum: Perspectives and practice.* New York: Longman.

Oliva, P. F. (1982). *Developing the curriculum.* Boston: Little, Brown.

Oliva, P. F., & Henson, K. T. (1980). What are the generic teaching competencies? *Theory into Practice, 19,* 117–121.

Pratt, D. (1980). *Curriculum design and development.* New York: Harcourt.

Renner, J. W., Bibens, R. F., & Shepherd, G. D. (1972). *Guiding learning in the secondary school.* New York: Harper & Row.

Schubert, W. H. (1986). *Curriculum: Perspectives, paradigm, and possibility.* New York: Macmillan.

Simon, S. B., Howe, L. W., & Kirschenbaum, H. (1972). *Values clarification.* New York: Hart.

Stinnett, T. M., & Henson, K. T. (1982). Updating the examination syndrome. *America's public schools in transition* (pp. 204–227). New York: Teachers College Press.

Vargas, J. S. (1972). *Writing worthwhile behavioral objectives.* New York: Harper & Row.

Wiles, J., & Bondi, J. C. (1984). *Curriculum development: A guide to practice* (2nd ed.). Columbus, Ohio: Merrill.

The Junior High Movement

As the twentieth century approached, the typical elementary school had grades Kindergarten (K) through 8, and the high school included grades 9 through 12. Common knowledge held that the purpose of grades 7 and 8 was to review the content covered in K through 6. Many saw this use of the seventh and eighth grade as a waste of time, but it was difficult to prove because American schools had no nationally accepted goals.

During the next 30 years, several national committees were established to set goals and measure the degree to which schools were meeting them. The first of these was the National Education Association (NEA) Committee of Ten, which reported its conclusions in 1893. The committee set the major purpose of secondary education as preparation for life, not just for college. Accordingly, it recommended that the secondary school's grades 10 through 12 be extended downward to include grades 7 through 12. This would make it possible to teach some secondary school subjects earlier.

In 1895 another major NEA report was issued (see Stinnett & Henson, 1982; Armstrong, Henson, & Savage, 1985). The NEA Department of Superintendents Committee of Fifteen also wanted the secondary school content to be lowered into grades 7 and 8, but it did not recommend changing the 8–12 grade pattern—in fact, it opposed this change. But four years later the NEA Department of Secondary Education issued a report by its Committee on College Requirements suggesting a 6–6 grade pattern. In 1918 the NEA Commission on the Reorganization of Secondary Education, which issued the Cardinal Principles of Secondary Education, also recommended a 6–6 system, but with an added alteration: the upper 6 was to be divided into a 3–3 pattern. This, along with the recommendation of several other committees, promoted the idea that a junior high school was needed to meet the instructional needs of seventh-, eighth-, and ninth-graders.

It would be easy to say that the concern for improving the curriculum for this age-group was the main cause for the development of the junior high school, but that would be an oversimplification. Many factors collectively caused the development of the junior high, and some of them had nothing to do with the quality of the curriculum and instruction. Evidence that the school resulted from causes other than educational can be seen in the fact that the early junior high schools were built *before* goals for junior high were identified.

There was some real concern for meeting the educational needs of this age-group. The NEA was quick to warn that merely regrouping the old elementary and secondary grades would not meet the needs of adolescent learners, and it provided a list of features needed to make a "real junior high school" (NEA Research Bulletin, 1923):

> A building of its own, housing grades 7, 8, and 9 or at least two of these grades
> A separate staff of teachers
> Recognition of individual differences among the students
> A reform of the progress of studies traditionally offered these grades
> Elective courses to be chosen by the students
> Student activities designed for the needs of early adolescents

Research on the nature of adolescence seemed to demand a special school for these students (especially Hall, 1904).

Practical reasons also gave impetus to the development of the junior high school. These included the need to relieve overcrowded high school classrooms caused by the post–World War I population boom, to reduce the high dropout rate, and to make more efficient use of the time spent in school.

From the start, junior high schools have varied in many ways. About half the earlier schools were located in the high school building, about one-third were housed in elementary schools, and the rest were located in separate buildings. The types of instruction in these schools were equally diverse. Therefore, it is not surprising that a majority of studies found little or no difference in the scholastic atttainment of junior high school students and their counterparts in the traditional high schools. There were many studies of the effect of the junior high pattern on the socialization and psychological welfare of the students, but the bulk of these studies found little difference between junior high school students and high school students in grades 7 through 9. By the middle of the twentieth century, studies of the junior high school had painted a dismal picture.

SUGGESTED READINGS

Armstrong, D. G., Henson, K. T., & Savage, T. (1985). *Education: An introduction* (2nd ed.). New York: Macmillan.

Hall, G. S. (1904). *Adolescence, its psychology, and its relations to physiology, anthropology, sociology, sex, crime, religion, and education.* Vols. I and II. New York: Appleton.

Stinnett, T. M., & Henson, K. T. (1982). *America's public schools in transition: Future trends and issues.* New York: Teachers College Press, Columbia University.

The Middle School Movement

Widespread dissatisfaction with the junior high schools, coupled with several other factors, gave rise to a new kind of school—the middle school. By 1950, many critics of the junior high believed it had lost sight of its original purpose: to serve the unique needs and interests of the adolescent. They felt that the junior high school had gradually become a miniature high school. It is important to note that educators were dissatisfied with the junior high school's failure to attain its goals but not with the goals themselves.

The time was ripe for a new type of school to replace the junior high school. Thus emerged the middle school, defined by Alexander as ''a school of some three to five years between the elementary and high school focused on the educational needs of students in these in-between years and designed to promote continuous educational progress for all concerned'' (Alexander, 1981, p. 3).

There were also positive forces that contributed to the development of the middle school—for example:

New research found that children in the seventh and eighth grades resembled children in the fifth and sixth grades more than they resembled ninth-graders.

Research showed that preadolescent children have special needs and interests.

Puberty was occurring earlier than ever before, each generation reaches puberty four months earlier than the previous generation. (Smart, 1978).

An educational program could be designed especially for this group.

Curricula for individualizing instruction could be developed.

The middle school could bridge the gap between the elementary and high schools.

Curricula could be designed to serve the whole child, not just the intellect.

Middle schools could have their own counselors.

Teacher education programs could be designed to prepare teachers to meet the interests and needs of this age-group.

The middle school could be an exploratory school.

HISTORY AND STATUS OF MIDDLE SCHOOLS

The first middle school was opened in Bay City, Michigan, in 1950. Middle schools grew modestly in number for about 15 years, but by the mid-1960s there was rapid growth. By 1980 the number of middle schools in the United States had reached 5,000. With such rapid expansion, it is not surprising that middle schools vary greatly. Some middle schools encompass grades 5 through 8, some have grades 6 through 8, and some 5 through 7. Some use interdisciplinary team-teaching, but most do not. Less than half the middle schools use flexible scheduling. Failure of states to pass legislation defining the role of the middle school and local concerns and priorities have undoubtedly contributed to the failure of middle schools to reach their goals. Another contributing factor has been the general failure of middle school principals to adjust their own perceptions and concepts of the middle school. Only a small minority have received any special training. Fortunately, middle school teachers have made more progress in adjusting their attitudes toward the middle school student. Unfortunately, the humanistic attitude of the middle school teacher has not always resulted in changing the middle school teacher's behavior.

Middle school teachers should realize that their role carries the responsibility for helping attain the general goals of the middle school. Some of these goals are:

1. To help students progress intellectually, socially, physically, and emotionally
2. To enhance the student's self-image
3. To provide opportunities for success
4. To promote active learning
5. To encourage exploration
6. To provide security

An understanding of the nature of the middle school student will help the teacher who wants to contribute to the goals of the middle school. For instance, middle school students are active by nature. Klingele (1979, p. 33), offered the following rationale for involving all middle school students:

1. Middle school students, by their very nature, need and desire a variety of challenging and flexible learning activities.
2. Middle school students both desire and are capable of accepting variable amounts of responsibility for learning.
3. Middle school students learn variable degrees of content, at different rates, and at different times.

4. Middle school students will learn more and better when actively involved in the learning activity.
5. Middle school students learn through various learning styles—no one style is necessarily effective for all students.
6. Middle school students learn best in environments characterized by a respectful, warm, informal, and personalized climate.

Clearly, a major responsibility of the middle school teacher is to find many and varied ways of involving all students, but this does not always happen. All too often the school practitioners, teachers and administrators both, have strayed from the purposes for which the middle school was originally designed. Lately this has led to considerable criticism of middle schools.

SUGGESTED READINGS

Alexander, W. M. (1981). *The exemplary middle school.* New York: Holt, Rinehart and Winston.
Klingele, W. E. (1979). *Teaching in middle schools.* Boston: Allyn & Bacon.
Smart, M. S., and Smart, R. C. (1978). *Adolescence* (2nd ed.). New York: Macmillan.

APPENDIX *C*

Teaching in Middle Schools

When polled about their prospective teaching assignments, only a very small percentage of pre-service teachers who are not participating in middle school programs express a desire to teach in the middle or junior high grades. Initially, almost all secondary education majors assume they will teach in the upper secondary grades. But this is before their student-teaching experience. In reality, more than half of all secondary education majors teach in the junior or middle school grades. Attrition alone assures that there are more grade 7–9 students than grade 10–12 students, excluding the middle schools. The result is that more than half of all students who plan to teach in the upper secondary grades actually become junior high teachers.

An interesting phenomenon occurs when students have an opportunity to student teach at junior and middle levels. By the end of their student-teaching program, most of these students know whether or not they want to teach at these levels. In fact, most students end their middle and junior high student-teaching program with either a very strong determination to teach early adolescents or an equally strong determination to avoid this age-group at all costs. Because there are these typically strong reactions, and because most of those who will actually teach these age-groups do not do so by choice, it is important to know as much as possible about this age-group and about the teacher's role in working with them.

TRANSESCENCE: AN UNKNOWN STAGE

Middle schools exist in varying grade patterns. Some span across grades 5 through 8, while other middle schools include as few as two grades (often 5 and 6, or 6 and 7, or 7 and 8). Because most junior highs involve grades 7 through 9, students are usually at the adolescent stage, but most middle schools cater to preadolescents. *Transescence* is a term that refers to the preadolescent to early-adolescent ages.

There is relatively little in the literature about the transescent student; few studies have focused on this age-group. Transescence is difficult to define because it is tied to our history and to our culture. For example, being a 12-year-old in the United States is different from being a 12-year-old in Japan. A few physical characteristics are shared, but these are complicated by the many different expectations of this age-group that come out of different cultural environments. Furthermore, being a 12-year-old in the late 1980s is different from being a 12-year-old in the 1950s. According to Elder (1970), "It is not possible to discuss adolescence outside a socio-historical perspective." From a psychological perspective, adolescence is an integration of past experiences, the development of a sense of individuality, and a growing awareness of personal destiny.

As youths enter the preadolescent ages, their goals may become less acute and their attention spans shorter. They often develop a keen sense of interdependence. But as we consider such "typical" characteristics, we must remember that many individual members of this age-group are perfect nonexamples of the stereotype. For instance, we might well think of middle school as a time of change (from child to adolescent and from home guidance to peer guidance), but a study of primarily middle-class suburban students reported that "stability, not change, is the overriding characteristic in the psychological patterns of reaction of these older adolescents" (Offer, 1969, p. 222).

While the terms *transescence* and *adolescence* are almost impossible to define, teachers of middle and junior high school students are quick to say that there is something unique about the preadolescent and early adolescent. This uniqueness makes teaching this group a real challenge—and extremely satisfying. The young adolescent is sometimes described as lonely and vulnerable (Konopka, 1973). Teachers of this age group will be surprised to learn how important teacher approval is to their students. Many middle and junior high school teachers find it very rewarding to teach this age group because of the opportunity it provides for influencing the lives of their students.

Another challenge that comes with the territory is determining how much in the way of intellectual demands one can make of these students. Research has shown that only a few individuals develop the ability to function well at the formal operations level (Neimark, 1975).

THE ROLE OF THE TEACHER

Studies show that there is a hiatus in brain growth between the ages of 12 to 14 (Epstein, 1976). One can therefore conclude that the middle school teacher should spend more time giving students opportunities to use the mental skills they have already developed rather than demanding that these students acquire new skills.

Further complicating the role of the middle and junior high teacher is a list of paradoxical demands made on these teachers. For example, in an attempt to make students feel secure and well adjusted, teachers may remove from their students "the springs of their intellectual and artistic productivity" (Hudson, 1966). Another middle school expert notes, "The mercurial nature of the transescent re-quires a fluid but structured atmosphere. It should provide students with the security of structure, but it should be sufficiently elastic to permit students to explore learning and socialization in a manner consistent with individual needs" (Eichhorn, 1980, p. 67). Since youths in the middle years are seeking greater independence, there should be provision for activities that allow students to ac-cept challenges, and support from the teacher to help them meet those challenges. Alexander (1968) emphasizes the need for activities at the middle level:

> Friendliness is a needed element in the school climate, [and] a variety of learning experiences should be provided . . . to permit students to pursue their curiosity and grow intellectually. Several middle school authorities have emphasized the need for making the middle school curriculum an ongoing set of activities for continued learning and organized knowledge.

As Alexander explained, student activities are most effective in friendly, personal classrooms. Although proponents of this need offer different packages—for ex-ample, core-curriculum versus non-core-curriculum—there are similar elements: personalization, sequential process, and organized knowledge. In other words, middle and junior high teachers should learn how to plan continuous curricula chock-full of activities, each one leading to the next. As for instructional skills, these teachers need to know how to relate personally to their students.

A PERSONAL CHALLENGE

As you continue your program, look into the world of middle and junior high school teaching. Consider its advantages and its frustrations. Take every opportu-nity you get to prepare yourself better for teaching at these levels. Consider the slogan of the U.S. Marines: "We need a few good men." America's middle and junior high schools need many good men and women who are mentally, emotion-ally, and academically prepared to accept this challenge.

SUGGESTED READINGS

Eichorn, D. H. (1980). The school. In M. Johnson (Ed.), *Toward adolescence*. 79th Year-book of the National Society for the Study of Education. Chicago: University of Chicago Press.

Epstein, H. T. (1976). A bibliography based framework for intervention projects. *Mental Retardation, 14,* 26–27.

Hudson, L. (1966). *Contrary imaginations: A psychological study of the English school-boy*. Middlesex, England: Penguin Books.

Knopka, G. (1973). Requirements for healthy development of adolescent youth. *Adoles-cence, 8,* 2.

Offer, D. (1969). *The psychological world of the teenager*. New York: Basic Books.

Neimark, E. (1975). In F. D. Horowitz (Ed.), *Review of child development research* (Vol. 4). Chicago: University of Chicago Press.

Directory
of Simulation Materials

Blue Wodjet Company. A business simulation having to do with the problems of pollution for industry.

Requirements	*Designer/Supplier*
25–30 players	Interact
4–6 hours	P.O. Box 1023
	Lakeside, CA 92040

Clug (Community Land Use Game). A simulation of urban land-use interactions that has been compared to combinations of chess and Monopoly and is capable of considerable elaboration.

Requirements	*Designer/Supplier*
9 players (minimum)	Systems Gaming Associates
3 hours (minimum)	Triphammer Road
Packaged materials and kit	Ithaca, NY 14850

Community Disaster. A simulation of a community hit by a localized natural disaster.

Requirements	*Designer/Supplier*
6–16 players	Western Publishing Co., Inc.
2–6 hours	School and Library Department
Packaged materials	850 Third Avenue
	New York, NY 10022

Conflict (preliminary edition). A simulation centered on a crisis that erupts in the year 1999 in a world disarmed by universal agreement and policed by three international councils (based on Waskow's peacekeeping model described in *Keeping the World Disarmed* and published by the Centre for the Study of Democratic Institutions).

Requirements	*Designer/Supplier*
24–36 players	World Law Fund
2–3 hours	11 West 42nd Street
Packaged materials	New York, NY 10036

Farming. A simulation of farm management in western Kansas at three different time periods. Part of Unit 2 of the High School Geography Project produced by the Association of American Geographers.

Requirements	*Designer/Supplier*
15–30 players	Macmillan Company
40–50 hours	866 Third Avenue
Packaged materials	New York, NY 10022

Galapagos (Evolution). A simulation of the evolution of Darwin's finches in which players fill a scientific role and are required to predict the evolution rate.

Requirements	*Designer/Supplier*
6–50 players	Abt Associates, Inc.
1–2 hours	14 Concord Lane
Mimeographed materials	Cambridge, MA 02138

Inner City Planning. A role-playing simulation of urban renewal processes involving various community interest groups.

Requirements	*Designer/Supplier*
18–35 players	Project Simile
5–6 hours	P.O. Box 1023
Kit of printed materials	La Jolla, CA 92037

Location of the Metfab Company. A simulation designed as an integral part of Unit 2 of the High School Geography Project produced by the Association of American Geographers. The central feature is a hypothetical metal-fabricating company facing the problem of determining a new site for a company branch.

Requirements	*Designer/Supplier*
5–10 players per group	Macmillan Company
4–6 hours (40-min.	866 Third Avenue
minimum periods)	New York, NY 10022
Packaged materials	

Low Bidder. A packaged simulation of contract bidding in the construction industry.

Requirements	*Designer/Supplier*
2–25 players, with 3–8 preferable	Entelek, Inc.
30 minutes (minimum)	42 Pleasant Street
Packaged materials	Newburyport, MA 01950

Manchester. A simulation of the impact on the agricultural population of major historical and social issues at the advent of the Industrial Revolution in England.

Requirements	*Designer/Supplier*
8–40 players	Abt Associates, Inc.
	(for Educational Services, Inc.)
1–2 hours	14 Concord Lane
Instructional manual	Cambridge, MA 02138

Marketplace. A simulation of the American economic system at work in a medium-size urban manufacturing community.

Requirements	*Designer/Supplier*
30–50 players	Joint Council on Economic Education
3–4 hours (minimum)	1212 Avenue of the Americas
Packaged materials	New York, NY 10036

Point Roberts. A simulation of international boundary arbitration procedures that is part of Unit 4 of the High School Geography Project produced by the Association of American Geographers.

Requirements	*Designer/Supplier*
30 players	Macmillan Company
30–50 hours	866 Third Avenue
Packaged Materials	New York, NY 10022

Politica. A political crisis simulation set in Latin America and involving major international conflicts.

Requirements	*Designer/Supplier*
40–80 players	Abt Associates, Inc.
2–4 hours	14 Concord Lane
Mimeographed materials	Cambridge, MA 02138

Portsville. An interactive game designed to simulate the growth of the city of Portsville in three different time periods, produced by the Association of American Geographers as part of Unit 1 of the High School Geography Project.

Requirements	*Designer/Supplier*
6 players per map board	Macmillan Company
8–10 players (40 min.	866 Third Avenue
minimum periods)	New York, NY 10022
Packaged materials	

Rutile and the Beach. A simulation of Australian mining, conservation, and recreation groups in competition for land. Part of Unit 5 of the High School Geography Project produced by the Association of American Geographers.

Requirements	*Designer/Supplier*
27 players roles	Macmillan Company
50–60 hours (40 min.	866 Third Avenue
minimum periods)	New York, NY 10022

Section. A simulation designed to provide students with an understanding of conflicts of interest among the sections of a political territory as they are expressed in the political process used in Unit 4 of the American High School Geography Project produced by the Association of American Geographers.

Requirements	*Designer/Supplier*
Over 30 players	Macmillan Company
5–6 hours	866 Third Avenue
Packaged materials	New York, NY 10022

Simulation of American Government. A simulation of certain hypothetical roles and relationships analogous to those found in various branches of the U.S. government.

Requirements	*Designer/Supplier*
9 players and above	Dale M. Garvey
2–4 hours	Division of Social Sciences
Mimeographed materials	Kansas State Teachers College
	Emporia, KA 66801

Solution for ACME Metal. A simulation of flood prevention planning designed as an integral part of Unit 5 of the High School Geography Project produced by the Association of American Geographers.

Requirements	*Designer/Supplier*
7–28 players	Macmillan Company
30–40 hours (40 min.	866 Third Avenue
minimum periods)	New York, NY 10022
Packaged materials	

Steam. A simulation of some of the economic aspects of steam engine development relevant to coal mining in England at the start of the nineteenth century.

Requirements	*Designer/Supplier*
6–15 players	Abt Associates, Inc.
1–2 hours	14 Concord Lane
Mimeographed materials	Cambridge, MA 02138

Venture. A school business game that is a total enterprise simulation covering many of the major decision-making areas of business and management.

Requirements	*Designer/Supplier*
20–35 players	Public Relations Department
4–5 hours	Education Services
Complete kit (available without	P.O. Box 599
charge in the U.S.)	Cincinnati, OH 45201

Yes, But Not Here. A role-playing simulation of an urban locational conflict involving a housing project for the elderly.

Requirements	*Designer/Supplier*
32 roles	Macmillan Company
2–3 hours	866 Third Avenue
Published materials	New York, NY 10022

Directory of Programs for Teaching Thinking Skills

Strategic Reasoning, edited by John J. Glade

Audience:
Ages 10 to adult. The program has instructional levels appropriate to students from fourth grade through adult education.

Most appropriate subjects in which to teach this project:
The program is usually taught in English/reading classes, but has also been taught in math and social studies classes.

Suggested schedule:
One class period per week.

Total hours required to complete program:
30 hours per instructional level.

Estimated cost of materials:
Classroom Starter Package is one-time cost of $198.00; additional student materials cost $4.50 per student per school year.

Address for further information:

Innovative Sciences, Inc.
P.O. Box 15129
Park Square Station
Stamford, CT 06901-0129
Tel.: (800) 243-9169

Purpose of goals:
To teach the conscious metacognitive and applied-thinking skills students must have to function effectively in school and real life, with an emphasis on the transfer of thinking skills to improving academic performance.

Motivational strategies:
By balancing group and individualized instruction, as well as analytical and creative-thinking experiences, the carefully sequenced learning activities guide students to improve their ability to think and demonstrate the benefits this has for enhanced academic achievement and life success.

Theoretical background:
The program is based upon the "Design for Thinking" theory of Dr. Albert Upton.

Curriculum for training teachers to use the program:
Full pre-service and in-service programs are conducted by specially trained consultants.

Evidence of success:
A large number of field research studies demonstrate improvements in such areas as academic achievement, problem solving, critical thinking, specific thinking skills, self-concept, and IQ.

Mastering Reading through Reasoning and Analytical Reading and Reasoning, a two-book series, both texts by Dr. Arthur Whimbey.

Audience:
Ages 12 to adult. *Mastering Reading through Reasoning* spans reading levels 6–9; *Analytical Reading and Reasoning* spans reading levels 9–12.

Most appropriate subjects in which to teach this project:
English/reading classes. The texts are appropriate for remedial, on-level, or advanced instruction. In addition, the texts are often used in special projects such as study skills classes or SAT/ACT exam preparation courses.

Suggested schedule:
One or more periods per week over an entire school year or intensive study for one semester.

Total hours required to complete program:
Approximately 35 hours per text.

Estimated cost of materials:
$12.95 per text.

Address for further information:

Innovative Sciences, Inc.
P.O. Box 15129
Park Square Station
Stamford, CT 06901-0129
Tel.: (800) 243-9169

Purpose of goals:
To improve students' vocabulary, reading comprehension, and cognitive abilities by developing their skills in reasoning with and about words and ideas.

Motivational strategies:
Strategies such as "thinking aloud" and "cooperative learning" are used to boost students' ability to develop their reasoning and reading abilities. High-interest materials, relevant to students' schoolwork in many disciplines, engage students' commitment to the program's goals.

Theoretical background:
The texts are founded on Dr. Whimbey's theory of "precise processing" and incorporate The Whimbey Method, an acclaimed instructional methodology reflecting current research in cognitive science and learning.

Curriculum for training teachers to use the program:
Full pre-service and in-service programs are conducted by specially trained consultants.

Evidence of success:
Field research studies show gains in such areas as vocabulary, reading comprehension, academic aptitude, specific thinking skills, Scholastic Aptitude Test (SAT) scores, and self-concept.

Think: A Thinking Skills Language Arts Program, edited by John J. Glade

Audience:
Ages 10 to adult. *Think* is designed to meet the special needs of typical Chapter I students, who may be performing three or more years below grade level. The program has a sequence of instructional reading levels ranging from functional illiteracy through grade 9.

Most appropriate subjects in which to teach this project:
The program is best suited to a "learning lab" setting, within English or reading classes.

Suggested schedule:
Three or more class periods per week.

Total hours required to complete program:
The program provides instruction for an entire school year. It is recommended
that students continue study of the program over successive school years, progressing through its sequential levels until they no longer require intensive remedial instruction.

Estimated cost of materials:
(The following figures are based upon 100 students participating in the program
and include all pre-service and in-service consulting expenses.) First year cost is
approximately $80.00–$100.00 per student; continuing years cost is approximately
$10.00–$12.00 per student.

Address for further information:

    Innovative Sciences, Inc.
    P.O. Box 15129
    Park Square Station
    Stamford, CT 06901-0129
    Tel.: (800) 243-9169.

Purpose of goals:
To remediate students' word attack, vocabulary, and comprehension language
skills by systematically improving thinking skills and reasoning processes. Cognitive development serves as the vehicle for improving language abilities.

Motivational strategies:
High-interest materials engage students in the instructional process. Language
skills are treated as the application and extension of thinking skills. A balance of
group and individualized instruction provides for both the social development of
language skills and individual learning progress in language and thinking ability.

Theoretical background:
The program is based on the "Design for Thinking" theory of Dr. Albert Upton,
and incorporates elements of Dr. J. P. Guilford's "Structure of Intellect" theory.

Curriculum for training teachers to use the program:
Full pre-service and in-service programs are conducted by specially trained consultants.

Evidence of success:
Substantial research evidence supports significant student gains in such areas as
word attack skills, vocabulary, comprehension, thinking skills, problem solving,
academic aptitude, and self-concept.

Intuitive Math: A Thinking Skills Mathematics Program, edited by Thomas P. Burke.

Audience:
Ages 10 to adult. *Intuitive Math* is designed to meet the special needs of typical Chapter I students, who may be performing three or more years below grade level. The program has a sequence of instructional mathematics levels ranging from functional illiteracy through pre-algebra.

Most appropriate subjects in which to teach this project:
The program is best suited to a "learning lab" setting within mathematics classes.

Suggested schedule:
Three or more class periods per week.

Total hours required to complete program:
The program provides instruction for an entire school year. It is recommended that students continue study of the program over successive school years, progressing through its sequential levels until they no longer require intensive remedial instruction.

Estimated cost of materials:
(The following figures are based upon 100 students participating in the program and include all pre-service and in-service consulting expenses.) First year cost is approximately $80.00–$100.00 per student; continuing years cost is approximately $10.00–$12.00 per student.

Address for further information:

Innovative Sciences, Inc.
P.O. Box 15129
Park Square Station
Stamford, CT 06901-0129
Tel.: (800) 243-9169

Purpose of goals:
To intensively remediate students' conceptual, computational, and problem-solving math skills by systematically improving thinking skills and reasoning processes. Cognitive development serves as the vehicle for improving mathematical abilities.

Motivational strategies:
High-interest materials engage students in the instructional process. Math skills are treated as the application and extension of thinking skills. Group and individu-

alized instruction provides opportunity for whole-class exploration of mathematics as well as individual learning progress in mathematical and thinking ability.

Theoretical background:
The program is based on the "Design for Thinking" theory of Dr. Albert Upton, and incorporates elements of Dr. J. P. Guilford's "Structure of Intellect" theory.

Curriculum for training teachers to use the program:
Full pre-service and in-service programs are conducted by specially trained consultants.

Evidence of success:
Substantial research evidence supports significant student gains in such areas as number concepts, computational abilities, problem solving, thinking skills, academic aptitude, and self-concept.

Odyssey: *A Curriculum for Thinking.*

Audience:
Ages 10 to 14. *Odyssey* can be introduced to students between grades 4 and 8. It is appropriate for all ability groups.

Most appropriate subjects in which to teach this project:
Odyssey focuses on fundamental thinking processes—classification, hierarchical classification, sequencing analogical reasoning—which are used in all curriculum areas.

Suggested schedule:
Foundations of reasoning should be taught first, then any other course or combination of courses.

Total hours required to complete program:
"Foundations of Reasoning": 30–35 hours approx. "Problem Solving": 15–20 hours. All other courses: 15–20 hours.

Estimated cost of materials:
"Foundations of Reasoning" student book is $5.00, all other student books cost $3.00; all teacher manuals cost $15.00.

Address for further information:

> Gary Chadwell, Director of Information and Training
> Mastery Education Corporation
> 85 Main Street
> Watertown, MA 02171

Purpose of goals:
To help students make the most productive use of their intellectual potential through lessons that encompass a broad range of highly productive thinking skills and processes.

Motivational strategies:
Because students learn best by doing, *Odyssey* instruction is highly interactive. It is designed to involve all students to the fullest extent possible in discussions, role-playing, simulations, and other problem-solving activities.

Theoretical background:
The *Odyssey* program approaches thinking as a life skill that involves performance, communication, attitudes, and values.

Curriculum for training teachers to use the program:
The *Odyssey* teacher manual provides detailed instructions for every lesson. This comprehensive support means that teachers can implement the program successfully without special training.

Evidence of success:
In controlled field tests of *Odyssey,* three standardized tests were used: CATTELL, OLSAT, and a battery of General Ability Tests (GATs). The gain of the experimental group was 20 percent greater than the gain of the control group on the CATTELL, 50 percent greater on the OLSAT, and 68 percent greater on the GATs.

Philosophy for Children: Harry Stottlemeier's Discovery (text); *Philosophical Inquiry* (instructional manual).

Audience:
Ages 11 to 12.

Most appropriate subjects in which to teach this project:
Language arts or as an independent subject.

Suggested schedule:
2 1/4 hours per week.

Total hours required to complete program:
75 hours.

Estimated cost of materials:
$10.00.

Address for further information:

> IAPC
> Montclair State College
> Upper Montclair, NJ 07043

Purpose of goals:
Strengthening reasoning, inquiry, concept formation, and translation skills.

Motivational strategies:
Classroom discussion, reading of novel (text) so as to form community of inquiry.

Theoretical background:
Bruner, Dewey, Vygotsky, Piaget, G. H. Mead.

Curriculum for training teachers to use the program:
Teacher education seminars, modeling sessions, and observations by workshop directors.

Evidence of success:
After one year, children in experimental classes gained 80 percent more in reasoning, 66 percent more in reading comprehension, and 36 percent more in mathematics proficiency than children not in the program.

Philosophy for Children: Lisa (text); *Ethical Inquiry* (instructional manual).

Audience:
Ages 13 to 14.

Most appropriate subjects in which to teach this project:
English, ethics.

Suggested schedule:
2 1/4 hours per week.

Total hours required to complete program:
75 hours.

Estimated cost of materials:
$10.00.

Address for further information:

> IAPC
> Montclair State College
> Upper Montclair, NJ 07043

Purpose of goals:
Teaching children strategies of moral reasoning and procedures of ethical inquiry.

Motivational strategies:
Converting classroom into a discussion community.

Theoretical background:
History of philosophical ethics.

Curriculum for training teachers to use the program:
Teaching education seminars (once a week for one year), plus modeling and observations by workshop director.

Philosophy for Children: Suki (text); *Writing: How and Why* (instructional manual).

Audience:
Ages 14 to 16.

Most appropriate subjects in which to teach this project:
English, writing.

Suggested schedule:
2 1/4 hours per week for at least one year.

Total hours required to complete program:
75 hours.

Estimated cost of materials:
$10.00.

Address for further information:

IAPC
Montclair State College
Upper Montclair, NJ 07043

Purpose of goals:
Stimulating children's writing.

Motivational strategies:
Promoting classroom discussion that can then be continued in written form.

Theoretical background:
Aesthetics, epistemology.

Curriculum for training teachers to use the program:
Teacher education seminars, modeling sessions, and observations by workshop directors.

Philosophy for Children: Mark (text); *Social Inquiry* (instructional manual).

Audience:
Ages 16 to 17.

Most appropriate subjects in which to teach this project:
Social studies.

Suggested schedule:
2 1/4 hours per week.

Total hours required to complete program:
37–75 hours.

Estimated cost of materials:
$10.00.

Address for further information:

   IAPC
   Montclair State College
   Upper Montclair, NJ 07043

Purpose of goals:
Encouraging reflection upon nature of society and citizenship.

Motivational strategies:
Converting classroom into community of social inquiry.

Theoretical background:
Philosophy of social sciences, sociology, contemporary civilization.

Curriculum for training teachers to use the program:
Teachers are taught in seminars; workshop directors model and observe in classrooms.

Directory of Materials for Multicultural Classes*

The Adventures of Billy Bean, Wesley Studie, Cross-Cultural Education Center (P. O. Box 66, Park Hill, OK 74451), 1982.

Produced by the Cherokee Bilingual Education Program, this collection of stories was published as a response to problems which Cherokee children have faced because of language deficiency and culture gap. These stories portray Billy Bean in such a way that he promotes the Indian culture and its value system as a priceless heritage.

The Girl on the Outside, Mildred Pitts Walker, Lothrop, Lee & Shepard, 1982.

Written against the background of the September, 1957, desegregation in Little Rock, Arkansas, this book presents an interesting comparison between the poor, black teen-age girl who will desegregate the school and the rich white teen-age girl who already attends the school. Black characters argue on valid grounds and white characters reveal the struggles of conscience as life in this country changed.

Tic Tac Toe and Other Three-in-a-Row Games from Ancient Egypt to the Modern Computer, Claudia Zaslavsky, T. Y. Crowell, 1982.

Games from China, the Philippines and Kenya, such as Nine-Men's Morris, Five Square and Shisima, are explained with diagrams. These games are suitable for children and many for adults. The African and Asian origins of the games are given as historical context.

Count on Your Fingers African Style, Claudia Zaslavsky, T. Y. Crowell, 1980.

This book has been recognized by the National Council of Christians and Jews and has received awards as a notable Social Studies and Outstanding Science Book.

My Mama Needs Me, Mildred Pitts Walker, illustrated by Pat Cummings, Lothrop, Lee & Shepard, 1983.

The illustrations in this book reveal that Jason lives in a neighborhood which is both black and white. This story deals with an older child's adjustment to the new baby in the family. It is a positive book with a simple text in which Jason grows to love his sister and support his mother with the new baby.

---

* Grace R. Bishop, The identification of multicultural materials for the middle school library: Annotations and sources, *American Middle School Education, 9* (Fall 1986).

Home Boy, Joyce Hansen, Clarion/Houghton Mifflin, 1982.

A youth and his family move to New York City from the Caribbean. The boy learns to fit in his new environment despite difficulties of time and place.

In Neuva York, Nicholosa Mohr, Dial, 1977.

A set of interrelated short stories provides good reading for young adults. The setting is a Puerto Rican Community in New York's lower east side.

Just My Luck, Emily Moore, Dutton, 1983.

The story of a middle-class black family provides humorous and refreshing reading for middle school teen-agers.

Music, Music for Everyone, Vera B. Williams, Greenwillow, 1984.

This book is the third in a series about Rosa, her mother, grandmother and friends. The beautiful illustrations add to the positive message, and this book includes not only interracial friendship but family affection and community cooperation.

Sweet Whispers, Brother Rush, Virginia Hamilton, Philomel, 1982.

A Newberry Honor Book for 1983 and recipient of the Coretta Scott King Award for that year, this book centers around a brother-sister relationship, and a relationship with a helpful ghost named Brother Rush.

Friends Till the End, Todd Strasser, Delacorte, 1981.

David visits a newcomer, Howie, who has leukemia and develops a very close friendship. Through his relationship with Howie, David gains an understanding of the meaning and value of life. An excellent book for any young person who has faced or may have to face a friend's death.

All the Colors of the Race, Arnold Adoff, Lothrop, Lee & Shepard, 1982.

This collection of poems pictures an interracial family through the eyes of the daughter. It emphasizes both the richness of cultural difference and the confusion which it causes outsiders. The poems are beautiful in their vision of racial harmony.

She Was There: Stories of Pioneering Women Journalists, Jean E. Collins, Messner, 1980.

Collins interviews 15 women journalists who were pioneers in their field. These stories include excerpts from their lives as well as short biographical accounts. The book leaves the reader wanting to learn more. A good book for teenagers, especially girls.

The Balancing Girl, Berniece Rabe, Dutton, 1981.

The touching story of a handicapped child who works toward acceptance from her peers in a "regular" classroom situation. This book has a positive tone.

Don't You Turn Back, Lee Bennett Hopkins, Knopf, 1969.

A collection of Langston Hughes' poetry which can be used to create student posters—art to celebrate poetry. (There is also a recording by Spoken Arts which can be used, **Langston Hughes Reads and Talks about His Poems**).

The Golda Meir Story, Margaret Davidson, Scribners, 1981.

The story of Golda Meir, the former Prime Minister of Israel, is a fascinating one. It focuses upon her experience as an American immigrant and her part in the founding of

Israel. This book is suitable for more mature readers and for teachers to use in introducing the accomplishments of a famous world figure, in this case, a woman.

Julie of the Wolves, Jean George, Harper & Rowe, 1972.

A fascinating story of an Eskimo girl set against the sparsely populated, expansive territory of Alaska.

The New Wind Has Wings: Poems from Canada. Oxford/Merrimack, 1975.

This prize winning collection includes poems about Canada, its history, its early settlers and its cultural blend of English and French speaking peoples.

A short article cannot do justice to the wealth of material available. Additional information can be obtained from the following centers and agencies (Tiedt and Tiedt, 1986).

American Library Association, 50 East Huron St., Chicago, IL 60611. **American Indians: A Bibliography of Sources,** a list of many materials. **Childrens Books of International Interest Printed in U.S.A.,** a selective list, (free).

Asia Society, 112 East 64th St., New York, NY 10021. Asia: **A Guide to Basic Books,** a list of basic books on Asia.

Augusta Baker, Office of Children's Services, New York Public Library, 8 East 40th St., New York, NY 10016. **The Black Experience in Children's Books,** a revision that includes 400 titles.

California Library Association, 1741 Solano Ave., Berkeley, CA 94707. **American Negro in Contemporary Society,** an annotated list of 121 titles, (free).

Centro Mexicano de Escritores, Apartado Postal 1298, Mexico, 1, D.F., Mexico. **Children's Books from Mexico,** a list of books for children in Spanish, (free).

David Cohen, chm. American Association of School Librarians, 50 East Huron St., Chicago, IL 60611. **Multi-ethnic Media: Selected Bibliographies,** (free).

Free Library of Philadelphia, 19th and Vine Sts., Philadelphia, PA 19103. **To Be Black in America,** a bibliographic essay arranged in broad categories; materials included suitable for use by junior and senior high school students, (free).

Barbara Jean Glancy, American Federation of Teachers, AFL-CIO, 1012 14th St. NW., Washington, DC 20036. **Children's Interracial Fiction,** an annotated unselected bibliography identifying 328 books with black characters.

The National Assessment and Dissemination Center for Bilingual/Bicultural Education (385 High St., Fall River, MA 02720) has Spanish, Portuguese, Oriental, Native American, Greek, Italian and French materials, (free).

The Dissemination Center for Bilingual/Bicultural Education (6504 Tracor Lane, Austin, TX 78721) has Spanish, Navajo, Portuguese and French materials, (free).

Another center funded by the National Institute of Education (NIE) and the Educational Products Exchange Institute (EPIE) has published informative volumes (EPIE Institute, 463 West St., New York, NY 10014).

Child of UNICEF. Eight children, each from a different country, tell of their experiences with UNICEF in separate booklets.

Information Center on Children's Cultures, United States Committee for UNICEF, 331 East 38th St., New York, NY 10016. **Africa: An Annotated List of Printed Materials Suitable for Children,** evaluation of all in-print English-language materials for children on the subject of Africa.

Name Index

Alexander, W. M., 371, 377
Alfke, D., 101
Althoff, R. H., 174
Alvins, J. J., 187
Anderson, L., 277
Arlin, M., 155
Armento, B. J., 36
Armstrong, D. G., 367

Baikov, F. I., 102
Ball, A. L., 156
Balzer, L., 97
Baughman, M. D., 273
Beasley, R., 277
Beauchamp, G., 37
Bell, L. C., 292
Benjamin, H., 104
Berg, R., 248
Berliner, D. C., 14, 89, 128, 280
Berry, K., 78
Bills, F. L., 96
Bingham, R. M., 95
Bishop, G. R., 208
Bittinger, M. L., 104
Block, J., 351
Bloom, B. S., 63, 94, 155, 333, 351
Boyer, E., 5
Braun, B. L., 187
Brooks, D. M., 122
Brophy, J. E., 121, 151, 158, 269, 271, 273
Brown, L. B., 96
Brown, R., 150
Brown, S. B., 96
Bruner, J. S., 122, 225
Buethe, C., 211, 212
Bull, B. L., 189
Bull, S. G., 100
Burns, R. B., 155
Buttery, T. J., 4, 225

Calderhead, J., 39
Calfee, R., 150
Cantor, L., 100
Carnahan, R. S., 36
Carpenter, T. P., 35
Carroll, J. B., 153, 155
Carruthers, S., 157
Carter, K., 324
Castaneda, A., 219
Cathey, F. M., 203
Cazden, C., 119
Centra, J., 150
Chambers, J. A., 247
Chansky, N. M., 279
Charles, C., 273
Chauldhari, U. S., 98
Cheyney, A., 202, 205
Chissom, B., 4, 225
Cinquino, D., 191
Clark, C. M., 35
Clark, L. H., 280
Clark, R. E., 225, 226
Clough, J. D., 300
Coffman, W. E., 324
Cohen, A., 155
Combs, A., 272
Commonwealth, V., 92
Copenhaver, R., 157
Cornbleth, C., 277
Corno, L., 39
Crabbe, A. B., 191
Crawford, J., 298
Curtis, L. T., 187
Curwin, R. L., 296
Cutts, N., 188

Dandridge, J. A., 204
Davis, D. M., 250
Davis, O. L., 15

Subject Index